P9-EMK-505

POWER

POWER

POWER

KeyQuest
PUBLISHING
www.entertainmentpower.com

THE PREMIER FASHION, FILM, MUSIC, SPORTS & TV DIRECTORY

*A Masterpiece for Taylor*

Published Exclusively by:

KeyQuest
PUBLISHING
Dackeyia Q. Sterling, Publisher
(323) 993-3354 • (323) 533-1971
www.entertainmentpower.com



***Art Director***: Dackeyia Q. Sterling/Key Quest Publishing
***Graphic Design By***: Starvin' Artist Graphic Design (www.starvinartist.net)
***Special Thanks***: God, for the strength, creativity & resources. Del, Taylor, Mom, Daddy, Shime, Jay, Nicholas, Jamie, Danielle, Olivia, Trace, Jahmal, Lori, Kay Pri, Keyandra, Nowling, Lecia, Larry, TaJuan, Marlon, Joacir, Maurice, Georgia, Kathryn & Hanson, Annie Mae & Cherita. R.I.P. Grams. I miss you!!!

*Disclaimer: Entertainment Power Players: Edition 4 is designed as a **catalyst** for established and emerging artists, executives, celebrities, athletes, college students, professors, career counselors, librarians and entertainment enthusiasts. Affectionately referred to throughout the industry as "EPP," this Directory contains 5,000+ Industry Contacts. Every effort has been made to provide our readers with a first-class publication that will aid and inspire those actively involved in the career and job arena. We make no guarantees of job or career success and claim no responsibility for, nor ownership of, any deals and/or interaction(s) our readers may have with the companies and Power Players featured in this Edition. We understand that there is no way we could list all the companies in the entertainment industry -- that would result in a 3,000+ page book. Therefore, what we've done is compiled a Comprehensive, Up-to-Date Directory that features an eclectic and POWERFUL mix of industry Information and Inspiration.*

*Please note that due to the fast-moving nature of the entertainment business that some numbers and addresses may have changed since this printing. Feel free to contact us for inclusion in future Editions.*

ISBN 13: 978-0-9679036-3-7 (Edition 4)
Printed in the USA
10 9 8 7 6 5 4 3 2 1

# PUBLISHER'S POWER PAGE

Welcome to *Edition 4*!

It's Fashion, Film, Music, Sports & TV from A-Z. Compiling this Edition was a lot of fun for the entrepreneur and tireless researcher in me. The challenge was figuring out how to present the information in a colorful, easy-to-use, first-class kind of way. I'm pleased to say that the 5,000+ updated Contacts, exclusive POWER PLAYER Interviews and Ads from our great sponsors, coupled with the introduction of our new FASHION Section, makes ***EPP: 4*** our best publication yet!

Our goal is that you use this Directory to THINK BOLD! THINK SUCCESS! THINK YOU! Use it to create your CAREER POWER PLAN, make new connections and keep moving your career forward! As you reach out to the companies listed in the Directory and read the POWER PLAYER articles, know that we're rooting for you and your success!

Special thanks to my family, friends, colleagues, legendary/mega-producer Lynda Obst and all of our Advertisers, Interviewees, industry organizations, colleges/universities, actors, directors, fashion designers, singers, songwriters, producers, models, athletes, college and high school students, counselors, professors, teachers, administrators, libraries, bookstores and industry POWER PLAYERS for supporting and embracing "EPP" the way you have. We're on a mission to become "the" entertainment go-to resource -- and you're helping us get there.

I look forward to meeting you on our ***EPP: 4*** Tour and hearing your success stories as you use the Directory to advance your career. If you need more information, log onto our new website - www.entertainmentpower.com - to get your downloadable digital ***Edition 4***.

Until the next Edition from the Key Quest Publishing House, create your legacy! Keep moving with POWER! Think Bold! Think Success! Think YOU!

Dackeyia Q. Sterling
CEO/Publisher

think bold.

think success.

think YOU.

# Table of Contents

Setting
YOUR
Industry Career Goals!

## *EPP: 4* is all about helping YOU!

## Use the 5,000+ Contacts in this Directory to:

### Create YOUR Career POWER PLAN

Outlining & Detailing

***Who** you will call, meet with, e-mail, etc.

***What** projects you will create, copyright, pitch and promote.

***When** you will complete one goal and move on to the next.

***Where** (and with whom) you want to work or intern.

***Why** succeeding in the industry so important to you.

**How** much time & money you're willing to commit to make your dreams come true.

There are no guarantees for success in this industry. Use *EPP: 4* as your resource for great Information & Inspiration....and keep working hard to achieve levels of success many only dream about!

BE INSPIRED!

## Take our *EPP: 4* Challenge here on the right!

*For ***Edition 4*** we've come up with a MASTERFUL equation to help motivate and inspire you to push past all fears and reach for super success.

**4** phone calls, resumes, headshots, CDs, DVDs or packages a day **to new people*

**x 5** days per week

**x 4** weeks per month

**x 5** months per year =

**4 x 5 x 4 x 5 = 400**

400 new contacts

400 new resources

400 new opportunities

to make something happen...

in a short period of time!!

The Possible Rewards & Results?

**New Jobs • New Deals • New Colleagues • Fresh Starts • Greater Inspiration!**

**TRY OUR *EPP 04* CHALLENGE TODAY &**
**CALL OR E-MAIL US WITH YOUR SUCCESS STORIES.**
**www.entertainmentpower.com**

4 STEPS TO **ENTERTAINMENT** SUCCESS

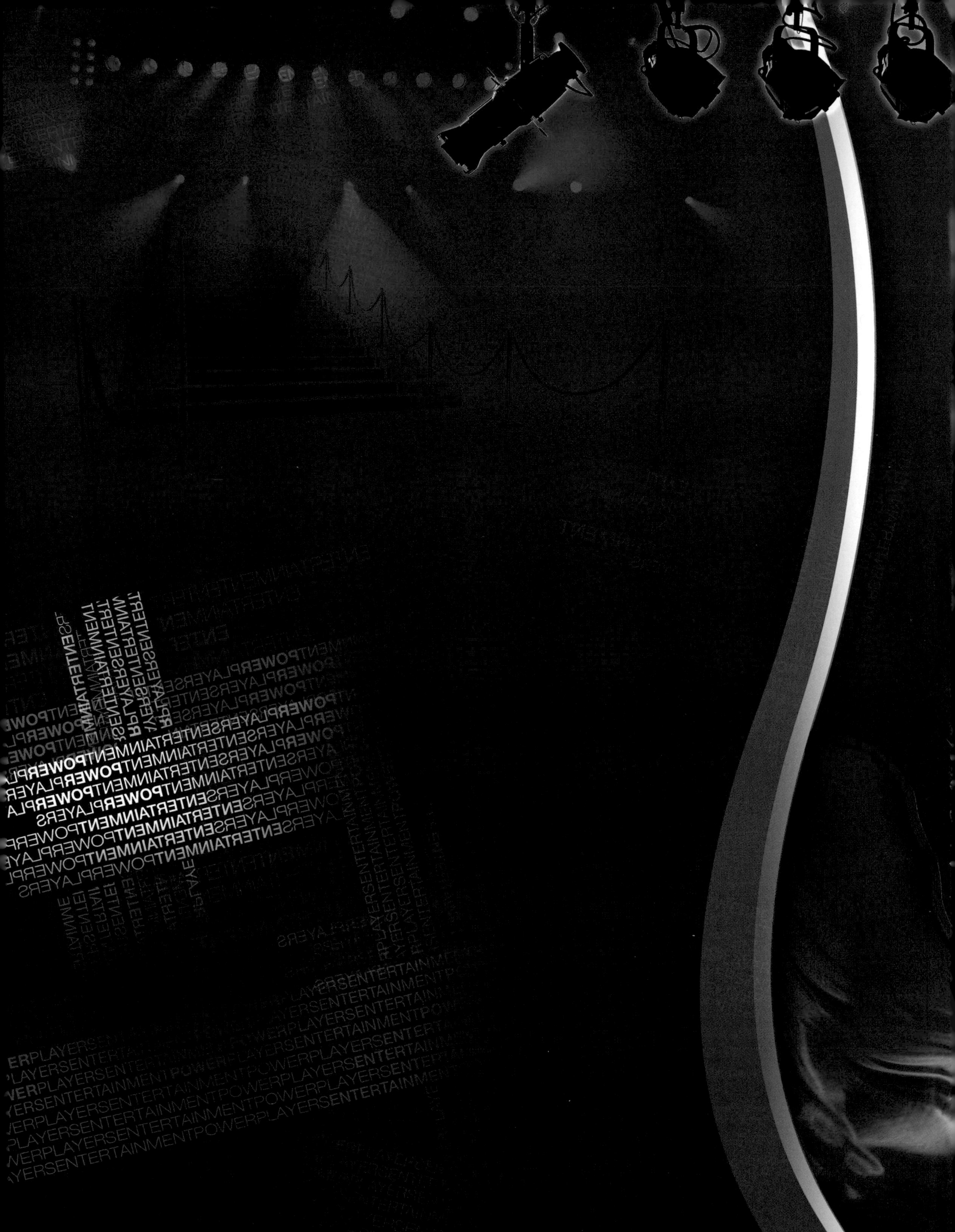

# FASHION

- » Accessories
- » Associations & Organizations
- » Celebrity Fashion & Fragrance Lines
- » Department & Retail Stores
- » Fashion Designers
- » Fashion Schools
- » Footwear Companies
- » Internships
- » The Jean Scene
- » Modeling Agencies
- » Trade Publications
- » Training Programs

**Avon Products, Inc.**
1345 Avenue of the Americas
New York, NY 10105
***Tel: (212) 282-5000***
***www.avoncompany.com***

**Bath & Body Works, Inc.**
7 Limited Parkway
Reynoldsburg, OH 43068
***Tel: (614) 856-6000***
***www.bathandbodyworks.com***

**The Body Shop**
5036 One World Way
Wake Forest, NC 27587
***Tel: (919) 554-4900***
***www.thebodyshop.com***

**Breitling USA, Inc.**
Hangar 7, 206 Danbury Road
Wilton, CT 06897
***Tel: (877) BREITLING***
***www.breitling.com***

**Bronner Bros.**
2141 Powers Ferry Road
Marietta, GA 30067
***Tel: (770) 988-0015***
***www.bronnerbros.com***

**BVULGARI**
***www.bulgari.com***

**Bulova Corporation**
1 Bulova Avenue
Woodside, NY 11377
***Tel. 718-204-3300***
***www.bulova.com***

**Carol's Daughter**
99 Hudson Street
New York, NY 10013
***Tel: (877) 540-2101***
***www.carolsdaughter.com***

**Cartier USA, Inc.**
2 East 52nd Street
New York, NY 10022
***Tel: (212) 753-0111***
***www.cartier.com***

**Coach, Inc.**
516 W. 34th Street
New York, NY 10001
***Tel: (212) 594-1850***
***www.coach.com***

**Christian Dior**
***www.dior.com***
***www.diorcouture.com***

**Dolce & Gabbana USA, Inc.**
148 Lafayette Street
New York, NY 10013
***Tel: (212) 750-0055***
***www.dolcegabanna.com***

**Dooney & Bourke Inc.**
1 Regent Street
Norwalk, CT 06855
***Tel: (203) 853-7515***
***www.dooney.com***

**Elizabeth Arden, Inc.**
200 Park Avenue S., 7th Fl.
New York, NY 10003
***Tel: (212) 261-1000***
***www.elizabetharden.com***

**Erickson Beamon**
***www.ericksonbeamon.com***

**Estée Lauder Companies, Inc.**
767 5th Avenue
New York, NY 10153
***Tel: (212) 572-4200***
***www.elcompanies.com***

**Fossil, Inc.**
2280 N. Greenville Ave.
Richardson, TX 75082
***Tel: (972) 234-2525***
***www.fossil.com***

**Gucci**
685 Fifth Avenue, 8th Fl.
New York, NY 10022
***Tel: (212) 750-5220***
***www.gucci.com***

**Hanesbrands Inc.**
1000 E. Hanes Mill Rd.
Winston-Salem, NC 27105
***Tel: (336) 519-4400***
***www.hanesbrands.com***
***Includes: Hanes; Bali; Barely There; Champion; Just My Size; L'eggs; Playtex & Wonderbra***

**kate spade**
48 W. 25th Street
New York, NY 10010
***Tel: (212) 739-6550***
***www.katespade.com***

**L'Occitane**
***www.loccitane.com***

**L'Oréal USA, Inc.**
575 Fifth Avenue
New York, NY 10017
***Tel: (212) 818-1500***
***www.lorealusa.com***
****25+ Brands Include: Garnier; Lancôme; Kiehl's Since 1851; Maybelline; Armani, Paloma Picasso & Ralph Lauren Fragrances***

**Louis Vuitton**
***www.louisvuitton.com***

**Luxottica**
***ww.luxottica.com***

**MAC Cosmetics**
***www.maccosmetics.com***
***www.macpro.com***

**Maidenform Brands, Inc.**
485 Rte. 1 South, Bldg. F
Iselin, NJ 08830
***Tel: (732) 621-2500***
***www.maidenform.com***

**Marchon Eyewear, Inc.**
35 Hub Drive
Melville, NY 11747
***Tel: (631) 755-2020***
***www.marchon.com***

**Mary Kay Inc.**
16251 Dallas Parkway
Addison, TX 75001
***Tel: (972) 687-6300***
***www.marykay.com***

**Movado Group, Inc.**
650 From Road
Paramus, NJ 07652
***Tel: (201) 267-8000***
***www.movadogroupinc.com***

**Irene Neuwirth**
***www.ireneneuwirth.com***

**Pandora**
***www.pandora-jewelry.com***

**Parlux Fragrances**
5900 N. Andrews Ave., Ste. 500
Ft. Lauderdale, FL 33309
***Tel: (954) 316-9008***
***www.parlux.com***
***Fragrances: Andy Roddick; babyGUND; Guess; Nicole Miller; Jessica Simpson; Paris Hilton XOXO; Queen by Queen Latifah***

**Jill Platner**
113 Crosby Street
New York, NY 10012
**Tel: (212) 324-1298**
***www.jillplatner.com***

**Prada USA Corp.**
609 W. 51 Street
New York, NY 10019
***Tel: (212) 307-9300***
***www.prada.com***

**Revlon, Inc.**
237 Park Avenue
New York, NY 10017
***Tel: (212) 527-4000***
***www.revlon.com***

**Rolex Watch USA, Inc.**
***Tel: (212) 758-7700***
***www.rolex.com***

**Sephora USA, Inc.**
525 Market Street, 11th Fl.
San Francisco, CA 94105
***Tel: (415) 284-3300***
***www.sephora.com***

**SoftSheen/Carson Products**
575 5th Avenue, 19th Fl.
New York, NY 10017
***Tel: (212) 818-1500***
***www.softsheen-carson.com***

**Spanx, Inc.**
3391 Peachtree Rd., Ste. 300
Atlanta, GA 30326
***Tel: (404) 321-1608***
***www.spanx.com***

**Sterling Jewelers Inc.**
375 Ghent Road
Fairlawn, OH 44333
***Tel: (330) 668-5000***
***www.sterlingjewelers.com***
***Includes: Kay; Jared's, Shaw's Jewelers***

**Stila Styles, LLC**
111 West Wilson Avenue
Glendale, CA 91203
***Tel: (818) 459-8000***
***www.stila.com***

**Koi Suwannagate**
1060 E. Cesar Chavez Ave.
Los Angeles, CA 90033
***Tel: (323) 224-9998***
***www.koisuwannagate.com***

**Tiffany & Co.**
727 5th Avenue
New York, NY 10022
***Tel. (212) 755-8000***
***www.tiffany.com***

**Ulta Beauty**
1000 Remington Blvd., Ste. 120
Bolingbrook, IL 60440
***Tel: (630) 410-4800***
***www.ulta.com***

**Under Armour, Inc.**
1020 Hull Street, 3rd Fl.
Baltimore, MD 21230
***Tel: (410) 454-6428***
***www.underarmour.com***

**Van Cleef & Arpels**
***Tel: (877) VAN-CLEEF (826-2533)***
***www.vancleef-arpels.com***

**Victoria's Secret**
3 Limited Parkway
Columbus, OH 43216
***Tel: (800) 411-5116***
***www.victoriassecret.com***

**The Warnaco Group, Inc.**
501 7th Avenue
New York, NY 10018
***Tel: (212) 287-8000***
***www.warnaco.com***
***Includes: Calvin Klein Jeans; Chaps; Olga; Speedo; Warner***

**Harry Winston**
***www.harrywinston.com***

# ASSOCIATIONS & ORGANIZATIONS

**American Apparel & Footwear Association**
1601 N. Kent St., 12th Fl.
Arlington, VA 22209
***Tel: (703) 524-1864***
***www.apparelandfootwear.org***

**American Assoc. of Textile Chemists and Colorists**
P.O. Box 12215
Research Triangle Park, NC 27709
***Tel: (919) 549-8141***
***www.aatcc.org***

**American Fiber Manufacturers Association**
1530 Wilson Blvd., Ste. 690
Arlington, VA 22209
***Tel: (713) 875-0432***
***www.fibersource.com***

**American Gem Trade Assoc.**
3030 LBJ Freeway, Ste. 840
Dallas, TX 75234
***Tel: (214) 742-4367***
***www.agta.org***

**American Purchasing Society**
8 E. Galena Blvd., Ste. 203
Aurora, IL 60506
***Tel: (630) 859-0250***
***www.american-purchasing.com***

**Association of Stylists & Coordinators**
18 East 18th St., #5E
New York, NY 10003
***www.stylistsasc.com***

**Cashmere & Camel Hair Manufacturers Institute**
6 Beacon Street, Ste. 1125
Boston, MA 02108
***Tel: (617) 542-7481***
***www.cashmere.org***

**Cosmetic Executive Women**
286 Madison Avenue, 19th Fl.
New York, NY 10017
***Tel: (212) 685-5955***
***www.cew.org***

**Costume Designers Guild Local #892**
11969 Ventura Blvd., 1st Fl.
Studio City, CA 91604
***Tel: (818) 752-2400***
***www.costumedesignersguild.com***

**Costume Society of America**
203 Towne Centre Drive
Hillsborough, NJ 08844
***Tel: (908) 359-1471***
***www.costumesocietyamerica.com***

**Cotton Council International**
1521 New Hampshire Avenue, NW
Washington, DC 20036
***Tel: (202) 745-7805***
***www.cottonusa.org***

**Council of Fashion Designers of America (CFDA)**
1412 Broadway, Ste. 2006
New York, NY 10018
***Tel: (212) 302-1821***
***www.cfda.com***

**Custom Tailors & Designers Association**
42732 Ridgeway Drive
Broadlands, VA 20148
***Tel:* (888) 248-CTDA**
***www.ctda.com***

**Embroiderers' Guild of America**
426 West Jefferson Street
Louisville, KY 40202
***Tel: (502) 589-6956***
***www.egausa.org***

**Fashion Accessories Shippers' Association, Inc.**
350 5th Avenue, Ste. 2030
New York, NY 10118
***Tel: (212) 947-3424***
***www.accessoryweb.com***

**Fashion Footwear Association of New York**
1414 Ave. of the Americas, Ste. 203
New York, NY 10019
***Tel: (212) 751-6422***

***www.ffany.org***

**Fashion Group Int'l., Inc.**
8 West 40th Street, 7th Fl.
New York, NY 10018
***Tel: (212) 302-5511***
***www.fgi.org***

**Footwear Distributors and Retailers of America**
1319 F Street, NW - Ste. 700
Washington, DC 20004
***Tel: (202) 737-5660***
***www.fdra.org***

**Garment Industry Development Corporation**
202 W 40th Street, 9th Fl.
New York, NY 10018
***Tel: (212) 366-6160***
***www.gidc.org***

**GenArt**
133 West 25th Street, 6th Fl.
New York, NY 10001
***Tel: (212) 255-7300***
***www.genart.org***

**GenArt**
3710 S. Robertson Blvd., Ste. 219
Culver City, CA 90232
***Tel: (323) 782-9367***
***www.genart.org***

**The Hosiery Association**
7421 Carmel Exec. Park, Ste. 200
Charlotte, NC 28226
***Tel: (704) 365-0913***
***www.hosieryassociation.com***

**International Textile & Apparel Association**
6060 Sunrise Vista Dr., Ste. 1300
Citrus Heights, CA 95610
***Tel: (916) 723-1628***
***www.itaaonline.org***

**Jewelers of America**
52 Vanderbilt Ave., 19th Fl.
New York, NY 10017
***Tel: (646) 658-0246***
***www.jewelers.org***

**MAGIC Int'l. (Men's Apparel Guild in California)**
6200 Canoga Ave., 2nd Fl.
Woodland Hills, CA 91367
***Tel: (818) 593-5000***
***www.magiconline.com***

**Men's Apparel Guild in California/MAGIC Int'l.**
MAGIC International
6200 Canoga Ave., 2nd Fl.
Woodland Hills, CA 91367
***Tel: (818) 593-5000***
***www.magiconline.com***

**National Association of Fashion and Accessory Designers**
Washington DC Chapter
P. O. Box 10058
Silver Spring, Maryland 20914
***www.nafaddc.org***

**National Cotton Council of America**
7193 Goodlett Farms Parkway
Cordova, TN 38016
***Tel: (901) 274-9030***
***www.cotton.org***

**National Shoe Retailers Association**
7150 Columbia Gateway Dr., Ste. G
Columbia, MD 21046
***Tel: (410) 381-8282***
***www.nsra.org***

**Personal Care Products Council**
1101 17th Street, NW - Ste. 300
Washington D.C. 20036-4702
***Tel: (202) 331-1770***
***www.personalcarecouncil.org***

**Public Relations Society of America (PRSA)**
33 Maiden Lane, 11th Fl.
New York, NY 10038
***Tel: (212) 460-1400***
***www.prsa.org***

**Public Relations Student Society of America (PRSSA)**
33 Maiden Lane, 11th Fl.
New York, NY 10038
***Tel: (212) 460-1474***
***www.prssa.org***

**Retail Design Institute**
25 North Broadway
Tarrytown, NY 10590
***Tel: (800) 379-9912***
***www.retaildesigninstitute.org***

**Retail Industry Leaders Association**
1700 N. Moore St., Ste. 2250
Arlington, VA 22209
***Tel: (703) 841-2300***
***www.rila.org***

**Shoe Service Institute of America**
18 School St.
North Brookfield, MA 01535
***Tel: (508) 867-7732***
***www.ssia.info***

**Textile Society of America**
P.O. Box 193
Middletown, DE 19709
***Tel. (302) 378-9636***
***www.textilesociety.org***

**UNITE HERE**
275 7th Avenue
New York, NY 10001
***Tel: (212) 265-7000***
***www.unitehere.org***

**United Scenic Artists**
29 West 38th Street, 15th Fl.
New York, NY 10018
***Tel: (212) 581-0300***
***www.usa829.org***

# CELEBRITY FASHION LINES

**Aneres**
4199 Maya Cay
Jupiter, FL 33458
***Tel: (561) 630-9400***
***www.aneresdesigns.com***
***Serena Williams***

**Apple Bottoms**
1385 Broadway, 16th Fl.
New York, NY 10018
***Tel: (212) 221-4700 - ext. 129***
***www.applebottoms***
***Nelly***

**Argyle Culture**
***www.argyleculture.com***
***Russell Simmons***

**Baby Phat & KLS**
512 7th Ave., 29th Fl.
New York, NY 10018
***Tel: (212) 798-3100***
***www.babyphat.com***
***www.kls.com***
***Kimora Lee Simmons***

**Mischa Barton for Stacey Lapidus**
Stacey Lapidus, LLC
18090 Collins Avenue, #T17-201
Sunny Isles Beach, FL 33160
***Tel: (305) 692-8609***
***www.staceylapidus.com***
***Mischa Barton***

**Benjamin Bixby**
***www.benjamin-bixby.com***
***André Benjamin/André 3000***

**Billionaires Boys Club**
***www.bbcicecream.com***
***Pharrell Williams***

**Brown Sugar**
***Tel: (212) 397-0981***
***www.simmonsjewelryco.com/brownsugar/***
***Justine Simmons***

**Celine Dion Parfums**
***www.celinedionbeauty.com***
***Celine Dion***

**Edun**
***www.edunonline.com***
***Bono***

**Eleven**
***www.elevenbyvenus.com***
***Venus Williams***

**Fancy Jessica Simpson**
Parlux Fragrances
5900 N. Andrews Ave., Ste. 500
Ft. Lauderdale, FL 33309
***Tel: (954) 316-9008***
***www.parlux.com***
***Jessica Simpson***

**Forever Your Girl Collection**
***www.paulaabdul.com***
***Paula Abdul***

**G-UNIT Clothing**
***www.g-unitclothing.com***
***Curtis Jackson/50-Cent***

**Halle**
***www.halleberryfragrances.com***
***Halle Berry***

**Steve Harvey Collection**
***www.steveharvey.com/collection***
***Steve Harvey***

**Hawk Clothing**
***www.hawkclothing.com***
***Tony Hawk***

**Faith Hill Parfums**
***www.faithhill.com/fragrances***
***Faith Hill***

**Nicky Hilton**
***www.nickyhilton.com***
***Nicky Hilton***

**Paris Hilton Fragrances**
Parlux Fragrances
5900 N. Andrews Ave., Ste. 500
Ft. Lauderdale, FL 33309
***Tel: (954) 316-9008***
***www.parlux.com***
***Paris Hilton***

**House of Dereon**
***Tel: (646) 308-5500***

***www.houseofdereon.com***
***Beyoncé Knowles***

**Ice Cream**
***www.bbcicecream.com***
***Pharrell Williams***

**Janet Jackson Intimate/Pleasure Principle**
9595 Wilshire Blvd., Ste. 900
Beverly Hills, CA 90212
***Tel: (310) 300-8428***
***www.jupicorp.com***
***Janet Jackson***

**JLO by Jennifer Lopez**
***www.jenniferlopezbeauty.com***
***Jennifer Lopez***

**L.e.i. Sundresses by Taylor Swift**
1441 Broadway
New York, NY 10018
***Tel: (212) 575-2571***
***www.leijeans.com***
***Taylor Swift***

**Lovely**
***www.sarahjessicaparkerbeauty.com***
***Sarah Jessica Parker***

**M Mariah Carey's Luscious Pink**
***www.mariahcarey.com/fragrance***
***Mariah Carey *(Forever fragrance too)***

**Mblem**
***www.mblem.net***
***Mandy Moore***

**McGraw Southern Blend**
***www.timmcgrawfragrances.com***
***Tim McGraw***

**Mary-Kate And Ashley Olsen**
Dualstar Entertainment Group
3760 Robertson Blvd., 2nd Fl.
Culver City, CA 90232
***Tel: (310) 553-9000***
***www.marykateandashley.com***
***Mary-Kate & Ashley Olsen***

**Pastry Kicks**
***Tel: (212) 542-3143***
***www.pastrykicks.com***
***Angela & Vanessa Simmons***

**Phat Fashions, LLC**
512 7th Ave., 29th Fl.
New York, NY 10018
***Tel: (212) 798-3100***
***www.phatfarm.com***
***Kimora Lee Simmons & Russell Simmons***

**Sarah Jessica Parker**
***www.sarahjessicaparkerbeauty.com***
***Sarah Jessica Parker***

**Queen by Queen Latifah**
Parlux Fragrances
5900 N. Andrews Ave., Ste. 500
Ft. Lauderdale, FL 33309
***Tel: (954) 316-9008***
***www.parlux.com***
***Queen Latifah***

**Joan Rivers Classics Collection**
***www.joanrivers.com***
***Joan Rivers***

**Rocawear**
***Tel: (800) 839-6016/(201) 601-4298***
***www.rocawear.com***
***Shawn "Jay-Z" Carter***

**Andy Roddick**
Parlux Fragrances
5900 N. Andrews Ave., Ste. 500
Ft. Lauderdale, FL 33309
***Tel: (954) 316-9008***
***www.parlux.com***
***Andy Roddick***

**Sean John**
1710 Broadway, 2nd Fl.
New York, NY 10019
***Tel: (212) 500-2200***
***www.seanjohn.com***
***Sean Combs/P. Diddy***

**Maria Sharapova by Cole Haan**
***www.colehaan.com***
***Maria Sharapova***

**Simmons Jewelry Co.**
***www.simmonsjewelryco.com***
***Russell Simmons***

**Jessica Simpson Collection**
***www.jessicasimpsoncollection.com***
***Jessica Simpson***

**Jaclyn Smith**
***www.jaclynsmith.com***
***Jaclyn Smith***

**Touch Clothing**
***www.alyssa.com/category/touch clothing***
***Alyssa Milano***

**Donald J. Trump Signature Collection**
The Trump Organization
725 Fifth Avenue
New York, NY 10022
***Tel: (212) 932-2000***
***www.trump.com***
***Donald Trump***

**Ivanka Trump Fine Jewelry**
685 Madison Avenue
New York, NY 10065
***Tel: (212) 756-9912***
***www.ivankatrumpcollection.com***
***Ivanka Trump***

**Usher**
Elizabeth Arden, Inc.
200 Park Avenue S., 7th Fl.
New York, NY 10003
***Tel: (212) 261-1000***
***www.elizabetharden.com***
***Usher Raymond***

**West Coast Choppers**
718 West Anaheim St.
Long Beach, CA 90813
**Tel: (562) 983-6666**
***www.westcoastchoppers.com/apparel***
***Jesse James***

**William Rast**
***Tel: (800) 977-9540***
***www.williamrast.com***
***Justin Timberlake***

# DEPARTMENT & RETAIL STORES

**Abercrombie & Fitch Co.**
6301 Fitch Path
New Albany, OH 43054
***Tel: (614) 283-6500***
***www.abercrombie.com***

**Aéropostale, Inc.**
112 W. 34th St., 22nd Fl.
New York, NY 10120
***Tel: (646) 485-5410***
***www.aeropostale.com***

**American Eagle Outfitters, Inc.**
77 Hot Metal Street
Pittsburgh, PA 15203
***Tel: (412) 432-3300***
***www.ae.com***

**Ann Taylor**
7 Times Square Tower, 15th Fl.
New York, NY 10036
***Tel: (212) 541-3300***
***www.anntaylorstorescorp.com***

**Banana Republic**
Gap Inc.
Two Folsom Street
San Francisco, CA 94105
***Tel: (650) 952-4400***
***www.gapinc.com***
***Includes: Banana Republic; Gap; Old Navy***

**Barneys New York, Inc.**
575 5th Avenue
New York, NY 10017
***Tel: (212) 339-7300***
***www.barneys.com***

**Belk**
2801 W. Tyvola Road
Charlotte, NC 28217
***Tel: (704) 357-4000***
***www.belk.com***

**Bergdorf Goodman**
754 Fifth Avenue
New York, NY 10019
***Tel: (800) 558-1855***
***www.bergdorfgoodman.com***

**The Bon-Ton Stores, Inc.**
2801 East Market Street
York, PA 17402
***Tel: (717) 757-7660***
***www.bonton.com***

**Burlington Coat Factory**
1830 Rt. 130
Burlington, NJ 08016
***Tel: (609) 387-7800***
***www.burlingtoncoatfactory.com***

**Caché, Inc.**
1440 Broadway, 5th Fl.
New York, NY 10018
***Tel: (212) 575-3200***
***www.cache.com***

**Catherines Plus Sizes**
450 Winks Lane
Bensalem, PA 19020
***Tel: (215) 245-9100***
***www.catherines.com***

**Charming Shoppes, Inc.**
450 Winks Lane
Bensalem, PA 19020
***Tel: (215) 245-9100***
***www.charmingshoppes.com***
***Includes: Catherines; Fashion Bug; Lane Bryant***

**Chico's FAS, Inc.**
11215 Metro Pkwy.
Fort Myers, FL 33966
***Tel: (239) 277-6200***
***www.chicos.com***

**Dillard's**
1600 Cantrell
Little Rock, AR 72201
***Tel: (501) 376-5200***
***www.dillards.com***

**Forever 21, Inc.**
2001 S. Alameda St.
Los Angeles, CA 90058
***Tel: (213) 741-5100***
***www.forever21.com***

**Gap Inc.**
Two Folsom Street
San Francisco, CA 94105
***Tel: (650) 952-4400***

**www.gapinc.com**
***Includes: Banana Republic; Gap; Old Navy***

**H & M (Hennes & Mauritz LP)**
215 Park Avenue S., 15th Fl.
New York, NY 10003
***Tel: (212) 564-9922***
***www.hm.com***

**Harrods**
***www.harrods.com***

**Ron Herman**
8100 Melrose Avenue
Los Angeles, CA 90046
***Tel: (323) 651-4129***
***www.ronherman.com***

**Hermes**
***www.hermes.com***

**Henri Bendel**
666 5th Avenue
New York, NY 10003
***Tel: (800) 423-6335***
***www.henribendel.com***

**Holt Renfrew**
***www.holtrenfrew.com***

**JC Penney**
6501 Legacy Drive
Plano, TX 75024
***Tel: (972) 431-8200***
***www.jcpenney.net/careers***

**J. Crew Group, Inc.**
770 Broadway
New York, NY 10003
***Tel: (212) 209-2500***
***www.jcrew.com***

**Kohl's**
N56 W17000 Ridgewood Dr.
Menomonee Falls, WI 53051
***Tel: (262) 703-7000***
***www.kohls.com***

**Lands' End**
5 Lands' End Lane
Dodgeville, WI 53595
***Tel: (608) 935-9341***
***www.landsend.com/jobs/opportunities/internship/***

**Lane Bryant**
3344 Morse Crossing
Columbus, OH 43219
***Tel: (614) 463-5200***
***www.lanebryant.com***

**L.L. Bean**
***www.llbean.com***

**Lord & Taylor**
424 5th Avenue
New York, NY 10018
***Tel: (212) 391-3344***
***www.lordandtaylor.com***

**Macy's, Inc.**
7 W. 7th Street
Cincinnati, OH 45202
***Tel: (513) 579-7000***
***www.federated-fds.com/macys/***

**The Men's Wearhouse, Inc.**
6380 Rogerdale Rd.
Houston, TX 77072
***Tel: (281) 776-7200***
***www.menswearhouse.com***

**The Neiman Marcus Group, Inc.**
1618 Main St.
Dallas, TX 75201
***Tel: (214) 743-7600***
***www.neimanmarcus.com***

**Nordstrom, Inc.**
1617 6th Avenue
Seattle, WA 98101
***Tel: (206) 628-2111***
***www.nordstrom.com***

**Sears Holdings Corporation**
3333 Beverly Rd.
Hoffman Estates, IL 60179
***Tel: (847) 286-2500***
***www.searsholdings.com***

**Saks Fifth Avenue**
12 East 49th Street
New York, NY 10017
***Tel: (212) 940 5305***
***www.saksfifthavenue.com***

**Ross Stores**
4440 Rosewood Dr.
Pleasanton, CA 94588
***Tel: (925) 965-4400***
***www.rossstores.com***

**Fred Segal**
420 Broadway
Santa Monica, CA 90401
***Tel: (310) 458-2800***
***www.fredsegal.com***

**Fred Segal Couture**
500 Broadway
Santa Monica, CA 90401
***Tel: (310) 458-8100***
***www.fredsegalcouture.com***

**Talbots**
The Talbots, Inc.
1 Talbots Dr.
Hingham, MA 02043
***Tel: (781) 749-7600***
***www.talbots.com***

**Von Maur**
6565 Brady Street
Davenport, IA 52806
***Tel: (563) 388-2200***
***www.vonmaur.com***

**White House | Black Market**
11215 Metro Parkway
Fort Myers, FL 33966
***Tel: (239) 277-6200***
***www.whitehouseblackmarket.com***

# FASHION DESIGNERS

**Giorgio Armani Corporation**
114 Fifth Avenue, 17th Fl.
New York, NY 10011
***Tel: (212) 366 9720***
***www.armanipress.com***

**Max Azria**
2761 Fruitland Avenue
Vernon, CA 90058
***Tel: (323) 589-2224***
***www.bcbgmaxazriagroup.com***

**BCBGMAXAZRIA**
2761 Fruitland Avenue
Vernon, CA 90058
***Tel: (323) 589-2224***
***www.bcbgmaxazriagroup.com***

**Geoffrey Beene, LLC**
37 West 57th Street
New York, NY 10019
***Tel: (212) 371-5570***
***www.geoffreybeene.com***

**Chris Benz**
307 W. 38th St., #1201
New York, NY 10018
***Tel: (212) 244-2020***
***www.chris-benz.com***

**Manolo Blahnik USA, Ltd.**
31 W. 54th Street
New York, NY 10019
***Tel: (212) 582-3007***
***www.manoloblahnik.com***

**Hugo Boss**
601 West 26th St., 8th Fl.
New York, NY 10001
***Tel: (212) 940-0600***
***www.hugoboss.com***
***www.valentinofashiongroup.com***

**Dana Buchman**
***www.danabuchman.com***

**Burberry**
***www.burberry.com***

**Roberto Cavalli**
***www.robertocavalli.com***

**Reco Chapple**
3459 Brainerd Road, Ste. B
Chattanooga, TN 3741
***Tel: (423) 475-6034***
***www.houseofchapple.com***

**CHANEL**
9 W. 57th Street Street
New York, NY 10019
***Tel: (212) 688-5055***
***www.chanel.com***

**David Chu**
DC Design International
25 E. 22nd Street
New York, NY 10010
***Tel: (212) 277-6400***
***www.davidchudesign.com***

**Liz Claiborne**
1441 Broadway
New York, NY 10018
***Tel: (212) 626-5200***
***www.lizclaiborneinc.com***
***Includes: Juicy Couture; Kate Spade; Lucky Brand Jeans***

**Kenneth Cole**
603 West 50th Street
New York, NY 10019
***Tel: (212) 265-1500***
***www.kennethcole.com***

**Robert Danes**
481 Greenwich St., #5B/5N
New York, NY 10013
***Tel: (212) 674-3252***
***www.robertdanes.com***

**Chloe Dao**
Dao Chloe Dao
1318 Blair Street
Houston, TX 77003
***Tel: (713) 863-7311***
***www.chloedao.com***

**Oscar de la Renta**
550 7th Avenue
New York, NY 10018
***Tel: (212) 354-6777***
***www.oscardelarenta.com***

"The Harder I Work, the Luckier I Get…unfortunately I can't take credit for this one though. It is a quote by the famous golfer Gary Player."

Ivanka Trump
Executive Vice President of
Development & Acquisitions
of The Trump Organization
Principle of Ivanka Trump Fine Jewelry

**Lyn Devon**
***www.lyndevon.com***

**Dolce & Gabbana USA Inc.**
148 Lafayette Street
New York, NY 10013
***Tel: (212) 750-0055***
***www.dolcegabanna.com***

**Marc Ecko Enterprises**
40 West 23rd Street
New York NY, 10010
***Tel: (917) 262-1002***
***www.marceckoenterprises.com***

**Evan-Picone**
498 7th Avenue
New York, NY 10018
***Tel: (212) 642-3780***
****Jones Apparel Group***

**Fendi**
Taramax USA Inc.
600 Warren Avenue
Spring Lake Heights, NJ 07762
***Tel: (732) 282-0300***
***www.fendi.com***

**Erin Fetherston**
252 W. 37th St., Ste. 1801
New York, NY 10018
***Tel: (212) 643-7537***
***www.erinfetherston.com***

**Fubu**
350 Fifth Avenue, Ste. 6617
New York, NY 10118
***Tel: (212) 273-3300***
***www.fubu.com***

**Jean-Paul Gaultier**
***www.jeanpaul-gaultier.com***

**Givenchy**
***www.givenchy.com***

**Gucci**
685 Fifth Avenue, 8th Fl.
New York, NY 10022
***Tel: (212) 750-5220***
***www.gucci.com***

**Kevan Hall**
8313 Beverly Blvd.
Los Angeles, CA 90048
***Tel: (323) 658-7979***
***www.kevanhalldesigns.com***

**Tim Hamilton**
***www.timhamilton.com***

**Carolina Herrera**
48 West 38th Street
New York, NY 10018
***Tel: (212) 719-3150***
***www.carolinaherrera.com***

**Tommy Hilfiger**
601 W 26th Street, Ste. 600
New York, NY 10001
***Tel: (212) 549-6000***
***www.tommy.com***

**Iconix Brand Group, Inc.**
1450 Broadway, 4th Fl.
New York, NY 10018
***Tel: (212) 730-0030***
***www.iconixbrand.com***

**Marc Jacobs International LLC**
72 Spring Street, 2nd Fl.
New York, NY 10012
***www.marcjacobs.com***

**Betsey Johnson**
498 7th Avenue, 21st Fl.
New York, NY 10018
***Tel: (212) 244-0843***
***www.betseyjohnson.com***

**Jones Apparel Group**
1411 Broadway
New York, NY 10018
***Tel: (212) 642-3860***
***www.jonesapparel.com***

**Donna Karan**
Donna Karan International Inc.
550 7th Avenue
New York, NY 10018
***Tel: (212) 789-1500***
***www.donnakaran.com***

**Calvin Klein**
205 W. 39th Street
New York, NY 10018
***Tel: (866) 214-6694***
***www.calvinklein.com***

**Michael Knight**
***www.mychaelknight.com***

**Christopher & Nicholas Kunz**
***www.nicholask.com***

**Lacoste**
***www.lacoste.com***

**Karl Lagerfeld**
***www.karllagerfeld.com***

**Ralph Lauren**
Polo Ralph Lauren Corporation
625 Madison Avenue
New York, NY 10022
***Tel: 212-318-7000***
***www.ralphlauren.com***

**Nanette Lepore**
225 W. 35th Street, 8th Fl.
New York, NY 10001
***Tel: (212) 594-0012/(212) 219-8265***
***www.nanettelepore.com***

**Marcella and Johan Lindeberg**
J. Lindeberg USA, LLC
57 E. 11th Street, Ste. 8A
New York, NY 10003
***Tel: (212) 625-8600***
***www.jlindeberg.com***

**Christian Louboutin**
***www.christianlouboutin.com***

**Bob Mackie**
Bob Mackie Design Group, Ltd.
230 Park Avenue, Ste. 446
New York, NY 10169
***Tel: (212) 813-1900***
***www.bobmackie.com***

**Stella McCartney**
***www.stellamccartney.com***

**Jessica McClintock, Inc.**
1400 16th Street
San Francisco, CA 94103
***Tel: (800) 711-8718***
***www.jessicamcclintock.com***

**Alexander McQueen**
***www.alexandermcqueen.com***

**Nicole Miller**
525 Seventh Avenue
New York, NY, 10018
***Tel: (212) 719-9200***
***www.nicolemiller.com***

**Badgley Mischka**
525 Seventh Avenue
New York, NY 10018
***Tel: (212) 921-1585***
***www.badgleymischka.com***

**Isaac Mizrahi**
Isaac Mizrahi Studio
475 Tenth Avenue, 4th Fl.
New York, NY 10018
***www.isaacmizrahiny.com***

**Thierry Mugler**
***www.thierrymugler.com***

**Irene Neuwirth**
***www.ireneneuwirth.com***

**The North Face**
2013 Farallon Drive
San Leandro, CA 94577
***Tel: (510) 618-3500***
***www.thenorthface.com***

**Phillips-Van Heusen**
1001 Frontier Road, MS#44
Bridgewater, NJ 08807
***Tel: (908) 231-6660***
***www.pvh.com***

**Loro Piana**
711 5th Ave., 11th Fl.
New York, NY 10022
***Tel: (212) 980-7960***
***www.loropiana.com***

**Maria Pinto**
135 N. Jefferson Street
Chicago, IL 60661
***Tel: (312) 648-1350***
***www.mariapinto.com***

**Zac Posen**
13-17 Laight Street
New York, NY 10013
***Tel: (212) 925-1263***
***www.zacposen.com***

**Prada USA Corp.**
609 W. 51 Street
New York, NY 10019
***Tel: (212) 307-9300***
***www.prada.com***

**Narciso Rodriguez**
***www.narcisorodriguez.com***

**Yves Saint Laurent**
3 East 57th Street, 4th Fl.
New York, NY 10022
***Tel: (212) 832-7100***
***www.ysl.com***

**Simon Spurr**
***www.spur.tv***

**Anna Sui**
***www.annasui.com***

**Albertus Swanepoel**
124 W. 30th Street, Rm. 304
New York, NY 10001
***Tel: (212) 629-1090***
***www.albertusswanepoel.com***

**Swarovski**
1 Kenney Drive
Cranston, RI 02920
***Tel: (401) 734-1800/(800) 426-3088***
***www.swarovski.com***

**Elie Tahari**
***www.elietahari.com***

**Rebecca Taylor**
307 W. 36th St., 15th Fl.
New York, NY 10018
***Tel: (212) 302-6485***
***www.rebeccataylor.com***

**Ellen Tracy**
1400 Broadway, 32nd Fl.
New York, NY 10018
***Tel: (212) 515-5300***
***www.ellentracy.com***

**Ivanka Trump**
685 Madison Avenue
New York, NY 10065
***Tel: (212) 756-9912***
***www.ivankatrumpcollection.com***

**Emanuel Ungaro**
***www.ungaro.com***

**Valentino**
11 W. 42nd Street, 26th Fl.
New York, NY 10036
***Tel: (212) 997-8100***
***www.valentino.com***

**Gloria Vanderbilt**
1441 Broadway
New York, NY 10018
***Tel: (212) 575-2571***
***www.gloria-vanderbilt.com***

**Versace**
***www.versace.com***

**Diane von Furstenberg**
DVF Studio
440 W. 14th Street
New York, NY 10014
***Tel: (212) 741-6607***
***www.dvf.com***

**Louis Vuitton**
***www.louisvuitton.com***
***www.lvmh.com***

**Vera Wang**
225 West 39th Street
New York, NY 10018
***Tel: (212) 575-6400***
***www.verawang.com***

**Jason Wu**
***Tel: (212) 643-0598***
***www.jasonwu.com***
***www.thewstudio.com***

# FASHION SCHOOLS

**Academy of Art University**
79 New Montgomery Street
San Francisco, CA 94105
***Tel: (415) 274-2200***
***www.academyart.edu***

**The Art Institutes**
***Tel: (888) 624-0300***
***www.artinstitutes.edu/campuslocations/***
***(*40+ Locations Nationwide. Call to Find a Campus Near You)***

**Art Institute of California Hollywood**
3440 Wilshire Blvd., 10th Fl.
Los Angeles, CA 90010
***Tel: (213) 251-3636***
***www.artinstitutes.edu/campuslocations/***

**Art Institute of California Los Angeles**
2900 31st Street
Santa Monica, CA 90405
***Tel: (310) 752-4700***
***www.artinstitutes.edu/campuslocations/***

**Art Institute of California San Francisco**
1170 Market Street
San Francisco, CA 94102
***Tel: (415) 865-0198***
***www.artinstitutes.edu/campuslocations/***

**Art Institute of Charlotte**
Three Lake Pointe Plaza
2110 Water Ridge Parkway
Charlotte, NC 28217
***Tel: (704) 357-802***
***www.artinstitutes.edu/campuslocations/***

**Art Institute of Dallas**
8080 Park Lane, Ste. 100
Dallas, TX 75231
***Tel: (214) 692-8080***
***www.artinstitutes.edu/campuslocations/***

**Art Institute of Houston**
1900 Yorktown Street
Houston, TX 77056
***Tel: (713) 623-2040***
***www.artinstitutes.edu/campuslocations/***

**Art Institute of New York**
75 Varick Street, 16th Fl.
New York, NY 10013
***Tel: (212) 226-5500***
***www.artinstitutes.edu/campuslocations/***

**Art Institute of Pittsburgh**
420 Boulevard of the Allies
Pittsburgh, PA 15219
***Tel: (412) 263-6600***
***www.artinstitutes.edu/campuslocations/***

**Art Institute of Seattle**
2323 Elliott Avenue
Seattle, WA 98121
***Tel: (206) 448-6600***
***www.artinstitutes.edu/campuslocations/***

**Art Institute of Washington**
1820 N. Fort Myer Drive
Arlington, VA 22209
***Tel: (703) 358-9550***
***www.artinstitutes.edu/campuslocations/***

**Bauder College**
384 Northyards Boulevard, NW
Suites 190 & 400
Atlanta, GA 30313
***Tel: (404) 237-7573***
***www.atlanta.bauder.edu***

**California College of the Arts**
1111 Eighth Street
San Francisco, CA 94107
***Tel: (415) 703-9500***
***www.cca.edu***

**California College of the Arts**
5212 Broadway
Oakland, CA 94618
***Tel: (510) 594-3600***

***www.cca.edu***

**Columbus College of Art & Design**
107 N. Ninth St.
Columbus, OH 43215
***Tel: (614) 224-9101***
***www.ccad.edu***

**Drexel University**
Antoinette Westphal College of Media Arts & Design
Nesbitt Hall
33rd and Market Streets
Philadelphia, PA 19104
***Tel: (215) 895-1834***
***www.drexel.edu/westphal/***

**Fashion Institute of Design & Merchandising (FIDM)**
919 S. Grand Avenue
Los Angeles, CA 90015
***Tel: (213) 624-1201***
***Tel: (800) 624-1200***
***www.fidm.edu***

**Fashion Institute of Design & Merchandising (FIDM)**
17590 Gillette Avenue
Irvine, CA 92614
***Tel: (949) 851-6200***
***Tel: (888) 974-3436***
***www.fidm.edu***

**Fashion Institute of Design & Merchandising (FIDM)**
55 Stockton Street
San Francisco, CA 94108
***Tel: (415) 675-5200***
***Tel: (800) 422-3436***
***www.fidm.edu***

**Fashion Institute of Design & Merchandising (FIDM)**
350 Tenth Avenue, 3rd Fl.
San Diego, CA 92101
***Tel: (619) 235-2049***
***Tel: (800) 243-3436***
***www.fidm.edu***

**Fashion Institute of Technology (FIT)**
Seventh Avenue @ 27th Street
New York, NY 10001
***Tel: (212) 217-7999***
***www.fitnyc.edu***

**Georgia Southern University**
College of Health & Human Sciences
Fashion Merch. & Apparel Design
P.O. Box 8073
Statesboro, GA 30460
***Tel: (912) 478-5322/(912) 478-5339***
***www.georgiasouthern.edu/majors***

**Int'l. Academy of Design & Technology - Chicago**
One North State Street, Ste. 500
Chicago, IL 60602
***Tel: (312) 980-9200***
***www.iadtchicago.edu***

**Int'l. Academy of Design & Technology - Detroit**
1850 Research Drive
Troy, MI 48083
***Tel: (248) 526-1700***
***www.iadtdetroit.com***

**Int'l. Academy of Design & Technology - Las Vegas**
2495 Village View Drive
Henderson, NV 89074
***Tel: (702) 990-0150***
***www.iadtvegas.com***

**Int'l. Academy of Design & Technology - Nashville**
1 Bridgestone Park
Nashville, TN 37214
***Tel: (615) 232-7384***
***www.iadtnashville.com***

**Int'l. Academy of Design & Technology - Orlando**
5959 Lake Ellenor Drive
Orlando, FL 32809
***Tel: (407) 857-2300***
***www.iadt.edu***

**Int'l. Academy of Design & Technology - Sacramento**
2450 Del Paso Road
Sacramento, CA 95834
***Tel: (916) 285-9468***
***www.iadtsacramento.com***

**Int'l. Academy of Design & Technology - San Antonio**
4511 Horizon Hill Boulevard
San Antonio, TX 78229
***Tel: (210) 530-9449***
***www.iadtsanantonio.com***

**Int'l. Academy of Design & Technology - Seattle**
645 Andover Park West
Seattle, WA 98188
***Tel: (206) 575-1865***
***www.iadtseattle.com***

**Int'l. Academy of Design & Technology - Schaumburg**
915 National Parkway
Schaumburg, IL 60173
***Tel: (847) 969-2800***
***www.iadtschaumburg.com***

**Int'l. Academy of Design & Technology - Tampa**
5104 Eisenhower Blvd.
Tampa, FL 33634
***Tel: (888) 315-6111***
***www.academy.edu***

**Kent State University**
School of Fashion Design & Merchandising
P.O. Box 5190
Kent, OH 44242
***Tel: (330) 672-3010***
***www.fashionschool.kent.edu***

**Massachusetts College of Art and Design**
621 Huntington Avenue
Boston, MA 02115
***Tel: (617) 879-7000***
***www.massart.edu***

**Miami Int'l. University of Art & Design**
1501 Biscayne Blvd., Ste. 100
Miami, FL 33132
***Tel: (800) 225-9023***
***www.artinstitutes.edu/miami/***

**North Carolina State University**
College of Textiles
2401 Research Drive/Box 8301
Raleigh, NC 27695
***Tel: (919) 515-3442***
***www.tx.ncsu.edu***

**Otis College of Art and Design**
9045 Lincoln Boulevard
Los Angeles, CA 90045
***Tel: (310) 665-6800***
***www.otis.edu***

**Paris Fashion Institute**
355 W. Fourth Street
Boston, MA 02127
***Tel: (617) 268-0026***
***www.parisfashion.org***

**Parsons The New School For Design**
66 Fifth Avenue
New York, NY 10011
***Tel: (212) 229-8900***
***www.parsons.edu***

**Pratt Institute**
200 Willoughby Avenue
Brooklyn, NY 11205
***Tel: (718) 636-3600***
***www.pratt.edu***

**Pratt Institute**
144 West 14th Street
New York, NY 10011
***Tel: (718) 636-3600***
***www.pratt.edu***

**Rhode Island School of Design**
Two College Street
Providence, RI 02903
***Tel: (401) 454-6100***
***www.risd.edu***

**Savannah College of Art & Design**
P.O. Box 3146
Savannah, GA 31402
***Tel: (912) 525-5000***
***Tel: (404) 253-2700***
***www.scad.edu/fashion/***

**Seattle Pacific University**
3307 Third Avenue W.
Seattle, WA 98119
***Tel: (206) 281-2000***
***www.spu.edu***

**University of Cincinnati**
College of Design, Architecture, Art & Planning
5470 Aronoff Center
P.O. Box 210016
Cincinnati, OH 45221
***Tel: (513) 556-1376***
***www.daap.uc.edu/schools***

**University of South Carolina**
College of Hospitality, Retail & Sports Management
Columbia, SC 29208
***Tel: (803) 777-4290***
***www.hrsm.sc.edu/retail***

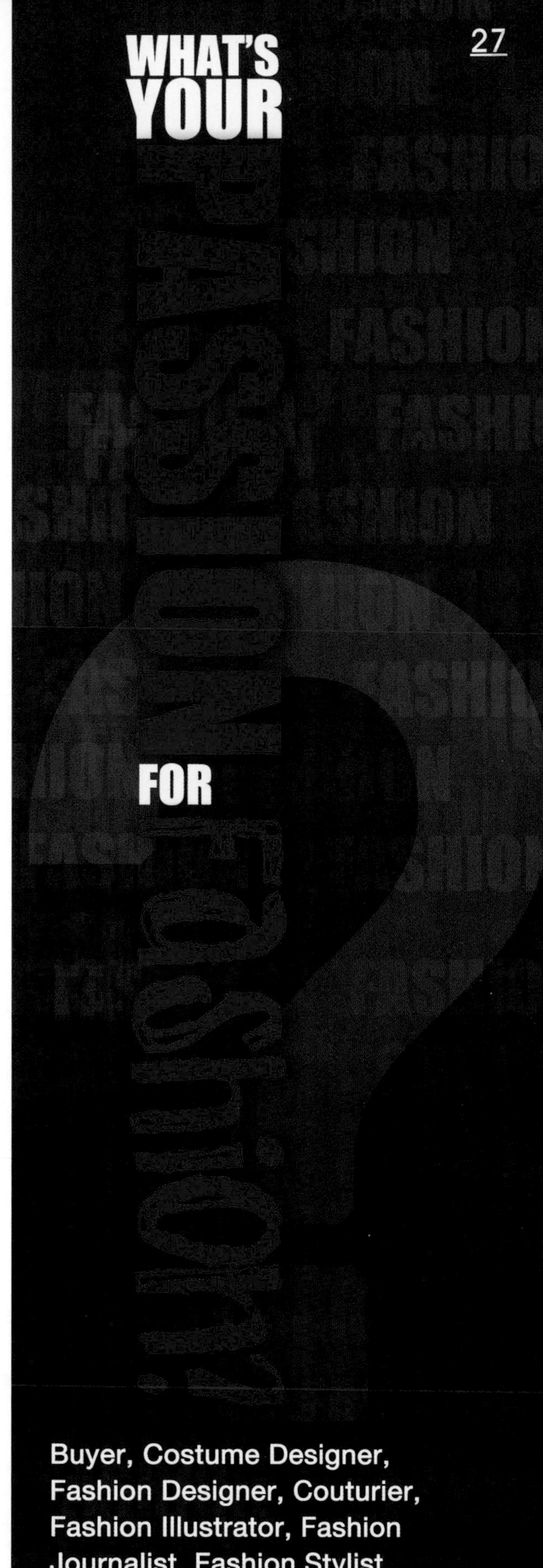
WHAT'S YOUR
PASSION
FOR
FASHION?

**Buyer, Costume Designer, Fashion Designer, Couturier, Fashion Illustrator, Fashion Journalist, Fashion Stylist, Haute Couture, Merchandiser, Pattern Maker, Runway Model, Textile Designer/Colorist?**

# FOOTWEAR COMPANIES

**Adidas America, Inc.**
5055 N.Greeley Avenue
Portland, OR 97217
***Tel: (971) 234-2300***
***www.adidas-group.com***

**American Sporting Goods Corp. Avia/Ryka/NSS**
101 Enterprise, Ste. 100
Alisa Viejo, CA 92656
***Tel: (949) 752-6688***

**ASICS America**
29 Parker, Ste. 100
Irvine, CA 92618
***Tel: (949) 727-7141***
***www.asics.com***

**Auri Footwear**
1200 North Coast Highway
Laguna Beach, CA 92651
***Tel: (949) 793-4045***
***www.aurifootwear.com***

**Ballard Custom Footwear**
7805 W. Sunset Blvd.
Hollywood, CA 90028
***Tel: (323) 876-7308/(323) 333-9137***
***www.ballardfootwear.com***

**BCBGMAXAZRIA Footwear**
1370 Ave. of the Americas, 8th Fl.
New York, NY 10019
***Tel: (212) 246-4735***
***www.bcbgmaxazriagroup.com***

**Birkenstock**
***www.birkenstockusa.com***

**Manolo Blahnik USA, Ltd.**
31 W. 54th Street
New York, NY 10019
***Tel: (212) 582-3007***
***www.manoloblahnik.com***

**Brown Shoe Company, Inc.**
Famous Footwear, Shoes.com
8300 Maryland Ave.
St. Louis, MO 63105
***Tel: (314) 854-4000***
***www.brownshoe.com***

**Bruno Magli**
75 Triangle Boulevard
Carlstadt, NJ 07072
***Tel: (201) 623-7800***
***www.brunomagli.it***

**René Caovilla**
***www.renecaovilla.com***

**Cels/Chinese Laundry**
3485 S. La Cienega Blvd.
Los Angeles, CA 90016
***Tel: (310) 838-2103/(310) 945-3299***
***www.chineselaundry.com***

**Jimmy Choo**
750 Lexington Avenue, 22nd Fl.
New York, NY10022
***Tel: (212) 319-1111***
***www.jimmychoo.com***

**Kenneth Cole**
603 West 50th Street
New York, NY 10019
***Tel: (212) 265-1500***
***www.kennethcole.com***

**Charles David**
5731 Buckingham Parkway
Culver City, CA 90230
***Tel: (310) 348-5050***
***www.charlesdavid.com***

**Cole Haan Holdings, Inc.**
1 Cole Haan Dr.
Yarmouth, ME 04096
***Tel: (207) 846-2500***
***www.colehaan.com***

**Collective Brands**
3231 SE Sixth Avenue
Topeka, KS 66607
***Tel: (785) 233-5171***
***www.collectivebrands.com***
***www.payless.com***
***Includes: Airwalk; Keds; Payless Shoe Source; Saucony; Sperry Top-Sider***

**Converse**
One High Street
North Andover, MA 01845
***Tel: (978) 983-3300***
***www.converse.com***

**Diadora**
*www.diadoraamerica.com*

**Dr. Martens**
*www.drmartens.com*

**Dusica Dusica**
67 Prince Street
New York, NY 10012
*Tel: (212) 966-1699*
*www.dusicadusica.com*

**The Finish Line, Inc.**
3308 N. Mitthoeffer Rd.
Indianapolis, IN 46235
*Tel: (317) 899-1022*
*www.finishline.com*

**Foot Locker, Inc.**
112 West 34th Street
New York, NY 10120
*Tel: (212) 720-3700*
*www.footlocker-inc.com*

**Harbor Footwear Group, Ltd.**
55 Harbor Park Drive
Port Washington, NY 11050
*Tel: (516) 621-8400*
*www.harborfootwear.com*

**Jack Schwartz Shoes, Inc.**
155 Sixth Avenue
New York, NY 10013
*Tel: (212) 691-4700*
*www.lugz.com*
*Includes: Lugz/JSSI/Snow/British Knights*

**Johnston & Murphy**
1415 Murfreesboro Rd./P.O. Box 731
Nashville, TN 37202
*Tel: (615) 367-7000*
*www.genesco.com*

**Jones Apparel Group**
1411 Broadway
New York, NY 10018
*Tel: (212) 642-3860*
*www.jonesapparel.com*
**Includes: Bandolino; Easy Spirit; Enzo Angiolini; Joan & David; Nine West & More*

**Michael Kors (USA), Inc.**
11 W. 42nd St., 21st Fl.
New York, NY 10036
*Tel: (212) 201-8100*
*www.michaelkors.com*

**K-Swiss**
31248 Oak Crest Drive
Westlake Village, CA 91361
*Tel: (818) 706-5100*
*www.kswiss.com*

**Christian Louboutin**
965 Madison Avenue
New York, NY 10021
*Tel: (212) 396-1884*
*www.christianlouboutin.com*

**LaDuca**
534 Ninth Avenue
New York, NY 10018
*Tel: (212) 268-6751/(212) 586-2079*
*www.laducashoes.com*

**Lanvin**
*www.lanvin.com*

**Steven Madden, Ltd.**
52-16 Barnett Ave.
Long Island City, NY 11104
*Tel: (718) 446-1800*
*www.stevemadden.com*

**Maxwell Shoe Company**
101 Sprague Street
Hyde Park, MA 02136
*Tel: (617) 364-5090*
*Brands: Mootsies Tootsies; Sam & Libby*

**Nike**
One Bowerman Drive
Beaverton, OR 97005
*Tel: (503) 671-6453*
*www.nike.com & www.nike.biz*

**Nine West Footwear**
1129 Westchester Ave.
White Plains, NY 10604
*Tel: (914) 640-6400*
*www.ninewest.com*

**Nina**
*www.ninashoes.com*

**Pastry Kicks**
*www.pastrykicks.com*

**PONY International LLC.**
1250 J Street, 2nd Fl.
San Diego, CA 92101
*Tel: (619) 814-5499*
*www.pony.com*

**Puma**
*www.puma.com*

**Reebok International**
1895 J. W. Foster Blvd.
Canton, MA 02021
*Tel: (781) 401-5000*
*www.reebok.com*

**Skechers U.S.A., Inc.**
228 Manhattan Beach Blvd.
Manhattan Beach, CA 90266
*Tel: (310) 318-3100*
*www.skx.com*

**Stacy Adams Shoe Company**
333 W. Estabrook Blvd.
Glendale, WI 53212
*Tel: (866) 523 8705*
*www.stacyadams.com*

**Ugg Australia**
*www.uggaustralia.com*

**Vans, Inc.**
15700 Shoemaker Avenue
Santa Fe Springs, CA 90670
*Tel: (562) 565-8267*
*www.vans.com*

**Vida Shoes International**
29 West 56th Street
New York, NY 10019
*Tel: (212) 246-1900*
*www.vidagroup.com*
*Brands: Baby Phat; Espirit; K1X; Pastry; Phat Farm; Run Athletics; Union Bay*

**Wolverine**
9341 Courtland Dr., NE
Rockford, MI 49351
*Tel: (616) 866-5500*
*www.wolverineworldwide.com*
*Includes: Bates; Cushe; Harley-Davidson; Hush Puppies; Patagonia; Wolverine*

**Guiseppe Zanotti**
*www.giuseppe-zanotti-design.com*

# EVERY LISTING

## in this DIRECTORY can be an Internship Opportunity.
## Here's our List to get you going!!!

**American Apparel & Footwear Association**
1601 N. Kent St., 12th Fl.
Arlington, VA 22209
***Tel: (703) 524-1864***
***www.apparelandfootwear.org***

**Betsey Johnson**
498 7th Avenue, 21st Fl.
New York, NY 10018
***Tel: (212) 244-0843***
***www.betseyjohnson.com***

**Bloomingdale's Internships**
Bloomingdale's Executive
Development Program
1000 Third Avenue, 3rd Fl.
New York, NY 10022
***Tel: (212) 705-2000***
***www.bloomingdalescollege.com***

**Bon-Ton Internship Program**
2801 East Market Street
York, PA 17402
***Tel: (717) 757-7660***
***www.careers.bonton.com***

**Coach, Inc.**
516 W. 34th Street
New York, NY 10001
***Tel: (212) 594-1850***
***www.coach.com***

**Condé Nast Publications Summer Internship Program**
4 Times Square
New York, NY 10036
***Tel: (212) 286-2860***
***www.condenastcareers.com***

**Fubu**
350 Fifth Avenue, Ste. 6617
New York, NY 10118
***Tel: (212) 273-3300***
***www.fubu.com***

**Gap Inc. Summer Internship Program**
Two Folsom Street
San Francisco, CA 94105
***Tel: (650) 952-4400***
***www.gapinc.com***
***Includes: Banana Republic; Gap; Old Navy***

**Guess?, Inc.**
1444 S. Alameda St.
Los Angeles, CA 90021
***Tel: (213) 765-3100***
***www.guessinc.com***

**Hanesbrands Inc.**
1000 E. Hanes Mill Rd.
Winston-Salem, NC 27105
***Tel: (336) 519-4400***
***www.hanesbrands.com***
***Includes: Hanes; Bali; Barely There; Champion; Just My Size; L'eggs; Playtex & Wonderbra***

**J. Crew Group, Inc.**
770 Broadway
New York, NY 10003
***Tel: (212) 209-2500***
***www.jcrew.com***

**Jones Apparel Group**
1411 Broadway
New York, NY 10018
***Tel: (212) 642-3860***
***www.jonesapparel.com***

**Lands' End**
5 Lands' End Lane
Dodgeville, WI 53595
***Tel: (608) 935-9341***
***www.landsend.com/jobs/opportunities/internship/***

**Liz Claiborne**
1441 Broadway
New York, NY 10018
***Tel: (212) 626-5200***
***www.lizclaiborneinc.com***
***Includes: Juicy Couture; Kate Spade; Lucky Brand Jeans***

**Lord & Taylor Internships**
424 5th Avenue
New York, NY 10018
***Tel: (212) 391-3344***
***http://lt.lordandtaylor.us/college/merchandisingCareerPaths.do***

**Louis Vuitton**
***www.louisvuitton.com***

**Macy's Internships**
***www.macyscollege.com***
***www.macysjobs.com/college/internships/***

**Macy's • Bloomingdale's Internships**
7 W. 7th Street
Cincinnati, OH 45202
***Tel: (513) 579-7000***
***www.macyscollege.com***
***www.bloomingdalescollege.com***
***www.macysjobs.com/college/careers/training/***

**MAGIC Int'l. (Men's Apparel Guild in California)**
6200 Canoga Ave., 2nd Fl.
Woodland Hills, CA 91367
***Tel: (818) 593-5000***
***www.magiconline.com***

**Marie Claire Magazine**
300 West 57th St., 34th Fl.
New York, NY 10019

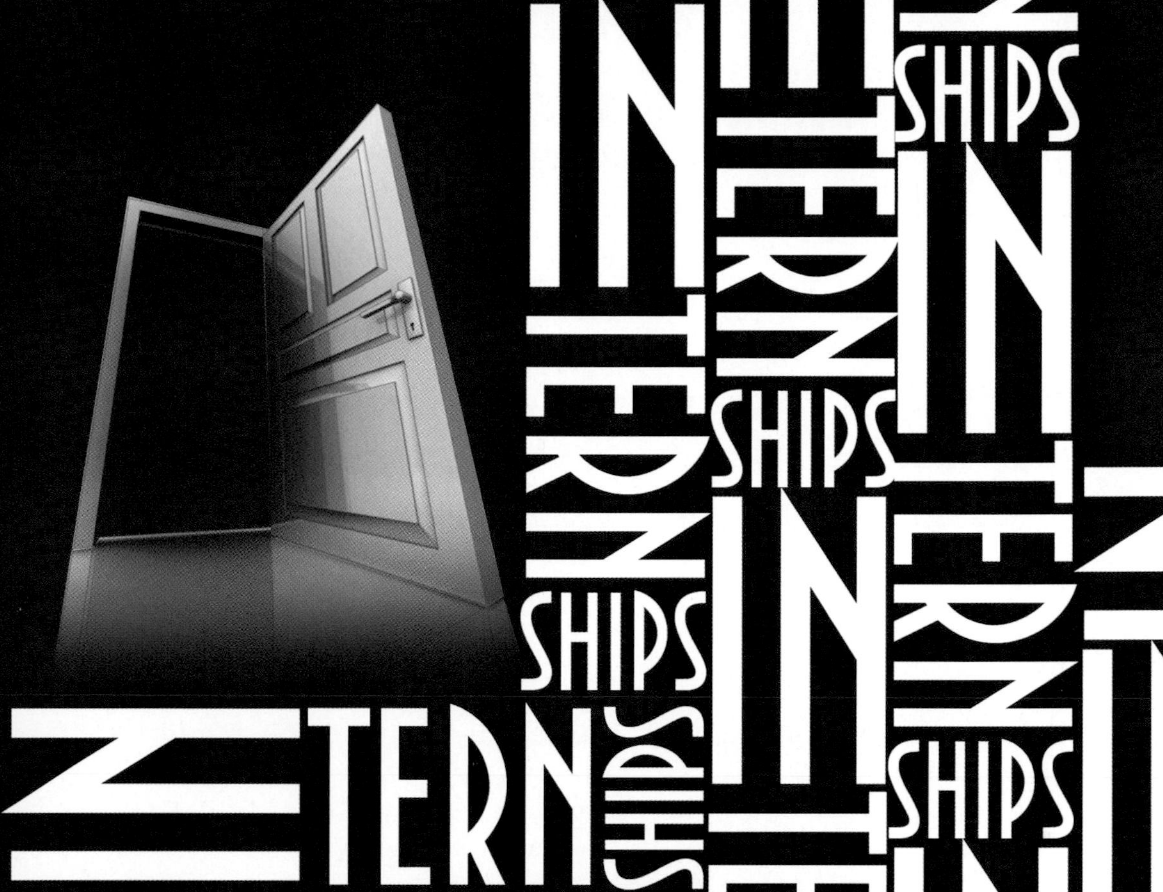


***Tel: (212) 649-2000***
***ww.marieclaire.com***

**Jessica McClintock, Inc.**
1400 16th Street
San Francisco, CA 94103
***Tel: (800) 711-8718***
***www.jessicamcclintock.com***

**NIKE Design Internship**
One Bowerman Drive, JR-1
Beaverton, OR 97005
***Tel: (503) 671-6453***
***www.nike.com***
****Interns Placed in Beaverton, OR; Chicago, Miami & New York***

**Phillips-Van Heusen**
1001 Frontier Road, MS#44
Bridgewater, NJ 08807
***Tel: (908) 231-6660***
***www.pvh.com***

**Sears Merchant Internship**
Sears Holdings Corporation
3333 Beverly Rd.
Hoffman Estates, IL 60179
***Tel: (847) 286-2500***
***www.searsholdings.com***
***www.searsholdings.com/careers/college/merchant_intern.htm***

**Under Armour, Inc.**
1020 Hull Street, 3rd Fl.
Baltimore, MD 21230
***Tel: (410) 454-6428***
***www.underarmour.com***
***www.uabiz.com/careers/interns.cfm***

**Vanity Fair**
Condé Nast Publications
4 Times Square
New York, NY 10036
***Tel: (212) 286-2860***
***www.vanityfair.com***

**Vogue**
Condé Nast Publications
4 Times Square
New York, NY 10036
***Tel: (212) 286-2860***
***www.style.com/vogue***

**Vera Wang**
225 West 39th Street
New York, NY 10018
***Tel: (212) 575-6400***
***www.verawang.com***

**WWD/Women's Wear Daily**
750 Third Avenue, 8th Fl.
New York, NY 10017
***Tel: (212) 630-3500***
***www.wwd.com***

# WHAT'S YOUR FAVORITE JEAN?

## MORE BRANDS THAN EVER ARE DOMINATING TODAY'S MARKETPLACE. HERE'S OUR *EPP* SHORT LIST.

**1921 Jeans**
***www.1921jeans.com***

**7 For All Mankind**
4440 East 26th Street
Los Angeles, CA 90023
***Tel: (323) 406-5300***
***www.7forallmankind.com***

**Agave**
1001 Main Street, Ste. D
Vancouver, WA 98660
***Tel: (360) 694-8494***
***www.agavejean.com***

**AG Adriano Goldschmied**
2741 Seminole Ave.
South Gate, CA 90280
***Tel: (323) 357-1111***
***www.agjeans.com***

**Antik Denim**
Blue Holdings, Inc.
4901 Zambrano Street
Commerce, CA 90040
***Tel: (323) 726-0297***
***www.antikdenim.com***

**Citizens of Humanity**
***Tel: (213) 489-2391***
***www.citizensofhumanity.com***

**Diesel**
***www.diesel.com***

**Earnest Sewn**
71 Gansevoort St., 3rd FL
New York, NY 10014
***Tel: (212) 675-0553***
***www.earnestsewn.com***

**Earnest Sewn**
MK Sportswear
127 E. Ninth St., #1203
Los Angeles, CA 90015
***Tel: (213) 623-3526***
***www.earnestsewn.com***

**Ellecid**
***www.ellecid.com***

**Evisu**
121 Greene Street, 2nd Fl.
New York, NY 10012
***Tel: (877) BUY-EVISU***
***www.evisu.com***

**Fortune Denim**
***Tel: (214) 549-5459***
***www.fortunedenim.com***

**Guess?, Inc.**
1444 S. Alameda St.
Los Angeles, CA 90021
***Tel: (213) 765-3100***
***www.guessinc.com***

**Habitual**
13344 S. Main Street, Ste. B
Los Angeles, CA 90061
***Tel: (310) 380-1510***
***www.habitual.com***

**Il Dolce Jeans**
SoBear, Inc.
P.O. Box 230
Houma, LA 70361
***Tel: (877) 762-3270***
***www.ildolceusa.com***

**J & Company Jeans, LLC**
1501 Rio Vista Avenue
Los Angeles, CA 90023
***Tel: (323) 881-3217***
***www.jandcompany.com***

**J Brand Denim Co.**
1201 East Washington Blvd.
Los Angeles, CA 90021
***Tel: (213) 749-3500***
***www.jbrandjeans.com***

**James Jeans**
500 Greenwich St., Ste. 202
New York, NY 10013
***Tel: (212) 221-4603***
***www.jamesjeans.com***

**Joe's Jeans Inc.**
5901 S. Eastern Ave.
Commerce, CA 90040
***Tel: (323) 837-3700***
***www.joesjeans.com***

**L.e.i.**
1441 Broadway
New York, NY 10018
***Tel: (212) 575-2571***
***www.leijeans.com***

**Levi Strauss & Co.**
1155 Battery Street
San Francisco, CA 94111
***Tel: (415) 501-6000***
***www.levistrauss.com***
****Levis & Dockers***

**Lucky Brand Jeans**
***www.luckybrand.com***

**Madewell**
***Tel: (434) 385-5792***
***www.madewell1937.com***

**Mavi Jeans**
550 Seventh Ave., 23rd Fl.
New York, NY 10018
***Tel: (212) 502-5885***
***www.mavi.com***

**Miss Me**
4715 S. Alameda Street
Los Angeles, CA 90058
***Tel: (323) 235-7351***
***www.missme.com***

**Paige Premium Denim**
10119 Jefferson Blvd.
Culver City, CA 90232
***Tel: (310) 733-2100***
***www.paigepremiumdenim.com***

**Paper Denim & Cloth**
*www.paperdenim.org*

**PRPS**
31 W. 34th St., Ste. 401
New York, NY 10018
*Tel: (212) 563-4999*
*www.prpsgoods.com*

**Ranahan Jeans**
*Tel: (213) 291-1710*
*www.ranahanjeans.com*

**Replay**
*www.replayjeans.com*

**Rock & Republic**
3523 Eastham Drive
Culver City, CA 90232
*Tel: (310) 839-3330*
*www.rockandrepublic.com*

**Rich & Skinny**
*www.richandskinnyjeans.com*

**Tag+ Jeans**
Fetish Group Inc.
3864 Santa Fe Ave.
Los Angeles, CA 90058
*Tel: (323) 587-7873*
*www.tagjeans.com*

**True Religion Apparel Inc.**
2263 E. Vernon Ave.
Vernon, CA 90058
*Tel: (323) 266-3072*
*www.truereligionbrandjeans.com*

**V.F. Corporation**
105 Corporate Center Blvd.
Greensboro, NC 27408
*Tel: (336) 424-6000*
*www.vfc.com*
**Includes: Lee; Riders, Rustler & Wrangler Jeans; Eagle Creek; Nautica & The North Face*

**William Rast**
*Tel: (800) 977-9540*
*www.williamrast.com*

**YMI Jeanswear**
2423 East 23rd Avenue
Los Angeles, CA 90058
*Tel: (323) 583-3083*
*www.ymijeans.com*

**City Model Management, Inc.**
500 Third Street, Ste. 525
San Francisco, CA 94107
***Tel: (415) 546-3160***
***www.citymodel.com***

**Click Models of Los Angeles**
9057 Nemo Street
West Hollywood, CA 90069
***Tel: (310) 246-0800***
***www.clickmodel.com***

**Click Models of Atlanta**
STUDIOPLEX
659 Auburn Ave. #123
Atlanta, GA 30312
***Tel: (404) 688-9700***
***www.clickmodel.com***

**Click Models of Boston**
222 Newbury Street, Ste. 3R
Boston, MA 02116
***Tel: (617) 266-1100***
***www.clickmodel.com***

**Click Model Management**
129 West 27th Street, 12th Fl.
New York, NY 10001
***Tel: (212) 206-1616***
***www.clickmodel.com***

**Click Models of Philadelphia**
216 Green Tree Drive
Westchester, PA 19382
***Tel: (610) 399-0700***
***www.clickmodel.com***

**DNA Model Management**
520 Broadway, 11th Fl.
New York, NY 10012
***Tel: (212) 226-0080***
***www.dnamodels.com***

**Elite Atlanta**
1708 Peachtree St., NW - Ste. 210
Atlanta, GA 30309
***Tel: (404) 872-7444***
***www.eliteatlanta.com***

**Elite Chicago**
58 W. Huron Street
Chicago, IL 60654
***Tel: (312) 943-3226***
***www.elitechicago.com***

**Elite Los Angeles**
345 N. Maple Dr., Ste. 397
Beverly Hills, CA 90210
***Tel: (310) 274-9395***
***www.elitemodel.com***

**Elite Miami**
119 Washington Ave., Ste. 501
Miami Beach, FL 33139
***Tel: (305) 674-9500***
***www.elitemiami.com***

**Elite Model Management**
404 Park Avenue S., 9th Fl.
New York, NY 10016
***Tel: (212) 529-9700***
***www.elitemodel.com***

**Ford Models**
9200 Sunset Blvd., Ste. 805
W. Hollywood, CA 90069
***Tel: (310) 276-8100***
***www.fordmodels.com***

**Ford Models**
291 Geary Street, Ste. 500
San Francisco, CA 94102
***Tel: (415) 777-9099***
***www.fordmodels.com***

**Ford Models**
1071 W. Washington, Ste. 2C
Chicago, IL 60607
***Tel: (312) 243-9400***
***www.fordmodels.com***

**Ford Models**
111 Fifth Avenue
New York, NY 10003
***Tel: (212) 219-6500***
***www.fordmodels.com***

**Ford Models**
807 N. Jefferson, Ste. 200
Milwaukee, WI 53202
***Tel: (414) 283-5600***
***www.fordmodels.com***

**ID Model Management**
110 Greene Street, Ste. 702
New York, NY 10012
***Tel: (212) 206-1818***
***www.idmodels.com***

**Ikon Model Management**
260 W. 39th Street
New York, NY 10018
***Tel: (212) 691-2363***
***www.ikonmodels.com***

**IMG Models**
304 Park Ave. S., PH North
New York, NY 10010
***Tel: (212) 253-8884***
***www.imgmodels.com***

**L.A. Models**
7700 Sunset Boulevard
Los Angeles, CA 90046
***Tel: (323) 436-7700***
***www.lamodels.com***

**Marilyn Model Agency**
32 Union Square E., PH
New York, NY 10003
***Tel: (212) 260-6500***
***www.marilyn-ny.com***

**MC2 Model Management**
6 W. 14th Street, 3rd Fl.
New York, NY 10011
***Tel: (646) 638-3330***
***www.mc2mm.com***

**MC2 Model Management**
1674 Alton Road, Ste. 500
Miami Beach, FL 33139
***Tel: (305) 672-8300***
***www.mc2mm.com***

**McDonald/Richards Connecticut**
5 River Road, Ste. 317
Wilton, CT 06897
***Tel: (203) 221-1401***
***www.imgco.com***

**New York Model Management**
596 Broadway, Ste. 701
New York, NY 10012
***Tel: (212) 539-1700***
***www.newyorkmodels.com***

**Next Model Management**
8447 Wilshire Blvd., PH
Beverly Hills, CA 90211
***Tel: (323) 782-0010***
***www.nextmodels.com***

**Next Model Management**
1688 Meridian Ave., Ste. 800
Miami Beach, FL 33139
***Tel: (305) 531-5100***
***www.nextmodels.com***

**Next Model Management**
15 Watts Street, 6th Fl.
New York, NY 10013
***Tel: (212) 925-5100***
***www.nextmodels.com***

**One Management**
9000 Sunset Blvd., Ste. 1550
Los Angeles, CA 90069
***Tel: (310) 270-1304***
***www.onemanagement.com***

**One Management**
42 Bond Street, 2nd Fl.
New York, NY 10012
***Tel: (212) 505-5545***
***www.onemanagement.com***

**Q New York**
354 Broadway
New York, NY 10013
***Tel: (212) 807-6777 (women)***
***Tel: (212) 807-6111 (men)***
***www.qmodels.com/nyc***

**Q Los Angeles**
8618 W. Third Street
Los Angeles, CA 90048
***Tel: (310) 205-2888***
***www.qmodels.com***

**Stars Model Management**
23 Grant Avenue, 4th Fl.
San Francisco, CA 94108
***Tel: (415) 421-6272***
***www.starsmodelmgmt.com***

**Supreme Management**
199 Lafayette Street, 7th Fl.
New York, NY 10012
***Tel: (212) 966-3840***
***www.suprememanagement.com***

**Trump Model Management**
91 5th Avenue
New York, NY 10003
***Tel: (212) 924-0990***
***www.trumpmodels.com***

**Wilhelmina Los Angeles**
7257 Beverly Boulevard
Los Angeles, CA 90036
***Tel: (323) 655-0909 (women)***
***Tel: (323) 655-6508 (men)***
***www.wilhelmina.com***

**Wilhelmina Miami**
2399 Collins Avenue
Miami Beach, FL 33139
***Tel: (305) 672-9344 (women/men)***
***Tel: (305) 531-5475 (kids)***
***www.wilhelmina.com***

**Wilhelmina New York**
300 Park Avenue South
New York, NY 10010
***Tel: (212) 473-0700***
***www.wilhelmina.com***

**Women Model Management**
199 Lafayette Street, Ste. 7
New York, NY 10012
***Tel: (212) 334-7480***
***www.womenmanagement.com***

# TRADE PUBLICATIONS

**Accessories Magazine**
1384 Broadway, 11th Fl.
New York, NY 10018
***Tel: (212) 686-4412***
***www.accessoriesmagazine.com***

**Allure**
Condé Nast Publications
4 Times Square
New York, NY 10036
***Tel: (212) 286-2860***
**www.allure.com**

**Apparel**
801 Gervais Street, Ste. 101
Columbia, SC 29201
***Tel: (803) 771-7500***
***www.apparelmag.com***

**Apparel News**
MnM Publishing Corp.
110 E. 9th St., Ste. A-777
Los Angeles, CA 90079
***Tel: (213) 627-3737***
***www.apparelnews.net***

**The Apparel Strategist**
12 Oak Way
Scarsdale, NY 10583
***Tel: (914) 713-4444***
***www.apparelstrategist.com***

**BODY**
617 W. 46th Street
New York, NY 10036
***Tel: (212) 541-9350***
***www.fmmg.com***

**Brides**
Condé Nast Publications
4 Times Square
New York, NY 10036
***Tel: (212) 286-2860***
***www.brides.com***

**California Apparel News**
MnM Publishing Corp.
110 E. 9th St., Ste. A-777
Los Angeles, CA 90079
***Tel: (213) 627-3737***
***www.apparelnews.net***

**The Costume Designer**
Costume Designers Guild
11969 Ventura Blvd., 1st Fl.
Studio City, CA 91604
***Tel: (818) 752-2400***
***www.costumedesignersguild.com***

**Council Magazine**
Council Communications
P.O. Box 4932
McLean, VA 22103
***Tel: (202) 731-4482***
***www.councilmag.com***

**Details**
Condé Nast Publications
4 Times Square
New York, NY 10036
***Tel: (212) 286-2860***
***www.men.style.com/details***

**Elle**
Hachette Filipacchi Media
1633 Broadway, 44th Fl.
New York, NY 10019
***Tel: (212) 767-6000***
***www.elle.com***

**Esquire**
300 West 57th Street, 21st Fl.
New York, NY 10019
***Tel: (212) 649-4020***
***www.esquire.com***

**ESSENCE**
135 W. 50th Street, 4th Fl.
New York, NY 10020
***Tel: (212) 522-1212***
***www.essence.com***

**Fashion Calendar**
153 E. 87th Street
New York, NY 10128
***Tel: (212) 289-0420***
***www.fashioncalendar.com***

**Fashion Magazine**
111 Queen St. E., Ste. 320
Toronto, ON M5C 1S2
***Tel: (416) 364-333***

Crystal Wright's

**Hair Makeup & Fashion Styling Career Guide,**
STILL the **ONLY** Complete Reference on the subject of working behind-the-scenes as a freelance Makeup, Hair, or Fashion Stylist.
www.CRYSTALWRIGHTLIVE.com

***If working in print, video, film and television has always been a dream of yours, then look no further than The Hair Makeup & Fashion Styling Career Guide for answers to ALL of your questions about becoming a celebrity stylist.***

## Making the Rules

*Crystal Wright is Founder and President of Crystal Agency, and creator of the Packaging Your Portfolio: Marketing Yourself as a Professional Makeup, Hair or Fashion Stylist workshop. Throughout the book, she illustrates her teaching with interviews, advice and anecdotes from well-known art directors, photographers, fashion editors, record company executives and agency owners in an effort to guide aspiring artists to success.*

## Learn the Secrets to a Successful Styling Career

*This comprehensive workbook is filled with practical advice and step-by-step instructions on:*
*Building a Portfolio*
*Testing with Photographers*
*Signing with an Agency;*
*Working with Record Labels, Magazines, Production Companies and more.*
*Included are examples on how to negotiate with creatives, an annotated list of resources from agencies to magazines to studio services and makeup schools.*

## What We Offer

- *A no nonsense approach to job hunting, career planning & development .*
- *Exposure to the exciting, lucrative, and creative fields of freelance styling.*
- *Guidance, advice and inside information.*
- *An indepth and honest picture of what it takes to create images for the stars of fashion, television, film and music.*

**CRYSTAL WRIGHT LIVE**
**OFC 323-299-0500 | FAX 323-443-3752**
**ISBN NO: 0964157241**
**$49.95**
**www.crystalwrightlive.com**

www.fashionmagazine.com

**Fashion Manuscript**
Mann Publications
1385 Broadway, Ste. 1102
New York, NY 10018
**Tel: (212) 840-6266**
**www.mannpublications.net**

**Fashion Market**
617 W. 46th Street
New York, NY 10036
**Tel: (212) 541-9350**
**www.fmmg.com**

**Fashion Update**
79 Pine Street, Ste. 129
New York, NY 10005
**Tel: (718) 897-0381**
**www.fashionupdate.com**

**Footwear Plus**
8 West 38th Street, Ste. 201
New York, NY 10018
**Tel: (646) 278-1550**
**www.footwearplusmagazine.com**

**Giant Magazine**
Interactive One
205 Hudson Street, 6th Fl.
New York, NY, 10013
**Tel: (212) 431-4477**
**www.giantmag.com**
**www.interactiveone.com**

**Glamour**
Condé Nast Publications
4 Times Square
New York, NY 10036
**Tel: (212) 286-2860**
**www.glamour.com**

**GQ**
Condé Nast Publications
4 Times Square
New York, NY 10036
**Tel: (212) 286-2860**
**www.gq.com**

**Hair, Makeup & Fashion Styling Career Guide**
7119 W. Sunset Blvd., Ste. 392
Los Angeles, CA 90046
**Tel: (323) 913-0500**
**www.makeuphairandstyling.com**

**Harper's Bazaar**
300 West 57th Street
New York, NY 10019
**Tel: (212) 903-5000**
**www.harpersbazaar.com**

**Le Book**
552 Broadway, 6th Fl.
New York, NY 10012
**Tel: (212) 334-5252**
**www.lebook.com**

**Marie Claire Magazine**
300 West 57th St., 34th Fl.
New York, NY 10019
**Tel: (212) 649-2000**
**ww.marieclaire.com**

**O, The Oprah Magazine**
1700 Broadway
New York, NY 10019
**Tel: (212) 903-5366**
**www.oprah.com**

**Southern Textile News**
9629 Old Nations Ford Rd
Charlotte, NC 28273
**Tel: (704) 527-5111**
**www.textilenews.com**

**Vanity Fair**
Condé Nast Publications
4 Times Square
New York, NY 10036
**Tel: (212) 286-2860**
**www.vanityfair.com**

**Vogue**
Condé Nast Publications
4 Times Square
New York, NY 10036
**Tel: (212) 286-2860**
**www.style.com/vogue**

**W**
Condé Nast Publications
4 Times Square
New York, NY 10036
**Tel: (212) 286-2860**
**www.style.com/w**

**WWD/Women's Wear Daily**
750 Third Avenue, 8th Fl.
New York, NY 10017
**Tel: (212) 630-3500**
**www.wwd.com**

# TRAINING PROGRAMS

**Adidas Design Academy**
Adidas America, Inc.
5055 N.Greeley Avenue
Portland, OR 97217
***Tel: (971) 234-2300***
***www.adidas-group.com***

**American Eagle Outfitters, Inc. Achieving Excellence Training Program**
77 Hot Metal Street
Pittsburgh, PA 15203
***Tel: (412) 432-3300***
***www.liveyourlifeloveyourjob.com/***

**American Eagle Outfitters, Inc. Merchandising Training Program**
77 Hot Metal Street
Pittsburgh, PA 15203
***Tel: (412) 432-3300***
***www.liveyourlifeloveyourjob.com/***

**American Eagle Outfitters, Inc. College Trek Program**
77 Hot Metal Street
Pittsburgh, PA 15203
***Tel: (412) 432-3300***
***www.liveyourlifeloveyourjob.com/***

**Ann Taylor Merchant Development Program**
7 Times Square Tower
New York, NY 10036
***Tel: (212) 541-3300***
***www.anntaylorcareers.com***

**Belk Executive Trainee Program**
2801 W. Tyvola Road
Charlotte, NC 28217
***Tel: (704) 357-4000***
***www.belk.com***

**Bloomingdale's Executive Development Program**
1000 Third Avenue, 3rd Fl.
New York, NY 10022
***Tel: (212) 705-2000***
***www.bloomingdalescollege.com***

**Bon-Ton Executive Training Programs**
2801 East Market Street
York, PA 17402
***Tel: (717) 757-7660***
***www.careers.bonton.com***

**California Institute of Jewelry**
5805 Windmill Way
Carmichael, CA 95608
***Tel: (800) 731-1122***
***www.jewelrytraining.com***

**Gap Inc. Retail Management Program**
Two Folsom Street
San Francisco, CA 94105
***Tel: (650) 952-4400***
***www.gapinc.com***

**Gap Inc. Manager in Training Program**
Two Folsom Street
San Francisco, CA 94105
***Tel: (650) 952-4400***
***www.gapinc.com***

**JC Penney Design Trainee Program**
6501 Legacy Drive
Plano, TX 75024
***Tel: (972) 431-8200***
***www.jcpenney.net/careers***

**JC Penney Merchandising Trainee Program**
6501 Legacy Drive
Plano, TX 75024
***Tel: (972) 431-8200***
***www.jcpenney.net/careers***

**Kmart Retail Management Trainee**
Sears Holdings Corporation
3333 Beverly Road
Hoffman Estates, IL 60179
***Tel: (847) 286-2500***
***www.searsholdings.com/careers/college/kmart_retail_mngm.htm***

# bloomingdale's

## EXECUTIVE DEVELOPMENT PROGRAM

"Everybody in our Program receives a mentor to talk about their career and help them progress through the company...."

Jerry Wu
*Manager of College Relations for Bloomingdale's*

**POWER**

For all emerging POWER PLAYERS looking for an incredible opportunity to become a high-powered Fashion Buyer, *EPP: 4* is pleased to shine our spotlight on the Bloomingdale's Executive Development Program headquartered in NYC. Upscale, cutting-edge and highly competitive, this exceptional Program teaches trainees the ins and outs of fashion, buying, and planning through exercises, case studies and real-world application. *EPP* caught up with Jerry Wu, Bloomingdale's manager of College Relations, the POWER PLAYER responsible for recruiting all junior level merchants accepted into the Program. Jerry gave us a quick overview of the Program's highlights, perks and application process.

## Here are the 123 At-a-Glance POWER Details to Get You Going:

**The Program Overview:**

- It's highly competitive. Up to 45 trainees are hired from about 2,000 applicants each year. No application fee. Diverse college graduates with strong leadership skills preferred.
- 8-week Program.
- Training courses led by expert executives who help guide your career.
- Each Bloomingdale's Trainee receives a mentor.
- Entry-level salary.
- Successful Trainees move on to become an Assistant Buyer, then Senior Assistant Buyer, then an Associate Planner. Positions typically takes anywhere between 1 to 1 1/2 years to complete.
- Great chance to build a solid foundation and launch your career as a Fashion Buyer.

To find out more about the Bloomingdale's Executive Development Program, or to apply online, visit www.bloomingdalescollege.com.

**Lord & Taylor Executive Trainee Training & Development Program**
424 Fifth Avenue
New York, NY 10018
***Tel: (212) 391-3344***
***http://lt.lordandtaylor.us/college/merchandisingCareerPaths.do***

**Macy's, Inc.**
**Macy's • Bloomingdale's Executive Development & Training Programs**
7 W. 7th Street
Cincinnati, OH 45202
***Tel: (513) 579-7000***
***www.macyscollege.com***
***www.bloomingdalescollege.com***
***www.macysjobs.com/college/careers/training/***

**Make-Up Designory**
129 S. San Fernando Blvd.
Burbank, CA 91502
***Tel: (818) 729-9420***
***www.mud.edu***

**Make-Up Designory**
375 W. Broadway
New York, NY 10012
***Tel: (212) 925-9250***
***www.mud.edu***

**Neiman Marcus Group Executive Development Program**
1618 Main Street
Dallas, TX 75201
***Tel: (214) 761-2300***
***www.neimanmarcuscareers.com***

**NIKE Marketing Development Program**
NIKE, Inc.
One Bowerman Drive
Beaverton, OR 97005
***Tel: (503) 671-6453***
***www.nike.com***

**Makeup Training**
Award Studio
3204 W. Magnolia Blvd.
Burbank, CA 91505
***Tel: (818) 980-2119***
***www.mediamakeupartists.com***

**Pure Fashion Model Training Program**
6445 Shiloh Road, Ste. B
Alpharetta, GA 30005
***Tel: (404) 550-0243***
***www.purefashion.com***

**Saks Fifth Avenue Executive Excellence Program**
12 East 49th Street
New York, NY 10017
***Tel: (212) 940-5305***
***www.saksincorporated.com/careers/executivetraining.asp***

**Sears Buyer Apprenticeship Program**
Sears Holdings Corporation
3333 Beverly Road
Hoffman Estates, IL 60179
***Tel: (847) 286-2500***
***www.searsholdings.com/careers/college/merchant_intern.htm***

**Sears Outlet Stores - Management Development Program**
Sears Holdings Corporation
3333 Beverly Road
Hoffman Estates, IL 60179
***Tel: (847) 286-2500***
***www.searsholdings.com/careers/college/sears_outlet_stores_retail_mngm.htm***

**Sears Retail Management Trainee**
Sears Holdings Corporation
3333 Beverly Road
Hoffman Estates, IL 60179
***Tel: (847) 286-2500***
***www.searsholdings.com/careers/college/sears_retail_mngm_trainee.htm***

**Studio Makeup Academy**
1438 N. Gower Street, #14
Hollywood, CA 90028
***Tel: (323) 465-4002***
***www.studiomakeupacademy.com***

**TJX Corporate Merchandise Training Program**
The TJX Companies, Inc.
770 Cochituate Road
Framingham, MA 01701
***Tel: (508) 390-1000***
***www.tjx.com/careers_merchandising_trainingprogram.asp***
***Includes: A.J. Wright; HomeGoods; Marshalls; T.J. Maxx***

**Von Maur Executive Training Program**
6565 Brady Street
Davenport, IA 52806
***Tel: (563) 388-2200***
***www.vonmaur.com***

## Step Up & Step Out

Step Up to YOUR Future!

Seize the Day/ the Spotlight/ the Opportunities

Get YOUR Resume/ YOUR Career & YOURself

Red Carpet & Runway Ready!

www.entertainmentpower.com

FILM
POWER
Animation Companies «
Associations & Organizations «
Awards, Events & Conferences «
Celebrity-Owned Companies «
Distribution Companies «
Equipment Companies «
Film Commissions «
Film Festivals «
Film Financing «
Film Schools «
Internships «
Libraries & Research «
Major Studios «
Media Giants «
300+ Production Companies «
Screenwriting Competitions «
25+ Resources for Screenwriters «
Screenwriting Software «
Specialty Bookstores «
Stock Footage Companies «
Theatre Chains «
Trade Publications & Magazines «
Training Programs «
Writing Workshops & Programs «

ANIMATION COMPANIES

**Aniboom**
***www.aniboom.com***
****7,000 Animators from 70+ Countries***

**Animation Design Center**
***www.animationdesigncenter.com***
***Credits: Piglet's Big Movie; Starship Troopers***

**Animation Entertainment**
3830 Valley Ctr. Dr., Ste. 705
San Diego, CA 92130
***Tel: (858) 793-1900***
***www.animationtrip.com***
***Footage: Animation & Special FX***

**Animotion**
501 W. Fayette Street
Syracuse, NY 13204
***Tel: (315) 471-3533***
***www.animotioninc.com***
***Credits: Scooby Doo; SpongeBob Squarepants***

**Artistic Image**
887 W. Marietta Street, NW/Studio D
Atlanta, GA 30318
***Tel: (404) 815-1550***
***www.artisticimage.com***
***Credits: Academy Awards on-air campaign; Atlanta Falcons Intro; Ford President's Day***

**Big Idea**
230 Franklin Rd., Bldg. 2A
Franklin, TN 37064
***Tel: (615) 224-2200***
***www.bigidea.com***
***Credits: VeggieTales***

**Blue Sky Studios**
One America Lane
Greenwich, CT 06831
***Tel: (203) 992-6000***
***www.blueskystudios.com***
***Credits: Bunny; Ice Age***

**Cartoon Network Studios**
300 N. Third Street
Burbank, CA 91502
***Tel: (818) 729-4000***
***www.cartoonnetwork.com***
***Credits: Batman; Star Wars: The Clone Wars***

**Cartoon Network**
1050 Techwood Dr., NW
Atlanta, GA 30318
***Tel: (404) 885-2263***
***www.cartoonnetwork.com***
***Credits: Stuart Little; The Powerpuff Girls***

**Cinesite Digital Studio**
***www.cinesite.com***
***Credits: Charlie & the Chocolate Factory; Wonderboys***

**Classic Media**
860 Broadway, 6th Fl.
New York, NY 10003
***Tel: (212) 659-1959***
***www.classicmedia.tv***
***Credits: Casper; Frosty the Snowman; Richie Rich***

**Cookie Jar**
4100 W. Alameda Ave., 4th Fl.
Burbank, CA 91505
***Tel: (818) 955-5400***
***www.thecookiejarcompany.com***
***Credits: Arthur; Care Bears; DoodleBops***

**Cookie Jar**
362 Fifth Avenue, Ste. 403
New York, NY 10001
***Tel: (212) 239-4437***
***www.thecookiejarcompany.com***
***Credits: Arthur; Care Bears; DoodleBops***

**Creative Capers Entertainment**
2233 Honolulu Ave., 2nd Fl.
Montrose, CA 91020
***Tel: (818) 658-7120***
***www.creativecapers.com***
***Credits: Mr. Magoo; Sitting Ducks; Thumbelina***

**Curious Pictures**
440 Lafayette Street, 6th Fl.
New York, NY 10003
***Tel: (212) 674-1400***
***www.curiouspictures.com***
***Credits: Codename: Kids Next Door; Disney's Little Einsteins***

**DNA Productions**
2201 W. Royal Lane, Ste. 275
Irving, TX 75063
***Tel: (214) 352-4694***
***www.dnahelix.com***
***Credits: Jimmy Neutron; Santa vs. Snowman***

**DreamWorks Animation SKG**
1000 Flower Street
Glendale, CA 91201
***Tel: (818) 695-5000***
***www.dreamworksanimation.com***
***Credits: Kung Fu Panda; Monsters vs. Aliens; The Prince of Egypt; Shrek; Spirit***

**Film Roman**
2950 N. Hollywood way
Burbank, CA 91505
***Tel: (818) 748-4000***
***www.filmroman.com***
***Credits: The Simpsons; King of the Hill; Wow! Wow! Wubbzy!***

**Frederator Studios**
231 W. Olive Ave.
Burbank, CA 91502
***Tel: (818) 736-3606***
***www.frederator.kz***
***Credits: Chalkzone; Oh Yeah! Cartoons! The Powerpuff Girls***

**Frederator Studios**
419 Park Avenue St., Ste. 807
New York, NY 10016
***Tel: (212) 779-4133***
***www.frederator.kz***
***Credits: Chalkzone; The Powerpuff Girls***

**Harvey Entertainment Company**
Classic Media
860 Broadway, 6th Fl.
New York, NY 10003
***Tel: (212) 659-3037***
***www.harvey.com***
***Credits: Casper; Richie Rich***

**Jim Henson Company**
1416 N. LaBrea Avenue
Hollywood, CA 90028
***Tel: (323) 802-1500***
***www.henson.com***
***Credits: Muppets; World of Dr. Seuss***

**Jim Henson Company**
627 Broadway, 9th Fl.
New York, NY10021
***Tel: (212) 794-2400***
***www.henson.com***
***Credits: Muppets; World of Dr. Seuss***

**Industrial Light & Magic**
P.O. Box 2459

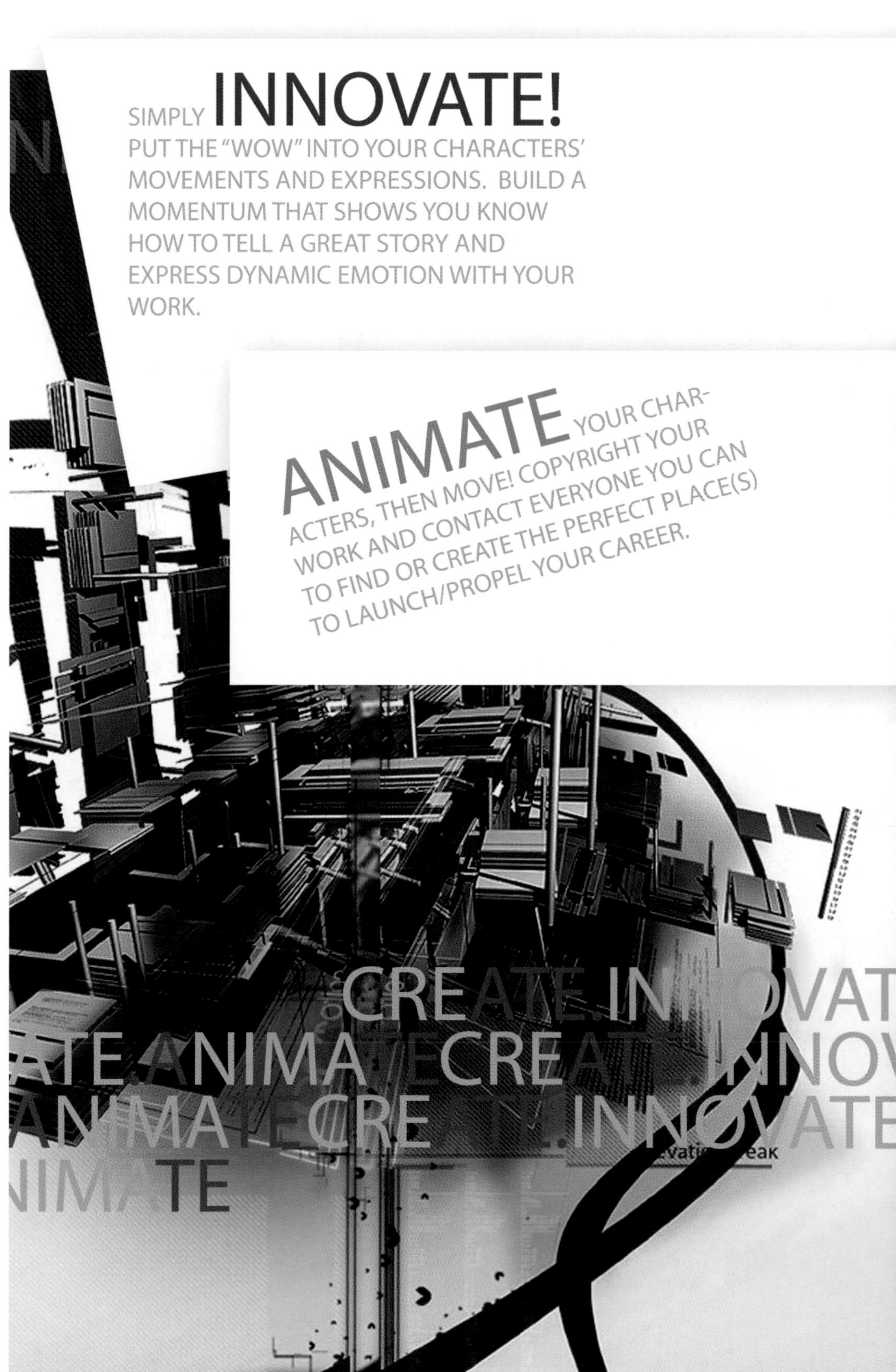
CREATE THE MOST DYNAMIC, HEAD-TURNING PORTFOLIO, DVD REELS, SKETCHBOOKS, SAMPLES, MODELS, COMPOSITIONS & WEBSITES. LABEL YOUR ARTWORK WITH YOUR NAME, TITLES OF YOUR WORK AND YOUR CONTACT INFORMATION.
SIMPLY INNOVATE! PUT THE "WOW" INTO YOUR CHARACTERS' MOVEMENTS AND EXPRESSIONS. BUILD A MOMENTUM THAT SHOWS YOU KNOW HOW TO TELL A GREAT STORY AND EXPRESS DYNAMIC EMOTION WITH YOUR WORK.
ANIMATE YOUR CHARACTERS, THEN MOVE! COPYRIGHT YOUR WORK AND CONTACT EVERYONE YOU CAN TO FIND OR CREATE THE PERFECT PLACE(S) TO LAUNCH/PROPEL YOUR CAREER.
CREATE.INNOVAT
ATE.ANIMATE.CREATE.INNOV
ANIMATE.CREATE.INNOVATE
NIMATE

local commercials
training videos
national commercials
independent films
vector 2033
music videos

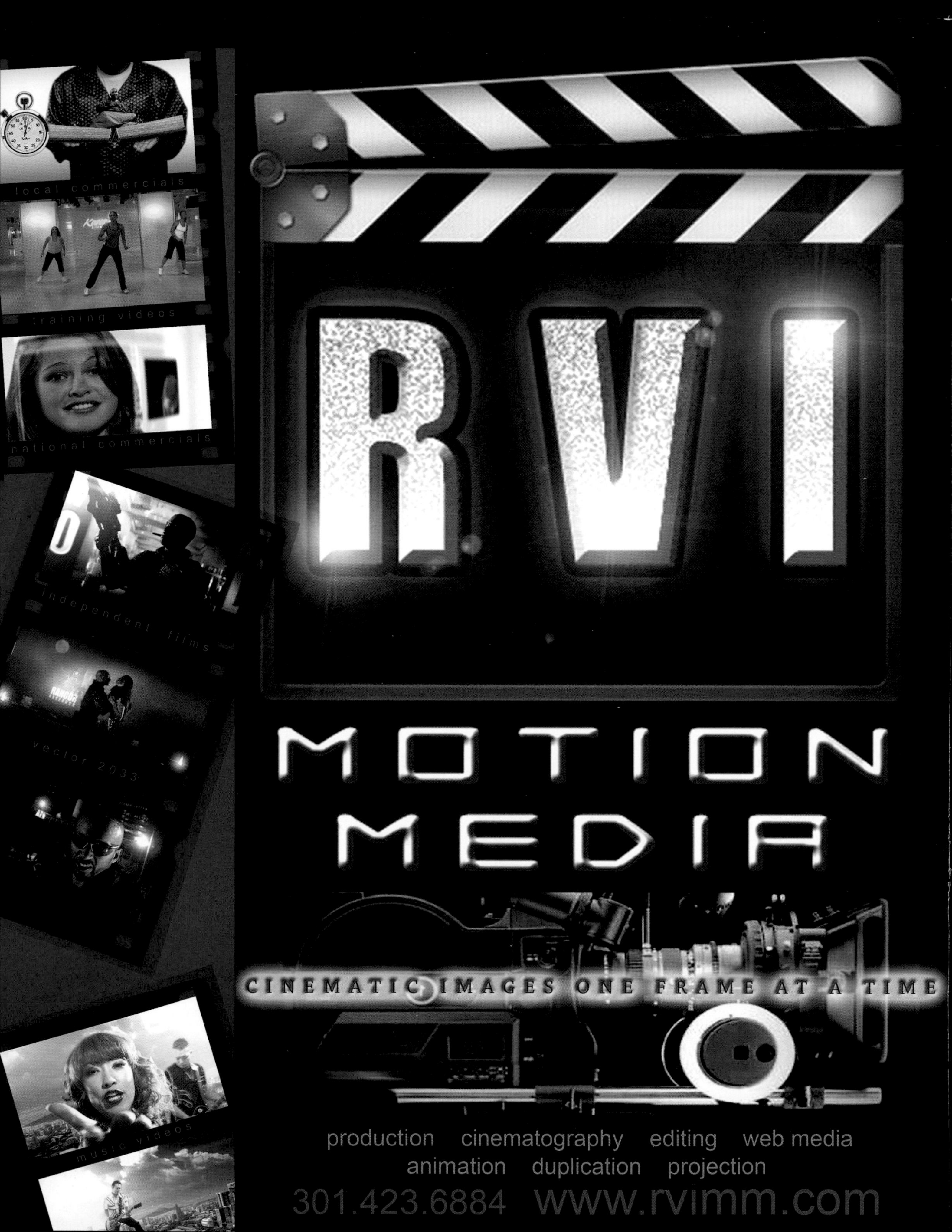

San Rafael, CA 94912
***Tel: (415) 746-3000***
***www.ilm.com/www.lucasfilm.com***
***Credits: Galaxy Quest; Rocky & Bullwinkle***

**Ka-Chew!**
1238 N. Highland Blvd.
Hollywood, CA 90038
***Tel: (323) 468-3020***
***www.kachew.com***
***Credits: Digimon; Ostrich FACTS; Rat***

**Klasky Csupo**
1238 N. Highland Blvd.
Hollywood, CA 90038
***Tel: (323) 468-2600***
***www.klaskycsupo.com***
***Credits: Duckman; Rugrats; The Simpsons; Wild Thornberrys***

**Marvel Entertainment Studios**
417 5th Avenue
New York, NY 10016
***Tel: (212) 576-4000***
***www.marvel.com***
***Credits: Blade; Hulk; Spider-Man; X-Men***

**Marvel Studios**
1600 Rosecrans Avenue
Bldg. 7, Ste. 110
Manhattan Beach, CA 90266
***Tel: (310) 234-8991***
***www.marvel.com***
***Credits: Blade; Hulk; Spider-Man; X-Men***

**Nickelodeon Animation Studio**
231 W. Olive Avenue
Burbank, CA, 91502
***Tel: (818) 736-3000***
***www.nick.com***
***Credits: Dora the Explorer; Hey Arnold!; SpongeBob Squarepants***

**Pixar Animation Studios**
1200 Park Avenue
Emeryville, CA 94608
***Tel: (510) 922-3000***
***www.pixar.com***
***Credits: Cars; Finding Nemo; The Incredibles; Ratatouille; Up; Wall-E***

**Pixel Magic**
10635 Riverside Drive
Toluca Lake, CA 91602
***Tel: (818) 760-0862***
***www.pixelmagicfx.com***
***Credits: Agent Cody Banks; Looney Tunes***

**PorchLight Entertainment**
11777 Mississippi Ave.
Los Angeles, CA 90025
***Tel: (310) 477-8400***
***www.porchlight.com***
***Credits: Jay Jay The Jet Plane; Tutenstein***

**POW! Entertainment**
9440 Santa Monica Blvd., Ste. 620
Beverly Hills, CA 90210
***Tel: (310) 275-9933***
***www.powentertainment.com***
***Credits: Legion of 5; Who Wants to Be A Superhero?***

**Rhythm & Hues**
5404 Jandy Place
Los Angeles, CA 90066
***Tel: (310) 448-7500***
***www.rhythm.com***
***Credits: Babe; Cat in the Hat; Scooby Doo***

**Ruby-Spears Productions**
3500 W. Olive Ave., Ste. 300
Burbank, CA 91505
***Tel: (818) 840-1234***
***www.rubyspears.com***
***Credits: Big Mouth; Jirimpimbira; Super Racing Fighting Frogs***

**Scholastic Entertainment**
577 Broadway
New York, NY 10012
***Tel: (212) 343-6100***
***www.scholastic.com***
***Credits: Clifford The Big Red Dog; Goosebumps; The Magic School Bus***

**Sesame Workshop**
One Lincoln Plaza
New York, NY 10023
***Tel: (212) 595-3456***
***www.sesameworkshop.org***
***Credits: Sesame Street; Dragon Tales***

**Sony Pictures Imageworks**
9050 W. Washington Blvd.
Culver City, CA 90232
***Tel: (310) 840-8000***
***www.imageworks.com***
***Credits: Stuart Little; Open Season; The ChubbChubbs; The Haunted Mansion; The Smurfs***

**Televix Entertainment**
449 S. Beverly Drive, 3rd Fl.
Beverly Hills, CA 90212
***Tel: (310) 788-5500***
***www.televix.com***
***Credits: Rollbots; TMNT: Back to the Sewer; Yugioh GX***

**Tippett Studio**
2741 10th Street
Berkeley, CA 94710
***Tel: (510) 649-9711***
***www.tippett.com***
***Credits: 6th Day; X-Men***

**TokyoPop**
5900 Wilshire Blvd., 20th Fl.
Los Angeles, CA 90036
***Tel: (323) 692-6700***
***www.tokyopop.com***
***Credits: GTO; Rave Master; Street Fury***

**Universal Cartoon Studios**
100 Universal City Plaza
Universal City, CA 91608
***Tel: (818) 777-1510***
***Credits: Alvin & The Chipmunks; The Land Before Time; Woody Woodpecker***

**Walt Disney Feature Animation**
500 S. Buena Vista Street
Burbank, CA 91521
***Tel: (818) 560-5000***
***www.disneyanimation.com***
***Credits: 101 Dalmations; A Bug's Life; Bolt; The Little Mermaid; The Princess & the Frog***

**Walt Disney Imagineering**
1401 Flower Street
Glendale, CA 91201
***Tel: (818) 544-1000***
***http://disney.go.com/disney careers/imaginations/ www.disneycollege.com***

**Warner Bros. Animation**
411 N. Hollywood Way
Burbank, CA 91505
***Tel: (818) 977-8700***
***www.warnerbros.com***
***Credits: Batman Beyond; Happy Feet; Scooby Doo; The Polar Express***

# ASSOCIATIONS & ORGANIZATIONS

**Academy of Motion Picture Arts & Sciences (Oscars)**
8949 Wilshire Boulevard
Beverly Hills, CA 90211
***Tel: (310) 247-3000***
***www.oscars.org***

**Actors Equity Association**
165 W. 46th Street
New York, NY 10036
***Tel: (212) 869-8530***
***www.actorsequity.org***

**Actors Equity Association**
6775 Hollywood Blvd., 5th Fl.
Hollywood, CA 90028
***Tel: (323) 978-8080 (Hollywood, CA)***
***Tel: (407) 345-8600 (Orlando, FL)***
***www.actorsequity.org***

**Actors Equity Association**
125 S. Clark St., Ste. 1500
Chicago, IL 60603
***Tel: (312) 641-0393***
***www.actorsequity.org***

**African American Women in Cinema**
545 Eighth Avenue, Ste. 401
New York, NY 10018
***Tel: (212) 769-7949***
***www.aawic.org***

**Alliance of Motion Picture & Television Producers (AMPTP)**
15501 Ventura Boulevard
Encino, CA 91436
***Tel: (818) 995-3600***
***www.amptp.org***

**American Cinema Editors (ACE)**
100 Universal City Plaza
Verna Fields Bldg. 2282, Rm. 190
Universal City, CA 91608
***Tel: (818) 777-2900***
***www.ace-filmeditors.org***

**American Cinema Foundation**
11400 W. Olympic Blvd. #200
Los Angeles, CA 90064
***Tel: (310) 914-0159***
***www.cinemafoundation.com***

**American Screenwriters Assoc.**
269 S. Beverly Drive, Ste. 2600
Beverly Hills, CA 902012
***Tel: (866) 265-9091/(513) 221-7014***
***www.goasa.com***

**American Society of Cinematographers (ASC)**
1782 N. Orange Drive
Hollywood, CA 90028
***Tel: (323) 969-4333***
***www.theasc.com***

**Art Directors Guild & Scenic, Title & Graphic Design**
11969 Ventura Blvd., 2nd Fl.
Studio City, CA 91604
***Tel: (818) 762-9995***
***www.artdirectors.org***

**Association of Film Commissioners International**
109 E. 17th St., Ste. 18
Cheyenne, WY 82001
***Tel: (307) 637-4422***
***www.afci.org***

**Association of Location Scouts & Managers**
***www.alsam.net***

**Association of Talent Agents**
9255 Sunset Blvd., Ste. 930
Los Angeles, CA 90069
***Tel: (310) 274-0628***
***www.agentassociation.com***

**Black Association of Documentary Filmmakers**
14431 Ventura Blvd., #115
Sherman Oaks, CA 91432
***Tel: (213) 534-6635***
***www.badwest.org***

**Black Entertainment & Sports Lawyers Association (BESLA)**
P.O. Box 441485
Fort Washington, MD 20749
***Tel: (301) 248-1818***
***www.besla.org***

**Black Filmmaker Foundation**
131 Varick Street, Ste. 937
New York, NY 10036
***Tel: (212) 253-1690***
***www.dvrepublic.com***

**Breaking Into Hollywood**
P.O. Box 3909
Hollywood, CA 90078
***Tel: (310) 712-3459***
***www.breakingintohollywood.org***

**Broadcast Film Critics Assoc.**
9220 Sunset Blvd., Ste. 220
Los Angeles, CA 90069
***Tel: (310) 860-2665***
***www.bfca.org***

**Casting Society of America**
606 N. Larchmont Blvd., Ste. 4B
Los Angeles, CA 90004
***Tel: (323) 463-1925***
***www.castingsociety.com***

**Casting Society of America**
311 W. 43rd St., 10th Fl.
New York, NY 10019
***Tel: (212) 868-1260***

**Christian Writers Guild**
5525 N. Union Blvd., Ste. 200
Colorado Springs, CO 80918
***Tel: (719) 495-5177***
***www.christianwritersguild.com***

**Coalition of Asian Pacifics in Entertainment**
P.O. Box 251855
Los Angeles, CA 90025
***Tel: (310) 278-2313***
***www.capeusa.org***

**Costume Designers Guild**
11969 Ventura Blvd., 1st Fl.
Studio City, CA 91604
***Tel: (818) 752-2400***
***costumedesignersguild.com***

**Directors Guild of America**
7920 Sunset Boulevard
Los Angeles, CA 90046
***Tel: (310) 289-2000***
***www.dga.org***

**Directors Guild of America**
400 N. Michigan Ave., Ste. 307
Chicago, IL 60611
***Tel: (312) 644-5050***
***www.dga.org***

**Directors Guild of America**
110 W. 57th Street
New York, NY 10019
***Tel: (212) 581-0370***
***www.dga.org***

**Entertainment Resources Marketing Association**
3401 Winona Avenue
Burbank, CA 91504
***Tel: (562) 694-3793***
***www.erma.org***

**Facets Multimedia**
1517 W. Fullerton Avenue
Chicago, IL 60614
***Tel: (773) 281-9075***
***www.facets.org***

**Film Artists Network**
P.O. Box 323
Canoga Park, CA 91305
***Tel: (818) 528-5938***
***www.filmartistsnetwork.com***

**Film Independent**
9911 W. Pico Boulevard, 11th Fl.
Los Angeles, CA 90035
***Tel: (310) 432-1200***
***www.filmindependent.org***

**Filmmakers Alliance**
1030 W. Hillcrest Blvd.
Inglewood, CA 90301
***Tel: (310) 568-0633***
***www.filmmakersalliance.com***

**Gen Art**
3710 S. Robertson Blvd., Ste. 219
Culver City, CA 90232
***Tel: (323) 782-9367***
***www.genart.org***

**GenArt**
133 W. 25th Street, 6th Fl.
New York, NY 10001
***Tel: (212) 255-7300***
***www.genart.org***

**Guild of Italian American Actors**
Canal Street Station
P.O. Box 123
New York, NY 10013
***Tel: (201) 344-3411***
***www.nygiaa.org***

**Harvardwood**
P.O. Box 5243
Santa Monica, CA 90409
harvardwood@harvardwood.org
***www.harvardwood.org***

**Hispanic Organization of Latin Actors (HOLA)**
107 Suffolk Street, Ste. 302
New York, NY 10002
***Tel: (212) 253-1015***
***www.hellohola.org***

**Hollywood Connect**
1763 North Gower Street
Hollywood, CA 90028
***www.hollywoodconnect.com***

**IFP (Independent Feature Project)**
68 Jay Street, Rm. 425
Brooklyn, NY 11201
***Tel: (212) 465-8200***
***www.ifp.org***

**Independent Film & TV Alliance**
10850 Wilshire Blvd., 9th Fl.
Los Angeles, CA 90024
***Tel: (310) 446-1000***
***www.ifta-online.org***

**Int'l. Alliance of Theatrical Stage Employees - IATSE Local 44**
12021 Riverside Drive
N. Hollywood, CA 91607
***Tel: (818) 769-2500***
***www.local44.org***

**Int'l Assoc. of Theatrical Stage Employees - IATSE Local 33**
1720 W. Magnolia Boulevard
Burbank, CA 91506
***Tel: (818) 841-9233***
***ia33.org***

**Int'l. Alliance of Theatrical Stage Employees (IATSE)**
10045 Riverside Drive
Toluca Lake, CA 91602
***Tel: (818) 980-3499***
***www.iatse-intl.org***

**Int'l. Alliance of Theatrical Stage Employees (IATSE)**
1430 Broadway, 20th Fl.
New York, NY 10018
***Tel: (212) 730-1770***
***www.iatse-intl.org***

**Int'l. Association of Lighting Designers**
The Merchandise Mart, Ste. 9-104
Chicago, IL 60654
***Tel: (312) 527-3677***
***www.iald.org***

**Int'l. Documentary Association**
1201 W. 5th Street, Ste. M270
Los Angeles, CA 90017
***Tel: (213) 534-3600***
***www.documentary.org***

**Media Education Foundation**
60 Masonic Street
Northhampton, MA 01060
***Tel: (413) 584-8500***
***www.mediaed.org***

**Media Fellowship International**
P.O. Box 82685
Kenmore, WA 98028
***Tel: (425) 488-3965***
***www.mediafellowship.org***

**Motion Picture Association of America (MPAA)**
15501 Ventura Blvd., Bldg. E
Sherman Oaks, CA 91403
***Tel: (818) 995-6600***
***www.mpaa.org***

**Motion Picture Association of America (MPAA)**
1600 I Street, NW
Washington, D.C. 20006
***Tel: (202) 293-1966***
***www.mpaa.org***

**Motion Picture Editors Guild**
7715 Sunset Blvd., Ste. 200
Hollywood, CA 90046
***Tel: (323) 876-4470***
***www.editorsguild.com***

**Motion Picture Editors Guild**
145 Hudson Street, Ste. 201
New York, NY 10013
***Tel: (212) 302-0700***
***www.editorsguild.com***

**Motion Picture Studio Mechanics (IA Local 52)**
326 W. 48th Street
New York, NY 10036
***Tel: (212) 399-0980***
***www.iatselocal52.org***

**Multicultural Motion Pic. Assoc.**
6100 Wilshire Boulevard, Ste. 230
Los Angeles, CA 90048
***Tel: (310) 358-8300***
***www.thediversityawards.org***

**National Association of Black Female Executives in Music & Entertainment (NABFEME)**
59 Maiden Lane, 27th Fl.
New York, NY 10038
***Tel: (212) 424-9568***
***www.nabfeme.org***

**National Association of Concessionaires**
35 E. Wacker Drive, Ste. 1816
Chicago, IL 60601
***Tel: (312) 236-3858***
***www.naconline.org***

**National Association Latino Independent Producers (NALIP)**
1323 Lincoln Blvd., Ste. 220
Santa Monica, CA 90401
***Tel: (310) 395-8880***
***www.nalip.org***

**National Association of Latino Independent Producers (NALIP)**
c/o POV
32 Broadway, 14th Fl.
New York, NY 10004
***Tel: (646) 336-6333***
***www.nalip.org***

**National Assoc. of Minority Media Executives**
7950 Jones Branch Dr., 3rd Fl.
McLean, VA 22107
***Tel: (888) 968-7658/(703) 854-7178***
***www.namme.org***

**National Association of Talent Representatives**
The Gage Group
315 W. 57th St., Ste. 48
New York, NY 10019
***Tel: (212) 541-5250***

**National Association of Theatre Owners (NATO)**
4605 Lankershim Blvd., Ste. 180
N. Hollywood, CA 91602
***Tel: (818) 506-1778***
***www.natoonline.org***

**National Association of Theatre Owners (NATO)**
750 First St., NE - Ste. 130
Washington D.C. 20002
***Tel. (202) 962-0054***
***www.natoonline.org***

**Nat'l. Hispanic Media Coalition**
55 S. Grand Avenue
Pasadena, CA 91105
***Tel: (626) 792-6462***
***www.nhmc.org***

**New York Celebrity Assistants**
459 Columbus Ave., #216
New York, NY 10024
***Tel: (212) 803-5444***
***ww.nycelebrityassistants.org***

**New York Film Critics Circle**
***www.nyfcc.com***

**New York Production Alliance**
876 6th Avenue, Ste. 1005
New York, NY 10001
***Tel: (646) 839-0431***
***www.nypa.org***

**New York Women in Film & TV**
6 E. 39th Street, Ste. 1200
New York, NY 10016
***Tel: (212) 679-0870***
***www.nywift.org***

**Organization of Black Screenwriters (OBS)**
Golden State Mutual Bldg.
1999 West Adams Blvd., Rm. Mezz.
Los Angeles, CA 90018
***Tel: (323) 735-2050***
***www.obswriter.com***

**Producers Guild of America**
8530 Wilshire Blvd., Ste. 450
Beverly Hills, CA 90211
***Tel: (310) 358-9020***
***www.producersguild.org***

**Producers Guild of America**
1000 Ave. of the Americas, 11th Fl.
New York, NY 10013
***Tel: (212) 894-4016***

**Production Equipment Rental Association**
101 W. 31st Street, Ste. 1005
New York, NY 10001
***Tel: (646) 839-0430***
***www.peraonline.org***

**Projectionists Union - IATSE 15**
***Tel: (206) 441-1515***
***www.ia15.org***

**Public Relations Society of America (PRSA)**
33 Maiden Lane, 11th Fl.
New York, NY 10038
***Tel: (212) 460-1400***
***www.prsa.org***

**Public Relations Student Society of America (PRSSA)**
33 Maiden Lane, 11th Fl.
New York, NY 10038
***Tel: (212) 460-1474***
***www.prssa.org***

**Screen Actors Guild (SAG)**
5757 Wilshire Blvd, 18th Fl.
Los Angeles, CA 90036
***Tel: (323) 954-1600***
***www.sag.org***

**Screen Actors Guild (SAG)**
360 Madison Avenue, 12th Fl.
New York, NY 10036
***Tel: (212) 944-1030***
***www.sag.org***

**Script Supervisors & Continuity Coordinators**
1159 Chandler Boulevard
N. Hollywood, CA 91601
***Tel: (818) 509-7871***
***www.ialocal871.org***

**Scriptwriters Network**
6404 Wilshire Blvd., #1640
Los Angeles, CA 90048
***Tel: (888) 796-9673***
***www.scriptwritersnetwork.com***

**Set Decorators Society**
1646 N. Cherokee Avenue
Hollywood, CA 90028
***Tel: (323) 462-3060***
***www.setdecorators.org***

**Society of Camera Operators**
***Tel: (818) 382-7070***
***www.soc.org***

**Society of Illustrators**
128 E. 63rd Street
New York, NY 10021
***Tel: (212) 838-2560***
***www.societyillustrators.org***

**Society of Motion Picture & Television Engineers (SMPTE)**
3 Barker Avenue, 5th Fl.
White Plains, NY 10601
***Tel: (914) 761-1100***
***www.smpte.org***

**Society of Stage Directors & Choreographers**
1501 Broadway, Ste. 1701
New York, NY 10036
***Tel: (212) 391-1070***
***www.ssdc.org***

**Stuntmen's Association of Motion Pictures**
10660 Riverside Dr., 2nd Fl. - Ste. E
Toluca Lake, CA 91602
***Tel: (818) 766-4334***
***www.stuntmen.com***

**Stuntwomen's Association of Motion Pictures**
***Tel: (818) 762-0907***
***www.stuntwomen.com***

**Theatrical Wardrobe Union**
545 W. 45th Street
New York, NY 10036
***Tel: (212) 957-3500***
***www.ia764.com***

**United Scenic Artists**
29 W. 38th Street, 15th Fl.
New York, NY 10018
***Tel: (212) 581-0300***
***www.usa829.org***

**University Film & Video Assoc.**
Peter J. Bukalski
Box 1777
Edwardsville, IL 62026
***Tel: (866) 647-8382***
***www.ufva.org***

**Women in Film**
8857 W. Olympic Blvd., Ste. 201
Beverly Hills, CA 90211
***Tel: (310) 657-5144***
***www.wif.org***

**Women in Film & TV Atlanta**
P.O. Box 52726
Atlanta, GA 30355
***Tel: (770) 621-5071***
***www.wifa.org***

**Women in Film & Video (WIFV)**
3628 12th Street, NE
Washington, DC 20017
***Tel: (202) 429-9438***
***www.wifv.org***

**Women Make Movies**
462 Broadway, Ste. WS
New York, NY 10013
***Tel: (212) 925-0606***
***www.wmm.com***

**Workplace Hollywood**
1201 W. 5th Street, Ste. T-550
Los Angeles, CA 90017
***Tel: (213) 250-9921***
***www.workplacehollywood.org***

**Writers Guild of America, east**
555 W. 57th St., Ste. 1230
New York, NY 10019
***Tel: (212) 767-7800***
***www.wgaeast.org***

**Writers Guild of America, west**
7000 W. Third Street
Los Angeles, CA 90048
***Tel: (323) 951-4000***
***www.wga.org***

**Academy Awards (The Oscars) & Student Academy Awards**
8949 Wilshire Boulevard
Beverly Hills, CA 90211-1972
***Tel: (310) 247-3000***
***www.oscars.org***
***www.oscars.org/saa/***

**Artios Awards**
Casting Society of America
606 N. Larchmont Blvd., Ste. 4-B
Los Angeles, CA 90004
***Tel: (323) 463-1925***
***www.castingsociety.com***

**ActorFest L.A.**
Back Stage
5055 Wilshire Boulevard
Los Angeles, CA 90036
***Tel: (323) 525-2225***
***www.backstage.com***

**ActorFest NY**
Back Stage
770 Broadway
New York, NY 10003
***Tel: (646) 654-5700***
***www.backstage.com***

**BET Awards**
1235 W Street, NE
Washington, D.C. 20018
***Tel: (202) 608-2000***
***www.bet.com***

**CINE Golden Eagle Award**
1112 16th Street, NW - Ste. 510
Washington, D.C. 20036
***Tel: (202) 785-1136***
***www.cine.org***

**Film, Stage & Showbiz Expo**
440 Ninth Avenue, 8th Fl.
New York, NY 10001
***Tel: (212) 404-2345***
***www.theshowbizexpo.com***

**Golden Globe Awards**
Hollywood Foreign Press. Assoc.
646 N. Robertson Boulevard
W. Hollywood, CA 90069
***Tel: (310) 657-1731***
***www.hfpa.org***

**Great American Pitch Fest**
12400 Ventura Blvd., #735
Studio City, CA 91604
***Tel: (877) 255-2528***
***www.pitchfest.com***

**Hollywood Pitch Fest**
Fade In Magazine
287 S. Robertson Blvd., #467
Beverly Hills, CA 90211
***Tel: (310) 275-0287***
***www.fadeinonline.com***

**Latino Media Market**
National Association of Latino Independent Producers (NALIP)
1323 Lincoln Blvd., Ste. 220
Santa Monica, CA 90401
***Tel: (310) 395-8880***
***www.nalip.org***

**Locations Trade Show**
Assoc. of Film Commissioners Int'l.
109 E. 17th Street, Ste. 18
Cheyenne, WY 82001
***Tel: (307) 637-4422***
***www.afci.org***

**NAACP Image Awards**
4929 Wilshire Blvd., Ste. #310
Los Angeles, CA 90010
***Tel: (323) 938-5268***
***www.naacpimageawards.net***

**NATPE Conference**
5757 Wilshire Boulevard, PH 10
Los Angeles, CA 90036
***Tel: (310) 453-4440***
***www.natpemarket.com/conference***

**NYILFF/NALIP Pitchathon**
New York Int'l. Latino Film Festival
419 LaFayette St., 6th Fl.
New York, NY 10003
***Tel: (646) 723-1428***
***www.nylatinofilm.com***

**ShoWest/ShoEast**
770 Broadway, 5th Fl.
New York, NY 10003
***Tel: (646) 654-7680***
***www.showest.com***

CELEBRITY-OWNED COMPANIES

**40 Acres & A Mule Filmworks**
75 S. Elliot Place
Brooklyn, NY 11217
***Tel: (718) 624-3703***
***www.40acres.com***
*Spike Lee*

**900 Films**
1203 Activity Drive
Vista, CA 92081
***Tel: (760) 477-2470***
***www.900films.com***
*Tony Hawk*

**Apostle**
568 Broadway, #301
New York, NY 10012
***Tel: (212) 541-4323***
***www.apostlenyc.com***
*Denis Leary*

**Appian Way**
9255 Sunset Blvd., Ste. 615
W. Hollywood, CA 90069
***Tel: (310) 300-1390***
*Leonardo DiCaprio*

**Attaboy Films**
8335 Sunset Blvd., Ste. 102
W. Hollywood, CA 90069
***Tel: (323) 337-9037***
***www.attaboyfilms.com***
*James Gandolfini*

**Bad Boy**
1710 Broadway, 2nd Fl.
New York, NY 10019
***Tel: (212) 500-2200***
***www.badboyonline.com***
*Sean Combs*

**Bankable Productions**
4000 Warner Boulevard
Bldg. 139, Rm. 207
Burbank, CA 91522
***Tel: (818) 954-1600***
*Tyra Banks*

**Bankable Productions**
221 W. 26th Street
New York, NY 10001
***Tel: (646) 638-5760***
*Tyra Banks*

**Banyan Tree Films**
One Worth Street, 2nd Fl.
New York, NY 10013
***Tel: (212) 966-1135***
*Matt Dillon*

**Barwood Films**
5670 Wilshire Blvd., Ste. 2400
Los Angeles, CA 90036
***Tel: (323) 653-1555***
*Barbra Streisand*

**Bay Films**
631 Colorado Avenue
Santa Monica, CA 90401
***Tel: (310) 319-6565***
*Michael Bay*

**Big Pita, Lil' Pita Productions**
500 S. Buena Vista Street
Animation Building 2A; Rooms 1 & 2
Burbank, CA 91521
***Tel: (818) 560-7668***
*Alicia Keys*

**Big Pita, Lil' Pita Productions**
240 W. 35th Street, 18th Fl.
New York, NY 10001
***Tel: (212) 244-4903***
*Alicia Keys*

**Black Folk Entertainment**
2533 N. Beachwood Drive
Los Angeles, CA 90068
***Tel: (323) 466-3828***
*John Salley*

**Blossom Films**
10201 W. Pico Blvd., Bldg. 45
Los Angeles, CA 90035
***Tel: (310) 369-5359***
*Nicole Kidman*

**Boxing Cat Films**
11500 Hart Street
N. Hollywood, CA 91605
***Tel: (818) 765-4870***
*Tim Allen*

**Brooksfilms Limited**
Culver Studios
9336 W. Washington Blvd.
Culver City, CA 90232
***Tel: (310) 202-3292***

*Mel Brooks*

**Bruckheimer Films**
1631 Tenth Street
Santa Monica, CA 90404
***Tel: (310) 664-6260***
***Jerry Bruckheimer***

**Busboy Productions**
375 Greenwich Street, 5th Fl.
New York, NY 10013
***Tel: (212) 965-4700***
***Jon Stewart***

**Carousel Productions**
Warner Bros. Pictures
4000 Warner Blvd., Bldg. 144
Burbank, CA 91522
***Tel: (818) 954-5769***
***Steve Carrell***

**Carrie Productions**
2625 Alcatraz Ave., Ste. 243
Berkeley, CA 94705
***Tel: (510) 450-2500***
***Danny Glover***

**The Thomas Carter Company**
3000 W. Olympic Blvd.
Santa Monica, CA 90404
***Tel: (310) 264-3990***
***Thomas Carter***

**Castle Rock Entertainment**
335 N. Maple Dr., Ste. 135
Beverly Hills, CA 90210
***Tel: (310) 285-2300***
***Rob Reiner***

**Cineson Productions, Inc.**
4519 Varna Avenue
Sherman Oaks, CA 91423
***Tel: (818) 501-8246***
***Andy Garcia***

**Dick Clark Productions Inc.**
2900 Olympic Boulevard
Santa Monica, CA 90404
***Tel: (310) 255-4600***
***www.dickclarkproductions.com***
***Dick Clark***

**Class 5 Films**
200 Park Avenue South, 8th Fl.
New York, NY 10003
***Tel: (917) 414-9404***
***Edward Norton***

**Conaco Productions**
100 Universal City Plaza
Bldg. 5166, 3rd Fl.
Universal City, CA 91608
***Tel: (818) 777-1000***
***Conan O'Brien***

**Cooper's Town Productions**
302A W. 12th Street, Ste. 214
New York, NY 10014
***Tel: (212) 255-7566***
***Phillip Seymour Hoffman***

**Coquette Productions**
8105 W. Third Street
W. Hollywood, CA 90048
***Tel: (323) 801-1000***
***Courtney Cox***

**Corymore Entertainment**
9171 Wilshire Blvd., Ste. 400
Beverly Hills, CA 90210
***Tel: (310) 274-7891***
***Angela Lansbury***

**Crescendo Productions**
252 N. Larchmont Blvd.
Los Angeles, CA 90004
***Tel: (323) 464-0870***
***Don Cheadle***

**Cube Vision**
9000 W. Sunset Blvd.
W. Hollywood, CA 90069
***Tel: (310) 461-3490***
***Ice Cube***

**Current TV**
118 King Street
San Francisco, CA 94107
***Tel: (415) 995-8200***
***www.current.tv***
***Al Gore***

**Denver and Delilah Films**
9220 Sunset Blvd., Ste. 305
Los Angeles, CA 90069
***Tel: (310) 601-2616***
***Charlize Theron***

**De Passe Entertainment**
9200 Sunset Blvd., Ste. 510
W. Hollywood, CA 90069
***Tel: (310) 858-3734***
***Suzanne de Passe***

**Destiny Hill**
6253 Hollywood Blvd., Ste. 501
Hollywood, CA 90028
***Tel: (323) 318-9090***
***Hill Harper***

**Dreyfuss/James Productions**
2420 Laurel Pass
Los Angeles, CA 90046
***Tel: (323) 822-0140***
***Richard Dreyfuss***

**Dualstar Entertainment Group**
3760 Robertson Blvd., 2nd Fl.
Culver City, CA 90232
***Tel: (310) 553-9000***
***www.mary-kateandashley.com***
***Mary-Kate and Ashley Olsen***

**Duke Media**
7510 Sunset Blvd., Ste. 523
Los Angeles, CA 90046
***Tel: (323) 850-9390***
***www.officialbillduke.com***
***Bill Duke***

**Echo Films**
c/o Aleen Keshishian/Brillstein
Partners
9150 Wilshire Blvd., Ste. 350
Beverly Hills, CA 90212
***Tel: (323) 935-2909***
***Jennifer Aniston***

**Edmonds Entertainment**
1635 N. Cahuenga Blvd., 6th Fl.
Los Angeles, CA 90028
***Tel: (323) 860-1550***
***www.edmondsent.com***
***Tracey Edmonds***

**El Dorado Pictures**
P.O. Box 8677
La Crescenta, CA 91224
***Tel: (818) 888-3700***
***www.alecbaldwin.com***
***Alec Baldwin***

**Electric Dynamite**
100 Universal City Plaza
Bungalow 4133
Universal City, CA 91608
***Tel: (818) 777-0999***
***www.electricdynamite.com***
***Jack Black***

**Entertainment Studios, Inc.**
9903 Santa Monica Blvd., Ste. 418
Beverly Hills, CA 90212
***Tel: (310) 277-3500***
***www.es.tv***
***Byron Allen***

**Face Productions**
335 N. Maple Dr., Ste. 175
Beverly Hills, CA 90210
***Tel: (310) 205-2746***
***Billy Crystal***

**Fair Dinkum Productions**
P.O. Box 49914
Los Angeles, CA 90049
***Tel: (310) 260-2122***
***Henry Winkler***

**Flavor Unit Entertainment**
155 Morgan Street
Jersey City, NJ 07302
***Tel: (201) 333-4883***
***Queen Latifah***

**Flower Films Inc.**
7630 Santa Monica Blvd.
W. Hollywood, CA 90046
***Tel: (323) 876-7400***
***Drew Barrymore***

**Fortis Films**
8581 Santa Monica Blvd., Ste. 1
W. Hollywood, CA 90069
***Tel: (310) 659-4533***
***Sandra Bullock***

**Foxx King Entertainment**
9220 W. Sunset Blvd., Ste. 830
W. Hollywood, CA 90069
***Tel: (310) 205-2800***
***Jamie Foxx***

**Foxy Brown Productions**
P.O. Box 3538
Granada Hills, CA 91394
***Tel: (818) 368-5545***
***Vivica A. Fox***

**Further Films**
100 Universal City Plaza, Bldg. 5174
Universal City, CA 91608
***Tel: (818) 777-6700***
***Michael Douglas***

**Further Films**
825 8th Ave., 30th Fl.
New York, NY 10019
***Tel: (212) 333-1421***
***Michael Douglas***

**Leeza Gibbons Enterprises**
7257 Beverly Blvd., Ste. 218
Los Angeles, CA 90036
***Tel: (323) 634-0581***
***www.leezagibbons.com***
***Leeza Gibbons***

**The Goatsingers**
177 W. Broadway, 2nd Fl.
New York, NY 10013
***Tel: (212) 966-3045***
***Harvey Keitel***

**Grammnet Productions**
23852 Pacific Coast Hwy., Ste. 350
Malibu, CA 90265
***Tel: (310) 317-4231***
***Kelsey Grammer***

**Gray Angel Productions**
74 Market Street
Venice, CA 90291
***Tel: (310) 581-0010***
***Angelica Houston***

**G-Unit Television & Films**
P.O. Box 1500
New York, NY 10016
***Tel: (212)359-3000***
***Curtis Jackson/50 Cent***

**Handsome Charlie Films**
1720 1/2 Whitley Avenue
Los Angeles, CA 90028
***Tel: (323) 462-6013***
***Natalie Portman***

**Harpo**
110 N. Carpenter Street
Chicago, IL 60607
***Tel: (312) 633-1000***
***Oprah Winfrey***

**Harpo Films**
345 N. Maple Dr., Ste. 315
Beverly Hills, CA 90210
***Tel: (310) 278-5559***
***Oprah Winfrey***

**Havoc Inc.**
16 W. 19th St., 12th Fl.
New York, NY 10011
***Tel: (212) 924-1629***
***Tim Robbins***

**HQ Pictures**
1635 N. Cahuenga Blvd.
Los Angeles, CA 90028
***Tel: (323) 465-3120***
***Tyrese Gibson***

**Humble Journey Films**
7656 W. Sunset Boulevard
Los Angeles, CA 90046
***Tel: (323) 882-6376***
***Eriq La Salle***

**Icon Productions, Inc.**
808 Wilshire Blvd., 4th Fl.
Santa Monica, CA 90401
***Tel: (310) 434-7300***
***Mel Gibson***

**Imagine Entertainment**
9465 Wilshire Blvd., 7th Fl.
Beverly Hills, CA 90212
***Tel: (310) 858-2000***
***Ron Howard***

**Irish Dreamtime**
3000 W. Olympic Blvd.
Building 4, Ste. 1221
Santa Monica, CA 90404
***Tel: (310) 449-3411***
***Pierce Brosnan***

**Is or Isn't Entertainment**
8391 Beverly Bldg., #125
Los Angeles, CA 90038
***Tel: (310) 854-0972***
***Lisa Kudrow***

**ISBE Productions**
500 S. Buena Vista Street
Old Animation Blvd., Rm. 1G-10
Burbank, CA 91521
***Tel: (818) 560-3861***
***Teri Hatcher***

**Ixtlan**
12233 W. Olympic Blvd., Ste. 322
Los Angeles, CA 90064
***Tel: (310) 826-7080***
***Oliver Stone***

**Jersey Films**
P.O. Box 491246
Los Angeles, CA 90029
***Tel: (310) 477-7704***
***Danny DeVito***

**JK Livin' Productions**
64 Market Street
Venice, CA 90291
***Tel: (310) 857-1555***
***Matthew McConaughey***

**Don Johnson Productions**
9663 Santa Monica Blvd., Ste. 278
Beverly Hills, CA 90212
***Tel: (310) 246-1452***
***Don Johnson***

**Magic Johnson Enterprises**
9100 Wilshire Blvd., Ste. 700E
Beverly Hills, CA 90212
***Tel: (310) 247-2033***
***Earvin "Magic" Johnson***

**Quincy Jones Productions**
3800 Barham Blvd., Ste. 503
Los Angeles, CA 90068
***Tel: (323) 874-2009***
***Quincy Jones***

**Kingsgate Films, Inc.**
8954 W. Pico Blvd., 2nd Fl.
Los Angeles, CA 90035
***Tel: (323) 937-6110***
***Nick Nolte***

**Last Straw Productions**
4000 Warner Blvd.
Building 133, Ste. 209
Burbank, CA 91522
***Tel: (818) 954-1064***
***Anthony LaPaglia***

**Lightstorm Entertainment**
919 Santa Monica Blvd.
Santa Monica, CA 90401
***Tel: (310) 656-6100***
***James Cameron***

**Lion Rock Productions**
2120 Colorado Ave., Ste. 225
Santa Monica, CA 90404
***Tel: (310) 309-2980***
***John Woo***

**Logo Entertainment**
10642 Santa Monica Blvd., Ste. 205
Los Angeles, CA 90025
***Tel: (310) 927-8831***
***Louis Gossett Jr.***

**Lucasfilm**
P.O. Box 29901
San Francisco, CA 94129
***Tel: (415) 662-7800***
***George Lucas***

**Malpaso Productions**
Warner Bros.
4000 Warner Blvd., Bldg. 81
Burbank, CA 91522
***Tel: (818) 954-3367***
***Clint Eastwood***

**The Martin/Stein Company**
1528 N. Curson Avenue
Los Angeles, CA 90046
***Tel: (323) 851-4870***
***Steve Martin***

**Midnight Entertainment**
11846 Ventura Blvd., Ste. 208
Studio City, CA 91604
***Tel: (818) 752-0197***
***Wes Craven***

**Milojo Productions**
850 3rd Ave, 10th Fl.
New York, NY, 10022
***Tel: (212) 548-5300***
***Kelly Ripa & Mark Consuelos***

**ML Management**
1740 Broadway, 15th Fl.
New York, NY 10019

**CELEBRITY CENTRAL**
**BEST WAYS** TO CONTACT YOUR FAVORITE CELEBRITY?

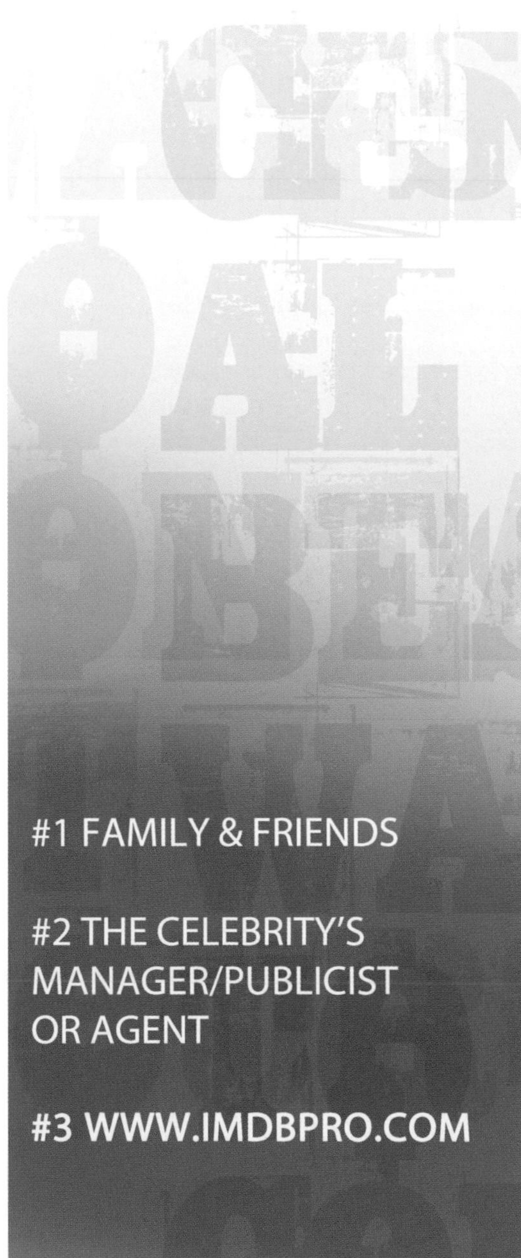

#1 FAMILY & FRIENDS
#2 THE CELEBRITY'S MANAGER/PUBLICIST OR AGENT
#3 WWW.IMDBPRO.COM

***Tel: (212) 333-5500***
***Eddie Murphy***

**New Crime Productions**
555 Rose Avenue
Venice, CA 90291
***Tel: (310) 396-2199***
***John Cusack***

**New Deal Productions**
3343 W. 43rd Street
Los Angeles, CA 90008
***Tel: (323) 299-2183***
***John Singleton***

**Nuyorican**
1100 Glendon Ave., Ste. 920
Los Angeles, CA 90024
***Tel: (310) 943-6633***
***Jennifer Lopez***

**Olmos Productions, Inc.**
c/o Walt Disney Studios
500 S. Buena Vista Street
Old Animation Bldg., 1G, MC 1675
***Tel: (818) 560-8651***
***Edward James Olmos***

**O'Taye Productions**
c/o Walt Disney Studios
500 S. Buena Vista St., MC 2290
Burbank, CA 91521
***Tel: (818) 560-6677***
***Taye Diggs***

**Our Stories Films**
1635 N. Cahuenga Blvd., 6th Fl.
Los Angeles, CA 90028
***Tel: (323) 817-0090***
***Robert L. Johnson; Tracey Edmonds***

**Overbrook Entertainment**
450 N. Roxbury Dr., 4th Fl.
Beverly Hills, CA 90210
***Tel: (310) 432-2400***
***Will Smith***

**OWN: The Oprah Winfrey Network**
5700 Wilshire Blvd., Ste. 120
Los Angeles, CA 90036
***Tel: (323) 602-5500***
***Oprah Winfrey***

**Parkway Productions**
7095 Hollywood Blvd., Ste. 1009
Hollywood, CA 90028
***Tel: (323) 874-6207***
***Penny Marshall***

**P.A.T. Productions**
10202 W. Washington Blvd.
David Lean Bldg., Ste. 230
Culver City, CA 90232
***Tel: (310) 244-8881***
***Pat Sajak***

**The Tyler Perry Company**
541 10th Street, Ste. 172
Atlanta, GA 30318
***Tel: (404) 222-6448***
***Tyler Perry***

**Tyler Perry Studios**
2769 Continental Colony Parkway
Atlanta, GA 30331
***Tel: (404) 222-6448***
***www.tylerperry.com***
***Tyler Perry***

**Platinum Dunes**
631 Colorado Avenue
Santa Monica, CA 90401
***Tel: (310) 394-9200***
***Michael Bay***

**Playtone Productions**
P.O. Box 7340
Santa Monica, CA 90406
***Tel: (310) 394-5700***
***Tom Hanks***

**Pretty Matches Productions**
1104 Ave. of the Americas
G26, Ste. 32
New York, NY 10036
***Tel: (212) 512-5755***
***Sarah Jessica Parker***

**Punch Productions**
11661 San Vicente Blvd., Ste. 222
Los Angeles, CA 90049
***Tel: (310) 442-4880***
***Dustin Hoffman***

**Red Bird Productions**
3791 Santa Rosalia Drive
Los Angeles, CA 90008
***Tel: (310) 202-1711***
***Debbie Allen***

**Red Hour Films**
629 N. LaBrea Avenue
Los Angeles, CA 90036
***Tel: (323) 602-5000***
***Ben Stiller***

**Red Om Films, Inc.**
3000 Olympic Blvd.
Bldg. 3, Ste. 2330
Santa Monica, CA 90404
***Tel: (310) 594-3467***
***Julia Roberts***

**Red Strokes Entertainment**
9465 Wilshire Blvd., Ste. 319
Beverly Hills, CA 90212
***Tel: (310) 786-7887***
***Garth Brooks***

**Tim Reid Productions**
One New Millennium Dr.
Petersburg, VA 23805
***Tel: (804) 957-4200***
***Tim Reid***

**Revelations Entertainment**
1221 2nd Street, 4th Fl.
Santa Monica, CA 90401
***Tel: (310) 394-3131***
***Morgan Freeman***

**Al Roker Productions**
250 W. 57th St., Ste. 1525
New York, NY 10019
***Tel: (212) 757-8500***
***Al Roker***

**Saturn Films**
9000 Sunset Blvd., Ste. 911
W. Hollywood, CA 90069
***Tel: (310) 887-0900***
***Nicolas Cage***

**Ryan Seacrest Productions**
5750 Wilshire Boulevard
Los Angeles, CA 90036
***Tel: (323) 954-2400***
***Ryan Seacrest***

**Seed Productions**
c/o 20th Century Fox
10201 W. Pico Blvd.

Bldg. 52, Rm. 101
Los Angeles, CA 90035
***Tel: (310) 369-1900***
***Nicolas Cage***

**Sigourney, Inc.**
P.O. Box 38
New York, NY 10150
***Tel: (212) 421-8293***
***Sigourney Weaver***

**Simmons Lathan Media Group**
6100 Wilshire Blvd., Ste. 1110
Los Angeles, CA 90048
***Tel: (323) 634-6400***
***Russell Simmons & Stan Lathan***

**Smoke House Pictures**
c/o Warner Bros.
4000 Warner Blvd., Bldg. 15
Burbank, CA 91522
***Tel: (818) 954-4840***
***George Clooney***

**Spirit Dance**
7336 Santa Monica Blvd., Ste. 34
W. Hollywood, CA 90046
***Tel: (323) 512-7988***
***Forest Whitaker***

**St. Amos Productions**
3480 Barham Blvd., Ste. 108
Los Angeles, CA 90068
***Tel: (323) 850-9872***
***John Stamos***

**Steamroller Productions, Inc.**
1438 N. Gower Street, Box 22
Hollywood, CA 90028
***Tel: (323) 468-3113***
***Steven Seagal***

**Martha Stewart Living Omnimedia, Inc.**
11 W. 42nd Street
New York, NY 10036
***Tel: (212) 827-8000***
***www.marthastewart.com***
***Martha Stewart***

**Superfinger Entertainment**
2660 W. Olive Avenue
Burbank, CA 91505
***Tel: (818) 526-5000***
***Dane Cook***

**Sundance Institute**
8530 Wilshire Blvd., 3rd Fl.
Beverly Hills, CA 90211
***Tel: (310) 360-1981***
***Robert Redford***

**Sundance Film Festival**
1825 Three Kings Drive
Salt Lake City, UT 84060
***Tel: (801) 328-3456***
***Robert Redford***

**TIG Productions**
4450 Lakeside Dr., Ste. 225
Burbank, CA 91505
***Tel: (818) 260-8707***
***Kevin Costner***

**Tribeca Productions**
375 Greenwich St., 8th Fl.
New York, NY 10013
***Tel: (212) 941-4040***
***Robert DeNiro***

**Trillium Productions**
P.O. Box 1560
New Canaan, CT 06840
***Tel: (203) 966-5540***
***Glenn Close***

**United Artists**
10250 Constellation Blvd., 11th Fl.
Los Angeles, CA 90067
***Tel: (310) 449-3777***
***Tom Cruise***

**Uppity Films**
3532 Hayden Avenue
Culver City, CA 90232
***Tel: (310) 558-6010***
***Samuel L. Jackson***

**Ventanarosa**
500 S. Buena Vista Street
Old Animation Building, 3F3
Burbank, CA 91521
***Tel: (818) 560-3950***
***Salma Hayek***

**Ventanazul**
10250 Constellation Blvd., 2nd Fl.
Los Angeles, CA 90067
***Tel: (310) 449-3300***
***Salma Hayek***

**Verdon-Cedric Productions**
P.O. Box 2639
Beverly Hills, CA 90212
***Tel: (310) 274-7253***
***Sidney Poitier***

**Meredith Vieira Productions**
888 Seventh Ave., Ste. 503
New York, NY 10106
***Tel: (212) 300-8928***
***Meredith Vieira***

**Jon Voight Entertainment**
1901 Ave. of the Stars, Ste. 605
Los Angeles, CA 90067
***Tel: (310) 843-0223***
***Jon Voight***

**Wayans Brothers Productions**
8730 Sunset Blvd., Ste. 290
W. Hollywood, CA 90069
***Tel: (323) 930-6720***
***Keenen Ivory Wayans; Marlon Wayans; Shawn Wayans***

**Whoop Inc./One Ho Productions**
333 W. 52nd Street, Ste. 602
New York, NY 10019
***Tel: (212) 245-6900***
***Credits: Hollywood Squares; Just for Kicks; Strong Medicine; Whoopi***

**Wildwood Enterprises**
725 Arizona Ave., Ste. 306
Santa Monica, CA 90401
***Tel: (310) 451-8050***
***Robert Redford***

**Worldwide Pants, Inc.**
1697 Broadway
New York, NY 10019
***Tel: (212) 975-5300***
***Tel: (323) 575-5600***
***David Letterman***

**Wyle/Katz Company**
1041 N. Formosa
Writers Bldg., Ste. 311
W. Hollywood, CA 90046
***Tel: (323) 850-2777***
***Noah Wyle***

DISTRIBUTION COMPANIES

**American World Pictures**
16027 Ventura Blvd., Ste. 320
Encino, CA 91436
***Tel: (818) 380-9100***
***www.americanworldpictures.com***

**Artistic License Films**
250 W. 57th Street, Ste. 606
New York, NY 10107
***Tel: (212) 265-9119***
***www.artlic.com***

**California Newsreel**
500 Third Street, Ste. 505
San Francisco, CA 91407
***Tel: (415) 284-7800***
***www.newsreel.org***

**Captive Entertainment**
450 N. Brand Ave., Ste. 600
Glendale, CA 91203
***Tel: (323) 658-7760***
***www.captive-entertainment.com***

**Cecchi Gori Pictures**
11990 San Vicente Blvd., Ste. 300
Los Angeles, CA 90049
***Tel: (310) 442-4777***
***www.cecchigoripictures.com***

**The Cinema Guild, Inc.**
115 W. 30th Street, Ste. 800
New York, NY 10001
***Tel: (212) 685-6242/(800) 732-5522***
***www.cinemaguild.com***

**CinemaNow, Inc.**
4553 Glencoe Ave., Ste. 380
Marina del Rey, CA 90292
***Tel: (310) 314-2000***
***www.cinemanow.com***

**Codeblack Entertainment**
111 Universal Hollywood Dr., Ste. 2260
Universal City, CA 91608
***Tel: (818) 286-8600***
***www.codeblackentertainment.com***

**Columbia Pictures**
10202 W. Washington Blvd.
Culver City, CA 90232
***Tel: (310) 244-4000***
***www.sonypictures.com***

**Crown International Pictures**
8701 Wilshire Boulevard
Beverly Hills, CA 90211
***Tel: (310) 657-6700***
***www.crownintlpictures.com***

**Dimension Films**
The Weinstein Company
345 Hudson St., 13th Fl.
New York, NY 10014
***Tel: (646) 862-3400/(212) 941-3800***
***www.weinsteinco.com***

**Distribution Video & Audio**
133 Candy Lane
Palm Harbor, FL 34683
***Tel: (727) 447-4147***
***www.dva.com***

**DreamWorks SKG Studios**
100 Universal City Plaza
Universal City, CA 91505
***Tel: (818) 733-7000***
***www.dreamworksstudios.com***

**Facets Multimedia**
1517 W. Fullerton Avenue
Chicago, IL 60614
***Tel: (773) 281-9075***
***www.facets.org***

**FilmEngine**
9220 Sunset Blvd., Ste. 301
Los Angeles, CA 90069
***Tel: (310) 205-9500***

**First Look Studios**
2000 Ave. of the Stars, Ste. 410
Century City, CA 90067
***Tel: (424) 202-5000***
***www.firstlookmedia.com***

**First Run Features**
630 Ninth Avenue, Ste. 1213
New York, NY 10036
***Tel: (212) 243-0600***
***www.firstrunfeatures.com***

**Focus Features**
100 Universal City Plaza
Universal City, CA 91608
***Tel: (818) 777-7373***
***www.filminfocus.com***

**Focus Features**
65 Bleecker St., 3rd Fl.
New York, NY 10012
***Tel: (212) 539-4000***
***www.filminfocus.com***

**Fox - Searchlight Pictures**
10201 W. Pico Blvd., Bldg. 38
Los Angeles, CA 90035
***Tel: (310) 369-1000***
***www.foxsearchlight.com***

**Gala Entertainment Corporation**
4536 E. Hastings Ave.
Orange, CA 92867
***Tel: (714) 974-9500***
***www.galaentertainmentcorp.com***

**Gigantic Releasing**
59 Franklin St., Ste. 401
New York, NY 10013
***Tel: (310) 315-1722***
***www.giganticdigital.com***

**GK Films**
1411 Fifth St., Ste. 200
Santa Monica, CA 90401
***Tel: (212) 219-3039***
***www.gkfilims.com***

**Goldcrest Films International**
1240 N. Olive Drive
Los Angeles, CA 90069
***Tel: (323) 650-4551***
***www.goldcrestfilms.com***

**Goldcrest Films International**
799 Washington Street
New York, NY 10014
***Tel: (212) 243-4700***
***www.goldcrestfilms.com***

**Alfred Haber Distribution**
111 Grand Avenue, Ste. 203
Palisades Park, NJ 07650
***Tel: (201) 224-8000***
***www.alfredhaber.com***

**Hearst Entertainment**
300 W. 57th Street
New York, NY 10019
***Tel: (212) 969-7553***
***www.hearstent.com***

**Hollywood Classics**
2450 Mission Street
San Marino, CA 91108
***Tel: (626) 403-8480***
***www.hollywoodclassics.com***

**IFM World Releasing**
1328 E. Palmer Ave.
Glendale, CA 91205
***Tel: (818) 243-4976***
***www.ifmfilm.com***

**IMAX Corporation**
3003 Exposition Blvd.
Santa Monica, CA 90404
***Tel: (310) 255-5500***
***Tel: (212) 821-0100 (NY)***
***www.imax.com***

**Image Entertainment**
20525 Nordhoff St., Ste. 200
Chatsworth, CA 91311
***Tel: (972) 671-5200***
***www.homevision.com***

**Independent Film Channel/IFC**
11 Penn Plaza, 15th Fl.
New York, NY 10001
***Tel: (212) 324-8500***
***www.ifctv.com***

**Indican Pictures**
8424A Santa Monica Blvd., #752
W. Hollywood, CA 90069
***Tel: (323) 650-0832***
***www.indicanpictures.com***

**IndieVest**
1416 N. La Brea Avenue
Los Angeles, CA 90028
***Tel: (888) 299-9961***
***www.indievest.com***

**IPA-Asia-Pacific**
1622 W. Oak Street
Burbank, CA 91506
***Tel: (818) 845-3480***
***www.ipaasia.biz***

**Karlin-Green Media, Inc.**
23480 Park Sorento, Ste. 117A
Calabasas, CA 91302
***Tel: (818) 224-3888***
***www.karlingreen.com***

**Keystone Entertainment**
23410 Civic Center Way, Ste. E-9
Malibu, CA 90265
***Tel: (310) 317-4883***
***www.keypics.com***

**Lakeshore International**
9268 W. Third Street
Beverly Hills, CA 90210
***Tel: (310) 867-8000***
***www.lakeshoreentertainment.com***

**Lantern Lane Entertainment**
P.O. Box 8187
Calabasas, CA 91372
***Tel: (818) 222-2309***
***www.lanternlane.com***

**Legendary Pictures**
4000 Warner Blvd., Bldg. 76
Burbank, CA 91522
***Tel: (818) 954-3888***
***www.legendarypictures.com***

**Lightyear Entertainment**
434 Ave. of the Americas, 6th Fl.
New York, NY 10011
***Tel: (212) 353-5084***
***www.lightyear.com***

**Lions Gate**
2700 Colorado Avenue
Santa Monica, CA 90404
***Tel: (310) 449-9200***
***www.lionsgate.com***

**Magnolia Pictures**
49 W. 27th Street, 7th Fl.
New York, NY 10001
***Tel: (212) 924-6701***
***www.magpictures.com***

**Magnolia Pictures**
1614 W. 5th Street
Austin, Texas 78703
***Tel: (512) 474-0303***
***www.magpictures.com***

**Mandalay Pictures**
4751 Wilshire Blvd., 3rd Fl.
Los Angeles, CA 90010
***Tel: (323) 549-4300***

*www.mandalay.com*

**Mandate Pictures**
2700 Colorado Ave., Ste. 501
Santa Monica, CA 90404
*Tel: (310) 360-1441*
*www.mandatepictures.com*

**Manga Entertainment**
521 Fifth Ave., Ste. 1900
New York, NY 10175
*Tel: (212) 905-4228*
*www.manga.com*

**Maverick Entertainment Group**
1191 E. Newport Ctr. Dr., Ste. 210
Deerfield Beach, FL 33442
*Tel: (954) 422-8811*
*www.maverickentertainment.cc*

**MGM Distribution**
10250 Constellation Blvd.
Los Angeles, CA 90067
*Tel: (310) 449-3000*
*www.mgm.com*

**Miramax Films**
8439 Sunset Blvd.
W. Hollywood, CA 90069
*Tel: (323) 822-4100*
*www.miramax.com*

**Miramax Films**
161 Avenue of the Americas
New York, NY 10013
*Tel: (917) 606-5500*
*www.miramax.com*

**Morgan Creek International**
10351 Santa Monica Blvd., Ste. 200
Los Angeles, CA 90025
*Tel: (310) 432-4848*
*www.morgancreek.com*

**Motion Picture Corporation of America**
10635 Santa Monica Blvd., Ste. 180
Los Angeles, CA 90025
*Tel: (310) 319-9500*

**Myriad Pictures**
3015 Main Street, Ste. 400
Santa Monica, CA 90405
*Tel: (310) 279-4000*
*www.myriadpictures.com*

**MySpace TV**
c/o Fox Interactive Media (FIM)
407 N. Maple Dr.
Beverly Hills, CA 90210
*Tel: (310) 969-7000*
*www.myspacetv.com*

**Namesake Entertainment**
P.O. Box 436492
Louisville, KY 40253
*Tel: (502) 243-3185*
*www.namesakeentertainment.com*

**National Geographic Giant Screen Film Distribution**
34 E.Putnam Ave., Ste. 103
Greenwich, CT 06830
*Tel: (203) 661-5678*
*www.nationalgeographic.com*

**Netflix**
100 Winchester Circle
Los Gatos, CA 9503
*Tel: (408)540-3700*
*www.netflix.com*

**New City Releasing**
5959 Topanga Canyon Blvd. Ste. 255
Woodland Hills, CA 91367
*Tel: (818) 348-2500*
*www.newcityreleasing.com*

**New Concorde International**
11600 San Vicente Blvd.
Los Angeles, CA 90049
*Tel: (310) 820-6733*
*www.newconcorde.com*

**New Line Cinema**
116 N. Robertson Blvd., Ste. 200
Los Angeles, CA 90048
*Tel: (310) 854-5811*
*www.newline.com*

**New Line Cinema**
888 Seventh Avenue, 30th Fl.
New York, NY 10106
*Tel: (212) 649-4900*
*www.newline.com*

**Newmarket Capital Group**
202 N. Canon Drive
Beverly Hills, CA 90210
*Tel: (310) 858-7472*
*www.newmarketfilms.com*

**next Pix Productions**
295 Greenwich St., Ste. 348
New York, NY 10007
*Tel: (212) 645-4600*
*www.nextpix.com*

**Nova Pictures**
6496 Ivarene Avenue
Hollywood, CA 90068
*Tel: (323) 462-5502*
*www.novapictures.com*

**Nu Image**
6423 Wilshire Blvd.
Los Angeles, CA 90048
*Tel: (310) 388-6900*
*www.nuimage.net*

**Palm Pictures**
76 Ninth Street, Ste. 1110
New York, NY 10011
*Tel: (212) 320-3600*
*www.palmpictures.com*

**Paramount Pictures**
5555 Melrose Avenue
Los Angeles, CA 90038
*Tel: (323) 956-5000*
*www.paramount.com*

**PBS**
2100 Crystal Drive
Arlington, VA 22202
*Tel: (703) 739-5000*
*www.pbs.org*

**Porchlight Entertainment**
11050 Santa Monica Blvd., 3rd Fl.
Los Angeles, CA 90025
*Tel: (310) 477-8400*
*www.porchlight.com*

**Promenade Pictures, LLC**
1149 Third St., Ste. 210
Santa Monica, CA 90403
*Tel: (310) 576-7555*
*www.promenadepictures.com*

**Pyramid Media**
P.O. Box 1048
Santa Monica, CA 90406
*Tel: (800) 421-2304/(310) 828-7577*
*www.pyramidmedia.com*

**Rainbow Film Company**
9165 Sunset Blvd., Ste. 300
Los Angeles, CA 90069
***Tel: (310) 271-0202***
***www.rainbowfilms.com***

**Relativity Media**
8899 Beverly Blvd., Ste. 510
Los Angeles, CA 90048
***Tel: (310) 859-1250***

**RKO Pictures**
1875 Century Park E., Ste. 2140
Los Angeles, CA 90067
***Tel: (310) 277-0707***
***www.rko.com***

**Roxie Releasing**
3125 16th Street
San Francisco, CA 94103
***Tel: (415) 431-3611***
***www.roxie.com/films***

**Samuel Goldwyn Films**
9570 W. Pico Blvd., 4th Fl.
Los Angeles, CA 90035
***Tel: (310) 860-3100***
***www.samuelgoldwynfilms.com***

**Samuel Goldwyn Films**
1133 Broadway, Ste. 926
New York, NY 10010
***Tel: (212) 367-9435***
***www.samuelgoldwynfilms.com***

**Screen Gems**
10202 W. Washington Blvd.
Culver City, CA 90232
***Tel: (310) 244-4000***

**Showcase Entertainment, Inc.**
21800 Oxnard Street, Ste. 150
Woodland Hills, CA 91367
***Tel: (818) 715-7005***
***www.showcaseentertainment.com***

**Sony Pictures Entertainment**
10202 W. Washington Blvd.
Culver City, CA 90232
***Tel: (310) 244-4000***
***www.sonypictures.com***

**Summit Entertainment**
1630 Stewart St., Ste. 120
Santa Monica, CA 90404
***Tel: (310) 309-8400***
***www.summit-ent.com***

**Starz!**
8900 Liberty Circle
Englewood, CO 80112
***Tel: (720) 852-7700***
***www.starz.com***

**Tapeworm Video Distribution**
25876 The Old Rd., #141
Stevenson Ranch, CA 91381
***Tel: (661) 257-4904***
***www.tapeworm.com***

**THINKFilm**
2121 Ave. of the Stars, Ste. 3000
Century City, CA 90067
***Tel: (310) 286-7200***
***www.thinkfilmcompany.com***

**Twentieth Century Fox**
10201 W. Pico Blvd.
Los Angeles, CA 90035
***Tel: (310) 369-1000***
***www.fox.com***

**Universal Pictures Distribution**
100 Universal City Plaza
Universal City, CA 91608
***Tel: (818) 777-1000***
***www.universalstudios.com***

**Vivendi Entertainment**
111 Universal Hollywood Dr., Ste. 400
Universal City, CA 91608
***Tel: (877) 252-4144***
***www.vivendient.com***

**The Walt Disney Company**
500 S. Buena Vista St.
Burbank, CA 91521
***Tel: (818) 560-1000***
***www.disney.com***

**Warner Bros. Distribution**
4000 Warner Boulevard
Burbank, CA 91522
***Tel: (818) 954-6000***
***www.warnerbros.com***

**The Weinstein Company**
375 Greenwich St., 3rd Fl.
New York, NY 10013
***Tel: (212) 941-3800***
***www.weinsteinco.com***

**The Weinstein Company**
345 Hudson St., 13th Fl.
New York, NY 10014
***Tel: (646) 862-3400***
***www.weinsteinco.com***

**The Weinstein Company**
375 Greenwich St., 3rd Fl.
New York, NY 10013
***Tel: (212) 941-3800***
***www.weinsteinco.com***

**The Weinstein Company**
5700 Wilshire Blvd., Ste. 600
Los Angeles, CA 90036
***Tel: (323) 207-3200***
***www.weinsteinco.com***

**Women Make Movies**
462 Broadway, Ste. 500 WS
New York, NY 10013
***Tel: (212) 925-0606***
***www.wmm.com***

**Xenon Pictures**
1440 Ninth Street
Santa Monica, CA 90401
***Tel: (301) 451-5510***
***www.xenonpictures.com***

**Yari Film Group**
10850 Wilshire Blvd, 6th Fl.
Los Angeles, CA 90024
***Tel: (310) 689-1450***
***www.yarifilmgroup.com***

**York Entertainment**
4565 Sherman Oaks Ave.
Sherman Oaks, CA 91403
***Tel: (818) 788-4050***
***www.yorkentertainment.com***

**YouTube**
***www.youtube.com***

**1st Call Studio Equipment**
12458 Gladstone Avenue
Sylmar, CA 91342
***Tel: (818) 771-9351/(818) 254-5217***
***www.1stcallequip.com***
***Booms, Lifts & More***

**Abel Cine Tech**
801 S. Main Street
Burbank, CA 91505
***Tel: (818) 972-9078***
***www.abelcine.com***
***Cameras & More***

**Abel CineTech**
509 Greenwich Street
New York, NY 10014
***Tel: (212) 462-0100***
***www.abelcine.com***
***Cameras***

**Abracadabra Video**
2250 N. Druid Hills Road
Ste. 123 & 125
Atlanta, GA 30329
***Tel: (404) 633-6002***
***www.abracadabravideo.com***
***Full Service Rentals***

**Absolute Rentals**
2633 N. San Fernando Blvd.
Burbank, CA 91504
***Tel: (818) 842-2828***
***www.absoluterentals.com***
***Full Service A-Z***

**Adolph Gasser**
181 Second St.
San Francisco, CA 94105
***Tel: (415) 495-3852***
***www.gassers.com***
***Cameras, Software, Tripods, Film & More***

**Alan Gordon Enterprises, Inc.**
5625 Melrose Avenue
Hollywood, CA 90038
**Tel: (323) 466-3561**
***www.alangordon.com***
***Camera Rentals; Video Assist Cameras***

**Albuquerque Studios**
5650 University Blvd., SE
Albuquerque, NM 87106
***Tel: (505) 227-2550***
***www.1stcallequip.com***
***Booms, Lifts & More***

**Altman Lighting Company**
57 Alexander Street
Yonkers, NY 10701
***Tel: (914) 476-7987***
***www.altmanltg.com***
***Stage, Studio & Location Lighting***

**Armanda Constanza**
240 Great Circle Rd., Ste. 328
Nashville, TN 37228
***Tel: (615) 256-2663***
***www.acincnashville.com***
***Cameras & more***

**Arri**
617 Route 303
Blauvelt, NY 10913
***Tel: (845) 353-1400***
***www.arri.com***
***Arriflex Cameras & Arri Lighting***

**Arri**
600 N. Victory Boulevard
Burbank, CA 91502
***Tel: (818) 841-7070***
***www.arri.com***
***Cameras & More***

**Arri Camera**
25 Enterprise Ave. N.
Secaucus, NJ 07094
***Tel: (212) 757-0906***
***www.cameraservice.com***
***Camera Rentals; Director's Finders***

**Arri Camera & Lighting FL**
2385 Stirling Road
Fort Lauderdale, FL 33312
***Tel: (954) 322-4545***
***www.cameraservice.com***
***Cameras & Lighting***

**Atlantic Television, Inc.**
524 Broadway, 4th Fl.
New York, NY 10012
***Tel: (212) 625-9327***
***www.atlantictv.com***
***Full Service Rentals***

**Avid**
One Park West
Tewksbury, MA 01876
***Tel: (978) 640-6789***
***www.avid.com***
***Editing & Media Composers***

**Barbizon Lighting Company**
101 Krog Street
Atlanta, GA 30373
***Tel: (404) 681-5124***
***www.barbizon.com***
***Lighting Equipment & Expendables***

**Barbizon Lighting Company**
456 W. 55th Street
New York, NY 10019
***Tel: (212) 586-1620***
***www.barbizon.com***
***Lighting Equipment & Expendables***

**Bexel Broadcast Services**
2701 N. Ontario Street
Burbank, CA 91504
***Tel: (818) 841-5051***
***www.bexel.com***
***Full Service Rentals***

**Bexel Broadcast Services**
5555 Oakbrook Pkwy. NW - Ste. 160
Norcross, GA 30093
***Tel: (770) 448-3000***
***www.bexel.com***
***Full Service Rentals***

**Bexel Broadcast Services**
625 W. 55th Street
New York, NY 10019
***Tel: (212) 246-5051***
***www.bexel.com***
***Full Service Rentals***

**Bexel Broadcast Services**
1001 N. Union Bower Rd., Ste. 130
Irving, TX 75061
***Tel: (972) 445-5051***
***www.bexel.com***
***Full Service Rentals***

**Birns & Sawyer**
6381 DeLongpre Avenue
Hollywood, CA 90028
***Tel: (323) 466-8211***
***www.birnsandsawyer.com***
***Cameras, Lighting & Grip Equipment***

**Birns & Sawyer**
5725 Craner Avenue
N. Hollywood, CA 91601
***Tel: (818) 766-2525***
***www.birnsandsawyer.com***
***Lighting & Grip Rentals***

**Birns, Inc.**
1720 Fiske Place
Oxnard, CA 93033
***Tel: (805) 487-5393***
***www.birns.com***
***Cameras & Lights***

**Boston Camera Rental Co.**
1284 Soldiers Field Road
Boston, MA 02135
***Tel: (617) 277-2200***
***www.rule.com***
***www.bostoncamera.com***
***Cameras***

**Camtec Motion Picture Cameras**
4221 W. Magnolia Blvd.
Burbank, CA 91505
***Tel: (818) 841-8700***
***www.camtec.tv***
***Camera Rentals***

**Canon, USA**
One Canon Plaza
Lake Success, NY 11042
***Tel: (516) 328-5000***
***www.usa.canon.com***
***Camera Rentals***

**Chesapeake Camera**
825 A-R N. Hammonds Ferry Rd.
Linthicum, MD 21090
***Tel: (410) 789-0894***
***www.chesapeakecamera.com***
***Camera Rentals***

**Cinema Rentals, Inc.**
25876 Old Road, Ste. 174
Stevenson Ranch, CA 91381
***Tel: (661) 222-7342***
***www.cinemarentals.com***
***Stunt & Underwater Cameras***

**CineQuipt**
2601 49th Avenue N. - Ste. 500
Minneapolis, MN 55430
***Tel: (612) 627-9080***
***www.cinequipt.com***
***Cameras; Generators; Lighting & More***

**Clairmont Camera**
4343 Lankershim Blvd.
N. Hollywood, CA 91602
***Tel: (818) 761-4440***
***www.clairmont.com***
***Camera Rentals***

**Day-1 Production Services**
225 Laredo Drive
Atlanta, GA 30030
***Tel: (404) 687-9511***
***www.day1productionservices.com***
***Lighting & Grip Equipment***

**Doggicam Systems**
1500 W. Verdugo Avenue
Burbank, CA 91504
***Tel: (818) 845-8470***
***www.doggicam.com***
***Doggicams, Body-Mounts***

**Entertainment Lighting Service**
11440 Sheldon Street
Sun Valley, CA 91352
***Tel: (818) 769-9800***
***www.elslights.com***
***Lighting Equipment***

**Feature Systems**
223 Veterans Blvd
Carlstadt, NJ 07072
***Tel: (201) 531-2299***
***Tel: (212) 736-0447***
***www.featuresystems.com***
***Lighting; Dollies, Trucks & More***

**The Film & Tape Works**
237 E. Ontario Street
Chicago, IL 60611
***Tel: (312) 280-2210***
***www.filmandtapeworks.com***
***Full Service***

**Film/Video Equipment Service**
800 S. Jason Street
Denver, CO 80223

***Tel: (303) 778-8616***
***www.fvesco.com***
***Cameras & Gear Support***

**Gear-Source, Inc.**
3101 Fairlane Farms Rd., Ste. 4
Wellington, FL 33414
***Tel: (561) 296-9555***
***www.gearsource.com***
***Camera Rentals & More***

**Geo Film Group**
7625 Hayvenhurst Ave., Ste. #46
Van Nuys, CA 91406
***Tel: (818) 376-6680***
***www.geofilm.com***
***Camera Rentals***

**Get-A-Grip Atlanta**
2421 Player Court
Duluth, GA 30096
***Tel: (678) 677-1257***
***www.getagripatlanta.com***
***Grip & Lighting Equipment***

**Hollywood Camera, Inc.**
3100 Damon Way
Burbank, CA 91505
***Tel: (818) 972-5000***
***www.hollywoodcamera.com***
***Camera & Video Assist Cameras***

**Hollywood Rentals**
12800 Foothhill Blvd.
Sylmar, CA 91342
***Tel: (818) 407-7800***
***www.hollywoodrentals.com***
***Lighting & Grip Rentals***

**Hollywood Rentals**
2616 Commerce Park Dr., Ste. 100
Orlando, FL 32819
***Tel: (407) 852-0164***
***www.hollywoodrentals.com***
***Lighting & Grip Rentals***

**Hollywood Rentals**
16333 George O'Neil Road
Baton Rouge, LA 70817
***Tel: (818) 407-7800***
***Lighting & Grip Rentals***

**Hollywood Rentals**
9100-C Perimeter Woods Dr.
Charlotte, NC 28216
***Tel: (704) 597-1808***
***www.hollywoodrentals.com***
***Lighting & Grip Rentals***

**HydroFlex**
301 E. El Segundo Blvd.
El Segundo, CA 90245
***Tel: (310) 301-8187***
***www.hyrdoflex.com***
***Underwater Camera Rentals***

**Innovision Optics**
1719 21st Street
Santa Monica, CA 90404
***Tel: (310) 453-4866***
***www.innovision-optics.com***
***Fiber Optic Lenses & Scopes***

**Kits and Expendables**
43-77 9th Street
Long Island City, NY 11101
***Tel: (212) 947-0700***
***Tel: (718) 482-1824***
***www.kitsandexpendables.com***
***Production Supplies***

**Koerner Camera Systems**
2323 N. Williams Avenue
Portland, OR 97227
***Tel: (503) 274-6533***
***www.koernercamera.com***
***Camera Packages***

**Koerner Camera Systems**
101 Nickerson, Ste. B500
Seattle, WA 98109
***Tel: (206) 285-7334***
***www.koernercamera.com***
***Camera Packages***

**Lee Utterbach**
126 Russ Street
San Francisco, CA 94103
***Tel: (415) 553-7700***
***www.lucamera.com***
***Cameras & Gear***

**Lighting and Grip NJ**
40 Hartz Way
Secaucus, NJ 07094
***Tel: (212) 757-0906***

**McCune Audio/Video/Lighting**
101 Utah Avenue
San Francisco, CA 94080
***Tel: (650) 873-1111***
***www.mccune.com***
***Audio; Lighting & Video***

**Moviola**
1135 N. Mansfield Avenue
Hollywood, CA 90038
***Tel: (323) 467-3107***
***www.moviola.com***
***Full Service Rentals***

**MPS Studios**
141 Regal Row
Dallas, TX 75247
***Tel: (214) 630-1655***
***www.mpsfilm.com***
***Full Service Rentals***

**Oppenheimer Cine Rental**
7400 Third Avenue S.
Seattle, WA 98108
***Tel: (206) 467-8666***
***www.oppenheimercamera.com***
***Camera Packages***

**Otto Nemenz**
870 N. Vine Street
Hollywood, CA 90038
***Tel: (323) 460-2774***
***www.ottonemenz.com***
***Cameras & Accessories***

**Panavision**
6735 Selma Avenue
Hollywood, CA 90028
***Tel: (323) 464-3800***
***www.panavision.com***
***Camera Packages***

**Panavision**
6219 DeSoto Ave.
Woodland Hills, CA 91367
***Tel: (818) 316-1000***
***www.panavision.com***
***Camera Packages***

**Panavision**
150 Varick Street, 2nd Fl.

New York, NY 10013
***Tel: (212) 606-0700***
***www.panavision.com***
***Camera Packages***

**Panavision**
One Technology Place
Homer, NY 13077
***Tel: (607) 749-2000***
***www.panavision.com***
***Camera Packages***

**Panavision Florida**
2000 Universal Studios Plza./Ste. 900
Orlando, FL 32819
***Tel: (407) 363-0990***
***www.panavision.com***
***Cameras; Lighting; Tractor Trailers & More***

**Paramount Pictures/Camera Dept.**
5555 Melrose Avenue
Hollywood, CA 90038
***Tel: (323) 956-5000***
***www.paramount.com***
***Cameras***

**PC & E (Production, Consulting & Equipment)**
2235 Defoor Hills Road
Atlanta, GA 30318
***Tel: (404) 609-9001***
***www.pce-atlanta.com***
***Full Service***

**Photo-Sonics, Inc.**
820 S. Mariposa St.
Burbank, CA 91506
***Tel: (818) 842-2141***
***www.photosonics.com***
***High-Speed Cameras***

**Pro8mm/Super8 Sound**
2805 Magnolia Blvd.
Burbank, CA 91505
***Tel: (818) 848-5522***
***www.pro8mm.com***
***Cameras, Film & Processing***

**R & R Lighting Company**
813 Silver Spring Avenue
Silver Spring, MD 20910
***Tel: (301) 589-4997***
***www.rrlighting.com***
***Lighting Equipment***

**RED Digital Cinema**
20291 Valencia Circle
Lake Forest, CA 92630
***Tel: (949) 206-7900***
***www.red.com***
***RED Cameras***

**Rule Boston Camera Rental Co.**
1284 Soldiers Field Road
Boston, MA 02135
***Tel: (617) 277-2200***
***www.rule.com***
***www.bostoncamera.com***
***Camera Packages***

**Schumacher Camera**
1147 W. Ohio Street, #303
Chicago, IL 50542
***Tel: (312) 243-3400***
***www.schumachercamera.com***
***Camera Packages***

**SpaceCam Systems**
31111 Via Colinas, Ste. 201
Westlake Village, CA 91362
***Tel: (818) 889-6060***
***www.spacecam.com***
***Helicopter Camera Mounts***

**TCS, Inc.**
341 W. 38th Street, 4th Fl.
New York, NY 10018
***Tel: (212) 247-6517***
***www.tcsfilm.com***
***Cameras, Sound & More***

**Tyler Camera Systems**
14218 Aetna St.
Van Nuys, CA 91401
***Tel: (818) 989-4420***
***www.tylermount.com***
***Helicopter Camera Mounts***

**Ultravision, Inc.**
1815 24th Street, Unit B
Santa Monica, CA 90404
***Tel: (310) 829-9130***
***www.ultravisioninc.com***
***Camera Packages***

**Video Edit Systems**
P.O. Box 950207
Mission Hills, CA 91395
***Tel: (818) 892-9236***
***www.videoeditsystems.com***
***Video Editing Systems***

**Vox-Cam**
813 Silver Spring Avenue
Silver Spring, MD 20910
***Tel: (301) 589-5377***
***www.voxcam.com***
***Cameras, Audio Pkgs. & More***

**The Washington Source For Lighting, Inc.**
5050 Lawrence Place
Hyattsville, MD 20781
***Tel: (301) 779.8185***
***www.thewashingtonsource.com***
***Grip, Lighting, Vehicles & More***

**Wooden Nickel Lighting & Camera**
6920 Tujunga Avenue
N. Hollywood, CA 91605
***Tel: (818) 761-9662***
***www.woodennickellighting.com***
***Camera & Lighting Packages***

# FILM COMMISSIONS

**Alabama Film Office**
*Tel: (334) 242-4195*
*www.alabamafilm.org*

**Alaska Film Program**
*Tel: (907) 269-8491*
*www.alaskafilm.org*

**Arizona Film Commission**
*Tel: (602) 771-1193*
*www.azcommerce.com*

**Arkansas Motion Picture Development Office**
*Tel: (501) 682-7326*
*www.arkansasedc.com*

**California Film Commission**
*Tel: (323) 860-2960*
*www.film.ca.gov*
*www.filmcafirst.com*

**Colorado Motion Picture & Television Commission**
*Tel: (303) 620-4500*
*www.coloradofilm.org*

**Connecticut Film Division**
*Tel: (860) 256-2800*
*www.ctfilm.com*

**Delaware Film Office**
*Tel: (302) 672-6857*
*www.state.de.us/dedo*

**D.C. Office of Motion Pictures & TV Development**
*Tel: (202) 727-6608*
*www.film.dc.gov*

**Florida Governor's Office of Film & Entertainment**
*Tel: (850) 410-4765*
*Tel: (818) 508-7772*
*www.filminflorida.com*

**Georgia Film, Video & Music**
*Tel: (404) 962-4052*
*www.filmgeorgia.org*

**Hawaii Film Office**
*Tel: (808) 586-2570*
*www.hawaiifilmoffice.com*

**Hawaii Big Island Film Office**
*Tel: (808) 327-3663*
*www.hawaiifilmoffice.com*

**Idaho Film Bureau**
*Tel: (208) 334-2470*
*www.filmidaho.com*

**Illinois Film Office**
*Tel: (312) 814-3600*
*www.filmillinois.state.il.us*

**Indiana Film Commission**
*Tel: (317) 234-2087*
*www.in.gov/film*

**Iowa Film Office**
*Tel: (515) 725-3021*
*www.filmiowa.com*

**Kansas Film Commission**
*Tel: (785) 296-2178*
*www.filmkansas.com*

**Kentucky Film Office**
*Tel: (502) 564-3456*
*www.kyfilmoffice.com*

**Louisiana Office of Film & Television Development**
*Tel: (225) 342-5403*
*www.lafilm.org*

**Maine Film Office**
*Tel: (207) 624-7631*
*www.filminmaine.com*

**Maryland Film Office**
*Tel: (410) 767-6340*
*www.marylandfilm.org*

**Massachusetts Film Office**
*Tel: (617) 423-1155*
*www.mass.gov/film*

**Michigan Film Office**
*Tel: (800) 477-3456*
*www.michiganfilmoffice.org*

**Minnesota Film & TV Board**
*Tel: (612) 767-0095*
*www.mnfilm.org*

**Mississippi Film Office**
*Tel: (601) 359-3297*
*www.visitmississippi.org/film*

**Missouri Film Commission**
*Tel: (573) 522-1288*
*www.missouribusiness.net/film/*

**Montana State Film Office**
*Tel: (406) 841-2876/(800) 553-4563*
*www.montanafilm.com*

**Nebraska Film Office**
*Tel: (402) 471-3746*

***VISIT** YOUR LOCAL FILM OFFICE TODAY!

***ASK** FOR A CALENDAR OF FILM & TV PROJECTS COMING TO TOWN (in the next 3-12 months).

***GET** FREE PRODUCTION GUIDES.

***NETWORK** WITH POWER PLAYERS IN YOUR CITY!

*www.filmnebraska.org*

**Nevada Film Office**
*Tel: (702) 486-2711*
*www.nevadafilm.com*

**New Hampshire Film & TV Office**
*Tel: (603) 271-2220*
*www.filmnh.org*

**New Jersey Motion Picture & TV Commission**
*Tel: (973) 648-6279*
*www.njfilm.org*

**New Mexico Film Office**
*Tel: (505) 476-5600*
*www.nmfilm.com*

**New York City Mayor's Office of Film, Theatre & Broadcasting**
*Tel: (212) 489-6710*
*www.nyc.gov/film*

**New York State Governor's Office of Motion Picture & Television Development**
*Tel: (212) 803-2330*
*www.nylovesfilm.com*

**North Carolina Film Commission**
*Tel: (919) 733-9900*
*www.ncfilm.com*

**North Carolina Film Office**
*Tel: (919) 733-9900*
*www.ncfilm.com*

**North Dakota Film Commission**
*Tel: (701) 328-2525*
*www.ndtourism.com*

**Ohio Film Office**
*Tel: (614) 466-2284*
*www.discoverohiofilm.com*

**Oklahoma Film & Music Office**
*Tel: (405) 230-8440*
*www.oklahomafilm.org*

**Oakland Film Commission**
*Tel: (510) 238-4734*
*www.filmoakland.com*

**Oregon Film & Video Office**
*Tel: (503) 229-5832*
*www.oregonfilm.org*

**Pennsylvania Film Office**
*Tel: (717) 783-3456*
*www.filminpa.com*

**Rhode Island Film & TV Office**
*Tel: (401) 277-3456*
*www.film.ri.gov*

**South Carolina Film Office**
*Tel: (803) 737-0492*
*www.filmsc.com*

**South Dakota Film Commission**
*Tel: (605) 773-3301*
*www.filmsd.com*

**Tennessee Film & Music Commission**
*Tel: (615) 741-3456*
*www.filmtennessee.com*

**Texas Film Commission**
*Tel: (512) 463-9200*
*www.texasfilmcommission.com*

**Utah Film Commission**
*Tel: (801) 538-8740*
*www.film.utah.org*

**Vallejo/Solano County Film Office**
*Tel: (707) 649-3510/(707)642-3653*
*Tel: (800) 4-VALLEJO*

**Vermont Film Commission**
*Tel: (802) 828-3618*
*www.vermontfilm.com*

**Virginia Film Office**
*Tel: (804) 545-5530*
*www.film.virginia.org*

**Washington State Film Office**
*Tel: (206) 256-6151*
*www.filmwashington.com*

**West Virginia Film Office**
*Tel: (304) 558-2200 ext. 382*
*www.wvfilm.com*

**Wisconsin Film Office**
*Tel: (414) 287-6235*
*www.filmwisconsin.org*

**Wyoming Film Office**
1520 Etchepare Circle
Cheyenne, WY 82007
*Tel: (307) 777-3400*
*www.filmwyoming.com*

**Academy of Motion Pictures Arts & Sciences Student Academy Awards**
8949 Wilshire Boulevard
Beverly Hills, CA 90211
***Tel: (310) 247-3000 ext. 131***
***www.oscars.org/saa/***

**AFI Los Angeles International Film Festival**
American Film Institute
2021 N. Western Ave.
Los Angeles, CA 90027
***Tel: (213) 856-7600/(866) AFI-FEST***
***www.afifest.com***

**AFI/Discovery Channel SilverDocs Film Festival**
AFI Silver Theatre & Cultural Ctr.
8633 Colesville Road
Silver Spring, MD 20910
***Tel: (301) 495-6720***
***www.silverdocs.com***

**African American Film Marketplace & S.E. Manly Short Showcase**
Black Hollywood Educational Resource Center
1875 Century Park E., Ste. 600
Los Angeles, CA 90067
***Tel: (310) 284-3170***
***www.bherc.org***

**African American Women in Cinema Film Festival**
545 Eighth Avenue, Ste. 401
New York, NY 10018
***Tel: (212) 769-7949***
***www.aawic.org***

**American Black Film Festival**
Film Life, Inc.
P.O. Box 1975
New York, NY 10113
***Tel: (646) 375-2144 ext. 1***
***www.abff.com***

**American Film Market (AFM)**
Independent Film & TV Alliance
10850 Wilshire Blvd., 9th Fl.
Los Angeles, CA 90024
***Tel: (310) 446-1000***
***www.ifta-online.org***

**Ann Arbor Film Festival**
308 1/2 State St., Ste 22
Ann Arbor, MI 48104
***Tel: (734) 995-5356***
***www.aafilmfest.org***

**Arizona Int'l. Film Festival**
The Screening Room
127 E. Congress
Tucson, AZ 85701
***Tel: (520) 882-0204***
***www.filmfestivalarizona.com***

**Ashland International Film Festival**
P.O. Box 218
Ashland, OR 97520
***Tel: (541) 488-3823***
***www.ashlandfilm.org***

**Asian American International Film Festival**
Asian CineVision, Inc.
133 W. 19th St., Ste. 300
New York, NY 10011
***Tel: (212) 989-1422***
***www.asiancinevision.org***

**Asian Pacific American Film Festival**
APA Film, Inc.
P.O. Box 58205
Washington, D.C. 20037
***Tel: (202) 330-5496***
***www.apafilm.org***

**Aspen Filmfest**
110 E. Hallan St., Ste. 102
Aspen, CO 81611
***Tel: (970) 925-6882***
***www.aspenfilm.org***

**Atlanta Film Festival**
535 Means Street, Ste. C
Atlanta, GA 30318
***Tel: (404) 352-4225***
***www.atlantafilmfestival.com***

**Austin Film Festival**
1801 Salina Street
Austin, TX 78702
***Tel: (512) 478-4795***
***www.austinfilmfestival.com***

# Power Quote

*" The films that win our competition usually go on and win many others."*

***Richard Miller***
*Awards Administration Director*

Saluting excellence in filmmaking, at the collegiate level, is what the Student Academy Awards is all about. Conducted by the Academy of Motion Pictures, Arts & Sciences and the Academy Foundation, this prestigious, national competition attracts over 500 college and university film students each year -- all vying for awards, cash prizes and a once-in-a-lifetime opportunity to shine as a new filmmaker in Animation, Documentary, Narrative and Alternative genres. Past winners include Spike Lee, Trey Parker, Bob Saget and Oscar winners John Lasseter and Robert Zemeckis.

"The biggest reward the Academy gives with the Student Academy Award is the encouragement," shares Richard Miller, the Awards Administration Director who runs the Program. "It's a pat on the back from the very top film professionals saying, 'We like your work.' Winning the Student Academy Award doesn't put you at the top of the industry; but, it can open some doors that might not be open otherwise."

What's Miller's POWER ADVICE for winning the competition? "It starts with a good story and it ends with the filmmakers' ability to take a good story and tell it on film," he shares. "There's no secret handshake filmmakers can learn and have their film get through. A good story is basically the formula for any film or any competition."

Application deadlines and more information can be found at **www.oscars.org/saa**.

**BACA Film & Video Festival**
Brooklyn Arts Council
55 Washington St., Ste. 218
Brooklyn, NY 11201
***Tel: (718) 625-0080***
***www.brooklynartscouncil.org***

**Beverly Hills Film Festival**
9663 Santa Monica Blvd., Ste. 777
Beverly Hills, CA 90210
***Tel: (310) 779-1206***
***www.beverlyhillsfilmfestival.com***

**Big Bear Lake Int'l. Film Festival**
P.O. Box 1981
Big Bear Lake, CA 92315
***Tel: (909) 866-3433***
***www.bigbearlakefilmfestival.com***

**Black Harvest Int'l. Festival of Film & Video**
Gene Siskel Film Center
164 N. State Street
Chicago, IL 60601
***Tel: (312) 846-2600***
***www.siskelfilmcenter.org***

**Campus Movie Fest**
***Tel: (404) 748-0012***
***www.campusmoviefest.com***

**Cannes Film Festival**
***www.festival-cannes.fr***

**Chicago International Documentary Festival**
1112 N. Milwaukee Avenue
Chicago, IL 60622
***Tel: (773) 486-9612***
***www.chicagodocfestival.org***

**Chicago International Film Fest.**
30 E. Adams Street, Ste. 800
Chicago, IL 60603
***Tel: (312) 683-0121***
***www.chicagofilmfestival.com***

**Chicago Latino Film Festival**
676 N. LaSalle Street, Ste. 520
Chicago, IL 60654
***Tel: (312) 431-1330***
***www.latinoculturalcenter.org***

**Cinema Expo International**
770 Broadway, 5th Fl.
New York, NY 10003
***Tel: (646) 654-7680***
***www.cinemaexpo.com***

**Cinequest Film Festival**
P.O. Box 720040
San Jose, CA 95127
***Tel: (408) 995-5033***
***www.cinequest.org***

**CineVegas Film Festival**
170 S. Green Valley Pkwy., Ste. 120
Henderson, NV 89012
***Tel: (702) 952-5555(888) 8-VEGAS***
***www.cinevegas.com***

**City Voices, City Visions Film Festival**
***cityvoicescityvisions.blogspot.com***

**CMJ FilmFest**
100 Fifth Avenue, 11th Fl.
New York, NY 10011
***Tel: (917) 277-7120***
***www.cmj.com***

**College Television Awards**
Academy of Television Arts & Sciences Foundation
5220 Lankershim Boulevard
N. Hollywood, CA 91601
***Tel: (818) 754-2820***
***www.emmys.tv/foundation***

**Crossroads Film Festival**
P.O. Box 22604
Jackson, MS 39225
***Tel: (601) 510-9148***
***www.crossroadsfilmfestival.com***

**D.C. Independent Film Market & Trade Show**
2950 Van Ness St., NW-Ste. 728
Washington DC, 20008
***Tel: (202) 686-8867***
***www.dciff.org***

**D.C. Shorts Film Festival**
1317 F Street, NW - Ste. 920
Washington, DC 20004
***Tel: (202) 393-4266***
***www.dcshorts.com***

**Denver Int'l. Film Festival**
Denver Film Society
900 Auraria Parkway
Denver, CO 80204
***Tel: (303) 595-3456***
***www.denverfilm.org***

**DIY Film Festival**
***www.diyconvention.com***

**Film Arts Festival**
145 Ninth Street, #101
San Francisco, CA 94103
***Tel: (415) 552-8760***
***www.filmarts.org***

**Filmfest D.C.**
P.O. Box 21396
Washington, D.C. 20009
***Tel: (202) 274-5782***
***www.filmfestdc.org***

**Film, Stage & Showbiz Expo**
440 Ninth Avenue, 8th Fl.
New York, NY 10001
***Tel: (212) 404-2345***
***www.theshowbizexpo.com***

**Florida Film Festival**
1300 S. Orlando Ave.
Maitland, FL 32751
***Tel: (407) 629-1088 ext. 225***
***www.floridafilmfestival.com***

**Freedom Film Festival**
American Cinema Foundation
11400 W. Olympic Blvd., #200
Los Angeles, CA 90064
***Tel: (310) 914-0159***
***www.cinemafoundation.com***

**Gen Art Film Festival**
133 W. 25th Street, 6th Fl.
New York, NY 10001
***Tel: (212) 255-7300***
***www.genart.org***

**Georgia BIG PICTURE Conference (GABPC) Film Festival**
6070 Stonebrook Lane
Austell, GA 30106
***Tel: (770) 726-9818***
***www.gabpc.com***

**Green Mountain Film Festival**
26 Main Street

Montpelier, VT 05602
***Tel: (802) 262 3423***
***www.greenmountainfilmfestival.org***

**Hawaii Int'l. Film Festival**
680 Iwilei Road, Ste. 100
Honolulu, HI 96813
***Tel: (808) 528-3456***
***www.hiff.org***

**Hollywood Black Film Festival**
8306 Wilshire Blvd., Ste. 2057
Beverly Hills, CA 90211
***Tel: (310) 407-3596***
***www.hbff.org***

**Hollywood Film Festival**
433 N. Camden Dr., Ste. 600
Beverly Hills, CA 90210
***Tel: (310) 288-1882***
***www.hollywoodfestival.com***
***www.hollywoodawards.com***

**Houston Black Film Festival**
***www.houstonblackfilmfestival.org***

**IFP/MNTV Short Film Competition**
2446 University Avenue W., Ste. 100
Saint Paul, MN 55114
***Tel: (651) 644-1912***
***www.ifpmn.org***

**Independent Feature Market**
68 Jay Street, Rm. 425
Brooklyn, NY 11201
***Tel: (212) 465-8200***
***www.ifp.org***

**Indian Film Festival of Los Angeles**
5657 Wilshire Blvd., #130
Los Angeles, CA 90036
***Tel: (310) 364-4403***
***www.indianfilmfestival.org***

**Indiefest Film Festival**
P.O. Box 148849
Chicago, IL 60614
***Tel: (773) 665-7600***
***www.indiefestchicago.com***

**International Diversity Market**
***www.onevibe.biz***

**International Family Film Festival**
4531 W. Empire Avenue, #200
Burbank, CA 91505
***Tel: (661) 257-3131/(818) 332-7951***
***www.iffilmfest.org***

**International Wildlife Film Fest.**
718 S. Higgins Avenue
Missoula, MT 59801
***Tel: (406) 728-9380***
***www.wildlifefilms.org***

**IVY Film Festival**
***www.ivyfilmfestival.com***

**Jewish Film Festival**
1219 S.W. Park Ave.
Portland, OR 97205
***Tel: (503) 221-1156***
***www.nwfilm.org***

**Kidfilm Festival**
6116 N. Central Expressway, Ste. 105
Dallas, TX 75206
***Tel: (214) 821-6300***
***www.usafilmfestival.com***

**Kodak Film School Competition**
Eastman Kodak Company
6700 Santa Monica Blvd.
Los Angeles, CA 90038
***Tel: (323) 464-6131***
***www.motion.kodak.com/US/en/motion/Education/Filmschool_Competition/***

**Kodak Film School Competition**
Eastman Kodak Company
360 W. 31st Street
New York, NY 10001
***Tel: (212) 631-3400/(585) 724-4000***
***www.motion.kodak.com/US/en/motion/Education/Filmschool_Competition/***

**L.A. Shorts Fest**
1610 Argyle Ave., #113
Los Angeles, CA 90028
***Tel: (323) 461-6300***
***www.lashortsfest.com***

**Los Angeles Asian Pacific Film Festival**
Visual Communications
Southern California Asian American Studies Central, Inc.
120 Judge John Aiso St.
Los Angeles, CA 90012
***Tel: (213) 680-4462 ext. 68***
***www.vconline.org***

**Los Angeles Film Festival**
9911 W. Pico Blvd.
Los Angeles, CA 90035
***Tel: (310) 432-1240***
***www.lafilmfest.com***

**Los Angeles Latino International Film Festival**
6777 Hollywood Blvd., Ste. 500
Los Angeles, CA 90028
***Tel: (323) 469-9066***
***www.latinofilm.org***

**Macon Film & Video Festival**
***www.maconfilmfestival.com***

**Malibu International Film Festival**
P.O. Box 1133
Malibu, CA 90264
***Tel: (310) 452-6688***
***www.malibufilmfestival.org***

**Manhattan Short Film Festival**
22 Prince Street, #110
New York, NY 10012
***Tel: (212) 529-8640***
***www.msfilmfest.com***

**Maryland Film Festival**
107 E. Read Street
Baltimore, MD 21202
***Tel: (410) 752-8083***
***www.mdfilmfest.com***

**Martha's Vineyard African American Film Festival**
Run & Shoot Filmworks
P.O. Box 1860
Denver, NC 28037
***www.mvaaff.com***

**Maui Film Festival**
***Tel: (808) 579-9244***
***www.mauifilmfestival.com***

**Memphis Film Festival**
***www.memphisfilmfestival.com***

**Miami Int'l. Film Festival**
25 NE 2nd Street, Ste. 5521
Miami, FL 33132
***Tel: (305) 237-FILM***
***www.miamifilmfestival.com***

**Mill Valley Film Festival**
1001 Lootens Place, Ste. 220
San Rafael CA 94901
***Tel: (415) 383-5256***
***www.cafilm.org***

**MIPCOM**
***Tel: (212) 284-5130***
***www.mipcom.com***

**MIPDOC**
***Tel: (212) 284-5130***
***www.mipdoc.com***

**MNTV Short Film Competition**
2446 University Avenue W., Ste. 100
Saint Paul, MN 55114
***Tel: (651) 644-1912***
***www.ifpmn.org***

**Nantucket Film Festival**
1633 Broadway, Ste. 15-310
New York, NY 10019
***Tel: (212) 708-1278***
***www.nantucketfilmfestival.org***

**Napa • Sonoma Wine Country Film Festival**
12000 Henno Road
P.O. Box 303
Glen Ellen, CA 95442
***Tel: (707) 935-FILM***
***www.wcff.us***

**Nashville Film Festival**
P.O. Box 24330
Nashville, TN 37202
***Tel: (615) 742-2500***
***www.nashvillefilmfestival.org***

**National Media Market**
P.O. Box 87410
Tucson, AZ 85754
***Tel: (520) 743-7735***
***www.nmm.net***

**NATPE/National Association of Television Program Executives**
5757 Wilshire Blvd., PH 10
Los Angeles, CA 90036
***Tel: (310) 453-4440***
***www.natpe.org***

**NATPE LATV Fest**
5757 Wilshire Blvd., PH 10
Los Angeles, CA 90036
***Tel: (310) 453-4440***
***www.natpe.org***

**New Jersey Int'l. Film Festival**
***Tel: (732) 932-8482***
***www.njfilmfest.com***

**New Orleans Film Festival**
900 Camp Street
New Orleans, LA 70130
***Tel: (504) 309-6633***
***www.neworleansfilmfest.com***

**Newport Beach Film Festival**
4540 Campus Drive
Newport Beach, CA 92663
***Tel: (949) 253-2880***
***www.newportbeachfilmfest.com***

**New York Film Festival**
Film Society of Lincoln Center
70 Lincoln Center Plaza
New York, NY 10023
***Tel: (212) 875-5610***
***www.filmlinc.com***

**New York International Independent Film & Video Festival**
505 E. Windmill Lane, Ste. 1B-102
Las Vegas, NV 89123
***Tel: (702) 361-1430/(702) 263-4480***
***www.nyfilmvideo.com***

**New York International Latino Film Festival**
419 Lafayette St., 6th Fl.
New York, NY 10003
***Tel: (646) 723-1428***
***www.nylatinofilm.com***

**NEXTFRAME Student Film Fest.**
Temple University
Dept. of Film & Media Arts
Annengerg Hall, Room 130
Philadelphia, PA 19122
***Tel: (215) 204-6740***
***www.temple.edu/nextframe***

**Northwest Film & Video Festival**
1219 S.W. Park Ave.
Portland, OR 97205
***Tel: (503) 221-1156***
***www.nwfilm.org***

**Oakland Int'l. Film Festival**
150 Frank H. Ogawa Plaza, 9th Fl.
Oakland, CA 94612
***Tel: (510) 238-4734***
***www.filmoakland.com***

**On Location: Memphis**
***www.memphisfilmforum.org***

**Oxford Film Festival**
P.O. Box 727
Oxford, MS 38655
***Tel: (877) 560-FILM***
***www.oxfordfilmfest.com***

**Palm Springs Int'l. Film Festival**
1700 E. Tahquitz Cnyn. Way, Ste. #3
Palm Springs, CA 92262
***Tel: (760) 322-2930***
***www.psfilmfest.org***

**Pan-African Film Festival/PAFF**
3775 Santa Rosalia Drive
Los Angeles, CA 90008
***Tel: (323) 295-1706***
***www.paff.org***

**Philadelphia Film Festival**
600 Chestnut St., Ste. 705
Philadelphia, PA 19106
***Tel: (215) 253-3599***
***www.phillyfests.com***

**Portland Int'l. Film Festival**
1219 S.W. Park Ave.
Portland, OR 97205
***Tel: (503) 221-1156***
***www.nwfilm.org***

**Portland Latin American Film Festival**
6128 SW Corbett Ave.
Portland, OR 97239
***Tel: (503) 245-8020***
***www.pdxlaff.org***

**Reel Sisters of the Diaspora Film Festival & Lecture Series**
c/o African Voices
270 West 96th Street
New York, NY 10025

***Tel: (347) 534-3304/(212) 865-2982***
***www.reelsisters.org***

**Rhode Island International Film Festival**
268 Broadway
Providence, RI 02903
***Tel: (401) 861-4445***
***www.film-festival.org***

**San Diego Film Festival**
7974 Mission Bonita Dr.
San Diego, CA 92120
***Tel: (619) 582-2368***
***www.sdff.org***

**San Francisco Int'l. Asian American Film Festival**
145 Ninth Street, Ste. 350
San Francisco, CA 94103
***Tel: (415) 863-0814***
***www.asianamericanfilmfestival.org***

**San Francisco Black Film Festival**
P.O. Box 15490
San Francisco, CA 94115
***Tel: (415) 400-4602***
***www.sfbff.org***

**San Francisco Int'l. Film Festival**
San Francisco Film Society
39 Mesa Street, Ste. 110
San Francisco, CA 94129
***Tel: (415) 561-5000***
***www.sffs.org***

**Santa Barbara Int'l. Film Festival**
1528 Chapala St., Ste. 203
Santa Barbara, CA 93101
***Tel: (805) 963-0023***
***www.sbfilmfestival.org***

**Seattle Int'l. Film Festival**
400 9th Avenue N.
Seattle, WA 98109
***Tel: (206) 464-5830***
***www.siff.net***

**Seattle Jewish Film**
***www.seattlejewishfilmfestival.org***

**SilverDocs Film Festival**
AFI Silver Theatre & Cultural Ctr.
8633 Colesville Road
Silver Spring, MD 20910
***Tel: (301) 495-6720***
***www.silverdocs.com***

**Gene Siskel Film Center**
164 N. State Street
Chicago, IL 60601
***Tel: (312) 846-2600***
***www.siskelfilmcenter.org***

**Slamdance Film Festival**
5634 Melrose Avenue
Los Angeles, CA 90038
***Tel: (323) 466-1786***
***www.slamdance.com***

**South By Southwest Film Festival & Conference (SXSW)**
P.O. Box 4999
Austin, TX 78765
***Tel: (512) 467-7979***
***www.sxsw.com***

**Spaghetti Junction Urban Film Festival**
***www.sjuff.net***

**Student Academy Awards**
Academy of Motion Picture Arts & Sciences
8949 Wilshire Boulevard
Beverly Hills, CA 90211
***Tel: (310) 247-3000 ext. 131***
***www.oscars.org/saa/***

**Sundance Film Festival**
1825 Three Kings Dr.
Park City, UT 84060
***Tel: (435) 658-3456***
***www.sundance.org***

**Sundance Film Festival**
8350 Wilshire Blvd., 3rd Fl.
Beverly Hills, CA 90211
***Tel: (310) 360-1981***
***www.sundance.org***

**Tallahassee Film Festival**
TCC Capitol Center
300 W. Pensacola St., Ste. 118C
Tallahassee, FL 32301
***Tel: (850) 201-9499***
***www.tallahasseefilmfestival.com***

**Telluride Film Festival**
800 Jones Street
Berkeley, CA 94710
***Tel: (510) 665-9494***
***www.telluridefilmfestival.org***

**Texas Black Film Festival**
***www.texasblackfilmfestival.com***

**Tribeca Film Festival**
375 Greenwich Street
New York, NY 10013
***Tel: (212) 941-2400***
***www.tribecafilmfestival.org***

**Urbanworld Film Festival**
375 Greenwich Street
New York, NY 10013
***Tel: (212) 231-7318***
***www.urbanworld.org***

**WIN Film Festival**
***www.winfemme.com***

**Wine Country Film Festival**
12000 Henno Road
P.O. Box 303
Glen Ellen, CA 95442
***Tel: (707) 935-FILM***
***www.wcff.us***

**Withoutabox**
***Tel: (818) 985-5999***
***www.withoutabox.com***

**WorldFest-Charleston Int'l. Film Festival**
9898 Bissonnet, Ste. 650
Houston, TX 77036
***Tel: (713) 965-9955***
***www.worldfest.org***

Be the Best!

Make YOUR mark in the industry by being the UNMISTAKABLE Best! No mediocrity. No excuses. Greatness Gets Recognized!

www.entertainmentpower.com

**Annenberg Media**
1301 Pennsylvania Ave., NW - #302
Washington, DC 20004
***Tel: (202) 783-0500***
***www.learner.org***

**Annenberg Media**
P.O. Box 55742
Indianapolis, IN 46205
***Tel: (317) 558-4834***
***Tel: (800) 532-7637***
***www.learner.org***

**Blue Rider Pictures**
2801 Ocean Park Blvd., Ste. 193
Santa Monica, CA 90405
***Tel: (310) 314-8405***
***www.blueriderpictures.com***

**California Arts Council**
1300 I Street, Ste. 930
Sacramento, CA 95814
***Tel: (916) 322-6555***
***www.cac.ca.gov***

**Center for Asian American Media (CAAM) Media Fund**
145 Ninth Street, Ste. 350
San Francisco, CA 94103
***Tel: (415) 863-0814***
***www.asianamericanmedia.org***

**Cinereach**
126 Fifth Avenue, 5th Fl.
New York, NY 10011
***Tel: (212) 727-3224***
***www.cinereach.org***

**Corporation for Public Broadcasting (CPB) Grants**
401 Ninth Street, NW
Washington, D.C. 20004
***Tel: (202) 879-9600***
***www.cpb.org***

**Creative Capital Foundation Grants**
65 Bleeker Street, 7th Fl.
New York, NY 10012
***Tel: (212) 598-9900***
***www.creative-capital.org***

**Roy Dean Film Grants**
From the Heart Productions
1455 Mandalay Beach Road
Oxnard, CA 93035
***Tel: (805) 984-0098***
***www.fromtheheartproductions.com***

**Documentary Educational Resources**
101 Morse Street
Watertown, MA 02472
***Tel: (617) 926-0491***
***www.der.org***

**Film Arts Foundation**
145 Ninth Street, Ste. 101
San Francisco, CA 94103
***Tel: (415) 552-8760***
***www.filmarts.org***

**Film Finances, Inc.**
9000 Sunset Boulevard, Ste.1400
Los Angeles, California 90069
***Tel: (310) 275-7323***
***www.ffi.com***

**Flicker Film Grant**
Richmond Moving Image Co-op
P.O. Box 7469
Richmond, VA 23221
***Tel: (804) 232-7642***
***www.rmicweb.org***

**Fractured Atlas Emerging Artists Fund**
248 W. 35th Street, Ste. 1202
New York, NY 10001
***Tel: (212) 277-8020***
***www.fracturedatlas.org***

**The Foundation Center**
79 Fifth Avenue/16th Street
New York, NY 10003
***Tel: (212) 620-4230***
***www.fdncenter.org***

**Gucci Tribeca Documentary Fund**
***Tel: (212) 274-8080 ext. 28***
***www.tribecafilminstitute.org***

**IFC Media Lab Studios**
11 Penn Plaza, 15th Fl.
New York, NY 10001
***Tel: (212) 324-8500***
***www.ifctv.com***

**IFP/Chicago Production Fund**
1104 S. Wabash, Ste. 403
Chicago, IL 60605
***Tel: (312) 235-0161***
***www.ifp.org***

**IFP Market Awards Emerging Narrative Award**
68 Jay Street, Rm. 425
Brooklyn, NY 11201
***Tel: (212) 465-8200***
***www.ifp.org***

**IFP Fresh Filmmakers Production Grant**
2446 University Avenue W., Ste. 100
Saint Paul, MN 55114
***Tel: (651) 644-1912***
***www.ifpmn.org***

**IFP Market Awards**
68 Jay Street, Rm. 425
Brooklyn, NY 11201
***Tel: (212) 465-8200***
***www.ifp.org***

**Illinois Arts Council Program Grants & Artist Fellowships**
James R. Thompson Center
100 West Randolph, Ste. 10-500
Chicago, IL 60601
***Tel: (312) 814-6750***
***www.state.il.us/agency/iac***

**Independent Television Service (ITVS)**
651 Brannan St., Ste. 410
San Francisco, CA 94107
***Tel: (415) 356-8383***
***www.itvs.org***

**IndieVest**
1416 N. La Brea Avenue
Los Angeles, CA 90028
***Tel: (888) 299-9961***
***www.indievest.com***

**Kodak Student Filmmaker Program**
6700 Santa Monica Blvd.
Los Angeles, CA 90038
***Tel: (323) 464-6131***
***www.kodak.com/go/student***

**Kodak Film School Competition**
6700 Santa Monica Blvd.
Los Angeles, CA 90038
***Tel: (323) 464-6131***
***www.motion.kodak.com/US/en/motion/Education/Filmschool_Competition/***

**Kodak Film School Competition**
Eastman Kodak Company
360 W. 31st Street
New York, NY 10001
***Tel: (212) 631-3400/(585) 724-4000***
***www.motion.kodak.com/US/en/motion/Education/Filmschool_Competition/***

**The John D. & Catherine T. Macarthur Foundation**
140 S. Dearborn Street
Chicago, IL 60603
***Tel: (312) 726-8000***
***www.macfdn.org***

**McKnight Artist Fellowships for Filmmakers**
IFP/Minneapolis
2446 University Avenue W., Ste. 100
Saint Paul, MN 55114
***Tel: (651) 644-1912***
***www.ifpmn.org***

**National Black Programming Consortium**
68 E. 131st Street, 7th Fl.
New York, NY 10037
***Tel: (212) 234-8200***
***www.nbpc.tv***

**National Endowment for the Arts**
1100 Pennsylvania Ave., NW
Washington, D.C. 20506
***Tel: (202) 682-5400***
***arts.endow.gov***

**National Latino Communications Center**
3171 Los Feliz Blvd., Ste. 200
Los Angeles, CA 90039
***Tel: (323) 663-8294***
***www.nlcc.com***

**New York State Council on the Arts' Electronic Media & Film Program**
175 Varick Street
New York, NY 10014
***Tel: (212) 627-4455***
***www.nysca.org***

**New York Women In Film & Television Film Finishing Fund**
6 East 39th Street, Ste. 1200
New York, NY 10016
***Tel: (212) 679-0870***
***www.nywift.org***

**Oppenheimer Camera New Filmmaker Equipment Grant Program**
7400 Third Avenue South
Seattle, WA 98108
***Tel: (206) 467-8666***
***www.oppenheimercamera.com***

**Pacific Islanders in Communications Funds**
1221 Kapiolani Blvd., Ste. 6A-4
Honolulu, HI 96814
***Tel: (808) 591-0059***
***www.piccom.org***

**Pacific Pioneer Fund**
P.O. Box 20504
Stanford, CA 94309
***Tel: (650) 996-3122***
***www.pacificpioneerfund.com***

**Panavision's New Filmmaker Program**
6219 De Soto Avenue
Woodland Hills, CA 91367
***Tel: (818) 316-1000***
***www.panavision.com***

**University Film & Video Assoc.**
Peter J. Bukalski
Box 1777
Edwardsville, IL 62026
***Tel: (866) 647-8382***
***www.ufva.org***

**Women in Film Foundation Film Finishing Fund**
8857 W. Olympic Blvd., Ste. 201
Beverly Hills, CA 90211
***Tel: (310) 657-5144***
***www.wif.org***

**Academy of Art University**
School of Motion Pictures & TV
79 New Montgomery Street
San Francisco, CA 94105
***Tel: (415) 274-2200***
***www.academyart.edu***

**American Film Institute (AFI)**
2021 N. Western Avenue
Los Angeles, CA 90027
***Tel: (323) 856-7600***
***www.afi.com***

**Ames Media Institute**
4280 Tamiami Trail E./Office 302F
Naples, FL 34112
***Tel: (239) 793-5255***
***www.amesmedia.org***

**Art Institute of California Hollywood**
3440 Wilshire Blvd., 10th Fl.
Los Angeles, CA 90010
***Tel: (213) 251-3636***
***www.artinstitutes.edu/campuslocations/***

**Art Institute of California Los Angeles**
2900 31st Street
Santa Monica, CA 90405
***Tel: (310) 752-4700***
***www.artinstitutes.edu/campuslocations/***

**Art Institute of California San Francisco**
1170 Market Street
San Francisco, CA 94102
***Tel: (415) 865-0198***
***www.artinstitutes.edu/campuslocations/***

**Art Institute of Charlotte**
Three Lake Pointe Plaza
2110 Water Ridge Parkway
Charlotte, NC 28217
***Tel: (704) 357-802***
***www.artinstitutes.edu/campuslocations/***

**Art Institute of Dallas**
8080 Park Lane, Ste. 100
Dallas, TX 75231
***Tel: (214) 692-8080***
***www.artinstitutes.edu***

**Art Institute of Houston**
1900 Yorktown Street
Houston, TX 77056
***Tel: (713) 623-2040***
***www.artinstitutes.edu***

**Art Institute of New York**
75 Varick Street, 16th Fl.
New York, NY 10013
***Tel: (212) 226-5500***
***www.artinstitutes.edu/campuslocations/***

**Art Institute of Pittsburgh**
420 Boulevard of the Allies
Pittsburgh, PA 15219
***Tel: (412) 263-6600***
***www.artinstitutes.edu***

**Art Institute of Seattle**
2323 Elliott Avenue
Seattle, WA 98121
***Tel: (206) 448-6600***
***www.artinstitutes.edu***

**Art Institute of Washington**
1820 N. Fort Myer Drive
Arlington, VA 22209
***Tel: (703) 358-9550***
***www.artinstitutes.edu/campuslocations/***

**Art Institute of Pittsburgh**
420 Boulevard of the Allies
Pittsburgh, PA 15219
***Tel: (800) 275-2470***
***www.aip.aii.edu***

**Boston University**
Dept. of Film & Television
640 Commonwealth Avenue
Boston, MA 02215
***Tel: (617) 353-3483***
***www.bu.edu***

**Brooklyn College**
Department of Film
2900 Bedford Ave./314 Plaza Bldg.
Brooklyn, NY 11210
***Tel: (718) 951-5664***
***www.brooklyn.edu***

**Brooks Institute Film & Video**
801 Alston Road
Santa Barbara, CA 93108
***Tel: (805) 966-3888***
***www.brooks.edu***

**California College of the Arts**
111 Eighth Street
San Francisco, CA 94107
***Tel: (415) 703-9500***
***www.cca.edu***

**California College of the Arts**
5212 Broadway
Oakland, CA 94618
***Tel: (510) 594-3600***
***www.cca.edu***

**California Institute of the Arts**
24700 McBean Parkway
Valencia, CA 91355
***Tel: (661) 255-1050***
***www.calarts.edu***

**California State University - Long Beach**
1250 Bellflower Boulevard
Long Beach, CA 90840
***Tel: (562) 985-4111***
***www.csulb.edu***

**California State University L.A.**
Dept. of Communication Studies
5151 State University Drive
Los Angeles, CA 90032
***Tel: (323) 343-4200***
***www.calstatela.edu***

**Center for Digital Imaging Arts at Boston University (CDIA)**
274 Moody Street
Waltham, MA 02453
***Tel: (781) 209-1700***
***www.cdiabu.com***

**Chapman University**
School of Film & TV
Cecil B. DeMille Hall
One University Drive
Orange, CA 92866
***Tel: (714) 997-6765***
***www.ftv.chapman.edu***

**City College of New York (CUNY)**
Media & Communications Arts Dept.
128th Street @ Convent Ave.
Shepard Hall, Rm. 472
New York, NY 10031
***Tel: (212) 650-7167***
***www.ccny.cuny.edu/mca***

**College of Santa Fe Moving Image Arts**
1600 St. Michael's Drive
Santa Fe, NM 87505
***Tel: (505) 473-6011***
***www.csf.edu***

**Columbia College Chicago**
600 S. Michigan Avenue
Chicago, IL 60605
***Tel: (312) 369-1000***
***www.colum.edu***

**Columbia College - Hollywood**
18618 Oxnard Street
Tarzana, CA 91356
***Tel: (818) 345-8414***
***www.columbiacollege.edu***

**Columbia University**
School of the Arts
513 Dodge Hall
2960 Broadway
New York, NY 10027
***Tel: (212) 854-2815***
***www.columbia.edu***

**Columbus College of Art & Design**
107 N. Ninth St.
Columbus, OH 43215
***Tel: (614) 224-9101***
***www.ccad.edu***

**De Anza College**
Film & Television Dept.
21250 Stevens Creek Blvd.
Cupertino, CA 95014
***Tel: (408) 864-8832***
***www.deanza.edu***

**Digital Film Academy**
630 Ninth Ave., Ste. 901
New York, NY 10036
***Tel: (212) 333-4013***
***www.digitalfilmacademy.com***

**Drexel University**
Antoinette Westphal College of Media Arts & Design
Nesbitt Hall
33rd and Market Streets
Philadelphia, PA 19104
***Tel: (215) 895-1834***
***www.drexel.edu/westphal/***

**Emerson College**
Visual & Media Arts
180 Tremont St., 13th Fl.
Boston, MA 02116
***Tel: (617) 824-8983***
***www.emerson.edu***

**Film Connection**
6253 Hollywood Blvd., Ste. 302
Los Angeles, CA 90028
***Tel: (310) 456-9624/(800) 755-7597***
***www.film-connection.com***

**The Film School**
2828 Boyer Avenue E.
Seattle, WA 98102
***Tel: (206) 709-2555***
***www.thefilmschool.com***

**Florida State University Film School**
University Center 3100 A
P.O. Box 3062350
Tallahassee, FL 32306
***Tel: (850) 644-7728/(888) 644-7728***
***film.fsu.edu***

**Full Sail University**
3300 University Boulevard
Winter Park, FL 32792
***Tel: (407) 679-6333/(800) 226-7625***

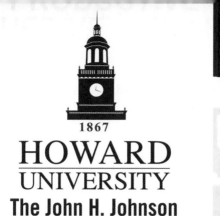

***www.fullsail.edu***

**Henry Cogswell College**
3002 Colby Avenue
Everett, WA 98201
***Tel: (425) 258-3351***
***www.henrycogswell.edu***

**Hollins University**
Screenwriting & Film Studies
Roanoke, VA 24020
***Tel: (540) 362-6575***
***www.hollins.edu***

**Hollywood Film Institute 2-Day Film School**
P.O. Box 481252
Los Angeles, CA 90048
***Tel: (818) 752-3456***
***www.hollywoodu.com***
***www.webfilmschool.com***

**Howard University**
John H. Johnson School of Communications
Department of Radio, TV & Film
525 Bryant Street, NW
Washington, D.C. 20059
***Tel: (202) 806-7927***
***www.soc.howard.edu***

**Industry Film School**
***Tel: (877) 593-8953***
***www.industryfilmschool.com***

**International Film Institute of New York**
2960 Broadway, Room 513
New York, NY 10027
***Tel: (866) 852-0569***
***www.nyfilmschool.com***

**The Juilliard School**
60 Lincoln Center Plaza
New York, NY 10023
***Tel: (212) 799-5000***
***www.juilliard.edu***

**Los Angeles Film School**
6363 Sunset Boulevard
Hollywood, CA 90028
***Tel: (323) 860-0789***
***www.lafilm.com***

**Loyola Marymount University**
School of Film & Television
One LMU Drive, MC 8230
Los Angeles, CA 90045
***Tel: (310) 338-2737***
***www.lmu.edu***

**Massachusetts College of Art & Design**
621 Huntington Avenue
Boston, MA 02115
***Tel: (617) 879-7000***
***www.massart.edu***

**The Motion Picture Institute Inc.**
1116 E. Big Beaver Rd.
Troy, MI 48083
***Tel: (248) 528-1760***
***www.mpifilm.com***

**New York Conservatory for Dramatic Arts**
School of Film & TV
39 West 19th Street
New York, NY 10011
***Tel: (888) 645-0030/(646) 216-2872***
***www.sft.edu***

**New York Film Academy**
100 E. 17th Street
New York, NY 10003
***Tel: (212) 674-4300/(818) 733-2600***
***www.nyfa.com***

**New York University (NYU)**
Tisch School of the Arts
721 Broadway, 9th Fl.
New York, NY10003
***Tel: (212) 998-1900***
***www.filmtv.tisch.nyu.edu***

**North Carolina School of the Arts**
School of Filmmaking
1533 S. Main Street
Winston-Salem, NC 27127
***Tel: (336) 770-1471***
***www.ncarts.edu***

**Northwestern University**
Dept. of Radio/Television/Film
Annie May Swift
1920 Campus Drive, 2nd Fl.
Evanston, IL 60208
***Tel: (847) 491-7315***
***www.communications.northwestern.edu/rtf***

**Ohio University**
School of Film
Lindley Hall 378
Athens, OH 45701
***Tel: (740) 593-1323***
***www.finearts.ohio.edu/film***

**Palm Beach Film School**
901 Northpoint Parkway, Ste. 303
West Palm Beach, FL 33407
***Tel: (561) 242-919***
***www.palmbeachfilmschool.com***

**Parsons The New School For Design**
The New School
66 West 12th Street
New York, NY 10011
***Tel: (212) 229-8903 (Media/Film)***
***Tel: (212) 229-5108 (Acting)***
***Tel: (212) 229-5611 (Writing)***
***www.parsons.edu***

**Platt College**
San Diego School of Design
6250 El Cajon Boulevard
San Diego, CA 92115
***Tel: (619) 265-0107/(866) 752-8826***
***www.platt.edu***

**Pratt Institute**
200 Willoughby Avenue
Brooklyn, NY 11205
***Tel: (718) 636-3633***
***www.pratt.edu/ad/media***

**Rutgers University**
Cinema Studies
72 Lipman Drive
New Brunswick, NJ 08901
***Tel: (732) 932-7355***
***www.rutgers.edu***

**San Diego State University**
School of Theatre, TV & Film
5500 Campanile Drive
San Diego, CA 92182
***Tel: (619) 594-1375***
***www.sdsu.edu***

**San Francisco State University**
Cinema Department
1600 Holloway Avenue
Fine Arts Bldg., Rm. 245
San Francisco, CA 94132
***Tel: (415) 338-1629***
***www.cinema.sfsu.edu***

**School of Visual Arts**
209 E. 23rd Street
New York, NY 10010
***Tel: (212) 592-2000***
***www.schoolofvisualarts.edu***

**Seattle Film Institute**
1709 23rd Avenue
Seattle, WA 98122
***Tel: (206) 568-4387***
***www.seattlefilminstitute.com***

**Sherwood Oaks ExperimentalCollege**
7095 Hollywood Blvd., Ste. 876
Los Angeles, CA 90028
***Tel: (323) 851-1769***
***www.sherwoodoakscollege.com***

**Sundance Institute**
P.O. Box 3630
Salt Lake City, UT 84110
***Tel: (801) 328-3456***
***www.sundance.org***

**Sundance Institute**
8530 Wilshire Blvd., 3rd Floor
Beverly Hills, CA 90211
***Tel: (310) 360-1981***
***www.sundance.org***

**TCU - Texas Christian University**
Radio, TV & Film Department
TCU Box 298030
Ft. Worth, TX 76129
***Tel: (817) 257-7630***
***www.rtvf.tcu.edu***

**Temple University**
School of Communications, Theater
Film & Media Arts
Annenberg Hall - Rm. 120
2020 N. 13th Street
Philadelphia, PA 19122
***Tel: (215) 204-3859***
***www.temple.edu/fma***

**The Art Institutes**
***www.education.org/artinstitutes***
****40+ Locations Nationwide***

**The New School**
66 W. 12th Street, 9th Fl.
New York, NY 10011
***Tel: (212) 229-8903***
***www.newschool.edu/mediastudies***

**TV Connection**
***www.tvconnection.com***

**University of California, Berkeley**
Film Studies
7408 Dwinelle Hall, #2670
Berkeley, CA 94270
***Tel: (510) 642-1415***
***filmstudies.berkeley.edu***

**University of California, Los Angeles (UCLA)**
School of Theater, Film & TV
102 E. Melnitz Hall/Box 951622
Los Angeles, CA 90095
***Tel: (310) 825-5761***
***www.tft.ucla.edu***

**University of Dallas**
College of Business
Sports & Entertainment Management Program
1845 E. Northgate Drive
Irving, TX 75062
***Tel: (972) 721-5000***
***www.thedallasmba.com***
***www.udallas.edu/gsm/se/***

**University of Kansas**
Department of Theatre & Film
1530 Naismith Dr. - Murphy Hall 356
Lawrence, KS 66045
***Tel: (785) 864-3511***
***www.ku.edu***

**University of Miami**
School of Communication
Frances Wolfson Bldg.
5100 Brunson Drive
Coral Gables, FL 33124
***Tel: (305) 284-2265***
***www.miami.edu***

**University of Michigan**
Dept. of Screen Arts & Cultures
505 S. State Street
Ann Arbor, MI 48109
***Tel: (734) 764-0147***
***www.lsa.umich.edu/filmvideo***

**University of New Orleans**
Dept. of Film, Theatre & Communications
Performing Arts Center
2000 Lakeshore Drive
New Orleans, LA 70148
***Tel: (504) 280-6317***
***www.uno.edu***

**University of Southern California (USC)**
School of Cinematic Arts
Film & Television Production
University Park, Luc 209
Los Angeles, CA 90089
***Tel: (213) 740-2804***
***www.cntv.usc.edu***

**Video Symphony**
266 Magnolia
Burbank, CA 91502
***Tel: (818) 845-1951***
***www.videosymphony.com***

**Watkins College of Art, Design & Film**
2298 Rosa L. Parks Blvd.
Nashville, TN 37228
***Tel: (615) 383-4848***
***www.watkins.edu***

*Featuring*

# Fashion, Film, Music, Sports & TV

» Creating YOUR Entertainment Career POWER PLAN.

» 10 Things You Can Do TODAY to POWER UP YOUR Career.

» How to Land the Perfect Entertainment Internship or Job.

» Make it Happen! Challenge

» 100+ Entertainment Job Websites.

» Prize Giveaways & More!

For more information about ***EPP: The Tour***, call (323) 533-1971.

**www.entertainmentpower.com**

# EVERY LISTING

## in this DIRECTORY can be an Internship Opportunity.
## Here's our List to get you going!!!

**The American Pavilion Cannes Film Program**
1526 14th Street, Ste. 109
Santa Monica, CA 90404
***Tel: (310) 576-6500***
***www.ampav.com***

**Cannes Film Internship Program**
Creative Minds in Cannes
7095 Hollywood Blvd., #571
Hollywood, CA 90028
***Tel: (310) 674-7466***
***www.creativemindsincannes.com***

**DreamWorks Animation SKG**
1000 Flower Street
Glendale, CA 91201
***Tel: (818) 695-5000***
***www.dreamworksanimation.com***

**Emma Bowen Foundation**
1299 Pennsylvania Ave., NW - 9th Fl.
Washington, DC 20004
***Tel: (202) 637-4494***
***www.emmabowenfoundation.com***

**Focus Features**
100 Universal City Plaza
Bldg. 9128, 2nd Fl.
Universal City, CA 91608
***Tel: (818) 777-7373***
***www.filminfocus.com***

**Focus Features**
65 Bleecker St., 3rd Fl.
New York, NY 10012
***Tel: (212) 539-4000***
***www.filminfocus.com***

**Harpo**
110 N. Carpenter Street
Chicago, IL 60607
***Tel: (312) 633-1000***
***www.harpocareers.com***

**Harpo Films**
345 N. Maple Dr., Ste. 315
Beverly Hills, CA 90210
***Tel: (310) 278-5559***
***www.harpocareers.com***

**The Hollywood Reporter**
5055 Wilshire Blvd., 6th Fl.
Los Angeles, CA 90036
***Tel: (323) 525-2000***
***www.hollywoodreporter.com***

**Lionsgate**
2700 Colorado Avenue
Santa Monica, CA 90404
***Tel: (310) 449-9200***
***www.lionsgate.com***

**Metro-Goldwyn-Mayer (MGM)**
10250 Constellation Blvd.
Los Angeles, CA 90067
***Tel: (310) 449-3000***
***www.mgm.com***
***www.mgm.com/employment.php***

**Mandalay Pictures**
4751 Wilshire Blvd., 3rd Fl.
Los Angeles, CA 90010
***Tel: (323) 549-4300***
***www.mandalay.com***

**Paramount Pictures**
5555 Melrose Avenue
Hollywood, CA 90038
***Tel: (323) 956-5000***
***www.paramount.com***

**Pixar Animation Studios**
1200 Park Avenue
Emeryville, CA 94608
***Tel: (510) 922-3000***
***www.pixar.com***

**Sony Pictures Entertainment**
10202 W. Washington Blvd.
Culver City, CA 90232
***Tel: (310) 244-4000***
***www.sonypicscareers.com***

**Twentieth Century Fox**
10201 W. Pico Blvd.
Los Angeles, CA 90035
***Tel: (310) 369-1000***
***www.foxcareers.com***
***www.foxmovies.com***

**Universal Pictures**
100 Universal City Plaza
Universal City, CA 91608
***Tel: (818) 777-1000***
***www.universalstudios.com***
***www.nbcunicareers.com***

**Walt Disney Company**
500 S. Buena Vista St.
Burbank, CA 91521
***Tel: (818) 560-1000***
***www.disneycareers.com***

**Academy of Motion Pictures Arts & Sciences**
Margaret Herrick Library
333 S. LaCienega Blvd.
Beverly Hills, CA 90211
***Tel: (310) 247-3020***
***www.oscars.org***

**Autry National Center**
4700 Western Heritage Way
Los Angeles, CA 90027
***Tel: (323) 667-2000***
***www.autry-museum.org***

**Baseline StudioSystems**
520 Broadway St., Ste. 230
Santa Monica, CA 90401
***Tel: (310) 393-9999***
***ww.blssi.com***
***www.studiosystem.com***

**Black Hollywood Education & Resource Center (BHERC)**
1875 Century Park East, 6th Fl.
Los Angeles, CA 90067
***Tel: (310) 284-3170***
***www.bherc.org***

**Black Talent News.com**
***www.blacktalentnews.com***

**Box Office Mojo.com**
***www.boxofficemojo.com***

**Burbank Central Library**
110 N. Glenoaks Boulevard
Burbank, CA 91502
***Tel: (818) 238-5600***
***www.burbank.lib.ca.us***

**California Film Commission**
Location Resource Library
7080 Hollywood Blvd., Ste. 900
Hollywood, CA 90028
***Tel: (323) 860-2960***
***www.film.ca.gov***

**Costume Designers Guild**
11969 Ventura Blvd., 1st Fl.
Studio City, CA 91604
***Tel: (818) 752-2400***
***costumedesignersguild.com***

**Film Arts Foundation**
149 Ninth Street, Ste. 101
San Francisco, CA 94103
***Tel: (415) 552-8760***
***www.filmarts.org***

**Film Independent Resource Library**
9911 W. Pico Boulevard
Los Angeles, CA 90035
***Tel: (310) 432-1200***
***www.filmindependent.org***

**Film Stew**
***www.filmstew.com***
***Tel: (310) 796-9245***

**The Futon Critic**
***www.thefutoncritic.com***

**Gene Siskel Film Center**
164 N. State Street
Chicago, IL 60601
***Tel: (312) 846-2600***
***www.siskelfilmcenter.org***

**Historic Films**
211 Third Street
Greenport, NY 11944
***Tel: (631) 477-9700***
***www.historicfilms.com***

**Hollywood Creative Directory Online Directory**
***www.hcdonline.com***

**Hollywood Entertainment Museum**
3200 Wilshire Blvd., Ste. 1680 S. Tower
Los Angeles, CA 90010
***Tel: (323) 465-7900***
***www.hollywoodmuseum.com***

**Internet Broadway Database**
***www.ibdb.com***

**Internet Movie Database**
***www.imdb.com***

**Eastman Kodak Company**
343 State Street
Rochester, NY 14650

***Tel: (585) 724-4000/(800) 698-3324***
***www.kodak.com***

**EUR Web (Electronic Urban Report)**
P.O. Box 412081
Los Angeles, CA 90041
***Tel: (323) 254-9599/(661) 250-7300***
***www.eurweb.com***

**Library of Congress Copyright Office/U.S. Copyright Office**
101 Independence Ave. SE
Washington, D.C. 20540
***Tel: (202) 707-3000/(202) 707-9100***
***www.copyright.gov***

**Library of Moving Images**
6671 Sunset Blvd., Bungalow 1581
Hollywood, CA 90028
***Tel: (323) 469-7499***
***www.libraryofmovingimages.com***

**Los Angeles Public Library**
630 W. 5th Street
Los Angeles, CA 90071
***Tel: (213) 228-7000***
***www.lapl.org***

**Louis B. Mayer Library**
American Film Institute
2021 N. Western Ave.
Los Angeles, CA 90027
***Tel: (323) 856-7654***
***www.afi.com***

**Moorland-Spingarn Research Center**
Howard University
Washington, D.C. 20059
***Tel: (202) 806-7240***
***www.founders.howard.edu/moorland-spingarn/***

**Music Library Association**
8551 Research Way, Ste. 180
Middleton, WI 53562
***Tel: (608) 836-5825***
***www.musiclibraryassoc.org***

**National Center For Film & Video Preservation**
American Film Institute
2021 N. Western Ave.
Los Angeles, CA 90027
***Tel: (323) 856-7708***
***www.afi.com***

**New York Public Library for the Performing Arts**
40 Lincoln Center Plaza
New York, NY 10023
***Tel: (212) 870-1630***
***www.nypl.org***

**The Numbers**
***www.the-numbers.com***

**The Paley Center for Media**
465 North Beverly Drive
Beverly Hills, CA 90210
***Tel: (310) 786-1025***
***www.paleycenter.org***

**The Paley Center for Media**
25 W. 52nd Street
New York, NY 10019
***Tel: (212) 621-6800***
***www.paleycenter.org***

**Schomburg Center for Research in Black Culture**
515 Malcolm X Blvd.
New York, NY 10037
***Tel: (212) 491-2200***
***www.nypl.org***

**Gene Siskel Film Center**
164 N. State Street
Chicago, IL 60601
***Tel: (312) 846-2600***
***www.siskelfilmcenter.org***

**Smithsonian Institution**
P.O. Box 37012
SI Bldg., Room 153, MRC 010
Washington, D.C. 20013
***Tel: (202) 633-1000***
***www.si.edu***

**StudioSystems**
520 Broadway St., Ste. 230
Santa Monica, CA 90401
***Tel: (310) 393-9999***
***ww.blssi.com***
***www.studiosystem.com***

**UCLA Film & TV Archive**
302 East Melnitz
Box 951323
Los Angeles, CA 90095
***Tel: (310) 206-5388***
***www.cinema.ucla.edu***

**UCLA Film & TV Archive**
1015 N. Cahuenga Boulevard
Hollywood, CA 90038
***Tel: (323) 462-4921***
***www.cinema.ucla.edu***

**Urban Film Premiere**
***www.urbanfilmpremiere.com***

**Warner Bros. Studios Research Library**
2777 N. Ontario Street
Burbank, CA 91504
***Tel: (818) 977-5050***

**Warner Research Collection Burbank Public Library**
110 N. Glenoaks Blvd.
Burbank, CA 91502
***Tel: (818) 238-5615***
***www.burbank.lib.ca.us***

**Western Costume Company**
11041 Vanowen Street
N. Hollywood, CA 91605
***Tel: (818) 760-0900***
***www.westerncostume.com***

**Who Represents.com**
***www.whorepresents.com***

**Writers Guild Foundation Shavelson-Webb Library**
7000 W. Third Street
Los Angeles, CA 90048
***Tel: (323) 782-4544***
***www.wga.org***

**Columbia Pictures**
10202 W. Washington Blvd.
Culver City, CA 90232
***Tel: (310) 244-4000***
***www.spe.sony.com***
***www.sonypicscareers.com***

**DreamWorks SKG**
100 Universal City Plaza, Bldg. 5121
Universal City, CA 91608
***Tel: (818) 733-7000***
***www.dreamworks.com***

**DreamWorks Animation SKG**
1000 Flower Street
Glendale, CA 91201
***Tel: (818) 695-5000***
***www.dreamworksanimation.com***

**Fox Searchlight Pictures**
10201 W. Pico Blvd., Bldg. 38
Los Angeles, CA 90035
***Tel: (310) 369-1000***
***www.foxsearchlight.com***
***www.foxcareers.com***

**Lionsgate**
2700 Colorado Avenue
Santa Monica, CA 90404
***Tel: (310) 449-9200***
***www.lionsgate.com***

**Metro-Goldwyn-Mayer (MGM)**
10250 Constellation Blvd.
Los Angeles, CA 90067
***Tel: (310) 449-3000***
***www.mgm.com***
***www.mgm.com/employment.php***

**Miramax Films**
8439 Sunset Boulevard
W. Hollywood, CA 90069
***Tel: (323) 822-4100***
***www.miramax.com***

**Miramax Films**
161 Avenue of the Americas
New York, NY 10013
***Tel: (917) 606-5500***
***www.miramax.com***

**Paramount Pictures**
5555 Melrose Avenue
Hollywood, CA 90038
***Tel: (323) 956-5000***
***www.paramount.com***

**Sony Pictures**
10202 W. Washington Blvd.
Culver City, CA 90232
***Tel: (310) 244-4000***
***www.spe.sony.com***
***www.sonypicscareers.com***

**Twentieth Century Fox**
10201 W. Pico Blvd.
Los Angeles, CA 90035
***Tel: (310) 369-1000***
***www.fox.com***
***www.foxmovies.com***
***www.foxcareers.com***

**Universal Studios**
100 Universal City Plaza
Universal City, CA 91608
***Tel: (818) 777-1000***
***www.universalpictures.com***
***www.universalstudios.com***
***www.nbcunicareers.com***

**The Walt Disney Studios**
500 S. Buena Vista St.
Burbank, CA 91521
***Tel: (818) 560-1000***
***www.disney.com***
***www.disneycareers.com***

**Warner Bros. Pictures**
4000 Warner Boulevard
Burbank, CA 91522
***Tel: (818) 954-6000***
***www.warnerbros.com***
***www.timewarnercareers.com***

**The Weinstein Company**
5700 Wilshire Blvd., Ste. 600
Los Angeles, CA 90036
***Tel: (323) 207-3200***
***www.weinsteinco.com***

**The Weinstein Company**
375 Greenwich St., 3rd Fl.
New York, NY 10013
***Tel: (212) 941-3800/Tel: (646) 862-3400***
***www.weinsteinco.com***

**NBC Universal**
100 Universal City Plaza
Universal City, CA 91608
***Tel: (818) 777-1000***
***www.nbcuni.com***
***www.nbcunicareers.com***
***www.ge.com/careers***

**News Corporation**
1211 Avenue of the Americas
New York, NY 10036
***Tel: (212) 852-7000***
***www.newscorp.com***
***careers.newscorp.com/***

**The Nielsen Company**
770 Broadway
New York, NY 10003
***Tel: (646) 654-5000***
***www.nielsen.com***

**Sony Corporation of America**
550 Madison Ave.
New York, NY 10022
***Tel: (212) 833-6800***
***www.sony.com***
***www.sonypicscareers.com***

**Time Warner, Inc.**
1 Time Warner Center
New York, NY 10019
***Tel: (212) 484-8000***
***www.timewarner.com***
***www.timewarnercareers.com***

**Viacom, Inc.**
1515 Broadway
New York, NY 10036
***Tel: (212) 258-6000***
***www.viacom.com***
***www.viacomcareers.com***

**Vivendi**
800 Third Avenue
New York, NY 10022
***Tel: (212) 572-7000***
***www.vivendi.com***

**Walt Disney Company**
500 S. Buena Vista St.
Burbank, CA 91521
***Tel: (818) 560-1000***
***www.disney.com***
***www.disneycareers.com***

### 1492 Pictures
1271 Ventura Blvd., Ste. 350
Studio City, CA 91604
***Tel: (818) 508-2055***
***Credits: Cheaper By the Dozen; Harry Potter Franchise; Night at the Museum***

### 21 Laps Entertainment
Twentieth Century Fox
10201 W. Pico Blvd.
Bldg. 41, Ste. 400
Los Angeles, CA 90035
***Tel: (310) 369-7170***
***Credits: A Night at the Museum; Cheaper by the Dozen 2; What Happens in Vegas***

### 2929 Productions
1437 7th Street, #250
Santa Monica, CA 90401
***Tel: (310) 309-5200***
***www.2929productions.com***
***Credits: Akeelah and the Bee; Good Night, and Good Luck***

### 3 Arts Entertainment
9460 Wilshire Boulevard, 7th Fl.
Beverly Hills, CA 90212
***Tel: (310) 888-3200***
***Credits: Biker Boyz; The Day the Earth Stood Still***

### 34th St. Films
8200 Wilshire Blvd., Ste. 300
Beverly Hills, CA 90211
***Tel: (323) 315-5743***

### 40 Acres & A Mule Filmworks
75 S. Elliot Place
Brooklyn, NY 11217
***Tel: (718) 624-3703***
***www.40acres.com***
***Credits: Do the Right Thing; Inside Man; Love and Basketball; Malcolm X***

### Acapella Pictures
8271 Melrose Ave., Ste. 101
Los Angeles, CA 90046
***Tel: (323) 782-8200***
***Credits: The Aviator; The House of Mirth***

### AEI-Atchity Entertainment, Int'l.
518 S. Fairfax Avenue
Los Angeles, CA 90036
***Tel: (323) 932-0407***
***www.aeionline.com***
***Credits: Dante's Inferno; Joe Somebody***

### Alcon Entertainment
10390 Santa Monica Blvd., Ste. 250
Los Angeles, CA 90025
***Tel: (310) 789-3040***
***Credits: P.S. I Love You; Racing Stripes; The Sisterhood of the Traveling Pants 1-2***

### The American Film Company
213 Rose Avenue, 2nd Fl.
Venice, CA 90291
***Tel: (310) 664-1999***
***www.americanfilmco.com***
***Credits: Citzen X; Gone in 60 Seconds; The Negotiator***

### The American Film Company
1414 Ave. of the Americas, 11th Fl.
New York, NY 10019
***Tel: (212) 941-1200***
***www.americanfilmco.com***
***Credits: Citzen X; Gone in 60 Seconds; The Negotiator***

### American Zoetrope
1641 N. Ivar
Los Angeles, CA 90028
***Tel: (323) 460-4420***
***www.zoetrope.com***
***Credits: Apocalypse Now; Bram Stoker's Dracula; Lost In Translation; The Rainmaker***

### American Zoetrope
916 Kearny Street
San Francisco, CA 94133
***Tel: (415) 788-7500***
***www.zoetrope.com***
***Credits: Apocalypse Now; Bram Stoker's Dracula; Lost In Translation; The Rainmaker***

### The Anschutz Film Group
1888 Century Park E., 14th Fl.
Century City, CA 90067
***Tel: (310) 887-1000***
***Credits: Journey to the Center of the Earth; Ray; The Chronicles of Narnia***

### Apatow Productions
11788 W. Pico Blvd.
Los Angeles, CA 90064
***Tel: (310) 943-4400***
***Credits: 40 Year-Old Virgin; Knocked Up; Pineapple Express; Talledega Nights***

Legendary film producer Lynda Obst is known the world over as an entertainment POWER PLAYER, for very good reasons. In the two plus decades since this native New Yorker started climbing the proverbial ladder, working first as a development assistant at the Geffen Film Company, then rising to her current mega-producer status, she has built a name and reputation for herself that is second to none. Her consistent string of blockbusters, including the iconic feature films *"Flashdance," "Sleepless in Seattle," "Contact"* and *"The Siege,"* to name a few, coupled with her bestselling memoir <u>Hello, He Lied</u> and her most recent films, *"This Side of the Truth," "How to Lose A Guy in 10 Days,"* and numerous others, sheds a bright and telling light on why A-list actors, directors, producers and every major studio and production company in the business call on Lynda Obst Productions to analyze scripts and identify hits.

Intrigued by her success and laudable credits, <u>*EPP*</u> asked Obst to share her thoughts on POWER and her advice for writers and producers. Here she is verbatim:

***<u>EPP</u>*:** What's your advice to screenwriters who want to pen the next blockbuster but suffer from writer's block?

***LO:*** Writing is a muscle. We tend to think of it as inspiration - but it's really perspiration. The more often you write, the easier it is to write. If you9re writing a screenplay, the days you spend researching and not writing are as important as the days you spend actually writing good pages. Remember that you don't have to put perfect stuff on the page, you just have to get things blocked out and on the page. If you spend those days you can't write in organizing and outlining, then you're writing. Give yourself a break."

***<u>EPP</u>*:** What's your definition of POWER and what's your real 123 POWER Advice for the emerging producer?

***LO:*** "Power is getting to make the things you want. And self respect. Your job as a producer is to find the best writers and directors that you know, and get them shooting, or writing. The most important thing is to figure out how you're going to get a good piece of material to control. Get control of a piece of material and get it made. It's a long road to getting it made; but, if you have nothing to get made you're not a producer."

***<u>EPP</u>*:** What are your POWER TOOLS as a mega-producer?

***LO:*** My #1 tool is humor because it helps with charm, survival and frustration tolerance - and it's good in a meeting. Technological tools? The computer, the iPhone, the Blackberry.

To read more about Lynda Obst, visit her website www.LyndaObstProductions.com, which is full of helpful career tips, information and inspiration.

**Apostle Pictures**
568 Broadway, #301
New York, NY 10012
***Tel: (212) 541-4323***
***Credits: Blow; Monument Avenue***

**Appian Way**
9255 Sunset Blvd., Ste. 615
W. Hollywood, CA 90069
***Tel: (310) 300-1390***
***Credits: The Assassination of Richard Nixon; Aviator***

**Ascendant Pictures**
406 Wilshire Boulevard
Santa Monica, CA 90401
***Tel: (310) 288-4600***
***www.ascendantpictures.com***
***Credits: Collateral Damage; Juwanna Man; Lucky Number Sleven; The Punisher; Wayne's World; Who's Your Caddy?***

**Atlas Entertainment**
9200 Sunset Blvd., 10th Fl.
Los Angeles, CA 90069
***Tel: (310) 786-4900***
***Credits: Batman Begins; The Dark Knight; Three Kings; Scooby Doo 1-2; Sister Act II***

**Atmosphere Entertainment**
4751 Wilshire Blvd., 3rd Fl.
Los Angeles, CA 90010
***Tel: (310) 860-5446***
***Credits: 300; The Spiderwick Chronicles; Godsend; Taking Lives; 300***

**Aurora Productions**
8642 Melrose Ave., Ste. 200
Los Angeles, CA 90069
***Tel: (310) 854-6900***
***Credits: Eddie & The Cruisers; The Rock***

**Automatic Pictures**
5225 Wilshire Blvd., Ste. 525
Los Angeles, CA 90036
***Tel: (323) 935-1800***
***Credits: There's Something About Mary***

**Avenue Pictures**
144 S. Beverly Drive, 5th Fl.
Beverly Hills, CA 90212
***Tel: (310) 860-5508***
***Credits: Angels in America; The Merchant of Venice; The Player***

**Back Lot Pictures**
1351 N. Genesee Avenue
Los Angeles, CA 90046
***Tel: (323) 876-1057***
***Credits: Eternal Sunshine of the Spotless Mind; Push; The Changeling***

**Bad Boy Films**
1710 Broadway, 2nd Fl.
New York, NY 10019
***Tel: (212) 500-2200***
***www.badboyonline.com***
***Credits: A Raisin in the Sun; Diddy Runs the City; Making the Band***

**Bad Hat Harry Productions**
4000 Warner Blvd.
Building 81, Ste. 200
Burbank, CA 91522
***Tel: (310) 244-8232***
***Credits: Superman Returns; Valkyrie; X-Men Franchise***

**The Badham Company**
16830 Ventura Blvd., Ste. 300
Encino, CA 91436
***Tel: (818) 990-9495***
***Credits: Drop Zone; Evel Knievel; War Games***

**John Baldecchi Productions**
2657 Greenfield Avenue
Los Angeles, CA 90064
***Tel: (310) 441-1496***
***Credits: Inspector Gadget; The Mexican; Up Close & Personal; Ultraviolet***

**Ballyhoo Inc.**
6738 Wedgewood Place
Hollywood, CA 90068
***Tel: (323) 874-3396***
***Credits: About Schmidt; Bounce; Seven Years In Tibet***

**Baltimore Pictures, Inc.**
8306 Wilshire Blvd., PMB 1012
Beverly Hills, CA 90211
***Tel: (310) 234-8988***
***Credits: Diner; Rain Man; The Natural; Wag the Dog***

**Barwood Films**
5670 Wilshire Blvd., #2400
Los Angeles, CA 90036
***Tel: (323) 653-1555***
***Credits: A Star Is Born; The Mirror Has Two Faces; Prince of Tides; Yentl***

**Carol Baum Productions**
8899 Beverly Blvd., Ste. 721
Los Angeles, CA 90048
***Tel: (310) 550-4575***
***Credits: Father of The Bride; Fly Away Home***

**Bay Films**
631 Colorado Avenue
Santa Monica, CA 90404
***Tel: (310) 319-6565***
***Credits: Armageddon; Bad Boys 1-2; Pearl Harbor; The Rock; Transformers***

**Bayonne Entertainment**
3815 Hughese Avenue
Culver City, CA 90232
***Tel: (310) 841-4355***
***Credits: Crossroads; Dean Koontz's Black River***

**Bazmark, Inq.**
***www.bazmark.com***
***Credits: Australia; Moulin Rouge; Romeo + Juliet***

**Beacon Pictures**
2900 W. Olympic Blvd., 2nd Fl.
Santa Monica, CA 90404
***Tel: (310) 260-7000***
***www.beaconpictures.com***
***Credits: Air Force One; Bring It On; Family Man; Ladder 49; The Hurricane***

**The Bedford Falls Company**
409 Santa Monica Blvd., PH
Santa Monica, CA 90401
***Tel: (310) 394-5022***
***Credits: Blood Diamond; Shakespeare in Love; The Last Samurai; Traffic***

**Lawrence Bender Productions**
8350 Wilshire Blvd., Ste. 500
Beverly Hills, CA 90211
***Tel: (323) 951-4600***
***Credits: An Inconvenient Truth; Kill Bill 1-2; Pulp Fiction; The Mexican***

**Benderspink**
110 S. Fairfax Ave., Ste. 350
Los Angeles, CA 90036
***Tel: (323) 904-1800***
***Credits: American Pie 1-3; Cats & Dogs; The Hangover; Monster-in-Law; Red Eye***

***EPP: 4*** salutes Liquid Soul Media for being a quiet giant in the entertainment industry. This award-winning, Atlanta-based lifestyle marketing firm, led by company CEO Tirrell Whittley and his team of principals and directors, is the behind-the scenes force busy masterminding creative ways to make millions of viewers stop and take notice of new projects, products and services.

With clients including Walt Disney Studios; Lionsgate; Sony Screen Gems; NBC Universal; Turner Broadcasting (TBS, TNT & CNN); the American Cancer Society; fellow ATL-based production company Rainforest Films, and a bevy of notable POWER PLAYERS in between, Liquid Soul Media's A-Z services range from grassroots marketing, digital platforms and social media consulting to a wide array of modern marketing tactics and strategies. The company has a reputation of bringing super-sized sizzle and creativity to dozens of TV and film projects, including Disney's newest fairy tale *"The Princess and The Frog,"* the Queen Latifah-led ensemble *"The Secret Life of Bees," "Notorious,"* the CNN *"Black in America"* series; Tyler Perry's *"House of Payne"* and *"Meet the Brown's"* and TNT's *"HawthoRNe"* - to name a few.

"We're always dripping with creativity," CEO Whittley shares when asked how Liquid Soul Media has built such an impressive client list and body of work. "We always look to over-deliver with quality and excellence."

Whittley says his POWER TOOLS include daily prayer, *Advertising Age* magazine, the entertainment blog ConcreteLoop.com, as well as non-stop CNN.com. Whittley also cites the management book Good to Great by James Collins as a great inspiration.

***EPP*** readers, be on the lookout for more superior marketing and media campaigns coming your way -- because just like the General Electric slogan from decades ago, Liquid Soul Media is busy bringing good things to life in the world of TV and film.

For more information about Liquid Soul Media, visit them online at www.LiquidSoulMedia.com.

**Harve Bennett Productions**
P.O. Box 825
Culver City, CA 90232
***Tel: (310) 306-7198***
***Credits: Rich Man, Poor Man; Star Trek II-V; The Jesse Owens Story***

**Berman Productions**
5555 Melrose Ave., Ste. 232
Los Angeles, CA 90038
***Tel: (323) 956-5037***
***Credits: Star Trek Franchise***

**Blue Bay Productions**
1119 Colorado Ave. Ste. 100
Santa Monica, CA 90401
***Tel: (310) 440-9904***
***Credits: Big Momma's House; In Good Company; The Honeymooners; Wild Things***

**Blue Rider Pictures**
2801 Ocean Park Blvd., Ste. 193
Santa Monica, CA 90405
***Tel: (310) 314-8405***
***Credits: Around the World in 80 Days; Call of the Wild; Hide and Seek***

**Blue Sky Studios**
One American Lane
Greenwich, CT 06831
***Tel: (203) 992-6000***
***Credits: Horton Hears a Who!; Ice Age 1-3; Robots***

**Blue Tulip Productions**
2128 Narcissus Court
Venice, CA 90291
***Tel: (310) 458-2166***
***Credits: Speed; Lara Croft Tomb Raider; Minority Report; Twister***

**Blueline Productions**
212 26th Street, Ste. 295
Santa Monica, CA 90402
***Tel: (310) 319-2421***
***Credits: Flight 93; Saving Jessica Lynch***

**Bona Fide Productions**
8899 Beverly Blvd. Ste. 804
Los Angeles, CA 90048
***Tel: (310) 273-6782***
***Credits: Cold Mountain; Election; Little Miss Sunshine; The Wood***

**Boneyard Entertainment**
863 Park Avenue, Ste. 11E
New York, NY10021
***Tel: (212) 628-8600***
***Credits: Illtown; Frogs for Snakes; Slingblade***

**Boxing Cat Productions**
11500 Hart Street
N. Hollywood, CA 91605
***Tel: (818) 765-4870***
***www.timallen.com***
***Credits: Joe Somebody; The Santa Clause 1-3; The Shaggy Dog***

**Boz Productions**
1822 Camino Palmero
Los Angeles, CA 90046
***Tel: (323) 876-3232***
***Credits: A Light in Darkness; Everything's Jake; Scary Movie; Soul Plane; Turistas***

**Braga Productions**
5555 Melrose Ave., Hart Bldg. #205
Los Angeles, CA 90038
***Tel: (323) 956-5799***
***Credits: Lara Croft: Tomb Raider; Mission: Impossible 2; Star Trek Franchise***

**Branded Entertainment/Batfilm Productions**
210 Bellevue Avenue
Upper Montclair, NJ 07043
***Tel: (973) 746-6476***
***Credits: Batman Franchise; Constantine; The Dark Night; National Treasure; The Spirit***

**Bregman Productions**
240 E. 39th Street
New York, NY 10022
***Tel: (212) 421-6161***
***Tel: (818) 954-9988***
***Credits: Dog Day Afternoon; Nothing to Lose; Scarface; The Bone Collector***

**Bristol Bay Productions**
1888 Century Park E., Ste. 1400
Los Angeles, CA 90067
***Tel: (310) 887-1000***
***Credits: Charm School; Ray; Sahara; Swimming Upstream***

**Broadway Video Entertainment**
5555 Melrose Avenue
Dressing Room Bldg., Ste. 105
Los Angeles, CA 90038
***Tel: (323) 956-8406***
***Credits: Baby Mama; Enigma; Mean Girls; Wayne's World***

**Brooklyn Films**
3815 Hughes Avenue
Culver City, CA 90232
***Tel: (310) 841-4300***
***Credits: 88 Minutes; Fried Green Tomatoes; Sky Captain & the World of Tomorrow; The Starter Wife; Up Close & Personal***

**Brooksfilms**
Culver Studios
9336 W. Washington Blvd.
Culver City, CA 90232
***Tel: (310) 202-3292***
***Credits: The Elephant Man; The Fly I-2; The Producers***

**Bonnie Bruckheimer Productions**
12439 Magnolia Blvd., Ste. 217
Valley Village, CA 91607
***Tel: (818) 761-0270***
***Credits: Beaches; For the Boys; Divine Secrets of the Ya-Ya Sisterhood***

**Jerry Bruckheimer Films**
1631 10th Street
Santa Monica, CA 90404
***Tel: (310) 664-6260***
***www.jbfilms.com***
***Credits: Bad Boys 1-2; Black Hawk Down; Confessions of a Shopaholic; National Treasure; Pirates of the Caribbean 1-3; Pearl Harbor; Remember the Titans***

**The Bubble Factory**
8840 Wilshire Blvd., 3rd Fl.
Beverly Hills, CA 90211
***Tel: (310) 358-3000***
***Credits: For Richer or Poorer; Flipper; McHale's Navy; Playing Mona Lisa***

**Bungalow 78 Productions**
1601 Cloverfield Blvd., Ste. 300S
Santa Monica, CA 90405
***Tel: (818) 560-4878***
***Credits: Coach; Catch Me If You Can; Patch Adams; Romy & Michelle's High School Reunion***

**Tim Burton Productions**
8033 Sunset Blvd., Ste. 7500
W. Hollywood, CA 90046

# Breaking Into Film

## *Starter Tips*:

Circulate YOUR Name • Circulate YOUR Resume
Land the Perfect Industry Job(s) & Internship(s)

**Call every production company in this Directory.**

- Call every Film Commission in this Directory.
- Create YOUR Career POWER PLAN.
- Find Jobs & Internships that interest YOU.
- Join Industry Assocations & Organizations.
- Meet Industry Players at Awards Shows, Film Festivals, Music Conferences & events like the Film, Stage & Showbiz Expo.
- Read *The Hollywood Reporter* & *Variety*.
- Read *Back Stage* & *Call Sheet*.
- Subscribe to & read *The Hollywood Creative Directory*.
- Subscribe to ImdbPro.com.
- WORK in the Industry!!!

**www.entertainmentpower.com**

*Tel: (310) 300-1670*
*Credits: Batman/Batman Returns; Charlie & the Chocolate Factory; Edward Scissorhands; Planet of the Apes*

**Butchers Run Films**
1041 N. Formosa Ave.
Santa Monica Bldg. E200
W. Hollywood, CA 90046
*Tel: (323) 850-2703*
*Credits: The Apostle; A Family Thing*

**C2 Pictures**
2308 Broadway
Santa Monica, CA 90404
*Tel: (310) 315-6000*
*Credits: Evita; Die Hard 3; I Spy; Terminator 3*

**John Calley Productions**
10202 W. Washington Blvd.
Crawford Building
Culver City, CA 90232
*Tel: (310) 244-7777*
*Credits: Closer; The Da Vinci Code; The Jane Austen Book Club*

**Camelot Pictures**
9255 W. Sunset Blvd., Ste. 711
W. Hollywood, CA 90069
*Tel: (310) 288-3000*
*Credits: Any Given Sunday; Fantastic Voyage; Nixon; S.W.A.T.*

**Cannell Studios**
7083 Hollywood Blvd., Ste. 600
Hollywood, CA 90028
*Tel: (323) 465-5800*
*www.cannell.com*
*Credits: The A-Team; 21 Jump Street; It Waits; The Garden*

**Capital Arts Entertainment**
17941 Ventura Blvd., Ste. 205
Encino, CA 91316
*Tel: (818) 343-8950*
*Credits: Addams' Family Reunion; My Best Friend's Wedding; The Cookout; The Family That Preys*

**Carrie Productions**
2625 Alcatraz Ave., Ste. 243
Berkeley, CA 94705
*Tel: (510) 450-2500*
*Credits: Buffalo Soldiers; Freedom Song*

**The Thomas Carter Company**
3000 W. Olympic Blvd.
Santa Monica, CA 90404
*Tel: (310) 264-3990*
*Credits: Coach Carter; Metro; Save the Last Dance; Swing Kids*

**Castle Rock Entertainment**
335 N. Maple Dr., Ste. 350
Beverly Hills, CA 90210
*Tel: (310) 285-2300*
*Credits: A Few Good Men; Miss Congeniality; In the Line of Fire; Michael Clayton; The Green Mile; The Polar Express*

**CBS Films**
11800 Wilshire Boulevard
Los Angeles, CA 90025
*Tel: (310) 575-7700*
*www.cbs.com*

**Cecchi Gori Pictures**
11990 San Vicente Blvd., Ste. 300
Los Angeles, CA 90049
*Tel: (310) 442-4777*
*Credits: Il Postino; La Vita Bella; Life is Beautiful; Seven; Taming Ben Taylor*

**Centropolis Entertainment**
1445 N. Stanley, 3rd Fl.
Los Angeles, CA 90046
*Tel: (323) 850-1212*
*Credits: 10,000 BC; Godzilla; Independence Day; The Day After Tomorrow; The Patriot*

**CFP Productions**
5555 Melrose Ave., Lucy Bung. 105
Los Angeles, CA 90038
*Tel: (323) 956-8866/(310) 470-0845*
*Credits: How to Lose a Guy in 10 Days; Out-of-Towners*

**Chartoff Productions**
1250 Sixth St., Ste. 101
Santa Monica, CA 90401
*Tel: (310) 319-1960*
*Credits: Raging Bull; Rocky 1-6*

**Chris/Rose Productions**
3131 Torreyson Place
Los Angeles, CA 90046
*Tel: (323) 851-8772*
*Credits: Down in the Delta; Kingfish; The Autobiography of Miss Jane Pittman*

**Chubbco Film Co.**
3532 Hayden Avenue
Culver City, CA 90232
*Tel: (310) 558-6510*
*Credits: Dark Blue; Eve's Bayou; Hoffa; Pootie Tang; The Crow; To Sleep with Anger*

**Cinecity Pictures**
9025 Wilshire Blvd., Ste. 500
Beverly Hills, CA 90211
*Tel: (310) 559-7410*
*Credits: Bopha!*

**Cinergi**
406 Wilshire Bloulevard
Santa Monica, CA 90401
*Tel: (310) 315-6000*
*Credits: Basic Instinct 2; Die Hard 3; Evita; Rambo 1-3; Stargate*

**Cinetic**
555 W. 25th Street
New York, NY 10001
*Tel: (212) 204-7979*
*Credits: Bowling for Columbine; Napoleon Dynamite; Super Size Me*

**Cineville**
3400 Airport Avenue
Santa Monica, CA 90405
*Tel: (310) 397-7150*
*Credits: Gas, Food Lodging; Mi Vida Loca; Swimming with Sharks*

**Code Entertainment**
9229 Sunset Blvd., Ste. 615
Los Angeles, CA 90069
*Tel: (310) 772-0008*
*www.codeentertainment.com*
*Credits: 50 First Dates; Barbershop; Palmetto*

**Codeblack Entertainment**
111 Universal Hollywood Dr.
Ste. 2260
Universal City, CA 91608
*Tel: (818) 286-8600*
*Credits: Mama, I Want to Sing! Preaching to the Choir; Shadow Boxer; Steve Harvey: Don't Trip, He Ain't Thru with Me Yet*

**The Collective**
9100 Wilshire B.vd, Ste. 700W
Beverly Hills, CA 90212
*Tel: (310) 288-8181*
*Credits: Big Momma's House 2; College*

*Road Trip; Pimp Chronicles*

**The Colleton Company**
20 Fifth Avenue, Ste. 13F
New York, NY 10011
***Tel: (212) 673-0916***
***Credits: Live from Baghdad; Renaissance Man; Riding in Cars with Boys***

**Company Films**
2629 Main Street, Ste. 167
Santa Monica, CA 90405
***Tel: (310) 399-2500***
***Credits: Face/Off; The Lord of the Rings; The Matrix***

**Concrete Entertainment**
468 N. Camden Dr., Ste. 200
Beverly Hills, CA 90210
***Tel: (310) 860-5611***
***Credits: Braceface; Excess Baggage***

**ContentFilm**
225 Arizona Ave., Ste. 250
Santa Monica, CA 90401
***Tel: (310) 576-1059***
***Credits: Never Die Alone; Open Range; Thank You for Smoking; The Cooler***

**Conundrum Entertainment**
325 Wilshire Blvd., Ste. 201
Santa Monica, CA 90401
***Tel: (310) 319-2800***
***Credits: Dumb & Dumber; Me, Myself & Irene; Osmosis Jones; Shallow Hal***

**Robert Cort Productions**
1041 N. Formosa Ave.
Administration Blvd., Ste. 196
W. Hollywood, CA 90046
***Tel: (323) 850-2644***
***Credits: Against the Ropes; Runaway Bride; Save the Last Dance 1-2; Something the Lord Made***

**Creative Entertainment**
132 B. Lasky Drive
Beverly Hills, CA 90212
***Tel: (310) 248-6360***
***Credits: Gideon; Joshua; The Patriot; Unchain My Heart: The Ray Charles Story***

**Cube Vision**
9000 W. Sunset Blvd.
W. Hollywood, CA 90069
***Tel: (310) 461-3490***
***Credits: Are We There Yet?; Barbershop Movies; First Sunday; Friday 1-3***

**Lee Daniels Entertainment**
315 W. 36th Street, 10th Fl.
New York, NY 10018
***Tel: (212) 334-8110***
***Credits: Monster's Ball; Precious; Shadowboxer; The Woodsman***

**Danjaq, Inc.**
2400 Colorado Ave., Ste. 310
Santa Monica, CA 90404
***Tel: (310) 449-3185***
***Credits: James Bond Films***

**Dark Horse Entertainment**
1438 N. Gower Street
Bldg. 28, 1st Fl.
Los Angeles, CA 90028
***Tel: (323) 655-3600***
***Credits: Alien vs. Predator; Hellboy; The Mask; Time Cop; Virus***

**Darkwoods Productions**
301 E. Colorado Blvd., Ste. 705
Pasadena, CA 91101
***Tel: (323) 454-4580***
***Credits: Collateral; Redemption; The Green Mile; The Mist; The Salton Sea***

**Davis Entertainment Company**
150 S. Barrington Place
Los Angeles, CA 90049
***Tel: (310) 556-3550***
***Credits: Daddy Day Care; Dr. Doolittle 1-5; Gulliver's Travels; Eragon; Fat Albert; Grumpy Old Men 1-2; I, Robot, The Firm***

**Davis Entertainment Company**
10201 W. Pico Blvd., Stes. 31-301
Los Angeles, CA 90064
***Tel: (310) 889-8000***
***Credits: See Above***

**Dino De Laurentiis Company**
100 Universal City Plaza, Bung. 5195
Universal City, CA 91608
***Tel: (818) 777-2111***
***www.ddlc.net***
***Credits: Bound; Conan the Barbarian; Dune; Hannibal; Red Dragon; U-571***

**Michael De Luca Productions**
10202 W. Washington Blvd.
Astaire Bldg., Ste. 302B
Culver City, CA 90232
***Tel: (310) 244-4990***
***Credits: Around the World in 80 Days; Ghost Rider; The Love Guru; Zathura***

**Di Bonaventura Pictures**
5555 Melrose Avenue
Dressing Room Bldg., Ste. 112
Los Angeles, CA 90038
***Tel: (323) 956-8282***
***Credits: Constantine; Derailed; Doom; Four Brothers; G.I. Joe; Transformers 1-2***

**Di Novi Pictures**
720 Wilshire Blvd., Ste. 300
Santa Monica, CA 90401
***Tel: (310) 458-7200***
***Credits: Batman Returns; Catwoman; The Sisterhood of the Traveling Pants 1-2***

**Digital Domain, Inc.**
300 Rose Avenue
Venice, CA 90291
***Tel: (310) 314-2800***
***Credits: A Beautiful Mind; Aeon Flux; The Day After Tomorrow; X-Men; XXX***

**Dimension Films**
The Weinstein Company
5700 Wilshire Blvd., Ste. 600
Los Angeles, CA 90036
***Tel: (323) 207-3200***
***Credits: Bad Santa; Grindhouse; The Long Shots; Scary Movie 1-4; Scream 1-3; Spy Kids 1-3; Superhero Movie***

**Dimension Films**
The Weinstein Company
345 Hudson Street, 13th Fl.
New York, NY 10014
***Tel: (646) 862-3400***
***Credits: See Above***

**Donley Pictures**
914 Westwood Blvd., Ste. 591
Los Angeles, CA 90024
***Tel: (310) 441-0834***
***Credits: Anastasia; Little Mermaid***

**The Donners' Company**
9465 Wilshire Blvd., Ste. 430
Beverly Hills, CA 90212
***Tel: (310) 777-4600***
***Credits: Lethal Weapon 1-4; The Secret Life of Bees; Wolverine; X-Men 1-3***

**Double Feature Films**
9465 Wilshire Blvd., Ste. 950
Beverly Hills, CA 90212
***Tel: (310) 887-1100***
***Credits: Be Cool; Freedom Writers; Reno 911!; World Trade Center***

**DreamWorks SKG**
1000 Flower Street
Glendale, CA 91201
***Tel: (818) 695-5000***
***Credits: A Beautiful Mind; Cast Away; Gladiator; Shrek 1-4; Transformers***

**DreamWorks Studios**
100 Universal City Plaza
Bldg. 5121
Universal City, CA 91608
***Tel: (818) 733-7000***
***Credits: A Beautiful Mind; Gladiator; Red Eye; Seabiscuit; Shrek 1-3; Transformers***

**The Edge/Jonathan Krane Motion Picture Organization**
7932 Woodrow Wilson Drive
Los Angeles, CA 90046
***Tel: (323) 650-6893***
***Credits: Face/Off; General's Daughter; Michael; Swordfish***

**Edmonds Entertainment**
1635 N. Cahuenga Blvd., 6th Fl.
Los Angeles, CA 90028
***Tel: (323) 860-1550***
***Credits: Hav Plenty; Light It Up; New in Town; Soul Food***

**Electric Entertainment**
940 N. Highland, Ste. A.
Los Angeles, CA 90028
***Tel: (323) 817-1300***
***Credits: Celluar; Godzilla; Independence Day; Stargate; The Patriot; Universal Soldier***

**Escape Artists**
10202 W. Washington Blvd.
Astaire Bldg., 3rd Fl.
Culver City, CA 90232
***Tel: (310) 244-8833***
***Credits: Seven Pounds; The Pursuit of Happyness; The Taking of Pelham 123***

**Esparza-Katz Productions**
1201 W. 5th Street, Ste. T210
Los Angeles, CA 90017
***Tel: (213) 542-4420***
***Credits: Introducing Dorothy Dandridge; Selena; The Milagro Beanfield War***

**The Robert Evans Company**
5555 Melrose Avenue
Lubitsch Bldg. Ste. 117
Los Angeles, CA 90038
***Tel: (323) 956-8800***
***Credits: Chinatown; How to Lose a Guy in 10 Days; The Godfather***

**Everyman Pictures**
3000 W. Olympic Blvd., Ste. 1500
Santa Monica, CA 90404
***Tel: (310) 460-7080***
***Credits: Austin Powers 1-3; Borat; Fifty First Dates; Meet the Fockers; Meet the Parents***

**Evolution Entertainment**
901 N. Highland Avenue
Los Angeles, CA 90038
***Tel: (323) 850-3232***
***Credits: John Q; Set It Off; Love Don't Cost a Thing; Love Inc.; Saw 1-5; The Sandlot***

**Face Prods./Jennilind Prods.**
335 N. Maple Dr., Ste. 175
Beverly Hills, CA 90210
***Tel: (310) 205-2746***
***Credits: Analyze That; Analyze This; City Slickers 1 & 2; Forget Paris***

**Edward S. Feldman Co.**
520 Evelyn Place
Beverly Hills, CA 90210
***Tel: (310) 246-1990***
***Credits: 101-2 Dalmations; K-19: The Widowmaker; The Truman Show; Witness***

**FGM Entertainment**
301 N. Canon Dr., Ste. 328
Beverly Hills, CA 90210
***Tel: (310) 205-9900***
***Credits: Internal Affairs; Ronin; Species***

**Film 44**
12233 W. Olympic Blvd., Ste. 352
Los Angeles, CA 90064
***Tel: (310) 689-2929***
***Credits: Bad Santa; Friday Night Lights; Intolerable Cruelty; The Ladykillers***

**Film Colony**
465 S. Sycamore Avenue
Los Angeles, CA 90036
***Tel: (323) 933-4670***
***Credits: Jackie Brown; Pulp Fiction; Reservoir Dog; The Bourne Identity***

**Film Engine**
9220 Sunset Blvd., Ste. 301
W. Hollywood, CA 90069
***Tel: (310) 205-9500***
***Credits: The Cleaner; Lucky Number Slevin; The Butterfly Effect; The Whale Hunter***

**Film Farm**
3204 Pearl Street
Santa Monica, CA 90405
***Tel: (310) 450-1220***
***Credits: Corina Corina; The Vagina Monologues***

**Wendy Finerman Productions**
144 S. Beverly Drive #304
Beverly Hills, CA 90212
***Tel: (310) 694-8088***
***Credits: Drumline; Forest Gump; P.S. I Love You; Stepmom; The Fan***

**Flashpoint Entertainment**
9150 Wilshire Blvd., Ste. 247
Beverly Hills, CA 90212
***Tel: (310) 205-6300***
***Credits: The Bourne Identity; The Bourne Supremacy; The Bourne Ultimatum***

**Flavor Unit Entertainment**
155 Morgan Street
Jersey City, NJ 07302
***Tel: (201) 333-4883***
***Credits: Beauty Shop; Bringing Down the House; The Cookout; The Perfect Holiday***

**Flower Films, Inc.**
7360 Santa Monica Blvd.
W. Hollywood, CA 90046
***Tel: (323) 876-7400***
***Credits: Charlie's Angels; First Fifty Dates; He's Just Not That Into You; Never Been Kissed***

**Focus Features**
100 Universal City Plaza
Universal City, CA 91608
***Tel: (818) 777-7373***
***Credits: 21 Grams; Dave Chappelle's Block Party; Lost in Translation; Milk; The Pianist***

**Focus Features**
65 Bleecker Street, 3rd Fl.
New York, NY 10012
***Tel: (212) 539-4000***
***Credits: 21 Grams; Dave Chappelle's Block Party; Lost in Translation; Milk; The Pianist***

**Fortis Films**
8581 Santa Monica Blvd. Ste. 1
W. Hollywood, CA 90069
***Tel: (310) 659-4533***
***Credits: All About Steve; Hope Floats; Practical Magic; Two Weeks' Notice***

**Forward Pass**
12233 W. Olympic Blvd., Ste. 340
Los Angeles, CA 90064
***Tel: (310) 207-7378***
***Credits: Ali; Collateral; Hancock; Miami Vice***

**David Foster Productions**
3003 Exposition Blvd.
Santa Moncia, CA 90404
***Tel: (310) 255-5530***
***Credits: Collateral Damage; The Core; The Fog; The Mask Of Zorro; The Thing***

**Fox Searchlight Pictures**
10201 W. Pico Blvd., Bldg. 38
Los Angeles, CA 90035
***Tel: (310) 369-4402***
***Credits: Last King of Scotland; Slumdog Millionaire; Notorious; The Secret Life of Bees; The Wrestler***

**Fuzzy Bunny Films**
5225 Wilshire Blvd., Ste. 305
Los Angeles, CA 90036
***Tel: (323) 692-0830***
***Credits: Brother; Crossroads; I Like It Like That***

**Generate**
1545 26th Street, 2nd Fl.
Santa Monica, CA 90404
***Tel: (310) 255-0460***
***Features; MIniseries, Specials & More***

**GK Films**
1411 Fifth Street, Ste. 200
Santa Monica, CA 90401
***Tel: (310) 315-1722***
***Credits: Ali; Blood Diamond; The Aviator; The Departed; Traffic***

**Gold Circle Films**
2000 Ave. of the Stars, Ste. 600N
Beverly Hills, CA 90067
***Tel: (310) 278-4800***
***Credits: Elysian Fields; My Big Fat Greek Wedding; New in Town; White Noise***

**Goldsmith-Thomas Productions**
655 Third Ave., 27th Fl.
New York, NY 10017
***Tel: (212) 243-2900***
***Credits: Kit Kittredge: An American Girl; Maid in Manhattan; Mona Lisa Smile***

**The Goldstein Company**
1644 Courtney Avenue
Los Angeles, CA 90046
***Tel: (310) 659-9511***
***Credits: Pretty Woman; The Hunted; The Mothman Prophecies; Under Siege***

**Samuel Goldwyn Films**
9570 W. Pico Blvd., Ste. 400
Los Angeles, CA 90035
***Tel: (310) 860-3100***
***Credits: American Violet; Man from Elysian Fields; Raising Victor Vargas; Super Size Me***

**Samuel Goldwyn Films**
1133 Broadway, Ste. 926
New York, NY 10010
***Tel: (212) 367-9435***
***Credits: American Violet; Man from Elysian Fields; Raising Victor Vargas; Super Size Me***

**Dan Gordon Productions**
2060-D Avenue Los Arboles, Ste. 256
Thousand Oaks, CA 91362
***Tel: (805) 496-2566***
***Credits: Passenger 57; The Hurricane; Wyatt Earp***

**Gracie Films**
10202 W. Washington Blvd.
Poitier Building
Culver City, CA 90232
***Tel: (310) 244-4222***
***Credits: Big; Jerry Maguire; Riding in Cars with Boys; The Simpsons Movie; Spanglish***

**Gran Via Productions**
1888 Century Park East, 14th Fl.
Los Angeles, CA 90067
***Tel: (310) 859-3060***
***Credits: Chronicles of Narnia; Donnie Brasco; My Dog Skip; The Notebook***

**Green Hat Films**
4000 Warner Blvd., Bldg. 66
Burbank, CA 91522
***Tel: (818) 954-3210***
***Credits: Road Trip; School for Scoundrels; Starsky & Hutch***

**Greenestreet Films**
609 Greenwich St., 6th Fl.
New York, NY 10014
***Tel: (212) 609-9000***
***Credits: Illuminata; I'm Not Rappaport***

**Haft Entertainment**
38 Gramercy Park N. - #2C
New York, NY 10019
***Tel: (212) 586-3881***
***Credits: Dead Poets Society; Emma; Hocus Pocus; Jakob the Liar; Last Dance***

**Harpo Films**
345 N. Maple Dr., Ste. 315
Beverly Hills, CA 90210
***Tel: (310) 278-5559***
***Credits: Beloved; Their Eyes Were Watching God; The Great Debaters; Tuesdays with Morrie***

**Havoc Films**
16 W. 19th St., 12th Fl.
New York, NY 10011
***Tel: (718) 858-7458***
***Credits: Dead Man Walking***

**HBO Films**
2500 Broadway, Ste. 400
Santa Monica, CA 90404
***Tel: (310) 382-3000***
***www.hbo.com/films***
***Credits: Elizabeth I; Idlewild; John Adams; Lackawanna Blues; Life Support***

**Jim Henson Pictures**
1416 N. LaBrea Ave.
Hollywood, CA 90238
***Tel: (323) 802-1500/(212) 794-2400***
***Credits: Elmo in Grouchland; Muppets***

**Icarus Productions**
1100 Madison Ave., Ste. 6A
New York, NY 10028
***Tel: (212) 581-3020***
***Credits: Angels in America; The Birdcage;***

***Closer***

**Icon Productions**
808 Wilshire Blvd., 4th Fl.
Santa Monica, CA 90401
***Tel: (310) 434-7300***
***Credits: Apocolypto; Braveheart; Hamlet; The Passion of the Christ; Push; We Were Soldiers; What Women Want***

**Imagemovers**
500 S. Buena Vista Street
Old Animation Blvd., #1A
Burbank, CA 91521
***Tel: (818) 560-6060***
***Credits: Beowulf; Cast Away; Forrest Gump; Last Holiday; What Lies Beneath***

**Imaginary Forces**
6526 Sunset Boulevard
Hollywood, CA 90028
***Tel: (323) 957-6868***
***Credits: Blade 1-2; Boys; Juice***

**Imaginary Forces**
530 W. 25th Street, 5th Fl.
New York, NY 10001
***Tel: (646) 486-6868***
***Credits: Blade 1-2; Boys; Juice***

**Imagine Entertainment**
9465 Wilshire Blvd., 7th Fl.
Beverly Hills, CA 90212
***Tel: (310) 858-2000***
***Credits: A Beautiful Mind; American Gangster; Apollo 13; Frost/Nixon; Life; The Cat in the Hat; The Changeling***

**IMAX Corporation**
3003 Exposition Blvd.
Santa Monica, CA 90404
***Tel: (310) 255-5500***
***www.imax.com***
***Credits: Deep Sea 3D; Michael Jordan; NASCAR 3D; Space Station 3D***

**Industry Entertainment Partners**
955 S. Carillo Dr., 3rd Fl.
Los Angeles, CA 90048
***Tel: (323) 954-9000***
***Credits: Eve's Bayou; Quills; Requiem for a Dream; The Player***

**InterMedia Film Equities**
9350 Civic Center Dr., Ste. 100
Beverly Hills, CA 90210
***Tel: (310) 777-0007***
***Credits: Adaptation; Basic Instinct 2; K-Pax; RV; Terminator 3; The Wedding Planner***

**Jaffilms**
2 Sackett Landing
Rye, NY 10580
***Tel: (212) 262-4700***
***Credits: Bad Company; Fatal Attraction; Kramer V. Kramer; Taps***

**Jersey Films**
P.O. Box 491246
Los Angeles, CA 90049
***Tel: (310) 550-3200***
***Credits: Erin Brockovich; Freedom Writers; Get Shorty; Out of Sight; Pulp Fiction***

**The Jinks/Cohen Company**
4000 Warner Boulevard
Bldg. 138, Rm. 1106
Burbank, CA 91522
***Tel: (818) 954-1072***
***Credits: American Beauty; Down with Love; Nothing to Lose; The Flintstones***

**Junction Entertainment**
500 S. Buena Vista St.
Animation Bldg., Ste. 1-B
Burbank, CA 91521
***Tel: (818) 560-2800***
***Credits: Instinct; National Treasure 1-2; Phenomenon; The Kid***

**Karz Entertainment**
4000 Warner Boulevard
Bldg. 138, Rm. 1205
***Tel: (818) 954-1698***
***Credits: First Daughter; Geppetto; Good Luck Chuck; Malibu's Most Wanted***

**The Kennedy/Marshall Company**
619 Arizona Avenue
Santa Monica, CA 90401
***Tel: (310) 656-8400***
***Credits: Seabiscuit; The Bourne Ultimatum; The Curious Case of Bengamin Buttons; The Sixth Sense***

**David Kirschner Productions**
12711 Ventura Blvd., Ste. 270
Studio City, CA 91604
***Tel: (818) 508-3424***
***Credits: Curious George; Hocus Pocus; Secondhand Lions; The Flintstones***

**Klasky Csupo**
6353 Sunset Boulevard
Los Angeles, CA 90028
***Tel: (323) 468-2600***
***www.klaskycsupo.com***
***Credits: The Rugrats Movies; The Wild Thornberrys Movie***

**Konwiser Brothers**
9333 Oso Avenue
Chatsworth, CA 91311
***Tel: (818) 887-0502***
***www.konwiserbros.com***
***Credits: Miss Evers' Boys; The Wash; The Shanghai Kid***

**Kopelson Entertainment**
1900 Avenue of the Stars, Ste. 500
Los Angeles, CA 90067
***Tel: (310) 407-1500***
***Credits: Eraser; Outbreak; Platoon; Seven; The Fugitive; U.S. Marshals***

**David Ladd Films**
9645 Wilshire Blvd., Ste. 910
Beverly Hills, CA 90212
***Tel: (310) 966-0610***
***Credits: Hart's War; Mod Squad; Serpent & The Rainbow***

**Lakeshore Entertainment Group**
9628 W. Third Street
Beverly Hills, CA 90210
***Tel: (310) 867-8000***
***Credits: Dance Flick; Fame; Million Dollar Baby; Runaway Bride***

**Larger Than Life Productions**
100 Universal City Plaza, Bldg. 5138
Universal City, CA 91608
***Tel: (818) 777-4004***
***Credits: Pleasantville; Seabiscuit***

**Latham Entertainment**
3200 Northline Ave., Ste. 210
Greensboro, NC 27408
***Tel: (336) 315-1440***
***Credits: The Original Kings of Comedy***

**Legendary Pictures**
4000 Warner Blvd., Bldg. 76
Burbank, CA 91522
***Tel: (818) 954-3888***
***Credits: 10,000 BC; 300; Lady in the Water; Superman Returns; The Dark Knight; The***

*Hangover*

**Licht Entertainment Corp.**
132 S. Lasky Dr., Ste. 200
Beverly Hills, CA 90212
***Tel: (310) 205-5500***
***Credits: The Cable Guy; Waterworld***

**Lighthouse Productions**
120 El Camino Dr., Ste. 212
Beverly Hills, CA 90212
***Tel: (310) 859-4923***
***Credits: Close Encounters; Mimic; Taxi Driver***

**Lightstorm Entertainment**
919 Santa Monica Blvd.
Santa Monica, CA 90401
***Tel: (310) 656-6100***
***Credits: Aliens; Abyss; Avatar; Solaris; Terminator; T2; Titanic***

**Lion Rock Productions**
2120 Colorado Ave., Ste. 225
Santa Monica, CA 90404
***Tel: (310) 309-2980***
***Credits: Bulletproof Monk; Face/Off; Mission Impossible 2; Windtalkers***

**Lions Gate Entertainment**
2700 Colorado Avenue
Santa Monica, CA 90404
***Tel: (310) 449-9200***
***Credits: Crash; Gladiator; Good Luck Chuck; Monster's Ball; Saw; Sicko; Why Did I Get Married?***

**Lucasfilm**
P.O. Box 29901
San Francisco, CA 94129
***Tel: (415) 662-7800***
***Credits: Star Wars Franchise***

**Macgillivray Freeman Films**
P.O. Box 205
Laguna Beach, CA 92652
***Tel: (949) 494-1055***
***Credits: IMAX Documentaries; Everest; To Fly!***

**Malpaso Productions**
4000 Warner Blvd., Bldg. 81
Burbank, CA 91522
***Tel: (818) 954-3367***
***Credits: Bridges of Madison County; Changeling; Flags of Our Fathers; Gran Torino; Letters from Iwo Jima; Million Dollar Baby; Unforgiven***

**Mandalay Pictures**
4751 Wilshire Blvd., 3rd Fl.
Los Angeles, CA 90010
***Tel: (323) 549-4300***
***Credits: Donnie Brasco; I Know/Still Know What You Did Last Summer; Seven Years in Tibet***

**Mandate Pictures**
8666 Wilshire Blvd.
Beverly Hills, CA 90211
***Tel: (310) 360-1441***
***Credits: Juno; Stranger Than Fiction; The Grudge 1-2***

**Mandeville Films**
500 S. Buena Vista Street
Animation Bldg., 2G
Burbank, CA 91521
***Tel: (818) 560-4077***
***Credits: Beauty Shop; Beverly Hills Chihuahua; Bringing Down the House; The Negotiator; Walking Tall***

**Mandy Films Inc.**
9201 Wilshire Blvd., Ste. 206
Beverly Hills, CA 90210
***Tel: (310) 246-0500***
***Credits: Charlie's Angels 1-2; Ground Zero; Sleeping with the Enemy; War Games***

**The Manhattan Project, Ltd.**
1775 Broadway, Ste. 410
New York, NY 10019
***Tel: (212) 258-2541***
***Credits: A Few Good Men; Deep Impact***

**Manifest Film Company**
812 16th Street, #12
Santa Monica, CA 90402
***Tel: (310) 899-5554***
***Credits: Joy Luck Club; People Vs. Larry Flynt***

**Laurence Mark Productions**
10202 W. Washington Blvd.
Poitier Bldg., Ste. 3111
Culver City, CA 90232
***Tel: (310) 244-5239***
***Credits: Dreamgirls; I, Robot; Jerry Maguire; Last Holiday; Simon Birch***

**Martin Chase Productions**
500 S. Buena Vista Street
Burbank, CA 91521
***Tel: (818) 560-3952***
***Credits: The Sisterhood of the Traveling Pants 1-2; The Cheetah Girls 1-2; The Princess Diaries 1-2***

**Marvel Studios, Inc.**
1600 Rosecrans Avenue
Manhattan Beach, CA 90266
***Tel: (310) 550-3100***
***Credits: Blade 1-3; Fantastic Four; Ghost Rider; Hulk; Iron Man 1-2; Spider-Man; X-Men Franchise***

**Mase/Kaplan Productions Inc.**
5314 Worster Avenue
Sherman Oaks, CA 91401
***Tel: (213) 304-5267***
***Credits: John Q.; The Notebook; The Patriot***

**Melee Entertainment**
144 S. Beverly Dr., Ste. 402
Beverly Hills, CA 90210
***Tel: (310) 248-3931***
***Credits: Friday; Next Day Air; You Got Served***

**Merchant-Ivory**
250 W. 57th St., Ste. 1825
New York, NY 10107
***Tel: (212) 582-8049***
***Credits: Le Divorce; Surviving Picasso***

**Metro-Goldwyn-Mayer (MGM)**
10250 Constellation Blvd.
Los Angeles, CA 90067
***Tel: (310) 449-3000***
***Credits: Barbershop 1-2; Die Another Day; Legally Blonde 1-2; The Pink Panther***

**Mirage Enterprises**
233 S. Beverly Dr., Ste. 200
Beverly Hills, CA 90212
***Tel: (310) 888-2830***
***Credits: Cold Mountain; How to Lose Friends and Alienate People; The Interpreter; Vicky Cristina Barcelona***

**Miramax Films**
8439 Sunset Boulevard
W. Hollywood, CA 90069
***Tel: (323) 822-4100***
***Credits: Doubt; Kill Bill 1-2; No Country for Old Men; Scary Movie Franchise***

**Miramax Films**
161 Avenue of the Americas
New York, NY 10013
***Tel: (917) 606-5500***
***Credits: Doubt; Kill Bill Movies; No Country for Old Men; Scary Movie Franchise***

**Mod3 Productions**
10390 Wilshire Blvd., Ste. 1104
Los Angeles, CA 90024
***Tel: (310) 285-8036***
***Credits: Agent Cody Banks 1-2; Dukes of Hazzard; The Island***

**The Montecito Picture Co.**
9465 Wilshire Blvd., Ste. 920
Beverly Hills, CA 90212
***Tel: (310) 247-9880/(805) 565-8590***
***Credits: 6 Days/7 Nights; Evolution; Hotel for Dogs; Road Trip; Space Jam***

**Morgan Creek Productions**
10351 Santa Monica Blvd., Ste. 200
Los Angeles, CA 90025
***Tel: (310) 432-4848***
***Credits: Ace Ventura 1-2; American Outlaws; Juwanna Mann; Major League 1-3***

**Mosaic Media Group**
9200 Sunset Blvd., 10th Fl.
Los Angeles, CA 90069
***Tel: (310) 786-4900***
***Credits: Batman Begins; Idlewild; Scooby Doo 1-2; The Dark Knight***

**Motion Picture Corp. of America**
10635 Santa Monica Blvd., Ste. 180
Los Angeles, CA 90025
***Tel: (310) 319-9500***
***Credits: Annie; Boat Trip; Dumb & Dumber***

**MTV Films**
5555 Melrose Ave.
Modular Building, #213
Los Angeles, CA 90038
***Tel: (323) 956-8023***
***Credits: Coach Carter; Dance Flick; Hustle & Flow; Save the Last Dance***

**Mutual Film Company**
8560 W. Sunset Blvd., Ste. 800
Los Angeles, CA 90069
***Tel: (310) 855-7355***
***Credits: Lara Croft Tomb Raider; Saving Private Ryan; Snakes on a Plane; Speed***

**Namesake Entertainment**
P.O. Box 436492
Louisville, KY 40253
***Tel: (502) 243-3185***
***Credits: Hangman's Curse; Left Behind***

**National Geographic Films**
9100 Wilshire Blvd., Ste. 401E
Beverly Hills, CA 90212
***Tel: (310) 858-5800***
***Credits: K-19: Widowmaker; Snow Dogs***

**Mace Neufeld Productions**
9100 Wilshire Blvd., Ste. 517 E
Beverly Hills, CA 90212
***Tel: (310) 401-6868***
***Credits: Clear & Present Danger; Invictus; Sahara; Sum of All Fears***

**New Line Cinema**
116 N. Robertson Blvd., Ste. 200
Los Angeles, CA 90048
***Tel: (310) 854-5811***
***Credits: Austin Powers 1-3; Blade 1-2; He's Just Not That Into You; Lord of the Rings Trilogy; Rush Hour 1-3; Sex and the City***

**New Millennium Studios**
One New Millennium Dr.
Petersburg, VA 23805
***Tel: (804) 957-4200***
***Credits: Asunder; Once Upon a Time...When We Were Colored***

**Newmarket Capital Group**
202 N. Canon Drive
Beverly Hills, CA 90210
***Tel: (310) 858-7472***
***Credits: Memento; Real Women Have Curves; The Passion of the Christ***

**Nickelodeon Movies**
2600 Colorado Ave.
Santa Monica, CA 90404
***Tel: (323) 310) 752-8000***
***Credits: Charlotte's Web; Jimmy Neutron: Boy Genius; Nacho Libre; Rugrats Movies***

**Nickelodeon Movies**
1515 Broadway, 44th Fl.
New York, NY 10036
***Tel: (212) 258-8000***
***Credits: See Above***

**Nuyorican**
1100 Glendon Ave., Ste. 920
Los Angeles, CA 90024
***Tel: (310) 943-6600***
***Credits: 3 Strikes; Bordertown; El Cantante; Siesta; The Cell; The Maid***

**Lynda Obst Productions**
10202 West Washington Blvd.
Astaire Bldg., Ste 1000
Culver City, CA 90232
***Tel: (310) 244-6112***
***Credits: Contact; Hope Floats; How to Lose a Guy in 10 Days; This Side of the Truth***

**Original Film**
11466 San Vicente Blvd.
Los Angeles, CA 90025
***Tel: (310) 575-6950***
***Credits: Made of Honor; The Fast & the Furious 1-4; S.W.A.T; Sweet Home Alabama; Torque; Vantage Point; XXX***

**Our Stories Films**
1635 N. Cahuenga Blvd., 6th Fl.
Los Angeles, CA 90028
***Tel: (323) 860-1550***
***Credits: Who's Your Caddy?***

**Overbrook Entertainment**
450 N. Roxbury Dr., 4th Fl.
Beverly Hills, CA 90210
***Tel: (310) 432-2400***
***Credits: Ali; Hancock; I, Robot; Seven Pounds; The Karate Kid; The Pursuit of Happyness; The Secret Life of Bees***

**Parkway Productions**
7095 Hollywood Blvd., Ste. 1009
Hollywood, CA 90028
***Tel: (323) 874-6207***
***Credits: A League of Their Own; Bewitched; Cinderella Man; Preacher's Wife***

**Participant Media**
335 N. Maple Dr., Ste. 245
Beverly Hills, CA 90210
***Tel: (310) 550-5100***
***Credits: An Inconvenient Truth; Darfur Now; Fast Food Nation; Syriana; The Soloist***

**Permut Presentations**
1801 Ave. of the Stars, Ste. 505
Los Angeles, CA 90067
***Tel: (310) 248-2792***
***Credits: Blind Date; Double Take; Dragnet;***

*Eddie; Face/Off*

**The Tyler Perry Company**
541 10th Street, Ste. 172
Atlanta, GA 30318
***Tel: (404) 222-6448***
***Credits: Diary of a Mad Black Woman; I Can Do Bad All By Myself; Madea Goes to Jail; Why Did I Get Married***

**Tyler Perry Studios**
2769 Continental Colony Parkway
Atlanta, GA 30331
***Tel: (404) 222-6448***
***Credits: Diary of a Mad Black Woman; I Can Do Bad All By Myself; Madea Goes to Jail; Why Did I Get Married***

**Peters Entertainment**
269 S. Beverly Dr., Ste. 2000
Beverly Hills, CA 90210
***Tel: (818) 954-2441***
***Credits: Ali; Batman; Rosewood; Superman Returns; The Color Purple***

**Phoenix Pictures**
9415 Culver Boulevard
Culver City, CA 90232
***Tel: (424) 298-2788***
***Credits: Holes; The People Vs. Larry Flynt; Thin Red Line; Zodiac***

**Platinum Dunes**
631 Colorado Avenue
Santa Monica, CA 90401
***Tel: (310) 394-9200***
***Credits: Friday the 13th; Texas Chainsaw Massacre Films***

**Marc Platt Productions**
100 Universal City Plaza, Bung. 5163
Universal City, CA 91608
***Tel: (818) 777-8811***
***Credits: Honey; Legally Blonde 1-2; Rachel Getting Married; Sound of Thunder***

**Punch Productions**
11661 San Vicente Blvd., Ste. 222
Los Angeles, CA 90049
***Tel: (310) 442-4888***
***Credits: Outbreak; Tootsie; Wag The Dog***

**Radar Pictures**
10900 Wilshire Blvd., Ste. 1400
Los Angeles, CA 90024
***Tel: (310) 208-8525***
***Credits: All About Steve; Swing Vote; Runaway Bride; The Chronicles of Riddick; This Side of the Truth; Zathura***

**Radiant Productions**
914 Montana Ave., 2nd Fl.
Santa Monica, CA 90403
***Tel: (310) 656-1400***
***Credits: Air Force One; Poseidon; The Perfect Storm; Troy***

**Raffaella Productions**
14320 Ventura Blvd., Ste. 617
Sherman Oaks, CA 91423
***Tel: (310) 472-0466***
***Credits: Daylight; Dragonheart; Sky Captain & the World of Tomorrow***

**Rainforest Films**
323-A Edgewood Avenue
Atlanta, GA 30312
***Tel: (770) 960-8733***
***Credits: Obsessed; Stomp the Yard; The Gospel; This Christmas***

**Random House Films**
1745 Broadway
New York, NY 10019
***Tel: (212) 782-9000***
***www.randomhouse.com***
*Credits: Reservation Road*

**Rat Entertainment**
5555 Melrose Avenue
Gloria Swanson Bldg. 307
Los Angeles, CA 90038
***Tel: (323) 956-8808***
***Credits: Money Talks; Rush Hour 1-3; The Family Man; X-Men: The Last Stand***

**Red Hour Films**
629 N. La Brea Avenue
Los Angeles, CA 90036
***Tel: (323) 602-5000***
***Credits: Dodgeball; Starsky & Hutch; The Cable Guy; Tropic Thunder; Zoolander***

**Red Om Films, Inc.**
***Tel: (310) 594-3467***
***Credits: Kit Kittredge: An American Girl; Mona Lisa Smile; Stepmom***

**Red Wagon Productions**
10202 W. Washington Blvd.
Hepburn Bldg. W.
Culver City, CA 90232
***Tel: (310) 244-4466***
***Credits: Bewitched; Gladiator; Spy Game; RV; Win a Date with Ted Hamilton***

**Regency Enterprises**
10201 W. Pico Boulevard, Bldg. 12
Los Angeles, CA 90035
***Tel: (310) 369-8300***
***Credits: Big Momma's House 1-2; Marley & Me; The Negotiator; What Happens in Vegas***

**Relevé Entertainment**
8200 Wilshire Blvd., Ste. 300
Beverly Hills, CA 90211
***Tel: (323) 468-9470***
***Credits: A Good Man is Hard to Find; In the Mix; Mama, I Want to Sing!; The Gospel***

**Revolution Studios**
2900 W. Olympic Blvd.
Santa Monica, CA 90404
***Tel: (310) 255-7000***
***Credits: Anger Management; Daddy Day Care; Hellboy; Mona Lisa Smile; Radio; XXX***

**RKO Pictures**
1875 Century Park E., Ste. 2140
Los Angeles, CA 90067
***Tel: (310) 277-0707***
***Credits: Are We Done Yet?; Citizen Cane; King Kong; Mighty Joe Young; Ritual***

**Scott Rudin Productions**
500 S. Buena Vista St.
Old Animation Bldg., Ste. 2H
Burbank, CA 91521
***Tel: (818) 560-4600/(212) 704-4600***
***Credits: First Wives Club; No Country for Old Men; There Will Be Blood; School of Rock; Shaft; The Firm; The Hours; The Queen***

**Arthur Sarkissian Productions**
9229 Sunset Blvd., Ste. 610
W. Hollywood, CA 90069
***Tel: (310) 550-6209***
***Credits: Last Man Standing; Rush Hour 1-3; While You Were Sleeping***

**Joel Schumacher Prods.**
3400 Riverside Dr., Ste. 900
Burbank, CA 91522
***Tel: (818) 260-6065***
***Credits: A Time To Kill; Batman Forever; Phone Booth; Veronica Guerin***

**Scott Free Productions**
614 N. La Peer Drive
W. Hollywood, CA 90069
***Tel: (310) 360-2250***
***Credits: American Gangster; Black Hawk Down; Enemy of the State; Gladiator***

**Screen Gems**
10202 W. Washington Blvd.
Culver City, CA 90232
***Tel: (310) 244-4000***
***Credits: Lakeview Terrace; Obsessed; Quarantine; Stomp the Yard; This Christmas***

**Silver Lion Films**
701 Santa Monica Blvd.
Santa Monica, CA 90401
***Tel: (310) 393-9177***
***Credits: Flipper; Man on Fire; McHale's Navy***

**Silver Pictures**
4000 Warner Blvd., Bldg. 90
Burbank, CA 91522
***Tel: (818) 954-4490***
***Credits: The Book of Eli; Die Hard 1-2; Lethal Weapon 1-4; Speed Racer; The Matrix 1-3***

**The Robert Simonds Company**
10202 W. Washington Blvd.
Astaire Bldg., Ste. 2110
Culver City, CA 90232
***Tel: (310) 244-5222***
***Credits: Billy Madison; Herbie: Fully Loaded; The Pink Panther; The Wedding Singer***

**Southern Skies Inc.**
1104 S. Holt Ave., Ste. 302
Los Angeles, CA 90035
***Tel: (310) 855-9833***
***Credits: Alien 3; City Slickers; Major League***

**Spyglass Entertainment**
10900 Wilshire Blvd., 10th Fl.
Los Angeles, CA 90024
***Tel: (310) 443-5800***
***Credits: 27 Dresses; Bruce Almighty; Memoirs of a Geisha; Reign of Fire; G.I. Joe; Seabiscuit; The Love Guru; The Sixth Sense***

**Stampede Entertainment**
3000 W. Olympic Blvd.
Los Angeles, CA 90404
***Tel: (310) 552-9977***
***Credits: City Slickers; Tremors I-4***

**Jane Startz Productions Inc.**
244 Fifth Ave., 11th Fl.
New York, NY 10001
***Tel: (212) 545-8910***
***Credits: Indian & The Cupboard; The Baby-Sitters Club; The Magic Schoolbus***

**State Street Pictures**
8075 W. Third St., Ste. 306
Los Angeles, CA 90048
***Tel: (323) 556-2240***
***Credits: Barbershop 1-2; Men of Honor; Notorious; Roll Bounce; Soul Food***

**Storyline Entertainment**
500 S. Buena Vista Street
Old Animation Bldg., Ste. 3D
Burbank, CA 91521
***Tel: (818) 560-2928***
***Credits: Chicago; Footloose; Hairspray; The Bucket List***

**Summit Entertainment**
1630 Stewart St., Ste. 120
Santa Monica, CA 90404
***Tel: (310) 309-8400***
***www.summit-ent.com***
***Credits: Knowing; Michael Clayton; Mr. & Mrs. Smith; P.S. I Love You; Vanilla Sky***

**Tapestry Films, Inc.**
9328 Civic Center Drive
Beverly Hills, CA 90210
***Tel: (310) 275-1191***
***Credits: Employee of the Month; The Wedding Planner; Wedding Crashers***

**Threshold Entertainment**
1649 11th Street
Santa Monica, CA 90404
***Tel: (310) 452-8899***
***Credits: Food Fight! Mortal Kombat 1-3***

**The Steve Tisch Company**
10202 W. Washington Blvd.
Astaire Bldg., 3rd Fl.
Culver City, CA 90232
***Tel: (310) 244-6612***
***Credits: American History X; Forrest Gump; Long Kiss Goodnight; The Postman***

**Tollin Productions**
10960 Ventura Blvd., 2nd Fl.
Studio City, CA 91604
***Tel: (818) 766-5004***
***Credits: Coach Carter; Good Burger; Radio; Varsity Blues; Wild Hogs***

**Totem Productions**
8009 Santa Monica Blvd.
Los Angeles, CA 90046
***Tel: (323) 650-4994***
***Credits: Crimson Tide; Deja Vu; Enemy of the State; Man on Fire***

**Tribeca Productions**
375 Greenwich St., 8th Fl.
New York, NY 10013
***Tel: (212) 941-4040***
***Credits: Analyze This/That; Meet the Fockers; Meet the Parents; Rent***

**Troublemaker Studios**
4900 Old Manor Road
Austin, TX 78723
***Tel: (512) 334-7777***
***www.loghooligans.com***
***Credits: El Mariachi; Desperado; Grindhouse; Spy Kids 1-3***

**Tulchin Entertainment**
11377 W. Olympic Blvd., 2nd Fl.
Los Angeles, CA 90064
***Tel: (310) 914-7900***
***Credits: The Mouse; To Sleep With Anger***

**Unique Features**
116 N. Robertson Blvd., Ste. 909
Los Angeles, CA 90048
***Tel: (310) 492-8009***

**Unique Features**
888 7th Avenue, 16th Fl.
New York, NY 10106
***Tel: (212) 649-4980***

**United Artists**
10250 Constellation Blvd., 11th Fl.
Los Angeles, CA 90067
***Tel: (310) 449-3777***
***Credits: Lions for Lambs; Valkyrie***

**Valhalla Motion Pictures**
3201 Cahuenga Blvd., W.
Los Angeles, CA 90068
***Tel: (323) 850-3030***
***Credits: Aliens; Armageddon; Terminator 1-2; The Incredible Hulk; The Punisher***

### View Askew Productions Inc.
P.O. Box 93339
Los Angeles, CA 90093
***Tel: (323) 969-9423***
***Credits: Chasing Amy; Clerks; Jersey Girl***

### Village Roadshow
3400 Riverside Dr., Ste. 900
Burbank, CA 91604
***Tel: (818) 260-6000***
***Credits: Gran Torino; Happy Feet; Ocean's 11-13; The Matrix 1-3; Training Day***

### Walden Media
1888 Century Park E., 14th Fl.
Los Angeles, CA 90067
***Tel: (310) 887-1000***
***Credits: Around the World in 80 Days; Charlotte's Web; Chronicles of Narnia; Journey to the Center of the Earth***

### Walden Media
294 Washington St., 7th Fl.
Boston, MA 02108
***Tel: (617) 451-5420***
***Credits: Around the World in 80 Days; Charlotte's Web; Chronicles of Narnia; Journey to the Center of the Earth***

### Warner Bros. Pictures
4000 Warner Blvd.
Burbank, CA 91522
***Tel: (818) 954-6000***
***Credits: 10,000 BC; 300; Around the World in 80 Days; Batman; Harry Potter; The Matrix; Ghosts of the Abyss***

### Weed Road Pictures
4000 Warner Boulevard
Building 81; Ste. 115
Burbank, CA 91522
***Tel: (818) 954-3771***
***Credits: Constantine; Deep Blue Sea; Hancock; I Am Legend; Starsky & Hutch***

### Weekend Films
2802 Main Street, Ste. 1
Santa Monica, CA 90405
***Tel: (310) 399-9577***
***Credits: Because of Winn Dixie; Groundhog Day; The League of Extraordinary Gentlemen***

### The Weinstein Company
5700 Wilshire Blvd., Ste. 600
Los Angeles, CA 90036
***Tel: (323) 207-3200***
***Credits: Clerks 2; Grindhouse; Scary Movie 4; Sicko; The Great Debaters***

### The Weinstein Company
375 Greenwich St., 3rd Fl.
New York, NY 10013
***Tel: (212) 941-3800***
***Credits: Clerks 2; Grindhouse; Scary Movie 4; Sicko; The Great Debaters***

### The Weinstein Company
345 Hudson Street, 13th Fl.
New York, NY 10014
***Tel: (646) 862-3400***
***Credits: Clerks 2; Grindhouse; Scary Movie 4; Sicko; The Great Debaters***

### Jerry Weintraub Prods.
4000 Warner Blvd., Bung. 1
Burbank, CA 91522
***Tel: (818) 954-2500***
***Credits: Karate Kid 1-4; Ocean's 11-13***

### Simon West Productions
5555 Melrose Avenue
Dressing Room Bldg., Rm. 109
Hollywood, CA 90038
***Tel: (323) 956-8994***
***Credits: Blackhawk Down; Con Air; Lara Croft: Tomb Raider; The General's Daughter***

### Wheelhouse Entertainment
15464 Ventura Blvd.
Sherman Oaks, CA 91403
***Tel: (818) 461-3599***
***Credits: Braveheart; Pearl Harbor; The Man in the Iron Mask; We Were Soldiers***

### Wildwood Enterprises Inc.
335 N. Maple Dr., Ste. 354
Beverly Hills, CA 90210
***Tel: (310) 246-7707***
***Credits: Lions for Lambs; Ordinary People; Quiz Show; The Horse Whisperer***

### Wind Dancer Productions
315 S. Beverly Dr., Ste. 502
Beverly Hills, CA 90212
***Tel: (310) 601-2720/(212) 765-4772***
***Credits: Thunder Alley; What Women Want***

### Winkler Films
190 N. Canon Dr., Ste. 302
Beverly Hills, CA 90210
***Tel: (310) 858-5780***
***Credits: Enough; Goodfellas; The Net; Raging Bull; Rocky***

### Winter Road Entertainment
10201 W. Pico Boulevard
Bldg. 732, Rm. 14
Los Angeles, CA 90035
***Tel: (310) 369-4723***
***Credits: Fantastic Four; Left Behind; Planet of the Apes; Star Trek; Wolverine; X-Men 1-3***

### Witt-Thomas-Harris Productions
11901 Santa Monica Blvd., Ste. 596
W. Los Angeles, CA 90025
***Tel: (310) 472-6004/(818) 762-7500***
***Credits: Dead Poets Society; Final Analysis; Insomnia; Three Kings***

### Working Title Films
9720 Wilshire Blvd., 4th Fl.
Beverly Hills, CA 90212
***Tel: (310) 777-3100***
***Credits: Bridget Jones's Diary; Fargo; Frost/Nixon; Notting Hill; The Soloist***

### Yari Film Group
10850 Wilshire Blvd., 6th Fl.
Los Angeles, CA 90024
***Tel: (310) 689-1450***
***Credits: Crash; Dave Chappelle's Block Party; Employee of the Month; Prime***

### The Zanuck Company
9465 Wilshire Blvd., Ste. 930
Beverly Hills, CA 90212
***Tel: (310) 274-0261***
***Credits: Charlie & the Chocolate Factory; Planet of the Apes; Rules of Engagement***

### Laura Ziskin Productions
10202 W. Washington Blvd.
Astaire Bldg., Ste. 1310
Culver City, CA 90232
***Tel: (310) 244-7373***
***Credits: As Good As It Gets; Pretty Woman; Spider-Man 1-3; To Die For; What About Bob?***

### Zucker Productions
1250 Sixth Street, Ste. 201
Santa Monica, CA 90401
***Tel: (310) 656-9202***
***Credits: Airplane!; First Knight; Ghost; My Best Friend's Wedding***

**American Cinema Foundation Screenwriting Competition**
11400 W. Olympic Blvd. #200
Los Angeles, CA 90064
***Tel: (310) 914-0159***
***www.cinemafoundation.com***

**American Screenwriters Assoc. Screenplay Competition**
269 S. Beverly Drive, Ste. 2600
Beverly Hills, CA 90212-3807
***Tel: (866) 265-9091***
***www.asascreenwriters.com***

**American Screenwriting Competition**
Flat Shoe Entertainment
311 N. Robertson Blvd., Ste. 172
Beverly Hills, CA 90211
***Tel: (888) 299-0234***
***www.flatshoe.com***

**American Zoetrope Screenplay Competition**
916 Kearny Street
San Francisco, CA 94133
***Tel: (415) 788-7500***
***www.zoetrope.com***

**Atlanta Film Festival Screenwriting Competition**
535 Means Street, Ste. C
Atlanta, GA 30318
***Tel: (404) 352-4225***
***www.atlantafilmfestival.com***

**Austin Film Festival Screenplay Competition**
1801 Salina Street
Austin, TX 78702
***Tel: (512) 478-4795***
***www.austinfilmfestival.com***

**Big Break International Screenwriting Contest**
Final Draft
26707 W. Agoura Rd., Ste. 205
Calabasas, CA 91302
***Tel: (818) 995-8995***
***www.finaldraft.com***

**Black Hollywood Entertainment Resource Center (BHERC) Screenwriting Contest**
1875 Century Park E., 6th Fl.
Los Angeles, CA 90067
***Tel: (310) 284-3170***
***www.bherc.org***

**Blue Cat Screenplay Competition**
P.O. Box 2635
Hollywood, CA 90028
***www.bluecatscreenplay.com***

**Cinequest Film Festival Screenplay Competition**
P.O. Box 720040
San Jose, CA 95172
***Tel: (408) 995-5033***
***www.cinequest.org***

**CineStory Screenplay Competition**
P.O. Box 3736
Idyllwild, CA 92549
***Tel: (909) 659-1180***
***www.cinestory.org***

**Cynosure Screenwriting Awards Competition**
BroadMind Entertainment
3699 Wilshire Blvd., Ste. 850
Los Angeles, CA 90010
***Tel: (310) 855-8730***
***www.broadmindent.com***

**D.C. Shorts Film Festival Screenwriting Competition**
1317 F Street, NW - Ste. 920
Washington, DC 20004
***Tel: (202) 393-4266***
***www.dcshorts.com***

**Disney | ABC Television Writing Fellowship**
Disney | ABC Television Group
Talent Development & Diversity
500 S. Buena Vista Street
Burbank, CA 91521
***www.disneyabctalentdevelopment.com***

**Film Independent Screenwriters Lab**
9911 W. Pico Boulevard
Los Angeles, CA 90035
***Tel: (310) 432-1200***
***www.filmindependent.org***

**Film*Makers*.com/Radmin Co. Screenwriting Contest**
P.O. Box 4678
Mission Viejo, CA 92690
***www.filmmakers.com***

**Final Draft's Big Break Int'l. Screenwriting Contest**
Final Draft
26707 W. Agoura Rd., Ste. 205
Calabasas, CA 91302
***Tel: (818) 995-8995***
***www.finaldraft.com***

**FOX Diversity Writers Initiative**
Diversity Outreach Program
P.O. Box 900
Beverly Hills, CA 90213
***Tel: (310) 369-1000***
***www.fox.com/diversity***

**Great Lakes Film Association Screenplay Competition**
P.O. Box 346
Erin, PA 16512
***Tel: (814) 873-5069***
***www.greatlakesfilmfest.com***

**Guy A. Hanks & Marvin Miller Screenwriting Program/The Cosby Program**
USC School of Cinematic Arts
900 W. 34th Street, Rm. 235
Los Angeles, CA 90089
***Tel: (213) 740-8194***
***www.cosbyprogram.com***

**Hollywood Nexus Screenwriting Contest**
***www.hollywoodnexus.com***

**Hollywood Screenplay Discovery Awards**
433 N. Camden Dr., Ste. 600
Beverly Hills, CA 90210
***Tel: (310) 288-1888***
***www.hollywoodawards.com***

**IC (Illinois/Chicago) Screenwriting Competition**
100 W. Randolph
Chicago, IL 60601
***Tel: (312) 814-3600***
***www.filmillinois.state.il.us***

**Kairos Prize**
5620 Paseo DeNorte, #127C-308
Carlsbad, CA 92008
***Tel: (310) 432-1200***
***www.kairosprize.com***

**L.A. Shorts Fest Screenplay Competition**
1610 Argyle Ave., #113
Los Angeles, CA 90028
***Tel: (323) 461-4400***
***www.lashortsfest.com***

**McKnight Artist Fellowships for Filmmakers**
IFP/Minneapolis
2446 University Avenue W., Ste. 100
Saint Paul, MN 55114
***Tel: (651) 644-1912***
***www.ifpmn.org***

**Monterey Screenwriting Competition**
Monterey County Film Commission
P.O. Box 111
Monterey, CA93942
***Tel: (831) 646-0910***
***www.filmmonterey.org***

**Nevada Film Office Screenwriters Competition**
555 E. Washington Ave., Ste. 5400
Las Vegas, NV 89101
***Tel: (702) 486-2711***
***www.nevadafilm.com***

**Nicholl Fellowships in Screenwriting**
Academy of Motion Pictures Arts & Sciences
8949 Wilshire Boulevard
Beverly Hills, CA 90211
***Tel: (310) 247-3010***
***www.oscars.org/nicholl***

**Nickelodeon Writing Fellowship**
231 W. Olive Ave.
Burbank, CA 91502
***Tel: (818) 736-3663***
***www.nickwriting.com***

**Ohio Independent Screenplay Awards**
Independent Pictures
1392 W. 65th Street
Cleveland, OH 44102
***Tel: (216) 651-7315***
***www.ohiofilms.com***

**Organization of Black Screenwriters (OBS) Screenwriting Contest**
Golden State Mutual Life Insur. Bldg.
1999 W. Adams Blvd., Rm. Mezz.
Los Angeles, CA 90018
***Tel: (323) 735-2050***
***www.obswriter.com***

**Page International Screenwriting Awards**
7510 Sunset Blvd., Ste. 610
Hollywood, CA 90046
***www.internationalscreenwritingawards.com***

**Screenplay Contests.com**
Cherub Productions
P.O. Box 540
Boulder, CO 80306
***Tel: (303) 629-3072***
***www.screenplaycontest.com***

**Screenwriting Expo**
Creative Screenwriting
6404 Hollywood Blvd., Ste. 415
Los Angeles, CA 90028
***Tel: (323) 957-1405***
***www.screenwritingexpo.com***

**Script Frenzy**
***www.scriptfrenzy.com***

**Scriptapalooza Screenwriting Competition**
***www.scriptapalooza.com***

**Script P.I.M.P.**
**(Pipeline Into Motion Pictures)**
**Scriptwriting Competition**
8033 Sunset Blvd., #3000
Los Angeles, CA 90046
***Tel: (310) 401-1155***
***www.scriptpimp.com***

**Scriptwriters Network**
6404 Wilshire Blvd., #1640
Los Angeles, CA 90048
***Tel: (888) 796-9673***
***www.scriptwritersnetwork.com***

**Scriptwriters Showcase**
Final Draft
26707 W. Agoura Rd., Ste. 205
Calabasas, CA 91302
***Tel: (818) 995-8995***
***www.finaldraft.com***

**Slamdance Screenplay Competition**
5634 Melrose Avenue
Los Angeles, CA 90038
***Tel: (323) 466-1786***
***www.slamdance.com***

**Sundance Screenwriters Lab**
Sundance Institute
8530 Wilshire Blvd., 3rd Fl.
Beverly Hills, CA 90211
***Tel: (310) 360-1981***
***www.sundance.org***

**Sundance Screenwriters Lab**
Sundance Institute
1825 Three Kings Dr.
Park City, UT 84060
***Tel: (435) 658-3456***
***www.sundance.org***

**Warner Bros. Writers Workshop**
4000 Warner Blvd.
Burbank, CA 91522
***Tel: (818) 954-5700***
***www2.warnerbros.com/writersworkshop/***

**Worldfest—Houston**
9494 SW Freeway, Ste. 200
Houston, TX 77074
***Tel: (713) 965-9955***
***www.worldfest.org***

**WriteMovies.com International Writing Contest**
***www.writemovies.com***

**Writers Network Screenplay & Fiction Competition**
*Fade In Magazine*
287 S. Robertson Blvd., Ste. 467
Beverly Hills, CA 90211
***Tel: (310) 275-0287***
***www.writemovies.com***

WILL
YOU
write
THE
NEXT
GREAT
SCREENPLAY
?

# 25+ RESOURCES FOR SCREENWRITERS

Below is our POWER LIST of websites where you can study blockbuster scripts and industry literary information, some for nominal fees and some for FREE!!! Writers can always use more information & inspiration. EPP is cheering you on as you write your ticket to the top!

**Creative Screenwriting**
***www.creativescreenwriting.com***

**The Daily Script**
***www.dailyscript.com***

**Done Deal Professional**
***www.donedealpro.com***

**Drew's Script-O-Rama**
***www.script-o-rama.com***

**Larry Edmunds Bookshop**
***www.larryedmunds.com***

**Fade In Magazine**
***www.fadeinmag.com***

**Film Tracker**
***www.filmtracker.com***

**Final Draft**
***www.finaldraft.com***

**The Guy A. Hanks & Marvin Miller Screenwriting Program**
***www.cosbyprogram.com***

**Michael Hauge's Screenplay Mastery**
***www.screenplaymastery.com***

**Inktip**
***www.inktip.com***

**iScriptDB**
***www.iscriptdb.com***

**MovieBytes.com**
***www.moviebytes.com***

**Movie Magic Screenwriter**
***www.write-bros.com***

**Movie Pitch.com**
***www.moviepitch.com***

**Nickelodeon Writing Fellowship**
***www.nickwriting.com***

**On the Page**
***www.onthepage.tv***

**Organization of Black Screenwriters**
***www.obswriter.com***

**Screenplay Contests.com**
***www.screenplaycontests.com***

**Screenwriters Utopia**
***www.screenwritersutopia.com***

**Screenwriting Expo**
***www.screenwritingexpo.com***

**Sci-Fi Scripts**
***www.scifiscripts.com***

**Script Crawler**
***www.scriptcrawler.net***

**Script Magazine**
***www.scriptmagazine.com***

**Script For Sale.com**
***www.scriptforsale.com***

**Script Shark**
***www.scriptshark.com***

**Sell A Script.com**
***www.sellascript.com***

**Showbiz Data**
***www.showbizdata.com***

**Simply Scripts**
***www.simplyscripts.com***

**Slamdance Coverage Service**
***www.slamdance.com***

**TV Writers Vault**
***www.tvwritersvault.com***

**United States Copyright Office**
***www.copyright.gov***
*****See Form FL 119 & others***

**Warner Bros. Writers Workshop**
***www.writersworkshop.warnerbros.com***

**Who's Buying What?.com**
***www.whosbuyingwhat.com***

**Winning Scripts.com**
***www.winningscripts.com***

**Write Brothers**
***www.write-bros.com***
***www.screenplay.com***

**Writers Boot Camp**
***www.writersbootcamp.com***

**Writers Guild of America, East**
***www.wgaeast.org***

**Writers Guild of America, West**
***www.wga.org***

## POWER QUOTE:

*"I've worked with writers who get $3 million a script, and I've worked with lots of writers trying to launch their careers. As a coach, it's about closing the gap between what the writer envisions on the screen and what they have on the page. Underneath all that, I've just been a huge, huge movie fan since I was 5 years old..."*

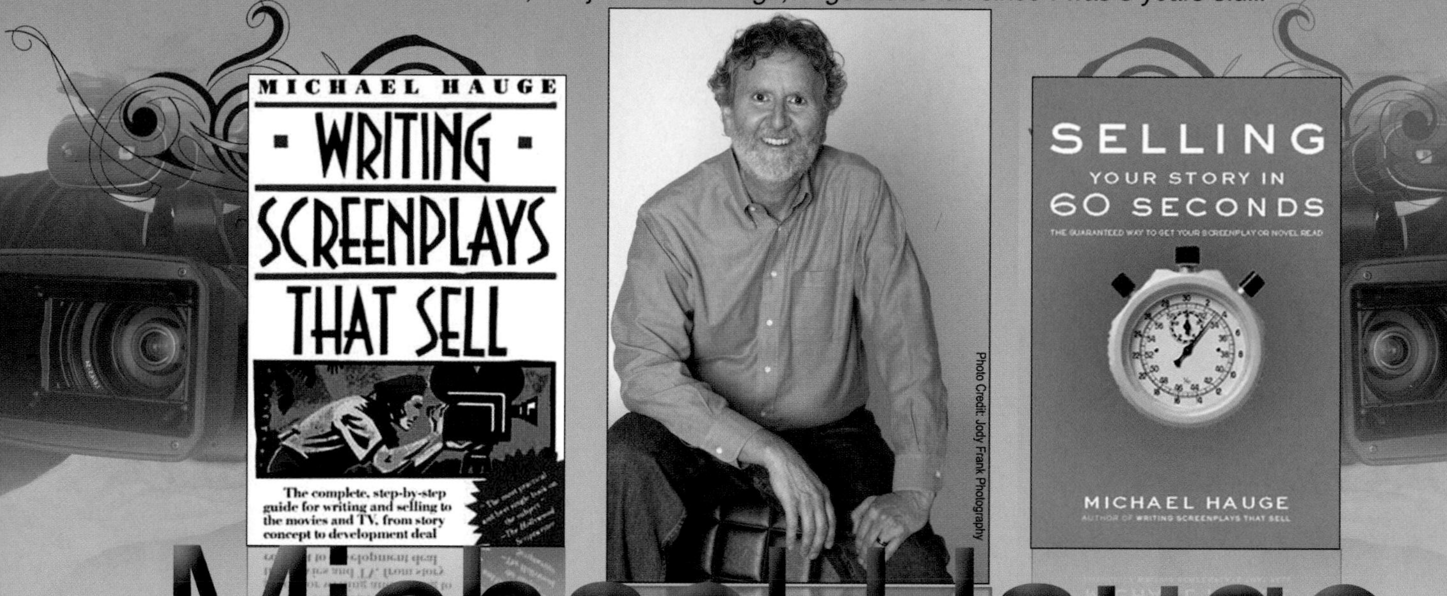


# Michael Hauge

### Author/Script Consultant

One conversation with Hollywood script consultant, author and lecturer Michael Hauge is like a refreshing master class in all things entertainment. His passion for the industry is contagious and he shares so many screenwriting success tips and techniques that his DVDs are must-buys in order to capture it all. ***EPP: 4*** caught up with Hauge, a native of Salem, Oregon, and the author of two bestselling books, *Selling Your Story in 60 Seconds* and *Writing Screenplays That Sell* (now in it's 33rd printing). We quickly found out why his day-to-day business consists of consulting with major studios, production companies, including Will Smith's Overbrook Productions, and a wide range of writers, filmmakers, directors and novelists. He's a screenwriting expert who doesn't mind sharing his mastery with the world.

**Here he is verbatim, sharing his 123 POWER ADVICE for Succeeding in Screenwriting:**

### ON GETTING STARTED:

*MH: "If you're considering becoming a screenwriter: #1 You've got to watch lots of movies. And see the good movies twice so you can figure out how the principles of screenwriting are being applied; #2 You MUST read scripts - two scripts a week until the end of time! You can download scripts for free off the Internet now, so there's no excuse whatsoever for not doing this. You will learn essential lessons – about style, how screenplays work, and how they differ from novels and other forms of writing – by actually reading them; #3 You must educate yourself about the craft of writing and storytelling, through books, lectures, seminars, CDs and DVDs; and most of all, #4 You've got to WRITE. Every single day."*

### ON WRITING SELLABLE SCREENPLAYS:

*MH: "The three most important elements your story has to possess are: #1 there has to be a hero that the audience cares about and empathizes with; #2 that hero has to be pursuing a very clear, visible goal or finish line that he is desperate to accomplish by the end of the movie. This is where most scripts fail, because writers aren't used to thinking about their stories that way; and #3 there have to be major, major obstacles standing between the hero and that goal. Emotion grows out of conflict, and the scenes where your hero is forced to confront these obstacles are the emotional moments of your story. As a writer and storyteller, your goal must be to create an emotional experience for the reader of the script or the audience of the movie."*

**If you're a screenwriter or novelist, log onto Michael Hauge's website www.screenplaymastery.com and get a wealth of information for advancing your career.**

# SCREENWRITING SOFTWARE

**Celtx**
***www.celtx.com***

**Final Draft**
26707 W. Agoura Rd., Ste. 205
Calabasas, CA 91302
***Tel: (818) 995-8995***
***www.finaldraft.com***

**Dramatica Pro**
Write Brothers
348 E. Olive Ave., Ste. H
Burbank, CA 91502
***Tel: (818) 843-6557/(800) 84-STORY***
***www.write-bros.com***

**HollyWord/Screenwriter Software**
P.O. Box 2048
Rancho Santa Fe, CA 92067
***Tel: (888) 234-6798***
***www.hollyword.com***

**Movie Magic Screenwriter**
Write Brothers
348 E. Olive Ave., Ste. H
Burbank, CA 91502
***Tel: (818) 843-6557/(800) 84-STORY***
***www.write-bros.com***
***www.screenplay.com***

**Showbiz Software/Media Services**
500 S. Sepulveda Blvd., Ground Fl.
Los Angeles, CA 90049
***Tel: (310) 440-9600***
***www.media-services.com***

**Screen Style**
***Tel: (917) 583-9470/(888) 627-8812***
***www.screenstyle.com***

**Scene Writer Pro**
***www.scenewriterpro.com***

**Scriptware Cinovation Inc.**
1282 Elden Ave.
Boulder, CO 80301
***Tel: (303) 786-7899***
***www.scriptware.com***

**ScriptWerx**
Parnassus Software
1923 Lyans Drive
La Canada, CA 91011
***Tel: (818) 952-2665***
***www.scriptwerx.com***

**Script Wizard**
***www.warrenassoc.com***

**Storybase**
***www.storybase.net***

**Storycraft**
***www.writerspage.com***

**Storyline Pro**
Truby's Writers Studio
664 Brooktree Road
Santa Monica, CA 90402
***Tel: (310) 573-9630***
***www.truby.com***

**Storyview**
Write Brothers
348 E. Olive Ave., Ste. H
Burbank, CA 91502
***Tel: (818) 843-6557/(800) 84-STORY***
***www.write-bros.com***

**Truby's Blockbuster**
664 Brooktree Road
Santa Monica, CA 90402
***Tel: (310) 573-9630***
***www.truby.com***

**Write Brothers**
348 E. Olive Ave., Ste. H
Burbank, CA 91502
***Tel: (818) 843-6557/(800) 84-STORY***
***www.write-bros.com***
***www.screenplay.com***

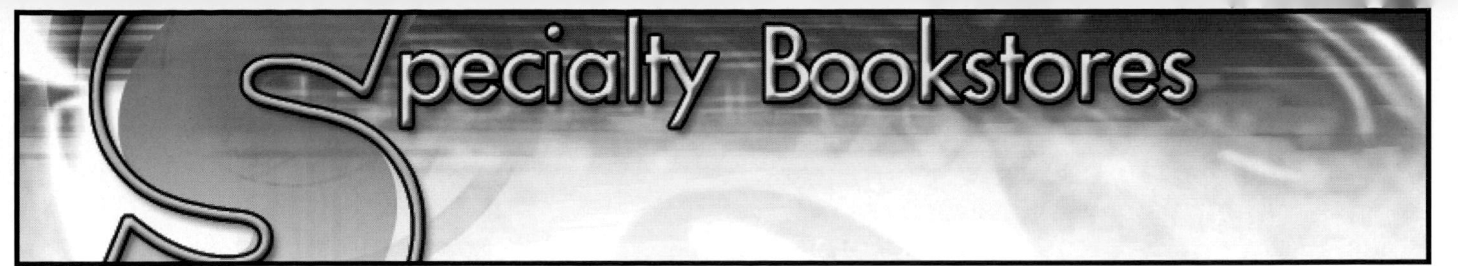






**ASC Store**
1313 Vine Street
Hollywood, CA 90028
***Tel: (323) 969-4333***
***www.theasc.com***

**Backstage**
545 8th Street, SE
Washington, D.C. 20003
***Tel: (202) 544-5744***
***www.backstagebooks.com***

**Book Castle**
212 N. San Fernando Blvd.
Burbank, CA 91502
***Tel: (818) 845-1563***
***www.bookcastlesmovieworld.com***

**Book City**
6627 Hollywood Boulevard
Hollywood, CA 90028
***Tel: (323) 466-2525***
***www.bookcity.net***

**Book City Script Shop**
8913 Lankershim Blvd.
Sun Valley, CA 91352
***Tel: (323) 466-2525***
***www.bookcity.net***

**Broadway New York**
1535 Broadway
New York, NY10036
***Tel: (212) 944-3724***
***www.broadwaynewyork.com***

**Drama Book Shop**
250 W. 40th Street
New York, NY 10018
***Tel: (212) 944-0595***
***www.dramabookshop.com***

**Hollywood Book & Poster Co.**
6562 Hollywood Boulevard
Hollywood, CA 90028
***Tel: (323) 465-8764***
***www.hollywoodbookandposter.com***

**Howard University Bookstore**
2225 Georgia Avenue, NW
Washington, D.C. 20059
***Tel: (202) 238-2640***
***www.bookstore.howard.edu***

**Larry Edmunds Bookshop**
6644 Hollywood Boulevard
Hollywood, CA 90028
***Tel: (323) 463-3273***
***www.larryedmunds.com***

**One Shubert Alley**
Shubert Alley (bet. 44th St./45th St.)
New York, NY 10036
***Tel: (212) 944-4133***
***www.broadwaynewyork.com***

**Paley Center for Media Shop**
465 N. Beverly Drive
Beverly Hills CA 90210
***Tel: (310) 786-1000***
***www.paleycenter.org***

**Paley Center for Media Shop**
25 W. 52nd Street
New York, NY 10019
***Tel: (212) 621-6880***
***www.paleycenter.org***

**Quixote Studio Store**
1000 Cahuenga Blvd.
Los Angeles, CA 90038
***Tel: (323) 876-3530***
***www.quixote.com***

**Samuel French Bookshop**
7623 Sunset Boulevard
Hollywood, CA 90046
***Tel: (323) 876-0570***
***www.samuelfrench.com***

**Samuel French Bookshop**
11963 Ventura Boulevard
Studio City, CA 91604
***Tel: (818) 762-0535***
***www.samuelfrench.com***

**Samuel French Bookshop**
45 W. 25th Street, 2nd Fl.
New York, NY 10010
***Tel: (212) 206-8990***
***www.samuelfrench.com***

**Shakespeare & Co. Booksellers**
716 Broadway
New York, NY 10003
***Tel: (212) 529-1330***
***www.shakeandco.com***

**Showbiz Software Store & Cafe**
500 S. Sepulveda Blvd., Ground Fl.
Los Angeles, CA 90049
***Tel: (310) 471-9330***
***www.showbizsoftware.com***

**Showbiz Store & Cafe**
19 W. 21st Street, Ground Fl.
New York, NY 10010
***Tel: (212) 366-9390***
***www.showbizsoftware.com***

**Theatre Circle**
268 W. 44th Street
New York, NY 10036
***Tel: (212) 391-7075***
***www.broadwaynewyork.com***

**UCLA BookZone**
308 Westwood Plaza
Los Angeles, CA 90024
***Tel: (310) 206-4041***
***www.uclastore.com***

**University of Southern California (USC) Bookstore**
840 Childs Way
Los Angeles, CA 90089
***Tel: (213) 740-0066***
***www.uscbookstore.com***

**The Writers Store**
2040 Westwood Boulevard
Los Angeles, CA 90025
***Tel: (310) 441-5151***
***www.writersstore.com***

**ABC News VideoSource**
125 West End Ave.
New York, NY 10023
***Tel: (212) 456-5421***
***www.abcnewsvsource.com***
***Footage: ABC News From 1963 to Present***

**Adventure Pictures**
350 Alabama Street, Ste. 1
San Francisco, CA 94110
***Tel: (415) 431-1122***
***www.adpix.com***
***Footage: Adventure Sports & Travel***

**Air Hollywood**
***Tel: (818) 890-6801***
***www.airhollywood.com***
***Footage: Airplanes & Airports***

**Alaska Stock Footage Library**
***www.akvideo.com***
***Footage: Alaska***

**All Stock**
***Tel: (310) 317-9996***
***www.all-stock.com***
***Footage: All Subjects***

**AM Stock-Cameo Film Library**
10513 Burbank Blvd.
N. Hollywood, CA 91601
***Tel: (818) 762-7865***
***www.amstockcameo.com***
***Footage: Nature; Skylines & Structures***

**Ambient Images**
***Tel: (310) 312-6640***
***www.ambientimages.com***
***Footage: California & New York***

**America by Air Stock Footage Library**
154 Euclid Boulevard
Lantana, FL 33462
***Tel: (800) 488-6359***
***www.americabyair.com***
***Footage: Aerials; Nature; World Culture***

**Animals Animals Enterprises**
17 Railroad Avenue
Chatham, NY 12037
***Tel: (518) 392-5500***
***www.animalsanimals.com***
***Footage: Animals & Earth Scenes***

**Ani Stock**
***Tel: (800) 901-3709***
***www.anistock.com***
***Footage: Animation & Special FX***

**Apex Stock**
6725 W. Sunset Blvd., Ste. 490
Hollywood, CA 90028
***Tel: (323) 443-2580***
***www.animationtrip.com***
***Footage: A-Z Subjects***

**Artbeats Digital Film Library**
***Tel: (541) 863-4429***
***www.artbeats.com***
***Footage: All Subjects***

**Battlegrounds**
***www.battlegroundsvideo.com***
***Footage: Military and Generic***

**BBC Motion Gallery**
747 Third Avenue, 29th Fl.
New York, NY 10017
***Tel: (212) 705-9399***
***www.bbcfootage.com***
***Footage: Art; News; Newsreels & More***

**BBC Motion Gallery**
4144 Lankershim Blvd., Ste. 200
N. Hollywood, CA 91602
***Tel: (818) 299-9720***
***www.bbcfootage.com***
***Footage: Art; Current Events; Travel & More***

**Best Shot**
***www.bestshotfootage.com***
***Footage: All Subjects***

**Blacklight Films**
3371 Cahuenga Blvd., W.
Los Angeles, CA 90068
***Tel: (323) 436-7070***
***www.blacklightfilms.com***
***Footage: All Subjects***

**Blue Fier Photography**
***Tel: (818) 344-5527***
***www.bluefier.com***

*Footage: Skylines; Sunsets; Water & More*

**Blue Sky Stock Footage**
*Tel: (310) 859-4709*
*www.blueskyfootage.com*
*Footage: Aerials; Clouds; Cityscapes*

**Broadcast Quality**
2334 Ponce De Leon Blvd., Ste. 200
Coral Gables, FL 33134
*Tel: (305) 461-5416*
*www.broadcastquality.com*
*Footage: All Subjects*

**Budget Films Stock Footage**
4427 Santa Monica Blvd.
Los Angeles, CA 90029
*Tel: (323) 660-0187*
*www.budgetfilms.com*
*Footage: Beauty; Current Events; Techno*

**Buyout Footage**
*Tel: (714) 693-1250*
*www.buyoutfootage.com*
*Footage: Classic - Contemporary*

**The C Group, Inc.**
*Tel: (919) 828-4086*
*www.cgfilm.com*
*Footage: N. Carolina Cities, Farms & More*

**CBS News Archives**
524 W. 57th Street
New York, NY 10019
*Tel: (212) 975-2875*
*Footage: CBS News 1954 To Present*

**The Cinema Guild, Inc.**
115 West 30th Street, Ste. 800
New York, NY 10001
*Tel: (800) 732-5522/(212) 685-6242*
*www.cinemaguild.com*
*Footage: All Subjects*

**Dick Clark Media Archives**
2900 Olympic Blvd.
Santa Monica, CA 90404
*Tel: (310) 253-4600*
*www.dickclarkproductions.com*
*Footage: 1950-Today Music Performances*

**Classic Images**
469 S. Bedford Drive
Beverly Hills, CA 90212
*Tel: (310) 277-0400*
*www.classicimg.com*
*Footage: Vintage & Contemporary Images*

**Clay Lacy Aviation**
*Tel: (818) 989-2900*
*www.claylacy.com*
*Footage: Aerials*

**CNN Image Source**
One CNN Ctr. 12th Fl./N. Tower
Atlanta, GA 30303
*Tel: (404) 827-3326*
*www.cnnimagesource.com*
*Footage: 1980 To Present Current Events*

**Collegiate Images**
*Tel: (954) 343-8000*
*www.collegiateimages.com*
*Footage: College Sports*

**COMPRO Stock**
*www.compro-atl.com*
*Footage: Landscapes & Structures*

**Compass Light**
*Tel: (207) 236-2078*
*www.compasslight.com*
*Footage: Classic*

**Corbis**
6060 Center Drive, Ste. 100
Los Angeles, CA 90045
*Tel: (323) 602-5750*
*Tel: (206) 373-6000 (Seattle)*
*www.corbismotion.com*
*Footage: All Subjects*

**Corbis**
902 Broadway
New York, NY 10010
*Tel: (212) 777-6200*
*www.corbismotion.com*
*Footage: All Subjects*

**Custom Medical Stock Photo**
3660 W. Irving Park Road
Chicago, IL 60618
*Tel: (773) 267-3100*
*www.cmsp.com*
*Footage: Medical & Science*

**Digital Juice**
*Tel: (352) 369-0930*
*www.digitaljuice.com*
*Footage: All Subjects*

**Documentary Educational Resources**
101 Morse Street
Watertown, MA 02472
*Tel: (617) 926-0491*
*www.der.org*
*Footage: Anthropology; Cultures & People*

**Eastman Kodak Company**
343 State Street
Rochester, NY 14650
*Tel: (800) 242-2424/(585) 724-4000*
*www.kodak.com*
*Footage: All Subjects*

**Easy Street Productions**
*Tel: (301) 471-8058*
*www.publicdomainfootage.com*
*Footage: All Subjects*

**F.I.L.M. Archives, Inc.**
35 W. 35th St., Ste. 504
New York, NY 10001
*Tel: (212) 696-2616*
*www.filmarchivesonline.com*
*Footage: 1896 To Present*

**Film & Video Stock Shot**
*Tel: (818) 760-2098*
*www.stockshots.com*
*Footage: Aerials; Cartoons; Locations*

**Fish Films Footage World**
*www.footageworld.com*
*Footage: All Subjects*

**FootageBank**
*Tel: (310) 822-1400*
*www.footagebank.com*
*Footage: Aerials, Animals, Underwater*

**Footage Hollywood**
10520 Magnolia Blvd.
N. Hollywood, CA 91601
*Tel: (818) 760-1500*
*www.footagehollywood.com*
*Footage: Vintage To Present Film Trailers*

**Footage, Inc.**
***Tel: (626) 395-9593***
***www.efootage.com***
*Footage: All Subjects*

**FootageHouseHD**
***Tel: (920-336-8937***
***www.footagehousehd.com***
*Footage: All Subjects/HD*

**Footage.Net**
28 Harrison Ave., Ste. 48
Englishtown, NJ 07720
***Tel: (732) 792-6710***
***www.footage.net***
*Footage: All Subjects*

**Freewheelin' Films Stock Footage**
***Tel: (970) 925-2640***
***www.fwf.com***
*Footage: Motor Sports*

**Getty Images**
6300 Wilshire Blvd., 16th Fl.
Los Angeles, CA 90048
***Tel: (323) 202-4200***
***Tel: (312) 344-4500 (Chicago)***
***Tel: (206) 925-5000 (Seattle)***
***www.gettyimages.com***
*Footage: All Subjects*

**Getty Images**
75 Varick Street
New York, NY 10013
***Tel: (646) 613-4000***
***www.gettyimages.com***
*Footage: All Subjects*

**Al Giddings Images**
***www.algiddings.com***
*Footage: Natural History & Oceans*

**Historic Films**
211 Third Street
Greenport, NY 11944
***Tel: (631) 477-9700***
***www.historicfilms.com***
*Footage: All Subjects*

**Hollywood Newsreel Syndicate**
***Tel: (323) 833-5920***
***www.hollywoodnewsreel.com***
*Footage: 1940s To Present Awards; Celebrities*

**Jalbert Productions Inc.**
***Tel: (631) 351-5878***
***www.jalbertfilm.com***
*Footage: Action & Olympic Sports*

**Jupiterimages Corporation**
6000 N. Forest Park Drive
Peoria, IL 61614
***Tel: (309) 687-0187***
***www.jupiterimages.com***
*Footage: All Subjects*

**Leonard Rue Video Productions**
138 Millbrook Road
Blairstown, NJ 07825
***Tel: (908) 362-6616***
***www.ruevideo.com***
*Footage: Scenics & Wildlife*

**Library of Moving Images**
6671 Sunset Blvd., Bungalow 1581
Hollywood, CA 90028
***Tel: (323) 469-7499***
***www.libraryofmovingimages.com***
*Footage: 1870s To Present*

**Lynn and Louis Wolfson II Florida Moving Image Archives**
***Tel: (305) 375-1505***
***www.fmia.org***
*Footage: Caribbean; Cuba; Florida; Space*

**MacGillivray Freeman Films**
P.O. Box 205
Laguna Beach, CA 92652
***Tel: (949) 494-1055***
***www.macfreefilms.com***
*Footage: Exotic/Tropical Locations; Nature*

**National Geographic Digital Motion**
1145 17th Street, NW
Washington, D.C. 20036
***Tel: (202) 857-7665***
***www.ngdigitalmotion.com***
*Footage: Archeology; Archival; Wildlife*

**NBC News Archives**
30 Rockefeller Plaza, Ste. 280E
New York, NY 10012
***Tel: (212) 664-3797***
***www.nbcnewsarchives.com***
*Footage: NBC News From 1940s To Present*

**Pan American Video**
***Tel: (707) 822-3800***
***www.panamvideo.com***
*Footage: Archive 1900-1970s*

**Photovault**
***Tel: (707) 775-2562***
***www.photovault.com***
*Footage: All Subjects*

**Producers Library**
10832 Chandler Blvd.
N. Hollywood, CA 91601
***Tel: (818) 752-9097***
***www.filmfootage.com***
*Footage: 1950s Americana; Film Outs & Hollywood*

**Reuters**
3 Times Square
New York, NY 10036
***Tel: (646) 223-4000***
***www.reuters.com***
*Footage: 1896 To Present News Archive*

**Shooting Star International**
1441 N. McCadden Place
Hollywood, CA 90028
***Tel: (323) 469-2020***
***www.shootingstaragency.com***
*Footage: Celebrities; Movie Stills & News*

**Shuttter Stock Images**
60 Broadway St., 30th Fl.
New York, NY 10004
***Tel: (646) 419-4452***
***www.footage.shutterstock.com***
*Footage: All Subjects*

**Ski Net**
***www.skinet.com***
*Footage: Aerials; Cities; Time Lapse; Water*

**Sony Stock Footage**
10202 W. Washington Blvd.
Culver City, CA 92032
***Tel: (310) 244-3704/(866) 275-6919***
***www.sonypicturesstockfootage.com***

Footage: All Subjects

**Source Stock Footage Library**
*Tel: (520) 298-4810*
*www.sourcefootage.com*
*Footage: Aerials; Destinations; Sports*

**Splash News & Picture Agency**
333 W. Washington Blvd., Ste. 508
Marina Del Rey, CA 90292
*Tel: (310) 821-2666*
*Tel: (305) 666-7778 (Miami)*
*Tel: (212) 619-2666 (New York)*
*www.splashnews.com*
*Footage: All Subjects*

**Stock Shop**
*Tel: (866) 663-1153*
*www.stockshop.com*
*Footage: All Subjects*

**StormStock Library**
*Tel: (817) 276-9500*
*www.stormstock.com*
*Footage: Floods; Hurricanes; Storms*

**Thought Equity Motion**
1530 16th Street, 6th Fl.
Denver, CO 80202
*Tel: (720) 382-2869*
*www.thoughtequity.com*
*Footage: All Subjects*

**Transtock**
*Tel: (310) 827-3440*
*www.transtock.com*
*Footage: Transportation Stock Footage*

**UCLA Film & TV Archive**
1015 N. Cahuenga Boulevard
Hollywood, CA 90038
*Tel: (323) 462-4921*
*www.cinema.ucla.edu*
*Footage: 1900s-Present Newsreels*

**Universal Studios Stock Footage Library**
100 Universal Plaza/Bldg. 2313/213
Universal City, CA 91608
*Tel: (818) 777-1695*
*www.universalstudios.com*
*Footage: All Subjects*

**U.S. Olympic Team**
USOC Broadcast Media
One Olympic Plaza
Colorado Springs, CO 80909
*Tel: (719) 632-5551*
*www.usolympicteam.com*
*Footage: Olympics*

**Vanderbilt Television News Archive**
110 21st Ave. South, Ste. 704
Nashville, TN 37203
*Tel: (615) 322-2927*
*www.tvnews.vanderbilt.edu*
*Footage: Olympics*

**Videometry**
330 Townsend Street, Ste. 117
San Francisco, CA 94103
*Tel: (415) 218-6742*
*www.videometry.com*
*Footage: Americana; Food; Locations*

**Video Tape Library**
1525 N. Crescent Drive, Ste. 2
Los Angeles, CA 90046
*Tel: (323) 656-4330*
*www.videotapelibrary.com*
*Footage: All Subjects; 2+ Million Images*

**WGBH Stock Sales**
One Guest Street
Boston, MA 02134
*Tel: (617) 300-3939*
*www.wgbhstocksales.org*
*Footage: All Subjects*

**Wings Wildlife Production, Inc.**
*www.wildlifelibrary.com*
*Footage: African & North American Wildlife*

**WireImage**
6300 Wilshire Blvd., 16th Fl.
Los Angeles, CA 90048
*Tel: (323) 202-4200*
*www.wireimage.com*
*Footage: All Subjects*

**WireImage**
75 Varick Street, 5th Fl.
New York, NY 10013
*Tel: (646) 613-4000*
*www.wireimage.com*
*Footage: All Subjects*

**Woodfin Camp & Associates**
341 W. 38th St., 7th Fl.
New York, NY 10018
*Tel: (212) 481-6900*
*Footage: Occupations; Politicians; Writers*

**WorldClips Stock Video Footage**
*www.worldclips.tv*
*Footage: Chicago & More*

**WPA Film Library**
16101 S. 108th Avenue
Orland Park, IL 60465
*Tel: (708) 460-0555*
*www.wpafilmlibrary.com*
*Footage: All Subjects*

**Wrightwood Laboratories**
*Tel: (702) 257-8822*
*www.wrightwood.com*
*Footage: All Subjects*

**WTTW Digital Archives**
5400 N. St. Louis Avenue
Chicago, IL 60625
*Tel: (773) 509-5412*
*www.wttwdigitalarchives.com*
*Footage: Chicago & More*

**AFI Silver Theatre**
8633 Colesville Road
Silver Spring, MD 20910
***Tel: (301) 495-6720***
***www.afi.com/silver***

**AMC Entertainment**
920 Main Street
Kansas City, MO 64105
***Tel: (816) 221-4000***
***www.amctheatres.com***
**Includes Magic Johnson Theatres*

**ArcLight Hollywood**
6360 Sunset Boulevard
Hollywood, CA 90028
***Tel: (323) 464-4226***
***www.arclightcinemas.com***

**B & B Theatres**
P.O. Box 825
Liberty, MO 64069
***Tel: (816) 407-7469***
***www.bandbtheatres.com***

**B & B Theatres**
P.O. Box 171
Salisbury, MO 65281
***Tel: (660) 388-5219***
***www.bandbtheatres.com***

**Carmike Cinemas**
1301 First Avenue /P.O. Box 391
Columbus, GA 31820
***Tel: (706) 576-3400***
***www.carmike.com***

**Chakeres Theatres**
P.O. Box 1200
Springfield, OH 45501
***Tel: (937) 323-6447***
***www.chakerestheatres.com***

**Cinemark USA, Inc.**
3900 Dallas Parkway, Ste. 500
Plano, TX 75093
***Tel: (972) 665-1000/(800) 246-3627***
***www.cinemark.com***

**Cineplex Entertainment**
1303 Yonge Street
Toronto, ON M4T 2Y9, Canada
***Tel: (416) 323-6600***
***www.cineplex.com***

**Dickinson Theatres**
6801 W. 107th Street
Overlook Park, KS 66212
***Tel: (913) 432-2334***
***www.dtmovies.com***

**Georgia Theatre Company**
500 Sea Island Rd.
St. Simons Island, GA 31522
***Tel: (912) 634-5192***
***www.georgiatheatrecompany.com***

**Harkins Theatres**
7511 E. McDonald Drive
Scottsdale, AZ 85250
***Tel: (480) 627-7777***
***www.harkinstheatres.com***

**Hollywood Theaters**
919 SW Taylor
Portland, OR 97205
***Tel: (503) 221-7090***
***www.gohollywood.com***

**Ice Theatres**
210 W. 87th Street, 2nd Fl.
Chicago, IL 60620
***Tel: (773) 892-3204***
***www.icetheatres.com***

**IMAX Corporation**
3003 Exposition Blvd.
Santa Monica, CA 90404
***Tel: (310) 255-5500***
***www.imax.com***

**Kerasotes Theatres**
224 N. Des Plaines
Chicago, IL 60661
***Tel: (312) 777-0480***
***www.kerasotes.com***

**Krikorian Premiere Theaters**
131 Palos Verdes Blvd.
Redondo Beach, CA 90277
***Tel: (310) 791-8688***
***www.krikoriantheatres.com***

**Laemmle Theatres**
11523 Santa Monica Blvd.
Los Angeles, CA 90025
***Tel: (310) 478-1041***
***www.laemmle.com***

**Landmark Theatre Corporation**
2222 S. Barrington Ave.
Los Angeles, CA 90064
***Tel: (310) 473-6701***
***www.landmarktheatres.com***

**Malco Theatres**
5851 Ridgeway Center Pkwy.
Memphis, TN 38120
***Tel: (901) 761-3480***
***www.malco.com***

**Mann Theatres**
16530 Ventura Blvd., Ste. 500
Encino, CA 91436
***Tel: (818) 784-6266***
***www.manntheatres.com***

## FILMMAKERS:

**THERE ARE ALMOST 40,000 MOVIE SCREENS IN AMERICA. ***EPP* CHALLENGES YOU TO MAKE A BETTER MOVIE AND GET IT SCREENED IN ANY ONE OF THESE THEATERS!!!**

**Marcus Theatres Corp.**
100 E. Wisconsin Ave., Ste. 2000
Milwaukee, WI 53203
***Tel: (414) 905-1500***
***www.marcustheatres.com***

**Muvico Theatres**
3101 N. Federal Hwy., 6th Fl.
Ft. Lauderdale, FL 33306
***Tel: (954) 564-6550***
***www.muvico.com***

**National Amusements**
200 Elm Street
P.O. Box 9126
Dedham, MA 02026
***Tel: (781) 461-1600***
***www.nationalamusements.com***

**Nickelodeon Theatres**
210 Lincoln Street
Santa Cruz, CA 95060
***Tel: (831) 426-7500***
***www.thenick.com***

**Pacific Theatres at The Grove**
189 The Grove Drive
Los Angeles, CA 90036
***Tel: (323) 692-0829***
***www.thegrovela.com***

**Pacific Theatres**
120 N. Robertson Blvd.
Los Angeles, CA 90048
***Tel: (310) 657-8420***
***www.pacifictheatres.com***

**Rave Motion Pictures**
3333 Welborn St., Ste. 100
Dallas, TX 75219
***Tel: (972) 692-1700***
***www.ravemotionpictures.com***

**Red Vic Movie House**
1727 Haight Street
San Francisco, CA 94117
***Tel: (415) 668-3994***
***www.redvicmoviehouse.com***

**Regal Cinemas**
7132 Regal Lane
Knoxville, TN 37918
***Tel: (865) 922-1123***
***www.regalcinemas.com***

**R/C Theatres**
231 W. Cherry Hill Court
P.O. Box 1056
Reisterstown, MD 21136
***Tel: (410) 526-4774***
***www.rctheatres.com***

**Roxie Theater**
3117 16th Street
San Francisco, CA 94103
***Tel: (415) 863-1087***
***www.roxie.com***

**Starplex Cinemas**
7502 Greenville Ave., Ste. 480
Dallas, TX 75231
***Tel: (214) 692-6494***
***www.starplexcinemas.com***

**Studio Movie Grill**
11300 N. Central Expwy., Ste. 200
Dallas, TX 75243
***Tel: (972) 388-7888***
***www.studiomoviegrill.com***

**Wehrenberg Theatres**
12800 Manchester Road
St. Louis, MO 63131
***Tel: (314) 822-4520***
***www.wehrenberg.com***

***Your #1 Resource for Theatre Ownership & Industry Information:***

**National Association of Theatre Owners**
750 First Street, NE - Ste. 1130
Washington, D.C. 20002
***Tel: (202) 962-0054***
***www.natoonline.org***

***Your #1 Resource for Cinema Advertising & In-Theatre Events:***

**National CineMedia**
9110 E. Nichols Ave., Ste. 200
Centennial, CO 80112
***Tel: (303) 792-3600***
***www.ncm.com***

**Academy Players Directory**
1313 N. Vine Street
Hollywood, CA 90028
***Tel: (310) 247-3058***
***www.playersdirectory.com***

**Advertising Age**
711 Third Avenue
New York, NY 10017
***Tel: (212) 210-0100***
***www.adage.com***

**Advertising Age**
6500 Wilshire Blvd., Ste. 2300
Los Angeles, CA 90048
***Tel: (323) 651-3710***
***www.adage.com***

**Adweek**
5055 Wilshire Blvd.
Los Angeles, CA 90036
***Tel: (323) 525-2270***
***www.adweek.com***

**Adweek**
770 Broadway, 7th Fl.
New York, NY 10003
***Tel: (646) 654-5421***
***www.adweek.com***

**American Cinematographer**
1782 N. Orange Drive
Hollywood, CA 90028
***Tel: (323) 969-4333***
***www.theasc.com***

**Animation Magazine**
30941 W. Agoura Rd., Ste. 102
Westlake Village, CA 91361
***Tel: (818) 991-2884***
***www.animationmagazine.net***

**Back Stage**
5055 Wilshire Boulevard
Los Angeles, CA 90036
***Tel: (323) 525-2356***
***www.backstage.com***

**Back Stage**
770 Broadway
New York, NY 10003
***Tel: (646) 654-5700***
***www.backstage.com***

**Black Talent News**
8306 Wilshire Blvd., Ste. 2057
Beverly Hills, CA 90211
***Tel: (310) 929-5297***
***www.blacktalentnews.com***

**Boxoffice Magazine**
9107 Wilshire Blvd., Ste. 450
Beverly Hills, CA 90210
***Tel: (310) 876-9090***
***www.boxoffice.com***

**Box Office Mojo.com**
***www.boxofficemojo.com***

**Breakdown Services**
2140 Cotner Avenue, 3rd Fl.
Los Angeles, CA 90025
***Tel: (310) 276-9166***
***www.breakdownservices.com***

**Breakdown Services**
850 7th Ave., Ste. 600
New York, NY 10019
***Tel: (212) 869-2003***
***www.breakdownservices.com***

**Call Sheet**
770 Broadway
New York, NY 10003
***Tel: (323) 525-2231***
***www.backstage.com/callsheet***

**Cinefantastique**
***www.cinefantastiqueonline.com***

**The Costume Designer**
Costume Designers Guild
11969 Ventura Blvd., 1st Fl.
Studio City, CA 91604
***Tel: (818) 752-2400***
***www.costumedesignersguild.com***

**Create Magazine**
***www.createmagazine.com***

**Creative Handbook**
10152 Riverside Drive
Toluca Lake, CA91602

WOULD YOU GO TO WORK
WITHOUT SHOES?
THERE ARE SOME THINGS YOU NEED IN LIFE...
The Hollywood Reporter
“A must-have for Entertainment Professionals”
SIGN UP FOR A 4-WEEK FREE TRIAL
866.525.2150 - 323.525.2150 - www.thr.com
THR digital edition

***Tel: (818) 752-3200***
***www.creativehandbook.com***

**Creative Screenwriting**
6404 Hollywood Blvd., Ste. 415
Los Angeles, CA 90028
***Tel: (323) 957-1405***
***www.creativescreenwriting.com***

**Debbie's Book**
P.O. Box 6488
Altadena, CA 91003
***Tel: (626) 798-7968***
***www.debbiesbook.com***

**DGA Magazine**
7920 Sunset Boulevard
Los Angeles, CA 90046
***Tel: (310) 289-2000***
***www.dga.org***

**Digital Video (DV) Magazine**
New Bay Media
810 Seventh Avenue, 27th Fl.
New York, NY 10019
***Tel: (212) 378-0400***
***www.dv.com***

**Ebony Magazine**
Johnson Publishing Company
820 S. Michigan Avenue
Chicago, IL 60605
***Tel: (312) 322-9200***
***www.ebony.com***

**Entertainment Today**
12021 Wilshire Blvd., Ste. 398
Los Angeles, CA 90025
***Tel: (213) 387-2060 ext 1***
***www.entertainmenttoday.net***

**Entertainment Weekly**
11766 Wilshire Blvd., Ste. #1700
Los Angeles, CA 90025
***Tel: (310) 268-7200***
***www.ew.com***

**Entertainment Weekly**
1675 Broadway
New York, NY 10019
***Tel: (212) 522-1400***
***www.ew.com***

**Essence**
135 W. 50th Street, 4th Fl.
New York, NY 10020
***Tel: (212) 522-1212***
***www.essence.com***

**EUR Web/Electronic Urban Report**
P.O. Box 412081
Los Angeles, CA 90041
***Tel: (323) 254-9599/(661) 250-7300***
***www.eurweb.com***

**Fade In Magazine**
287 S. Robertson Blvd., Ste. 467
Beverly Hills, CA 90211
***Tel: (323) 653-6065***
***www.fadeinmag.com***

**Film & Video Magazine**
110 William Street, 11th Fl.
New York, NY 10038
***Tel: (212) 621-4900***
***www.filmandvideomagazine.com***

**Film Comment**
Film Society of Lincoln Center
70 Lincoln Center Plaza
New York, NY 10023
***Tel: (212) 875-5610***
***www.filmlinc.com***

**Film Journal**
770 Broadway, 7th Fl.
New York, NY 10003
***Tel: (646) 654-7680***
***www.filmjournal.com***

**Filmmaker Magazine**
68 Jay Street, Rm. 425
Brooklyn, NY 11201
***Tel: (212) 465-8200***
***www.filmmakermagazine.com***

**Film Score Monthly**
6311 Romaine St., Ste. 7109
Hollywood, CA 90038
***Tel: (310) 461-2240***
***www.filmscoremonthly.com***

**Film/Tape World**
21 Orinda Way, Ste. C#343
Orinda, CA 94563
***Tel: (415) 543-6100***
***www.filmtapeworld.com***

**Film & TV Music Guide**
7510 Sunset Blvd., #1041
Los Angeles, CA 90046
***Tel: (818) 995-7458***
***www.musicregistry.com***

**Film Threat**
***www.filmthreat.com***

**Hair, Makeup & Fashion Styling Career Guide**
7119 W. Sunset Blvd., Ste. 392
Los Angeles, CA 90046
***Tel: (323) 913-0500***
***www.makeuphairandstyling.com***

**Hollywood Creative Directory**
5055 Wilshire Boulevard
Los Angeles, CA 90036
***Tel: (323) 525-2369***
***www.hcdonline.com***

**Hollywood Life**
Mail.com Media Corporation
9800 S. La Cienega Blvd., 14th Fl.
Los Angeles, CA 90301
***Tel: (310) 321-5000***
***www.hollywoodlife.com***

**The Hollywood Reporter**
5055 Wilshire Blvd., 6th Fl.
Los Angeles, CA 90036
***Tel: (323) 525-2000***
***www.hollywoodreporter.com***

**The Hollywood Reporter Blu-Book**
5055 Wilshire Blvd., 6th Fl.
Los Angeles, CA 90036
***Tel: (323) 525-2000/(323) 525-2369***
***www.hcdonline.com/blubook***

**Hollywood Scriptwriter Magazine**
P.O. Box 3761
Cerritos, CA 90703
***Tel: (310) 283-1630***

POWER
THINK BOLD.
THINK SUCCESS.
THINK YOU!
Dear Writer,
Want to Write for
Entertainment
Magazines
& Publications?

Step 1: Gather your best clips from all previous writing gigs (including high school and/or college newspaper articles).
Step 2: Create the hippest blog.* *(optional but highly recommended)*
Step 3: Approach editors at your favorite publication and simply ASK for a freelance assignment.

Once you get your "Byline" in print, repeat Step 3!

***www.hollywoodscriptwriter.com***

**InCamera Magazine**
Kodak Student Filmmaker Program
6700 Santa Monica Blvd.
Los Angeles, CA 90038
***Tel: (323) 464-6131***
***www.kodak.com/go/student***

**InCamera Magazine**
Eastman Kodak Company
343 State Street
Rochester, NY 14650
***Tel: (585) 724-4000***
***www.kodak.com/go/student***

**In Focus**
***www.infocus-magazine.com***

**The Independent**
***www.aivf.org***
***www.independent-magazine.org***

**Inside Film Magazine**
8421 Wilshire Blvd., Ste. 200
Beverly Hills, CA 90211
***Tel: (323) 852-0434***
***www.insidefilm.com***

**Jet Magazine**
Johnson Publishing Company
820 S. Michigan Avenue
Chicago, IL 60605
***Tel: (312) 322-9200***
***www.ebonyjet.com***

**Kemps Production Services Handbook**
***www.kftv.com***

**LA 411**
5900 Wilshire Blvd., Ste. 3100
Los Angeles, CA 90036
***Tel: (323) 617-9100***
***www.la411.com***

**LA 411**
360 Park Ave. South
New York, NY 10010
***Tel: (646) 746-6891***
***www.la411.com***

**Locations Magazine**
Association of Film
Commissioners International
109 E. 17th St., Ste. 18
Cheyenne, WY 82001
***Tel: (307) 637-4422***
***www.afci.org***

**Media Week**
770 Broadway, 7th Fl.
New York, NY 10003
***Tel: (646) 654-5553***
***www.mediaweek.com***

**Millimeter Magazine**
***Tel: (818) 236-3667***
***www.millimeter.com***
***www.digitalcontentproducer.com***

**Motion Picture TV & Theatre Directory**
P.O. Box 276
Tarrytown, NY 10591
***Tel: (212) 245-0969***
***www.mpe.net***

**MovieMaker Magazine**
174 Fifth Ave., Ste. 300
New York, NY 10010
***Tel: (212) 766-1100***
***www.moviemaker.com***

**New York Production Guide**
50 N. Main Street, 2nd Fl.
Norwalk, CT 06854
***Tel: (212) 243-0404/(203) 299-1330***
***www.nypg.com***

**NY 411**
360 Park Avenue S., 17th Fl.
New York, NY 10010
***Tel: (646) 746-6400***
***Tel: (646) 746-6891***
***www.newyork411.com***

**P3 Update**
1438 N. Gower, Box 65
Hollywood, CA 90028
***Tel: (323) 315-9477***
***www.p3update.com***

**Playbill**
525 Seventh Avenue
New York, NY 10018
***Tel: (212) 557-5757***
***www.playbill.com***

**Post Magazine**
***www.postmagazine.com***

**Premiere Magazine**
1633 Broadway
New York, NY 10019
***Tel: (212) 767-5400***
***www.premieremag.com***

**Production Hub**
1809 E. Winter Park Rd.
Orlando, FL 32803
***Tel: (407) 629-4122***
***www.productionhhub.com***

**Production Weekly**
3001 Bridgeway Blvd.
Sausality, CA 94965
***Tel: (415) 223-3994***
***www.productionweekly.com***

**Reel Directory**
P.O. Box 1910
Boyes Hot Springs, CA 95416
***Tel: (415) 531-9760***
***www.reeldirectory.com***

**Release Print**
Film Arts Foundation
145 Ninth Street, Ste. 101
San Francisco, CA 94103
***Tel: (415) 552-8760***
***www.filmarts.org***

**Screen Actor Magazine**
Screen Actors Guild
5757 Wilshire Blvd., 7th Fl.
Los Angeles, CA 90036
***Tel: (323) 549-6654***
***www.sag.org***

**Screen Magazine**
340 B Quadrangle Drive
Bolingbrook, IL 60440
***Tel: (312) 640-0800***
***www.screenmag.tv***

**Script Magazine**
Final Draft
26707 W. Agoura Rd. Ste. 205
Calabasas, CA 91302
***Tel: (818) 995-8995***
***www.scriptmag.com***

**Script Magazine**
5638 Sweet Air Road
Baldwin, MD 21013
***Tel: (888) 245-2228***
***www.scriptmag.com***

**Shoot**
650 N. Brunson Ave., #B140
Los Angeles, CA 90004
***Tel: (323) 960-8035***
***www.shootonline.com***

**Shoot**
21st Charles St., Ste. 203
Wesstport, CT 06880
***Tel: (203) 227-1699***
***www.shootonline.com***

**Showbiz Labor Guide**
500 S. Sepulveda Blvd., 4th Fl.
Los Angeles, CA 90049
***Tel: (310) 471-9330***
***www.showbizsoftware.com***

**Shutterbug**
1419 Chaffee Drive, Ste. 1
Titusville, FL 32780
***Tel: (321) 269-3212***
***www.shutterbug.com***

**SMPTE Motion Imaging Journal**
3 Barker Avenue
White Plains, NY 10601
***Tel: (914) 761-1100***
***www.smpte.org***

**The Hollywood Reporter**
5055 Wilshire Blvd., 6th Fl.
Los Angeles, CA 90036
***Tel: (323) 525-2000***
***www.hollywoodreporter.com***

**The Independent**
***www.aivf.org***
***www.independent-magazine.org***

**UPSCALE**
600 Bronner Brothers Way, SW
Atlanta, GA 30310
***Tel: (404) 758-7467***
***www.upscalemagazine.com***

**US Weekly**
1290 Ave. of the Americas, 2nd Fl.
New York, NY 10104
***Tel: (212) 484-1616***
***www.usmagazine.com***

**Variety**
5900 Wilshire Blvd., Ste. 3100
Los Angeles, CA 90036
***Tel: (323) 617-9100***
***www.dailyvariety.com***

**Variety**
360 Park Ave. South
New York, NY 10010
***Tel: (646) 746-7001***
***www.variety.com***

**Written By Magazine**
7000 W. Third Street
Los Angeles, CA 90048
***Tel: (323) 951-4000***
***www.wga.org***

WILL
YOU
write
THE
NEXT
GREAT
ARTICLE
?

**American Film Institute (AFI) Directing Workshop for Women**
2021 N. Western Avenue
Los Angeles, CA 90027
*Tel: (323) 856-7600*
*www.afi.com/education/dww/*

**The American Pavilion Cannes Film Program**
1526 14th Street, Ste. 109
Santa Monica, CA 90404
*Tel: (310) 576.6500*
*www.ampav.com*

**Cinema Makeup School**
3780 Wilshire Blvd., Ste. 300
Los Angeles, CA 90010
*Tel: (213) 368-1234*
*www.cinemamakeup.com*

**Creative Artists Agency Agent Trainee Program**
2000 Avenue of the Stars
Los Angeles, CA 90067
*Tel: (424) 288-2000*
*www.caa.com*

**Directors Guild Assistant Directors Training Program**
15301 Ventura Blvd., Bldg E #1075
Sherman Oaks, CA 91403
*Tel: (818) 386-2545*
*www.trainingplan.org*

**Directors Guild Producer Training Plan**
15301 Ventura Blvd., Bldg E #1075
Sherman Oaks, CA 91403
*Tel: (818) 386-2545*
*www.trainingplan.org*

**Disney | ABC Directing Fellowship Program**
500 S. Buena Vista Street
Burbank, CA 91521
*www.disneyabctalentdevelopment.com*

**Disney | ABC Institute of American Indian Arts Summer TV & Film Workshop**
*Tel: (505) 424-5716*
*www.disneyabctalentdevelopment.com*
*www.iaia.edu/newmedia*

**Disney | ABC Talent Development Programs**
Disney | ABC Television Group
Talent Development & Diversity
500 S. Buena Vista Street
Burbank, CA 91521-4016
*www.disneyabctalentdevelopment.com*

**Film Independent Screenwriters Lab**
9911 W. Pico Boulevard
Los Angeles, CA 90035
*Tel: (310) 432-1200*
*www.filmindependent.org*

**FOX Entertainment Group Programs**
*www.foxcareers.com*
*www.fox.com/diversity*

**FOX Writers Initiative**
FOX Broadcasting Company
Diversity Outreach Program
P.O. Box 900
Beverly Hills, CA 90213
*Tel: (310) 369-1000*
*www.fox.com/diversity*

**GE/NBC Universal Leadership Program**
*www.gecareers.com*

**Guy A. Hanks & Marvin Miller Screenwriting Program/The Cosby Program**
USC School of Cinematic Arts
900 W. 34th Street, Rm. 235
Los Angeles, CA 90089
*Tel: (213) 740-8194*
*www.cosbyprogram.com*

**Hollywood Cinema Production Resources (CPR)**
9700 S. Sepulveda Blvd.
Los Angeles, CA 90045
*Tel: (310) 258-0123*
*www.hollywoodcpr.org*

**Hollywood Mentorship Program**
*www.hollywoodmentorship program.org*

*"We're always looking for writers who are ready to pop. That means strong writers with unique voices who have been working on their writing professionally. People who have taken time to learn the industry and have been trying to make their way."*

**Doreene Hamilton**
Executive Director

The Guy Hanks & Marvin Miller Screenwriting Program, known and respected throughout the industry as "The Cosby Program," is sailing toward its second decade of propelling emerging and established tv and feature film writers to the next level of their writing careers.

Named in honor of Mrs. Camille Cosby's father, Guy Hanks and the late Marvin Miller, a veteran producer who worked with Dr. William H. Cosby, this privately-funded, intensive 15-week Program meets twice weekly with up to 15 Program participants on the campus of the University of Southern California (USC), beginning each February. Evening classes focus on writing instruction, lectures and discussions about African-American history, culture and iconography.

## Call All Great Writers!

### Here is the Cosby Program Overview to Get You Going:

- Tuition is free.
- Up to 15 writers are chosen from @ 200 applicants each year.
- Writers who complete the Program are armed with sellable screenplays, strong spec scripts and strong writing samples that can help move your career forward.
- Although there is no stipend, workshop participation and books are provided free of charge.
- Participants must reside in the Los Angeles area while attending the Program.
- Success Stories & Possible Perks? Writers who've completed the Cosby Program have secured literary agents, optioned their work, gained acceptance into other Programs, have secured full-time writing assignments and work as show runners.

**For more information or to obtain an application visit www.CosbyProgram.com.**

**ICM Agent Trainee Program**
10250 Constellation Blvd.
Los Angeles, CA 90067
***Tel: (310) 550-4000***
***www.icmtalent.com***

**ICM Agent Trainee Program**
825 8th Avenue, 26th Fl.
New York, NY 10019
***Tel: (212) 556-5600***
***www.icmtalent.com***

**IFP Independent Filmmaker Lab**
68 Jay Street, Rm. 425
Brooklyn, NY 11201
***Tel: (212) 465-8200***
***www.ifp.org***

**Inner City Filmmakers**
68 Jay Street, Rm. 425
Brooklyn, NY 11201
***Tel: (310) 264-3992***
***www.innercityfilmmakers.com***

**Kodak Cinematography Workshop**
343 Eighth Street
Rochester, NY 14650
***Tel: (585) 724-4000***
***www.kodak.com/us/en/motion/education***

**Kodak Student Filmmaker Program**
6700 Santa Monica Blvd.
Hollywood, CA 90038
***Tel: (323) 464-6131***
***www.kodak.com/go/student***

**New York DGA Assistant Director Training Program**
1697 Broadway, Ste. 600
New York, NY 10019
***Tel: (212) 397-0930***
***www.dgatrainingprogram.org***

**Nicholl Fellowships In Screenwriting**
Academy of Motion Pictures, Arts & Sciences
8949 Wilshire Boulevard
Beverly Hills, CA 90211
***Tel: (310) 247-3010***
***www.oscars.org/nicholl***

**The Nielsen Company Emerging Leaders Program**
770 Broadway
New York, NY 10003
***Tel: (646) 654-5000***
***www.nielsen.com***

**Sony Pictures Imageworks Professional Academic Excellence Program (IPAX)**
9050 W. Washington Blvd.
Culver City, CA 90232
***Tel: (310) 840-8000***
***www.sonypictures.com/imageworks***

**Peter Stark Producing Program**
USC School of Cinematic Arts
University Park, SCA 366
900 W. 34th Street
Los Angeles, CA 90089
***Tel: (213) 740-3304***
***cinema.usc.edu/stark***

**Streetlights Production Assist. Program**
Raleigh Studios
662 N. Van Ness Ave., Rm. 105
Hollywood, CA 90004
***Tel: (323) 960-4540***
***www.streetlights.org***

**Sundance Screenwriters Lab**
Sundance Institute
8530 Wilshire Blvd., 3rd Fl.
Beverly Hills, CA 90211
***Tel: (310) 360-1981/(801) 328-3456***
***www.sundance.org***

**United Talent Agency Agent Training Program**
9560 Wilshire Boulevard
Beverly Hills, CA 90212
***Tel: (310) 273-6700***
***www.unitedtalent.com/training***

**Walt Disney Feature Animation Talent Development & Associates Program**
500 S. Buena Vista Street
Burbank, CA 91521
***Tel: (818) 560-5000***
***www.disneyanimation.com/careers***

**Walt Disney Imagineering**
1401 Flower Street
Glendale, CA 91201
***Tel: (818) 544-1000***
***www.disney.go.com/disneycareers/imaginations***

**Warner Bros. Feature Production Management Trainee Program**
4000 Warner Blvd.
Burbank, CA 91505
***Tel: (818) 954-6000***
***www.warnerbroscareers.com***

**Warner Bros. STARS (Students Taking A Right Step) Program**
4000 Warner Blvd.
Burbank, CA 91505
***Tel: (818) 954-6000***
***www.warnerbroscareers.com***

**William Morris Endeavor Ent. Agent Training Program**
One William Morris Place
Beverly Hills, CA 90212
***Tel: (310) 859-4000/(310) 285-9000***
***www.wmeentertainment.com***

**William Morris Endeavor Ent. Agent Training Program**
1325 Ave. of the Americas, 15th Fl.
New York, NY 10019
***Tel: (212) 586-5100***
***www.wmeentertainment.com***

**William Morris Endeavor Ent. Agent Training Program**
1600 Division Street, Ste. 300
Nashville, TN 37203
***Tel: (615) 963-3000***
***www.wmeentertainment.com***

**Workplace Hollywood**
1201 W. 5th Street, Ste. T-550
Los Angeles, CA 90017
***Tel: (213) 250-9921***
***www.workplacehollywood.org***

*POWER QUOTE #1:* *"Our Trainees establish their reputation and experience by working with a host of different motion picture, television and commercial teams and production people, different kinds of projects -- so that when they graduate in a business that is driven by reputation and contacts, we have provided the foundation for a wide range of both."*

*POWER QUOTE #2:* *"If you're the kind of person that thrives on change and spontaneity, welcome to film."*

***Sandra Forman***
***Administrator***

The New York DGA Assistant Director Training Program is an intense two-year program that equips trainees to become Assistant Directors (AD's) of motion pictures, television shows and commercials. Each year, five to seven trainees are rigorously tested, interviewed and ultimately selected from a pool of about 300-400 applicants. The trainees then work under the supervision of Directors Guild of America (DGA) members, Second Assistant Directors, First Assistant Directors and Unit Production Managers, learning on the job how to make schedules, attend to the cast, direct extras, oversee the crew as each shot is prepared, create detailed reports and a list of other important duties the AD is responsible for during production. Upon completion of the Program, trainees are eligible to join the DGA as Second Assistant Directors.

## Perks of the Program:

> $673 per week salary, based on a 54 hour work week. (Overtime kicks in after 54 hrs.)
> Trainees are part of a collaborative process, making tons of industry connections
> Trainees learn from DGA members
> Monthly seminars with industry professionals

Do you have what it takes to become a DGA Assistant Director Trainee? Trainees are:

> Friendly and collegial.
> Team players who work well in a team setting.
> Smart.
> Quick-thinking.
> Able to juggle many responsibilities at once. Mult-tasking is critical.
> Able to flourish in a fast-paced, turn-on-a-dime environment.

If you're interested in learning more about 2nd Assistant Directing, visit the DGA Assistant Director Training Program online at **www.DGATrainingProgram.org**. Also, check out filmmaker Terry Gilliam's documentary *"Lost in LaMancha,"* narrated by Jeff Bridges. It's a behind-the-scenes look at the making of this film, in which everything that could go wrong went wrong and the 1st Assistant Director is very prominently featured as a part of the process.

*Talent* DEVELOPMENT...

...it reflects on all of us

# NALIP National Signature Programs

**Dedicated to improving the skills and relationships of our members as they advance their documentary and narrative projects to production and release**

## Latino Writers Lab™

Designed to assist up-and-coming Latino writers who aspire to create independent feature scripts, or work in the film and television industry, but who need skills development and mentoring in order to advance their craft. The LWL is a ten day intensive experience: 5 days in May, 5 days in September with script rewrites completed in between. It is a unique curriculum with direct professional mentoring to help develop strong, viable screenplays for production or sale.

## Latino Producers Academy™

An 11-day intensive residential program each August designed for documentary and narrative producers and directors with projects in development or production. Documentaries that are in post-production edit and score sequences with intensive mentoring on their rough cuts and completion plans. Narrative projects in pre-production work with professional crews and SAG actors to rehearse, shoot, edit and score scenes from their upcoming feature films. Documentary and narrative producers with projects in development spend the Academy working on comprehensive skills development, acquiring strategies to guide projects forward through production and release.

## Doing Your Doc: Diverse Visions, Regional Voices™

If you are stuck in the cutting room or have a trailer that doesn't bring you money, here is a chance to change that. Internationally known story consultant Fernanda Rossi, the Documentary Doctor, teaches you how to create a trailer that will maximize your ability to get funding and how to structure your documentary. Every weekend includes a case study, technical and fundraising advice, plus one-on-one mentorship of all participating projects by artists and industry professionals.

## Latino Media Resource Guide™

NALIP's Latino Media Resource Guide is a directory of Latino filmmakers and resources, filled with information that support independent media makers, including funding resources, diversity jobs opportunities, film school programs, distributors and Latino production companies. It also assembles credits and contact information for Latino/a media artists nationwide, along with their filmographies. Use the LMRG to take your project and career to a new level. Latino/a filmmakers can update their professional profiles and connect with crew around the country. Employers can research and hire Latino professionals.
Visit www.lmrg.nalip.org today!

    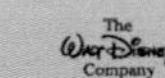   

## Latino Media Market™

The Latino Media Market is designed to bring funders, studio executives, distributors, dealmakers, agents, mentors and employers together with NALIP members and their projects. Select producers can pitch scripts or concepts, show trailers or marketing materials, and otherwise 'sell' their projects, one-on-one, to decision makers interested in Latino projects. Held concurrent to the NALIP National Conference.

**For applications and more information go to www.nalip.org or email Signature Programs Director Octavio Marin at moramar@msn.com**

# WRITING WORKSHOPS

**The COSBY Program/Guy A. Hanks & Marvin Miller Screenwriting Program**
USC School of Cinematic Arts • 900 W. 34th Street, Rm. 235 • Los Angeles, CA 90089 • Tel: (213) 740-8194
*www.cosbyprogram.com*

**Disney | ABC Writing Fellowship Program**
500 S. Buena Vista Street • Burbank, CA 91521 • *www.disneyabctalentdevelopment.com*

**FOX Entertainment Group Writers Initiative**
P.O. Box 900 • Beverly Hills, CA 90213 • Tel: (310) 369-1000 • *www.fox.com/diversity*

**Gotham Writers' Workshop**
555 8th Avenue, Ste. 1402 • New York, NY 10023 • Tel: (212) 974-8377 • *www.writingclasses.com*

**Michael Hauge's Screenplay Mastery**
P.O. Box 57498 • Sherman Oaks, CA 91413 • Tel: (818) 995-4209 • *www.screenplaymastery.com*

**Hollywood Film Institute**
P.O. Box 481252 • Los Angeles, CA 90048 • Tel: (310) 399-6699 • *www.hollywoodu.com*

**Robert McKee Story Seminar**
P.O. Box 452930 • Los Angeles, CA 90045 • Tel: (888) 676-2533 • *www.mckeestory.com*

**New York Film Academy**
100 E. 17th Street • New York, NY 10003 • Tel: (212) 674-4300 • *www.nyfa.com*

**Nickelodeon Writing Fellowship**
231 W. Olive Avenue • Burbank, CA 91502 • (818) 736-3663 • *www.nickwriting.com*

**On the Page**
13907 Ventura Blvd., Ste. 101 • Sherman Oaks, CA 91423 • (818) 905-8124 • *www.onthepage.tv*

**Planet DMA**
14622 Ventura Blvd., #333 • Sherman Oaks, CA 91403 • Tel: (818) 461-9211 • *www.planetdma.com*

**Truby's Writers Studio**
664 Brooktree Road • Santa Monica, CA 90402 • Tel: (310) 573-9630 • *www.truby.com*

**UCLA Extension**
10995 Le Conte Avenue • Los Angeles, CA 90024 • Tel: (310) 825-9971 • *www.uclaextension.edu*

**Writers Boot Camp**
Bergamot Station Arts Center • 2525 Michigan Ave., Bldg. I • Santa Monica, CA 90404 • Tel: (800) 800-1733
*www.writersbootcamp.com*

**Writers on the Verge**
*www.nbcunicareers.com/earlycareersprogram/writersontheverge.shtml*

SESAC's **MUSIC BUSINESS 101.**

**LESSON #1**

It's cool to write songs.
It's even cooler to get paid for it.

Find out how to write a hit song.

# MUSIC

- » Associations & Organizations
- » Awards, Conferences & Events
- » Concert Venues
- » Distribution Companies
- » Duplication & Manufacturing
- » Internships
- » Music & Sound Effects Libraries
- » Music Schools
- » Radio Networks
- » Record Labels
- » Recording Studios
- » Retail Outlets
- » Songwriting Competitions
- » Trade Publications

**Academy of Country Music**
5500 Balboa Blvd., Ste. 200
Encino, CA 91316
***Tel: (818) 788-8000***
***www.acmcountry.com***

**Alliance of Artists & Recording Companies**
700 N. Fairfax St., Ste. 601
Alexandria, VA 22314
***Tel: (703) 535-8101***
***www.aarcroyalties.com***

**American Association of Independent Music**
853 Broadway, Ste. 1406
New York, NY 10003
***Tel: (212) 999 6113***
***www.a2im.org***

**American Federation of Musicians**
3550 Wilshire Blvd., Ste. 1900
Los Angeles, CA 90010
***Tel: (213) 251-4510***
***www.afm.org***

**American Federation of Musicians**
1501 Broadway, Ste. 600
New York, NY 10036
***Tel: (212) 869-1330***
***www.afm.org***

**American Federation of TV & Radio Artists (AFTRA)**
5757 Wilshire Blvd., 9th Fl.
Los Angeles, CA 90036
***Tel: (323) 634-8100***
***www.aftra.org***

**American Federation of TV & Radio Artists (AFTRA)**
260 Madison Ave., 7th Fl.
New York, NY 10016
***Tel: (212) 532-0800***
***www.aftra.org***

**American Guild of Variety Artists**
4741 Laurel Canyon Blvd., Ste. 208
Valley Village, CA 91607
***Tel: (818) 508-9984***

**American Guild of Variety Artists**
363 Seventh Ave., 17th Fl.
New York, NY 10001
***Tel: (212) 675-1003***

**American Guild of Musical Artists**
1430 Broadway, 14th Fl.
New York, NY 10018
***Tel: (212) 265-3687***
***www.musicalartists.org***

**American Music Conference**
5790 Armada Drive
Carlsbad, CA 92008
***Tel: (760) 431-9124***
***www.amc-music.com***

**American Women in Radio & TV**
1760 Old Meadow Road, Ste. 500
McLean, VA 22102
***Tel: (703) 506-3290***
***www.awrt.org***

**Americana Music Association**
411 E. Iris Drive
P.O. Box 128077
Nashville, TN 37204
***Tel: (703) 506-3290***
***www.americanamusic.org***

**Artists For Literacy**
3737 Fillmore Street, #303
San Francisco, CA 94123
***Tel: (415) 307-3181***
***www.artistsforliteracy.org***

**ASCAP**
7920 Sunset Boulevard, 3rd Fl.
Los Angeles, CA 90046
***Tel: (323) 883-1000***
***www.ascap.com***

**ASCAP**
Two Music Square W.
Nashville, TN 37203
***Tel: (615) 742-5000***
***www.ascap.com***

**ASCAP**
One Lincoln Plaza
New York, NY 10023
***Tel: (212) 621-6000***
***www.ascap.com***

Smokey Robinson

Beyoncé

Stevie Wonder

Keyshia Cole

Mary J. Blige

Johnta Austin

Stargate

Diddy

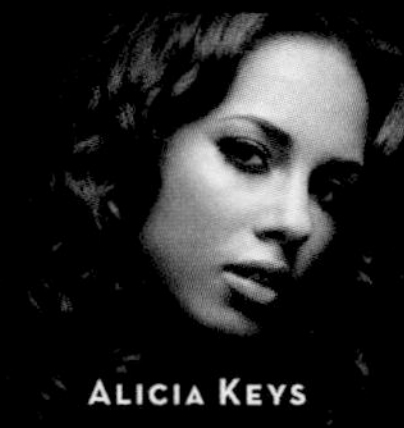
Alicia Keys

Pharrell Williams

We Thank You...
For sharing your soul, thru your music or your pen.
We know it's not easy to delve deep within.
Let us honor you with royalties
and service that knows no end.

Lionel Ritchie

Mary Mary

We Thank You...
For the songs that you write.
Polished 'til just right.
You're the reason why
we continue our fight
against any movement attempting
to devalue your worth.

Usher

Ne-Yo

ASCAP's Rhythm & Soul Creative Team... At Your Service!
Atlanta - 404.685.8699
Los Angeles - 323.883.1000
New York - 212.621.6000

Missy Elliott

Jay Z

Jimmy Jam & Terry Lewis

Ludacris

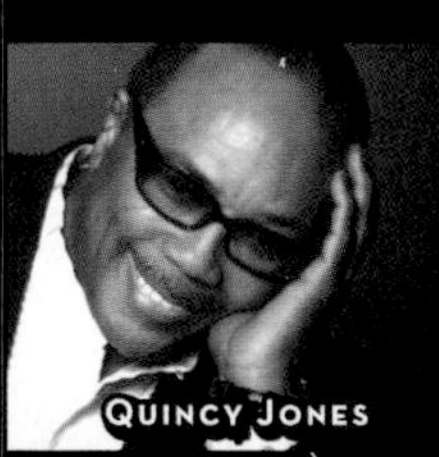
Quincy Jones

Jermaine Dupri

Smokie Norful

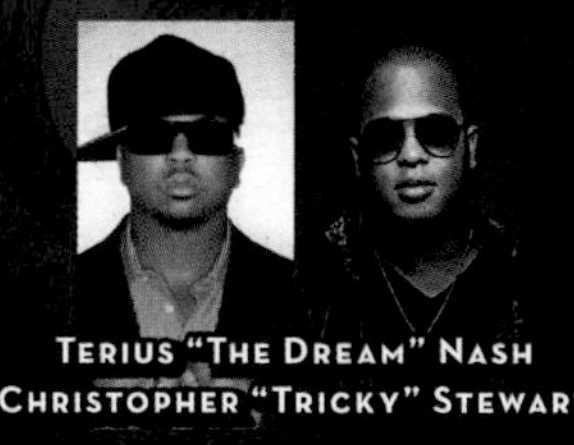
Terius "The Dream" Nash
Christopher "Tricky" Stewart

Chaka Khan

Timbaland

**Association for Women in Communications**
3337 Duke Street
Alexandria, VA 22314
***Tel: (703) 370-7436***
***www.womcom.org***

**Association of Independent Music Publishers**
P.O. Box 69473
Los Angeles, CA 90069
***Tel: (818) 771-7301***
***www.aimp.org***

**Association of Independent Music Publishers**
5 W. 37th Street, 6th Fl.
New York, NY 10018
***Tel: (212) 391-2532***
***www.aimp.org***

**Association of Music Producers**
3 West 18th St., 5th Fl.
New York, NY 10011
***Tel: (212) 924-4100***
***www.ampnow.com***

**Association of Performing Arts Presenters**
1211 Connecticut Ave., NW - Ste. 200
Washington, D.C. 20036
***Tel: (202) 833-2787***
***www.artspresenters.org***

**Association of Talent Agents**
9255 Sunset Blvd., Ste. 930
Los Angeles, CA 90069
***Tel: (310) 274-0628***
***www.agentassociation.com***

**Audio Engineering Society**
60 E. 42nd St., Ste. 2520
New York, NY 10165
***Tel: (212) 661-8528***
***www.aes.org***

**Black Entertainment & Sports Lawyers Association (BESLA)**
P.O. Box 441485
Ft. Washington, MD 20749
***Tel: (301) 248-1818***
***www.besla.org***

**Black Rock Coalition**
P.O. Box 1054/Cooper Station
New York, NY 10276
***Tel: (212) 713-5097***
***www.blackrockcoalition.org***

**Broadcast Music Inc. (BMI)**
8730 Sunset Blvd., 3rd Fl.
Los Angeles, CA 90069
***Tel: (310) 659-9109***
***www.bmi.com***

**Broadcast Music Inc. (BMI)**
320 W. 57th Street
New York, NY 10019
***Tel: (212) 586-2000***
***www.bmi.com***

**Broadcast Music Inc. (BMI)**
10 Music Square E.
Nashville, TN 37203
***Tel: (615) 401-2000***
***www.bmi.com***

**Christian Music Trade Assoc.**
1205 Division Street
Nashville, TN 37203
***Tel: (615) 242-0303***
***www.cmta.com***

**Church Music Publishers Association**
P.O. Box 158992
Nashville, TN 37215
***Tel: (615) 791-0273***
***www.cmpamusic.org***

**College Music Society**
312 E. Pine Street
Missoula, MT 59802
***Tel: (406) 721-9616***
***www.music.org***

**Collegiate Broadcasters, Inc.**
UPS - Hershey Square Center
1152 Mae Street
Hummelstown, PA 17036
***Tel: (713) 348-2935***
***www.collegebroadcasters.org***

**Concert Industry Consortium**
4697 W. Jacquelyn Ave.
Fresno, CA 93722
***Tel: (559) 271-7900***
***www.pollstaronline.com***

**Content Delivery & Storage Association**
182 Nassau Street, Ste. 204
Princeton, NJ 08542
***Tel: (609) 279-1700***
***www.contentdeliveryandstorage.org***

**Country Music Association**
1 Music Circle S.
Nashville, TN 37203
***Tel: (615) 244-2840***
***www.cmaworld.com***

**Country Radio Broadcasters**
819 18th Avenue South
Nashville, TN 37203
***Tel: (615) 327-4487***
***www.crb.org***

**Federal Communications Commission**
445 12th Street, SW
Washington, DC 20554
***Tel: (888) 225-5322***
***www.fcc.gov***

**Gospel Music Association**
1205 Division Street
Nashville, TN 37203
***Tel: (615) 242-0303***
***www.gospelmusic.org***

**Gospel Music Workshop of America**
3908 W. Warren Ave.
Detroit, MI 48208
***Tel: (313) 898-6900***
***www.gmwanational.net***

**Grammy University Network**
The Recording Academy
National Academy of
Recording Arts & Sciences (NARAS)
3030 Olympic Blvd.
Santa Monica, CA 90404
***Tel: (310) 392-3777***

*www.grammy.com*
*www.myspace.com/grammyu*
*www.grammy365.com*

**The Harry Fox Agency**
601 W. 26th St., Ste. 500
New York, NY 10001
*Tel: (212) 834-0100*
*www.harryfox.com*

**Heritage Music Foundation**
*www.hmfgospel.com*

**Hip Hop Summit Action Network**
*www.hsan.org*

**Holy Hip Hop Music Alliance**
*www.holyhiphop.com*

**Home Recording Rights Coalition**
*www.hrrc.org*

**IFCO International Fan Club Organization**
P.O. Box 40328
Nashville, TN 37204
*Tel: (615) 371-9596*
*www.ifco.org*

**International Bluegrass Assoc.**
2 Music Square S., Ste. 100
Nashville, TN 37203
*Tel: (615) 256-3222*
*www.ibma.org*

**International Entertainment Buyers Association**
9 Music Square W.
Nashville, TN 37203
*Tel: (615) 251-9000*
*www.ieba.org*

**Los Angeles Music Network**
P.O. Box 2446
Toluca Lake, CA 91610
*Tel: (818) 769-6095*
*www.lamn.com*

**Media Fellowship International**
P.O. Box 82685
Kenmore, WA 98028
*Tel: (425) 488-3965*
*www.mediafellowship.org*

**Metropolitan Opera Guild**
70 Lincoln Center Plaza
New York, NY 10023
*Tel: (212) 769-7000*
*www.metoperafamily.org*

**Mr. Holland's Opus Foundation**
4370 Tujunga Ave., Ste. 330
Studio City, CA 91604
*Tel: (818) 762-4329*
*www.mhopus.org*

**Music Distributors Association**
14070 Proton Road, Ste. 100 LB 9
Dallas, TX 75244
*Tel: (972) 233-9107 ext. 20*
*www.musicdistributors.org*

**Music Educators National Conference (MENC)**
1806 Robert Fulton Drive
Reston, VA 20191
*Tel: (703) 860-4000*
*www.menc.org*

**Music Library Association**
8551 Research Way, Ste. 180
Middleton, WI 53562
*Tel: (608) 836-5825*
*www.musiclibraryassoc.org*

**Music Publishers Association**
243 Fifth Ave., Ste. 236
New York, NY 10016
*Tel: (212) 327-4044*
*www.mpa.org*

**Music Teachers National Assoc.**
441 Vine Street, Ste. 505
Cincinnati, OH 45202
*Tel: (513) 421-1420*
*www.mtna.org*

**Music Video Production Association**
201 N. Occidental Street
Los Angeles, CA 90026
*Tel: (213) 387-1590*
*www.mvpa.com*

**Musicians Contact Service**
P.O. Box 788
Woodland Hills, CA 91365
*Tel: (818) 888-7879*
*www.musicianscontact.com*

**Nashville Songwriters Assoc.**
1701 Roy Acuff Place
Nashville, TN 37203
*Tel: (615) 256-3354*
*www.nashvillesongwriters.com*

**National Academy of Popular Music**
330 W. 58th St., Ste. 411
New York, NY 10019
*Tel: (212) 957-9230*
*www.songhall.org*

**National Academy of Recording Arts & Sciences/NARAS**
The Recording Academy
3030 Olympic Blvd.
Santa Monica, CA 90404
*Tel: (310) 392-3777*
*www.grammy.com*
**12 Chapters Nationwide*

**National Alliance For Media Arts & Culture**
145 Ninth Street, Ste. 205
San Francisco, CA 94103
*Tel: (415) 431-1391*
*www.namac.org*

**National Association for Music Educators**
1806 Robert Fulton Drive
Reston, VA 20191
*Tel: (703) 860-4000*
*www.menc.org*

**National Assoc. of Black Female Execs in Music & Entertainment (NABFEME)**
59 Maiden Lane, 27th Fl.
New York, NY 10038
*Tel: (212) 424-9568*
*www.nabfeme.org*

**National Association of Broadcasters (NAB)**
1771 N St. NW
Washington, D.C. 20036
***Tel: (202) 429-5300***
***www.nab.org***

**National Association of Record Industry Professionals (NARIP)**
P.O. Box 2446
Toluca Lake CA 91610
***Tel: (818) 769-7007***
***www.narip.com***

**National Association of Music Merchants**
5790 Armada Drive
Carlsbad, CA 92008
***Tel: (760) 438-8001***
***www.namm.org***

**National Association of Recording Merchandisers**
9 Eves Drive, Ste. 120
Marlton, NJ 08053
***Tel: (856) 596-2221***
***www.narm.com***

**National Association of Schools of Music**
11250 Roger Bacon Dr., Ste. 21
Reston, VA 20190
***Tel: (703) 437-0700***
***www.nasm.arts-accredit.org***

**National Convention of Gospel Choirs & Choruses**
***www.ncgccinc.com***

**National Gospel Announcers Guild**
9009 Shetland Court
Indianapolis, IN 46276
***Tel: (313) 898-6900***
***www.nationalgag.org***

**National Music Publishers Association**
101 Constitution Ave., NW, Ste. 705E
Washington, D.C. 20001
***Tel: (202) 742-4375***
***www.nmpa.org***

**National Religious Broadcasters**
9510 Technology Drive
Manassas, VA 20110
***Tel: (703) 330-7000***
***www.nrb.org***

**PROMAX BDA**
1522e Cloverfield Blvd.
Santa Monica, CA 90404
***Tel: (310) 788-7600***
***www.promax.bda.org***

**Radio Advertising Bureau Inc.**
1320 Greenway Dr., Ste. 500
Irving, TX 75038
***Tel: (800) 232-3131***
***www.rab.com***

**The Recording Academy**
National Academy of Recording Arts & Sciences (NARAS)
1702 Union Street
San Francisco, CA 94123
***Tel: (415) 749-0779***
***www.grammy.com***

**The Recording Academy**
National Academy of Recording Arts & Sciences (NARAS)
3030 Olympic Blvd.
Santa Monica, CA 90404
***Tel: (310) 392-3777***
***www.grammy.com***
****12 Chapters Nationwide***

**The Recording Academy**
National Academy of Recording Arts & Sciences (NARAS)
529 14th Street, NW - Ste. 840
Washington, D.C. 20045
***Tel: (202) 662-1341***
***www.grammy.com***

**The Recording Academy**
National Academy of Recording Arts & Sciences (NARAS)
311 Lincoln Rd., Ste. 301
Miami Beach, FL 33139
***Tel: (305) 672-4060***
***www.grammy.com***

**The Recording Academy**
National Academy of Recording Arts & Sciences (NARAS)
3290 Northside Parkway, Ste. 280
Atlanta, GA 30327
***Tel: (404) 816-1380***
***www.grammy.com***

**The Recording Academy**
National Academy of Recording Arts & Sciences (NARAS)
303 W. Erie St., Ste. 210
Chicago, IL 60654
***Tel: (312) 786-1121***
***www.grammy.com***

**The Recording Academy**
National Academy of Recording Arts & Sciences (NARAS)
11 West 42nd St., 27th Fl.
New York, NY 10036
***Tel: (212) 245-5440***
***www.grammy.com***

**The Recording Academy**
National Academy of Recording Arts & Sciences (NARAS)
200 S. Broad Street, Ste. 410
Philadelphia, PA 19102
***Tel: (215) 985-5411***
***www.grammy.com***

**The Recording Academy**
National Academy of Recording Arts & Sciences (NARAS)
493 S. Main St., Ste. 101
Memphis, TN 38103
***Tel: (901) 525-1340***
***www.grammy.com***

**The Recording Academy**
National Academy of Recording Arts & Sciences (NARAS)
1904 Wedgewood Ave.
Nashville, TN 37212
***Tel: (615) 327-8030***
***www.grammy.com***

**The Recording Academy**
National Academy of Recording Arts & Sciences (NARAS)
3601 S. Congress Ave., G-500
Austin, TX 78704

***Tel: (512) 328-7997***
***www.grammy.com***

**The Recording Academy**
National Academy of Recording
Arts & Sciences (NARAS)
159 Western Ave. West, Ste. 485
Seattle, WA 98119
***Tel: (206) 834-1000***
***www.grammy.com***

**Recording Industry Association of America (RIAA)**
1025 F. Street, NW - 10th Fl.
Washington, D.C. 20004
***Tel: (202) 775-0101***
***www.riaa.org***

**Recording Musicians Association**
817 Vine St., Ste. 209
Hollywood, CA 90038
***Tel: (323) 426-4762***
***www.rmaweb.org***

**Rhythm & Blues Foundation**
100 S. Broad St., Ste. 460
Philadelphia, PA 19110
***Tel: (215) 568-1080***
***www.rhythm-n-blues.org***

**Rock & Roll Hall of Fame & Museum**
1100 Rock and Roll Blvd.
Cleveland, OH 44114
***Tel: (216) 781-ROCK/(216) 515-1939***
***www.rockhall.com***

**SESAC**
501 Santa Monica Blvd., Ste. 450
Santa Monica, CA 90401
***Tel: (310) 393-9671***
***www.sesac.com***

**SESAC**
152 W. 57th Street, 57th Fl.
New York, NY 10019
***Tel: (212) 586-3450***
***www.sesac.com***

**SESAC**
55 Music Square E.
Nashville, TN 37203
***Tel: (615) 320-0055***
***www.sesac.com***

**Society of Composers & Lyricists**
8447 Wilshire Blvd., Ste. 401
Beverly Hills, CA 90211
***Tel: (310) 281-2812***
***www.thescl.com***

**Society of Professional Audio Recording Services (SPARS)**
P. O. Box 822643
Dallas, TX 75382
***Tel: (800) 771-7727***
***www.spars.com***

**Society of Singers**
15456 Ventura Blvd., Ste. 304
Sherman Oaks, CA 91403
***Tel: (818) 995-7100***
***www.singers.org***

**Songwriters Guild of America**
1560 Broadway, Ste. 408
New York, NY 10036
***Tel: (917) 309-7869***
***www.songwritersguild.com***

**Songwriters Guild of America**
209 10th Ave. South - Ste. 534
Nashville, TN 37203
***Tel: (615) 742-9945***
***www.songwritersguild.com***

**Songwriters Hall of Fame**
330 W. 58th St., Ste. 411
New York, NY 10019
***Tel: (212) 957-9230***
***www.songhall.org***

**SoundExchange**
1121 14th Street., NW - Ste. 700
Washington, D.C. 20005
***Tel: (202) 640-5858***
***www.soundexchange.com***

**Taxi**
5010 N. Pkwy. Calabasas, Ste. 200
Calabasas, CA 91302
***Tel: (818) 888-2111/(800) 458-2111***
***www.taxi.com***

**Texas Music Office**
P.O. Box 13246
Austin, TX 78711
***Tel: (512) 463-6666***
***www.governor.state.tx.us/music***

**University Musical Society**
Burton Memorial Tower
801 N. University Avenue
Ann Arbor, MI 48109
***Tel: (734) 764-2538***
***www.ums.org***

**Washington Area Music Association**
5263 Occoquan Forest Dr.
Manassas, VA 20112
***Tel: (202) 338-1134***
***www.wamadc.com***

**West Coast Songwriters**
1724 Laurel Street, Ste. 120
San Carlos, CA 94070
***Tel: (650) 654-3966***
***www.westcoastsongwriters.org***

**Women In Music National Network**
1450 Oddstad Drive
Redwood City, CA 94063
***Tel: (866) 305-7963***
***www.womeninmusic.com***

**Young Concert Artists**
250 W. 57th St., Ste. 1222
New York, NY 10019
***Tel: (212) 307-6655***
***www.yca.org***

* A&R Executives
* Artists
* Music Executives
* Producers

& More Contacts for Your Music Career!

A & R Live Hookup!
*www.armusic1.com*

A & R Music1
*www.armusic1.com*

A & R Select
*www.arselect.com*

ASCAP
*www.ascap.com*

BMI
*www.bmi.com*

National Academy of Popular Music
*www.songhall.org*

SESAC
*www.sesac.com*

Society of Composers & Lyricists
*www.thescl.com*

Song Ramp
*www.songramp.com*

SongU
*www.songu.com*

Songwriter 101
*www.songwriter101.com*

Songwriters Boot Camp
*www.christianmusiciansummit.com*

Songwriters Guild of America
*www.songwritersguild.com*

Songwriters Hall of Fame
*www.songhall.org*

TAXI
*www.taxi.com*

**Academy of Country Music Awards**
5500 Balboa Blvd., Ste. 200
Encino, CA 91316
*Tel: (818) 788-8000*
*www.acmcountry.com*

**All Eyes on Me Achievement Awards**
*Tel: (713) 957-6991*
*www.dasouth.com/awards*

**American Music Awards**
Dick Clark Productions
2900 Olympic Blvd.
Santa Monica, CA 90404
*Tel: (310) 255-4600*
*www.dickclarkproductions.com*

**American Drummers Achievement Awards/Zildjian**
22 Longwater Drive
Norwell, MA 02061
*Tel: (800) 229-8672*
*www.zildjian.com*

**American Music Conference**
5790 Armada Drive
Carlsbad, CA 92008
*Tel: (760) 431-9124*
*www.amc-music.com*

**Americana Music Conference**
411 E. Iris Drive
Nashville, TN 37204
*Tel: (615) 386-6936*
*www.americanamusic.org*

**APAP Conference**
Assoc. of Performing Arts Presenters
1211 Connecticut Ave., NW - Ste. 200
Washington, D.C. 20036
*Tel: (202) 833-2787*
*www.artspresenters.org*

**ASCAP Film & Television Music Awards**
7920 W. Sunset Blvd., Ste. 300
Los Angeles, CA 90046
*Tel: (323) 883-1000*
*www.ascap.com*

**ASCAP "I Create Music" Expo**
7920 W. Sunset Blvd., 3rd Fl.
Los Angeles, CA 90046
*Tel: (323) 883-1000*
*Tel: (212) 621-6000*
*www.ascap.com/eventsawards*

**ASCAP Pop Music Awards**
7920 W. Sunset Blvd., 3rd Fl.
Los Angeles, CA 90046
*Tel: (323) 883-1000*
*www.ascap.com*

**ASCAP Rhythm & Soul Awards**
7920 W. Sunset Blvd., 3rd Fl.
Los Angeles, CA 90046
*Tel: (323) 883-1000*
*www.ascap.com*

**Aspen Music Festival & School**
2 Music School Road
Aspen, CO 81611
*Tel: (970) 925-3254*
*www.aspenmusicfestival.com*

**Association of Performing Arts Presenters Conference**
1211 Connecticut Ave., NW - Ste. 200
Washington, D.C. 20036
*Tel: (202) 833-2787*
*www.artspresenters.org*

**Atlantis Music Conference & Festival**
50 Barrett Pkwy., Ste. 1200/PMB 342
Marietta, GA 30066
*Tel: (770) 499-8600*
*www.atlantismusic.com*

**Bandwidth Technology Conference**
P.O. Box 170602
San Francisco, CA 94117
*Tel: (415) 823-4540*
*www.bandwidthconference.com*

**BET Awards**
One BET Plaza
1235 W Street, NE
Washington, D.C. 20018
*Tel: (202) 608-2000*
*www.bet.com*

**Billboard Awards**
770 Broadway
New York, NY 10003
***Tel: (646) 654-4625***
***www.billboardevents.com***

**Billboard Back Stage Pass Conference**
770 Broadway
New York, NY 10003
***Tel: (646) 654-4660***
***www.billboardevents.com***

**Billboard Film & TV Music Conference**
770 Broadway
New York, NY 10003
***Tel: (646) 654-4660***
***www.billboardevents.com***

**Billboard Latin Music Conference & Awards**
770 Broadway
New York, NY 10003
***Tel: (646) 654-4660***
***www.billboardevents.com***

**Billboard Music & Money Symposium**
770 Broadway
New York, NY 10003
***Tel: (646) 654-4660***
***www.billboardevents.com***

**Billboard R & B/Hip Hop Conference & Awards**
770 Broadway
New York, NY 10003
***Tel: (646) 654-4660***
***www.billboardevents.com***

**BMI Awards**
8730 Sunset Blvd., 3rd Fl. West
Los Angeles, CA 90069
***Tel: (310) 659-9109***
***www.bmi.com***

**BMI Christian Music Awards**
10 Music Square East
Nashville, TN 37203
***Tel: (615) 401-2000***
***www.bmi.com***

**BMI Country Awards**
10 Music Square East
Nashville, TN 37203
***Tel: (615) 401-2000***
***www.bmi.com***

**BMI Film & Television Awards**
8730 Sunset Blvd., 3rd Fl. West
Los Angeles, CA 90069
***Tel: (310) 659-9109***
***www.bmi.com***

**BMI Latin Awards**
5201 Blue Lagoon Dr., Ste. 310
Miami, FL 33126
***Tel: (305) 266-3636***
***www.bmi.com***

**BMI Student Composer Awards**
320 W. 57th Street
New York, NY 10019
***Tel: (212) 586-2000***
***www.bmi.com***

**BMI Urban Awards**
3340 Peachtree Road, NE - Ste. 570
Atlanta, GA 30326
***Tel: (404) 261-5151***
***www.bmi.com***

**Chicago Blues Festival**
**Chicago Country Music Festival**
**Chicago Gospel Music Festival**
Mayor's Office of Special Events
121 N. LaSalle Street, Rm. 806
Chicago, IL 60602
***Tel: (312) 744-3315***
***www.cityofchicago.org/specialevents***

**Chicago MOBFest**
***www.chicagomobfest.com***

**CIC Conference - Concert Industry Consortium**
4697 W. Jacquelyn Ave.
Fresno, CA 93722
***Tel: (209) 271-7900***
***www.pollstaronline.com***

**Christian Musician Summit**
4227 S. Meridian Ste. C#275
Puyallup, WA 98373
***Tel: (253) 770-0650***
***www.christianmusiciansummit.com***

**CMJ Music Marathon**
100 5th Avenue, 11th Fl.
New York, NY 10011
***Tel: (212) 277-7120***
***www.cmj.com***

**Coachella**
***www.coachella.com***

**College Broadcasters Conference**
Collegiate Broadcasters, Inc.
P.O. Box D
Austin, TX 78713
***Tel: (713) 348-2935***
***www.collegebroadcasters.org***

**COMDEX/MediaLive Int'l.**
795 Folsom Street, 6th Fl.
San Francisco, CA 94107
***Tel: (415) 905-2300***
***www.comdex.com***

**Concert Industry Consortium/CIC**
4697 W. Jacquelyn Ave.
Fresno, CA 93722
***Tel: (209) 271-7900***
***www.pollstaronline.com***

**Country Music Awards**
One Music Circle South
Nashville, TN 37203
***Tel: (615) 244-2840***
***www.cmaworld.com***
***www.cmaawards.com***

**Country Music Expo**
***Tel: (317) 842-9550***
***www.countrymusicexpo.com***

**Country Radio Seminar (CRS)**
Country Radio Broadcaster's, Inc.
819 18th Avenue South
Nashville, TN 37203
***Tel: (615) 327-4487***
***www.crb.org***

**Cutting Edge Music Business Conference**
1524 N. Claiborne Avenue
New Orleans, LA 70116
*Tel: (504) 945-1800*
*www.jass.com/cuttingedge*

**DIY Music Festival**
*www.diymusicfestival.com*

**Dove Awards**
Gospel Music Association
1205 Division Street
Nashville, TN 37203
*Tel: (615) 242-0303*
*www.doveawards.com*

**Ella Awards**
Society of Singers
15456 Ventura Blvd., Ste. 304
Sherman Oaks, CA 91403
*Tel: (818) 995-7100*
*www.singers.org*

**Emergenza**
*www.emergenza.net*

**Essence Music Festival**
135 W. 50th Street, 4th Fl.
New York, NY 10020
*Tel: (212) 522-1212*
*www.essencemusicfestival.com*

**Film, Stage & Showbiz Expo**
440 Ninth Avenue, 8th Fl.
New York, NY 10001
*Tel: (212) 404-2345*
*www.theshowbizexpo.com*

**Folk Alliance Conference**
510 S. Main Street
Mempis, TN 38103
*Tel: (901) 522-1170*
*www.folkalliance.org*

**Gospel Heritage Foundation Praise & Worship Conference**
*www.gospelheritage.org*

**Gospel in the Rockies/ Gospel Music Association**
1205 Division Street
Nashville, TN 37203
*Tel: (615) 242-0303*
*www.gospelmusic.org*

**Gospel Music Association Music Week**
1205 Division Street
Nashville, TN 37203
*Tel: (615) 242-0303*
*www.gospelmusic.org*

**Grammy Awards**
The Recording Academy/
National Academy of Recording Arts & Sciences (NARAS)
3030 Olympic Blvd.
Santa Monica, CA 90404
*Tel: (310) 392-3777*
*www.grammy.com*

**The Hollywood Reporter/ Billboard Film & TV Music Conference**
5055 Wilshire Boulevard, 6th Fl.
Los Angeles, CA 90036
*Tel: (323) 525-2000/(646) 654-5000*
*www.billboardevents.com*

**I Hear Music in the Air**
9910 Coventry Court
Mason, OH 45040
*Tel: (513) 573-9596*
*www.ihearmusicintheair.com*

**INFOCOMM**
11242 Waples Mill Road, Ste. 200
Fairfax, VA 22030
*Tel: (703) 273-7200*
*www.infocomm.org*

**IFCO Fun Fest**
International Fan Club Organization
P.O. Box 40328
Nashville, TN 37204
*Tel: (615) 371-9596*
*www.ifco.org*

**Independent Music Conference**
304 Main Ave., PMB 287
Norwalk, CT 06851
*Tel: (203) 606-4649*
*www.indiemusicon.com*

**Independent Music World Series**
Disc Makers
7905 N. Route 130
Pennsauken, NJ 08110
*Tel: (800) 468-9353*
*www.discmakers.com*

**International Bluegrass Music Association World of Bluegrass**
2 Music Circle S., Ste. 100
Nashville, TN 37203
*Tel: (615) 256-3222*
*www.ibma.org*

**International CES**
Consumer Electronics Association
1919 S. Eads Street
Arlington, VA 22202
*Tel: (301) 631-3983*
*www.cesweb.org*

**Latin Alternative Music Conference**
10627 Burbank Blvd.,
N. Hollywood, CA 91601
*Tel: (818) 763-1397*
*www.latinalternative.com*

**Long Beach Jazz Festival**
*www.longbeachjazzfest.com*

**Mid-Atlantic Music Conference**
Wholeteam Enterprises
5588 Chamblee Dunno - PMB 110
Dunwoody, GA 30338
*Tel: (888) 755-0036*
*www.midatlanticmusic.com*

**MIDEM/Reed MIDEM**
360 Park Avenue S., 14th Fl.
New York, NY 1000
*Tel: (212) 284-5142*
*www.midem.com*

**Millennium Music Conference**
P.O. Box 1012
Harrisburg, PA 17108
***Tel: (717) 221-1124***
***www.musicconference.net***

**MTV Movie Awards**
**MTV Video Music Awards**
2600 Colorado Ave.
Santa Monica, CA 90404
***Tel: (310) 752-8000***
***www.mtv.com***

**MTV Movie Awards**
**MTV Video Music Awards**
1515 Broadway
New York, NY 10036
***Tel: (212) 258-8000***
***www.mtv.com***

**MUSEXPO**
A & R Worldwide
8370 Wilshire Blvd. Ste. 350
Beverly Hills, CA 90211 USA
***Tel: (323) 782-0770***
***www.musexpo.net***

**Music Educators National Conference (MENC)**
1806 Robert Fulton Drive
Reston, VA 20191
***Tel: (703) 860-4000***
***www.menc.org***

**Music Video Production Association Awards & Director's Cut**
201 N. Occidental Street
Los Angeles, CA 90026
***Tel: (213) 387-1590***
***www.mvpa.com***

**MusikFest**
ArtsQuest
25 W. Third Street
Bethlehem, PA 18015
***Tel: (610) 332-1300***
***www.musikfest.org***

**NAMM International Music Market**
5790 Armada Drive
Carlsbad, CA 92008
***Tel: (760) 438-8001***
***www.namm.com***

**National Association for Campus Activities Convention**
13 Harbison Way
Columbia, SC 29212
***Tel: (803) 732-6222***
***www.naca.org***

**National Association of Record Industry Professionals (NARIP) Workshops & Seminars**
P.O. Box 2446
Toluca Lake, CA 91610
***Fax: (818) 769-7007***
***www.narip.com***

**National Association of Recording Merchandisers (NARM) Conference**
9 Eves Drive, Ste. 120
Marlton, NJ 08053
***Tel: (856) 596-2221***
***www.narm.com***

**National Association of Broadcasters (NAB) Convention**
1771 N Street, NW
Washington, D.C. 20036
***Tel: (202) 429-5300***
***www.nab.org***

**National Quartet Convention**
815 John Harper Hwy., Ste. 8
Louisville, KY 40165
***Tel: (800) 846-8499***
***www.natqc.com***

**Radio-Television News Directors (RTNDA) Association Convention**
529 14th Street, NW - Ste. 425
Washington, DC 20045
***Tel: (202) 659-6510***
***www.rtnda.org***

**Rock 'N Roll Fantasy Camp**
***Tel: (888) 762-2263***
***www.rockandrollfantasycamp.com***

**Songwriter Boot Camp**
4227 S. Meridian Ste. C#275
Puyallup, WA 98373
***Tel: (253) 770-0650***
***www.christianmusiciansummit.com***

**Stellar Gospel Music Awards**
Central City Productions
212 E. Ohio Street, Ste. 300
Chicago, IL 60611
***Tel: (312) 654-1100***
***www.thestellarawards.com***

**SXSW Music Festival**
P.O. Box 4999
Austin, TX 78765
***Tel: (512) 467-7979***
***www.sxsw.com***

**TED Conferences**
Technology Entertainment Design
55 Van Dam Street, 16th Fl.
New York, NY 10013
***Tel: (212) 346-9333***
***www.ted.com***

**Trumpet Awards**
101 Marietta Street, Ste. 1010
Atlanta, GA 30303
***Tel: (404) 878-6738***
***www.trumpetfoundation.org***

**Urban Network Music, Marketing & Entertainment Summit**
3255 Wilshire Blvd., Ste. 815
Los Angeles, CA 90010
***Tel: (213) 388-4155***
***www.urbannetwork.com***

**West L.A. Music Weekly Series**
11345 Santa Monica Blvd.
Los Angeles, CA 90025
***Tel: (310) 477-1945***
***www.westlamusic.com***

**1st Mariner Arena**
201 W. Baltimore Street
Baltimore, MD 21201
***Tel: (410) 347-2020***
***www.baltimorearena.com***

**9:30 Club**
815 V Street, NW
Washington, D.C. 20001
***Tel: (202) 265-0930***
***www.930.com***

**Adams Center**
University of Montana Campus
32 Campus Drive, Campus Ctr. 103
Missoula, MT 59812
***Tel: (406) 243-5355***
***www.adamseventcenter.com***

**AEG**
800 West Olympic Blvd., Ste. 305
Los Angeles, CA 90015
***Tel: (213) 763-7700***
***www.aegworldwide.com***

**Ahmanson Theatre**
Music Center, Performing Arts Center of Los Angeles County
135 S. Grand Avenue
Los Angeles, CA 90012
***Tel: (213) 972-7211***
***www.musiccenter.org***

**Alamodome**
100 Montana Street
San Antonio, TX 78203
***Tel: (210) 207-3663***
***www.alamodome.com***

**Time Warner Cable Music Pavilion at Walnut Creek**
3801 Rock Quarry Road
Raleigh, NC 27610
***Tel: (919) 831-6400***
***www.livenation.com***

**American Airlines Arena**
601 Biscayne Boulevard
Miami, FL 33132
***Tel: (786) 777-1000***
***www.aaarena.com***

**American Airlines Center**
2500 Victory Avenue
Dallas, TX 75219
***Tel: (214) 222-3687***
***www.americanairlinescenter.com***

**Anaheim Convention Center**
800 West Katella Avenue
Anaheim, CA 92802
***Tel: (714) 765-8950***
***www.anaheimconventioncenter.com***

**Apollo Theater**
253 W. 125th Street
New York, NY 10027
***Tel: (212) 531-5300***
***www.apollotheater.com***

**Aramark Amphitheaters & Convention Centers**
1101 Market Street
Philadelphia, PA 19106
***Tel: (215) 238-3000***
***www.aramarkentertainment.com***

**ARCO Arena**
One Sports Parkway
Sacramento, CA 95834
***Tel: (916) 928-0000***
***www.arcoarena.com***

**Arena at Harbor Yard**
600 Main Street, 2nd Fl.
Bridgeport, CT 06604
***Tel: (203) 345-2300***
***www.arenaatharboryard.com***

**ArenaNetwork**
32129 Lindero Canyon Rd., Ste. 105
Westlake Village, CA 91361
***Tel: (818) 707-8421***
***www.arenanetwork.net***

**Arie Crown Theater**
2301 S. Lakeshore Drive
Chicago, IL 60616
***Tel: (312) 791-6511***
***www.ariecrown.com***

**Assembly Hall**
University of Illinois
1800 S. First Street

Champaign, IL 61820
***Tel: (217) 333-2923***
***www.uofiassemblyhall.com***

**Atlanta Civic Center Theatre**
395 Piedmont Avenue, NE
Atlanta, GA 30308
***Tel: (404) 523-6275***
***www.atlantaciviccenter.com***

**Austin Music Hall**
208 Nueces Street
Austin, TX 78701
***Tel: (512) 263-4146***
***www.austinmusichall.com***

**Avalon Hollywood**
1735 N. Vine Street
Hollywood, CA 90028
***Tel: (323) 462-8900***
***www.avalonhollywood.com***

**Bill Graham Civic Auditorium**
99 Grove Street
San Francisco, CA 94102
***Tel: (415) 974-4060***
***www.billgrahamcivic.com***

**Bank Atlantic Center**
One Panther Parkway
Sunrise, FL 33323
***Tel: (954) 835-7000***
***www.bankatlanticcenter.com***

**Calvin Simmons Theatre**
10 Tenth Street
Oakland, CA 94607
***Tel: (510) 238-7765***
***www.livenation.com***

**Capa**
247 College Drive
New Haven, CT 06510
***Tel: (203) 624-1825***
***www.capa.com***

**Capa**
55 E. State Street
Columbus, OH 43215
***Tel: (614) 469-1045***
***www.capa.com***

**Carnegie Hall**
881 Seventh Avenue
New York, NY 10019
***Tel: (212) 903-9600***
***www.carnegiehall.com***

**Cedar Fair Entertainment Co.**
One Cedar Point Drive
Sandusky, OH 44870
***Tel: (419) 627-2233***
***www.cedarfair.com***

**Cerritos Center for the Performing Arts**
12700 Center Court Drive
Cerritos, CA 90703
***Tel: (562) 916-8510***
***www.cerritoscenter.com***

**Chastain Park Amphitheatre**
4469 Stella Drive, NW
Atlanta, GA 30309
***Tel: (404) 733-4900***
***www.classicchastain.org***

**Clear Channel Entertainment**
200 E. Basse Road
San Antonio, TX 78209
***Tel: (210) 822-2828***
***www.clearchannel.com***

**Concord Pavilion**
2000 Kirker Pass Road
Concord, CA 94521
***Tel: (925) 676-8742***
***www.livenation.com***

**Cow Palace**
2600 Geneva Avenue
Daly City, CA 94014
***Tel: (415) 404-4107***
***www.cowpalace.com***

**Cox Arena**
San Diego State University
5500 Canyon Crest Drive
San Diego, CA 92182
***Tel: (619) 594-0234***
***www.cox-arena.com***

**Cramton Auditorium**
2455 Sixth Street, NW
Washington, D.C. 20059
***Tel: (202) 806-7194***
***www.cramtonauditorium.org***

**DAR Constitution Hall**
1776 D Street, NW
Washington, D.C. 20006
***Tel: (202) 628-1776***
***www.dar.org***

**Dorothy Chandler Pavilion**
Music Center, Performing Arts Center of Los Angeles County
135 S. Grand Avenue
Los Angeles, CA 90012
***Tel: (213) 972-7211***
***www.musiccenter.org***

**DTE Energy Music Theatre**
7773 Pine Road
Clarkston, MI 48348
***Tel: (248) 377-8256***
***www.palacenet.com***

**Edwards Jones Dome**
701 Convention Plaza
Saint Louis, MO 63101
***Tel: (314) 342-5201***
***www.edwardjonesdome.org***

**El Rey Theatre**
5515 Wilshire Boulevard
Los Angeles, CA 90036
***Tel: (323) 936-6400***
***www.theelrey.com***

**Festival Productions**
336 Camp Street, Ste. 250
New Orleans, LA 70130
***Tel: (504) 410-4100***
***www.fpi-no.com***

**The Fillmore**
1805 Geary Boulevard
San Francisco, CA 94115
***Tel: (415) 346-6000***
***www.livenation.com***

**The Fillmore Miami Beach at the Jackie Gleason Theater**
1700 Washington Avenue
Miami Beach, FL 33139
***Tel: (305) 673-7300***

www.gleasontheater.com

**John Anson Ford Amphitheatre**
2580 E. Cahuenga Blvd.
Hollywood, CA 90028
*Tel: (323) 856-5793*
*www.fordamphitheater.org*

**Ford Amphitheatre**
4802 US 301 North
Tampa, FL 33610
*Tel: (813) 740-2446*
*www.livenation.com*

**Georgia Dome**
One Georgia Dome Drive
Atlanta, GA 30313
*Tel: (404) 223-9200*
*www.gadome.com*

**Gibson Amphitheatre**
100 Universal City Plaza
Universal City, CA 91608
*Tel: (818) 622-4440*
*www.livenation.com*

**Global Spectrum**
3601 S. Broad Street
Philadelphia, PA 19148
*Tel: (215) 389-9587*
*www.global-spectrum.com*

**Bill Graham Civic Auditorium**
99 Grove Street
San Francisco, CA 94102
*Tel: (415) 974-4060*
*www.billgrahamcivic.com*

**Grand Ole Opry House**
2802 Opryland Drive
Nashville, TN 37214
*Tel: (615) 871-OPRY*
*www.opry.com*

**Greek Theatre**
University of California
Cal Performances
101 Zellerbach Hall # 4800
Berkeley, CA, 94720-4800
*Tel: (510) 809-0100/(510) 642-1212*
*facilities.calperfs.berkeley.edu/greek/*

**Greek Theatre**
2700 North Vermont
Los Angeles, CA 90027
*Tel: (323) 665-5857*
*www.greektheatrela.com*

**The Grove of Anaheim**
2200 E. Katella Avenue
Anaheim, CA 92806
*Tel: (714) 712-2700*
*www.thegroveofanaheim.com*

**Hahn Plaza**
USC Program Board
University Park STU, B-5
Los Angeles, CA 90089
*Tel: (213) 740-5656*
*www.scf.usc.edu/~prgbrd*

**Hampton Coliseum**
P.O. Box 7309
1000 Coliseum Drive
Hampton, VA 23666
*Tel: (757) 838-5650*
*www.hampton.gov/coliseum*

**HiFi Buys Amphitheatre**
2002 Lakewood way
Atlanta, GA 30315
*Tel: (404) 850-5090*
*www.hob.com/venues*

**Hollywood Bowl**
2301 N. Highland Avenue
Los Angeles, CA 90068
*Tel: (323) 850-2000*
*www.hollywoodbowl.org*

**Hollywood Palladium**
6215 Sunset Boulevard
Hollywood, CA 90028
*Tel: (323) 962-7600*
*www.livenation.com*

**Honda Center**
2695 E. Katella Avenue
Anaheim, CA 92806
*Tel: (714) 704-2400*
*www.hondacenter.com*

**House of Blues**
6255 W. Sunset Blvd., 16th Fl.
Hollywood, CA 90028
*Tel: (323) 769-4600*
*www.houseofblues.com*

**HP Pavilion at San Jose**
525 W. Santa Clara Street
San Jose, CA 95113
*Tel: (408) 999-5725*
*www.hppsj.com*

**Humphrey's Concerts by the Bay**
2241 Shelter Island Drive
San Diego, CA 92106
*Tel: (619) 220-8497*
*www.humphreysconcerts.com*

**Edwards Jones Dome**
701 Convention Plaza
Saint Louis, MO 63101
*Tel: (314) 342-5201*
*www.edwardjonesdome.org*

**Kellogg Arena**
One McCamly Square
Battle Creek, MI 49107
*Tel: (269) 963-4800*
*www.kelloggarena.com*

**Kemper Arena**
Convention & Entertainment Facilities
301 W. 13th Street, Ste. 100
Kansas City, MO 64105
*Tel: (816) 513-5000*
*www.kcconvention.com*

**Kennedy Center for the Performing Arts**
2700 F Street, NW
Washington, D.C. 20566
*Tel: (202) 467-4600*
*www.kennedy-center.org*

**Kings Dominion Amphitheatres**
Cedar Fair
One Cedar Point Drive
Sandusky, OH 44870
*Tel: (419) 627-2233*
*www.cedarfair.com*

**Knitting Factory**
7021 Hollywood Blvd.
Hollywood, CA 90028
*Tel: (323) 463-0204*

***www.knittingfactory.com***

**Knitting Factory**
74 Leonard Street
New York, NY 10013
***Tel: (212) 219-3132***
***www.knittingfactory.com***

**Kodak Theatre**
6801 Hollywood Blvd.
Hollywood, CA 90028
***Tel: (323) 308-6300***
***www.kodaktheatre.com***

**Lincoln Center for the Performing Arts**
70 Lincoln Center Plaza
New York, NY 10023
***Tel: (212) 875-5000***
***www.lincolncenter.org***

**The Lincoln Theatre**
1215 U Street, NW
Washington, D.C. 20009
***Tel: (202) 328-6000***
***www.thelincolntheatre.org***

**Live Nation**
9348 Civic Center Drive
Beverly Hills, CA 90210
***Tel: (310) 867-7000***
***www.livenation.com***

**Louisiana Superdome**
Sugar Bowl Drive
New Orleans, LA 70112
***Tel: (504) 587-3663***
***www.superdome.com***

**Madison Square Garden**
4 Pennsylvania Plaza
New York, NY 10001
***Tel: (212) 465-6741***
***www.thegarden.com***

**Mark Taper Forum**
Music Center, Performing Arts Center of Los Angeles County
135 S. Grand Avenue
Los Angeles, CA 90012
***Tel: (213) 972-7211***
***www.musiccenter.org***

**Merriweather Post Pavilion**
10475 Little Patuxent Parkway
Columbia, MD 21044
***Tel: (410) 715-5550***
***www.merriweathermusic.com***

**MGM Grand Garden Arena**
3799 Las Vegas Blvd., South
Las Vegas, NV 89109
***Tel: (702) 891-7801***
***www.mgmgrand.com***

**Music Center**
135 N. Grand Avenue
Los Angeles, CA 90012
***Tel: (213) 972-7211***
***www.musiccenter.org***

**Music Center at Strathmore**
5301 Tuckerman Lane
N. Bethesda, MD 20852
***Tel: (301) 581-5100***
***www.strathmore.org***

**Nederlander Concerts**
6233 Hollywood Blvd., Ste. 222
Los Angeles, CA 90028
***Tel: (323) 468-1700***
***www.nederlanderconcerts.com***

**Nissan Pavilion @ Stone Ridge**
707800 Cellar Door Drive
Bristow, VA 20136
***Tel: (703) 754-6400***
***www.nissanpavilion.com***

**Nokia Theatre L.A. Live**
777 Chick Hearn Court
Los Angeles, CA 90015
***Tel: (213) 763-6000***
***www.nokiatheatrelalive.com***

**NOKIA Theatre Times Square**
1515 Broadway at W. 44th Street
New York, NY 10036
***Tel: (212) 930-1950***
***www.nokiatheatrenyc.com***

**Orlando Centroplex**
600 W. Amelia Street
Orlando, FL 32801
***Tel: (407) 849-2001***
***www.orlandocentroplex.com***

**Orpheum Theatre**
1182 Market Street, Ste. 200
San Francisco, CA 94102
***Tel: (415) 551-2075***
***www.shnsf.com***

**Orpheum Theatre**
842 S. Broadway
Los Angeles, CA 90014
***Tel: (213) 749-5171***
***www.laorpheum.com***

**Pantages Theater**
6233 Hollywood Blvd., Ste. 222
Los Angeles, CA 90028
***Tel: (323) 468-1700***
***www.nederlanderconcerts.com***

**Paramount Theatre of the Arts**
2025 Broadway
Oakland, CA 94612
***Tel: (510) 893-2300***
***www.paramounttheatre.com***

**The Paramount Theatre**
911 Pine Street
Seattle, WA 98101
***Tel: (206) 467-5510***
***www.theparamount.com***

**Philips Arena**
One Philips Drive
Atlanta, GA 30303
***Tel: (404) 878-3000***
***www.philipsarena.com***

**Pioneer Center for the Performing Arts**
100 S. Virginia Street
Reno, NV 89501
***Tel: (775) 686-6610***
***www.pioneercenter.com***

**PNC Bank Arts Center**
Exit 116 Garden State Parkway
Holmdel, NJ 07733
***Tel: (732) 203-2500***
***www.pncbankartscenter.com***

**Portland Center for the Performing Arts**
111 SW Broadway
Portland, OR 97201
***Tel: (503) 248-4335***
***www.pcpa.com***

**Qualcomm Stadium**
9449 Friars Road
San Diego, CA 92108
***Tel: (619) 641-3100***
***www.sandiego.gov/qualcomm***

**Radio City Music Hall**
1260 6th Ave. (Ave. of the Americas)
New York, NY 10020
***Tel: (212) 247-4777***
***www.radiocity.com***

**Red Rocks Amphitheatre**
18300 W. Alameda Parkway
Morrison, CO 80465
***Tel: (303) 865-2494***
***www.redrocksonline***

**Reliant Park**
One Reliant Park
Houston, TX 77054
***Tel: (832) 667-1400***
***www.reliantpark.com***

**Ryman Auditorium**
116 Fifth Avenue N.
Nashville, TN 37219
***Tel: (615) 889-3060***
***www.ryman.com***

**Shoreline Amphitheatre**
One Amphitheatre Parkway
Mountain View, CA  94043
***Tel: (650) 967-3000***
***www.shorelineamp.com***

**SMG Worldwide**
300 Conshohocken State Rd.
Suite 770
W. Conshohocken, PA 19428
***Tel: (610) 729-7900***
***www.smgworld.com***

**Staples Center**
1111 S. Figueroa
Los Angeles, CA 90015
***Tel: (213) 742-7100***
***www.staplescenter.com***

**Strathmore**
5301 Tuckerman Lane
N. Bethesda, MD 20852
***Tel: (301) 581-5100***
***www.strathmore.org***

**Target Center**
600 First Avenue N.
Minneapolis, MN 55403
***Tel: (612) 673-1300***
***www.targetcenter.com***

**The Wiltern**
3790 Wilshire Boulevard
Los Angeles, CA 90010
***Tel: (213) 388-1400***
***www.wiltern.com***

**Times Union Center**
51 S. Pearl Street
Albany, NY 12207
***Tel: (518) 487-2000***
***timesunioncenter-albany.com***

**UCLA Royce Hall**
B100 Royce Hall
Box 95129
Los Angeles, CA 90095
***Tel: (310) 825-4401***
***www.uclalive.org***

**US Airways Center**
201 E. Jefferson Street
Phoenix, AZ 85004
***Tel: (602) 379-2000***
***www.usairwayscenter.com***

**USO World Headquarters**
2111 Wilson Blvd., Ste. 1200
Arlington, VA 22201
***Tel: (703) 908-6400/(703) 908-6480***
***www.uso.org***

**Verizon Center**
601 F Street, NW
Washington, D.C. 20004
***Tel: (202) 661-5000***
***www.verizoncenter.com***

**Verizon Wireless Amphitheater**
8808 Irvine Centre Drive
Irvine, CA 92618
***Tel: (949) 855-8095***
***www.verizonamphitheater.com***

**Verizon Wireless Amphitheater**
16765 Lookout Road
Selma, TX 78154
***Tel: (210) 657-8300***
***www.vwatx.com***

**Walt Disney Concert Hall**
Music Center, Performing Arts Center
of Los Angeles County
135 S. Grand Avenue
Los Angeles, CA 90012
***Tel: (213) 972-7211***
***www.musiccenter.org***

**Warner Theatre**
1299 Pennsylvania Ave., NW - Ste. 111
Washington, D.C. 20004
***Tel: (202) 783-4000***
***www.warnertheatre.com***

**Washington Convention Center**
801 Mount Vernon Place, NW
Washington, D.C. 20004
***Tel: (202) 249-3000***
***www.dcconvention.com***

**Wilshire Ebell Theatre**
4401 W. 8th Street
Los Angeles, CA 90005
***Tel: (323) 939-1128***
***www.wilshireebelltheatre.org***

**Wolf Trap**
1551 Trap Road
Vienna, VA 22182
***Tel: (703) 255-1900***
***www.wolftrap.org***

**Allegro Corporation**
20048 NE San Rafael
Portland, OR 97230
***Tel: (503) 257-8480/(800) 288-2007***
***www.allegro-music.com***

**Alliance Entertainment Corporation**
4250 Coral Ridge Drive
Coral Springs, FL 33065
***Tel: (800) 329-7664***
***www.aent.com***

**Alternative Distribution Alliance (ADA)**
3300 Pacific Avenue
Burbank, CA 91505
***Tel: (818) 977-0552***
***www.ada-music.com***

**Alternative Distribution Alliance (ADA)**
800 Washington Avenue N., Ste. 701
Minneapolis, MN 55401
***Tel: (612) 338-1022***
***www.ada-music.com***

**Alternative Distribution Alliance (ADA)**
72 Spring Street, 12th Fl.
New York, NY 10012
***Tel: (800) 239-3232***
***www.ada-music.com***

**Amazon MP3**
72 Spring Street, 12th Fl.
New York, NY 10012
***Tel: (800) 239-3232***
***www.amazonmp3.com***
***www.createspace.com***

**Baker & Taylor**
2550 W. Tyvola Rd., Ste. 300
Charlotte, NC 28217
***Tel: (704) 998-3100***
***www.btol.com***

**BFM Digital**
***www.bfmdigital.com***

**theBizmo.com**
***www.thebizmo.com***

**Caroline Distribution**
104 W. 29th Street, 4th Fl.
New York, NY 10001
***Tel: (212) 886-7500***
***www.carolinedist.com***

**CD Baby**
5925 NE 80th Avenue
Portland, OR 97218
***Tel: (503) 595-3000***
***www.cdbaby.com***

**Central South Distribution**
3730 Vulcan Drive
Nashville, TN 37211
***Tel: (615) 833-5960***
***www.centralsouthdistribution.com***

**City Hall Records**
101 Glacier Pointe, Ste. C
San Rafael, CA 94901
***Tel: (415) 457-9080***
***www.cityhallrecords.com***

**CNI Distribution**
5584 Mt. View Road
Nashville, TN 37013
***Tel: (615) 641-5550***
***www.cnidist.com***

**Crystal Clear Distribution**
10486 Brockwood Road
Dallas, TX 75238
***Tel: (214) 349-5057***
***www.crystalcleardistribution.com***

**EMI Christian Music Group**
101 Winners Circle
Brentwood, TN 37024
***Tel: (615) 371-4300***
***www.emicmg.com***

**EMI Distribution**
150 Fifth Avenue
New York, NY 10010
***Tel: (212) 786-8700***
***www.emigroup.com***

**EMI Label Services**
104 W. 29th Street, 4th Fl.
New York, NY 10001
***Tel: (212) 886-7500***
***www.emilabelservices.com***

**Fontana Distribution**
111 Universal Hollywood Dr., Ste. 500
Universal City, Ca 91608
***Tel: (877) 878-FONTANA***
***www.fontanadistribution.com***

**Goldenrod Music**
1310 Turner Street

Lansing, MI 48906
***Tel: (517) 484-1712***
***www.goldenrod.com***

**iMeem**
***www.imeem.com***

**IODA - Independent Online Distribution Alliance**
539 Bryant Street, Ste. 303
San Francisco, CA 94107
***Tel: 415.777.IODA***
***www.iodalliance.com***

**Koch Entertainment Distribution**
22 Harbor Park Drive
Port Washington, NY 11050
***Tel: (516) 484-1000***
***www.kochent.com***

**Music City Record Distributors**
25 Lincoln Street
Nashville, TN 37210
***Tel: (615) 255-7315***
***www.mcrd.com***

**MySpace**
***www.myspacee.com***

**Nail Distribution**
20048 NE San Rafael
Portland, OR 97230
***Tel: (888) NAIL-INC***
***www.naildistribution.com***

**Navarre Corporation**
7400 49th Avenue, N.
New Hope, MN 55428
***Tel: (763) 535-8333***
***www.navarre.com***

**New Day Christian Distributors**
126 Shivel Drive
Henderson, TN 37075
***Tel: (615) 822-3633/(800) 251-3633***
***www.newdaychristian.com***

**The Orchard**
23 E. 4th Street, 3rd Fl.
New York, NY 10003
***Tel: (212) 201-9280***
***www.theorchard.com***

**Provident Music Group**
741 Cool Springs Blvd.
Franklin, TN 37067
***Tel: (615) 261-6500***
***www.providentintegrity.com***

**RED Distribution**
79 Fifth Avenue, 15th Fl.
New York, NY 10003
***Tel: (212) 404-0600***
***www.redmusic.com***

**Redeye Distribution**
449-A Trollingwood Road
Haw River, NC 27258
***Tel: (877) REDEYE 1/(877) 733-3931***
***www.redeyeusa.com***

**Reverb Nation**
***www.reverbnation.com***

**Ryko Distribution**
30 Irving Place, 3rd Fl.
New York, NY 10003
***Tel: (212) 287-6100***
***www.rykodisc.com***

**Select-O-Hits Inc.**
1981 Fletcher Creek Dr.
Memphis, TN 38133
***Tel: (901) 388-1190***
***www.selectohits.com***

**Song Cast**
***www.songcastmusic.com***

**Sony Music Entertainment**
550 Madison Avenue
New York, NY 10022
***Tel: (212) 833-8000***
***www.sonymusic.com***

**Sparrow Distribution**
P.O. Box 5010
Brentwood, TN 37024
***Tel: (615) 371-6800***
***www.sparrowrecords.com***

**Spring Arbor Distributors**
One Ingram Blvd.
LaVergne, TN 37086
***Tel: (615) 213-5192/(800) 395-4340***
***www.springarbor.com***

**Tune Core**
55 Washington, Ste. 822
Brooklyn, NY 11201
***www.tunecore.com***

**Tyscot Records**
5501 71st Street, Ste. 3
Indianapolis, IN 46220
***Tel: (317) 926-6271***
***www.tyscot.com***

**Universal Music Group Distribution**
1755 Broadway
New York, NY 10019
***Tel: (212) 841-8000***
***www.universalmusic.com***

**Warner Music Group**
3400 W. Olive Avenue
Burbank, CA 91505
***Tel: (818) 238-6500***
***www.wmg.com***

**Warner Music Group**
75 Rockefeller Plaza
New York, NY 10019
***Tel: (212) 275-2000***
***www.wmg.com***

**Word Distribution**
25 Music Square West
Nashville, TN 37203
***Tel: (615) 251-0600***
***www.worddistribution.com***

**YouTube**
***www.youtube.com***

# DUPLICATION & MANUFACTURING COMPANIES

**1Stop CD Duplication**
5645 Hollywood Blvd
Los Angeles, CA 90028
***Tel: (626) 320-1051***
***www.onestopmediashop.com***
****20+ Nationwide Locations***

**1Stop CD Duplication**
8539 W. Sunset Blvd, Ste. #6
Los Angeles, CA 90069
***Tel: (310) 694-8155***
***www.onestopmediashop.com***
****20+ Nationwide Locations***

**1Stop CD Duplication Atlanta**
780 N. Highland Avenue, NE
Atlanta, GA 30306
***Tel: (404) 921-0164***
***www.onestopmediashop.com***
****20+ Nationwide Locations***

**1Stop CD Duplication New York**
575 Lexington Avenue
New York, NY 10022
***Tel: (917) 210-1706***
***www.onestopmediashop.com***
****20+ Nationwide Locations***

**A to Z Audio**
P.O. Box 26087
21929 Lorain Road
Fairview Park, OH 44126
***Tel: (440) 333-0040***
***www.atozaudio.com***

**ABACAB Audio**
245 Fischer Ave., Ste. A-9
Costa Mesa, CA 92626
***Tel: (714) 432-1745***
***www.abacabaudio.com***

**Abbey Tape Duplicators Inc.**
6855 Vineland Avenue
N. Hollywood, CA 91605
***Tel: (800) 346-3827***
***www.abbeytape.com***

**Abet Disc Plus**
411 E. Huntington Dr., Ste. #107-372
Arcadia, CA 91006
***Tel: (866) 574-0275***
***www.abetdisc.com***

**AccuPress**
128 E. Cypress Street
P.O. Drawer 990
Ville Platte, LA 70586
***Tel: (337) 363-2104/(800) 542-8283***
***www.accupress.com***

**Acutrack**
350 Sonic Avenue
Livermore, CA 94551
***Tel: (925) 579-5000***
***www.acutrack.com***

**American Mastering Labs**
38 Miller Avenue, #111
Mill Valley, CA 94941
***Tel: (888) 9-CDLABS***
***www.americanmastering.com***

**Armadillo Digital Audio**
6855 Vineland Avenue
N. Hollywood, CA 91605
***Tel: (818) 980-6895***
***www.armadillodigital.com***

**Audio Duplicating Service**
2613 N. Andrews Avenue
Wilton Manors, FL 33311
***Tel: (954) 568-5385***
***www.audiodups.com***

**Bay Records**
1741 Alcatraz Avenue
Berkeley, CA 94703
***Tel: (510) 428-2002***
***www.bayrecords.com***

**C & C Music**
220 Knickerbocker Avenue
Bohemia, NY 11716
***Tel: (800) 289-9155***
***www.candcmusic.com***

**CD Baby**
5925 NE 80th Avenue
Portland, OR 97218
***Tel: (503) 595-3000***
***www.cdbaby.net***

**CD FX**
5307 E. Mockingbird Lane, Ste. 900
Dallas, TX 75205

***Tel: (214) 826-1803/(800) 903-1673***
***www.cdfx.com***

**CD Lab**
23335 N. 18th Dr., Ste. B-140
Phoenix, AZ 85027
***Tel: (623) 334-9277***
***www.cd-lab.com***

**CD Marksman**
2105 S. McClintock
Tempe, AZ 85282
***Tel: (877) 890-5470***
***Tel: (480) 377-9191***
***www.cdmarksman.com***

**CDRom 2 Go**
US Digital Media
1929 W. Lone Cactus Drive
***Tel: (623) 587-4900***
***www.cdrom2go.com***

**Cinram**
***www.cinram.com***

**Creative Sound Corporation**
5515 Medea Valley Drive
Agoura Hills, CA 91301
***Tel: (818) 707-8986***
***www.csoundcorp.com***

**CRT Custom Products Inc.**
7532 Hickory Hills Ct.
Whites Creek, TN 37189
***Tel: (615) 876-5490***
***www.crtcustomproducts.com***

**DB Plus Digital Services Inc.**
250 W. 57th Street, Ste. 725
New York, NY 10107
***Tel: (212) 397-4099***
***www.dbplus.com***

**Digital Domain**
931 N. S.R. 434, Ste. 1201-168
Altamonte Springs, FL 32714
***Tel: (407) 831-0233***
***www.digido.com***

**Digital Video Services**
4592 40th Street, SE
Grand Rapids, MI 49512
***Tel: (616) 975-9911***
***www.digivid.com***

**DiskDuper**
2620 Walnut Avenue, Unit D.
Tustin, CA 92780
***Tel: (800) 397-7890***
***www.diskduper.com***

**Disc Makers**
7905 N. Route 130
Pennsauken, NJ 08110
***Tel: (856) 663-9030/(866) 707-0012***
***www.discmakers.com***

**DiscMasters**
5N279 Wooley Road
Maple Park, IL 60151
***Tel: (630) 365-0600***
***www.discmasters.com***

**Disc Services**
3102 Bernardo Lane, Ste. 200
San Diego, CA 92029
***Tel: (760) 432-8999***
***www.discservices.com***

**Disk Factory**
2805 McGraw Avenue
Irvine, CA 92614
***Tel: (949) 477-1700***
***www.diskfactory.com***

**Duplic8Media**
200 Spring Garden St., Unit B
Philadelphia PA, 19123
***Tel: (215) 923-2545***
***www.duplic8media.com***

**Duplium**
2029 Westgate Drive, Ste. 120
Carrollton, TX 75006
***Tel: (972) 512-0014***
***www.duplium.com***

**ESP**
37 John Glenn Drive
Buffalo, NY 14228
***Tel: (716) 691-7631***
***www.esp-cd.com***

**Forge Recording**
100 Mill Road
Oreland, PA 19071
***Tel: (215) 885-7000***
***www.forgerecording.com***

**Furnace Manufacturing**
P.O. Box 3268
Merrifield, VA 22116
***Tel: (703) 205-0007***
***www.furnacecd.com***

**GlobalDisc**
10 W. 135th Street, Ste. 14P
New York, NY 10007
***Tel: (212) 234-8333***
***www.globaldisc.com***

**Groove House Records**
5029 Serrania Avenue
Woodland Hills, CA 91364
***Tel: (888) 476-6838/(877) 447-3472***
***www.groovehouse.com***

**Imagitrax Recording Co.**
5 E. Moody
St. Louis, MO 63119
***Tel: (314) 497-1631***
***www.imagitrax.com***

**Imperial Media Services**
3303 Pico Blvd., Ste. A
Santa Monica, CA 90404
***Tel: (310) 396-2008***
***www.imperialmedia.com***

**IRT - In Record Time**
575 8th Avenue, Ste. 1900
New York, NY 10018
***Tel: (212) 262-4414***
***www.inrecordtime.com***

**JamSync**
1232 17th Avenue S.
Nashville, TN 37212
***Tel: (615) 320-5050***
***www.surroundeffects.com***

**KABA Audio Productions**
24 Commercial Blvd.
Novato, CA 94949
***Tel: (415) 883-5041***
***www.kabaaudio.com***

**Klarity Multimedia, Inc.**
1 Maple Street/P.O. Box 160
N. Vassalboro, ME 04962
***Tel: (207) 873-3911***
***www.klarity.com***

**Miami Tape Inc.**
6200 W. 21st Court
Hialeah, FL 33016
***Tel: (305) 558-9211***
***www.miamitape.com***

**Moon Valley Media**
10409 N. 21st Ave., Ste. 1
Phoenix, AZ 85021
***Tel: (602) 870-3987***
***www.moonvalleymedia.com***

**Morphius Disc Manufacturing**
100 E. 23rd Street
Baltimore, MD 21218
***Tel: (410) 662-0112***
***www.morphius.com***

**NationWide Disc**
7370 Dogwood Park
Richland Hills, TX 76118
***Tel: (817) 885-8855***
***www.nationwidedisc.com***

**Northeastern Digital**
2 Hidden Meadow Lane
Southboro, MA 01172
***Tel: (508) 481-9322***
***www.northeasterndigtal.com***

**NYCD.com**
555 Eighth Ave., 17th Fl.
New York, NY 10018
***Tel: (212) 502-0588***
***www.nycd.com***

**Oasis Disc Manufacturing**
7905 N. Crescent Boulevard
Delair, NJ 08110
***Tel: (866) 409-8170***
***www.oasiscd.com***

**Oasis Disc Manufacturing**
250 W. 57th St., Ste. 1218
New York, NY 10107
***Tel: (212) 395-9460***
***www.oasiscd.com***

**Oasis Disc Manufacturing**
5400 Carolina Place
Springfield, VA 22151
***Tel: (703) 642-3757***
***www.oasiscd.com***

**Odds On**
14 Sunset Way
Henderson, NV 89014
***Tel: (702) 318-6001***
***www.oddsonrecording.com***

**PHATEfx**
1782 N. Spring Street
Los Angeles, CA 90031
***Tel: (323) 276-5060***
***www.phatefx.com***

**Planet Dallas Recording Studios**
P.O. Box 191447
Dallas, TX 75219
***Tel: (214) 521-2216***
***www.planetdallasstudios.com***

**ProAction Media**
9014 N. 23rd Ave., Ste. 3
Phoenix, AZ 85021
***Tel: (602) 277-2011***
***www.proactionmedia.com***

**Rain Tree**
109 W. Main Street
Annville, PA 17003
***Tel: (717) 867-5617***
***www.raintree.com***

**S & J CD Duplication**
999 Blanding Blvd., Ste. 10
Orange Park, FL 32065
***Tel: (904) 272-0580***
***www.snjcd.com***

**Superdups**
68 H Stiles Road
Salem, NH 03079
***Tel: (800) 617-3877***
***www.superdups.com***

**Tape Specialty, Inc.**
24831 Avenue Tibbitts
Valencia, CA 91355
***Tel: (800) 310-0800***
***www.cdmanufacturing.com***

**The Mastering House**
1002 Ridge Rd.
Pottstown, PA 19465
***Tel: (610) 469-1050***
***www.masteringhouse.com***

**Triple Disc**
11827 Main Street
Fredericksburg, VA 22408
***Tel: (800) 414-7564***
***www.tripledisc.com***

**We Make Tapes & Discs**
118 16th Avenue South, Ste. 1
Nashville, TN 37203
***Tel: (615) 244-4236***
***www.wemaketapes.com***

**Wings Digital Corporation**
10 Commercial Street
Hicksville, NY 11801
***Tel: (516) 933-2500***
***www.wingsdigital.com***

**World Media Group Inc.**
6737 E. 30th Street
Indianapolis, IN 46219
***Tel: (317) 549-8484***
***www.worldmediagroup.com***

**World Replication Group**
46000 Witmer Industrial Estates #2
Niagra Falls, NY 14305
***Tel: (800) 463-9493***
***www.worldreplication.com***

# EVERY LISTING

## in this DIRECTORY can be an Internship Opportunity. Here's our List to get you going!!!

**Apollo Theater**
253 W. 125th Street
New York, NY 10027
***Tel: (212) 531-5300***
***www.apollotheater.com***

**Bad Boy**
1710 Broadway, 2nd Fl.
New York, NY 10019
***Tel: (212) 500-2200***
***www.badboyonline.com***

**Billboard**
5055 Wilshire Boulevard
Los Angeles, CA 90036
***Tel: (323) 525-2300***
***www.billboard.com***

**Billboard**
770 Broadway
New York, NY 10003
***Tel: (646) 654-4400***
***www.billboard.com***

**Capitol Records**
1750 N. Vine Street
Hollywood, CA 90028
***Tel: (323) 462-6252***
***www.hollywoodandvine.com***

**CBS Radio**
1515 Broadway
New York, NY 10036
***Tel: (212) 846-3939***
***www.cbsradio.com***

**CBS Radio**
40 West 57th Street
New York, NY 10019
***Tel: (212) 846-3939***
***www.cbsradio.com***

**Clear Channel**
200 E. Basse Road
San Antonio, TX 78209
***Tel: (210) 822-2828***
***www.clearchannel.com***

**Cox Radio**
6205 Peachtree Dunwoody Rd.
Atlanta, GA 30328
***Tel: (678) 645-0000***
***www.coxradio.com***

**EMI Christian Music Group**
101 Winners Circle
Brentwood, TN 37024
***Tel: (615) 371-4300***
***www.emicmg.com***

**EMI Group**
150 Fifth Avenue
New York, NY 10011
***Tel: (212) 786-8000***
***www.emigroup.com***

**EMI Music**
1750 N. Vine St.
Los Angeles, CA 90028
***Tel: (323) 871-5000***
***www.emigroup.com***

**EMI U.S. Latin**
404 Washington Ave., #700
Miami Beach, FL 33139
***Tel: (305) 674-7529***
***www.emilatin.com***

**Emmis Communications**
One Emmis Plaza
40 Monument Circle, Ste. 700
Indianapolis, IN 46204
***Tel: (317) 266-0100***
***www.emmis.com***

**Hidden Beach Recordings**
3030 Nebraska Ave., Penthouse
Santa Monica, CA 90404
***Tel: (310) 453-1400***
***www.hiddenbeach.com***

**Kennedy Center for the Performing Arts**
2700 F Street, NW
Washington, D.C. 20566
***Tel: (202) 416-8000***
***www.kennedy-center.org***

**MTV**
2600 Colorado Avenue
Santa Monica, CA 90404
***Tel: (310) 752-8000***
***www.mtvncareers.com***

**MTV**
1515 Broadway
New York, NY 10036
***Tel: (212) 258-8000***
***www.mtvncareers.com***

**National Public Radio**
635 Massachusetts Ave., NW
Washington, D.C. 20001
***Tel: (202) 513-2000***
***www.npr.org***

**Philadelphia Int'l. Records**
309 S. Broad Street
Philadelphia, PA 19107
***Tel: (215) 985-0900***
***www.gamble-huffmusic.com***

**Provident Music Group**
741 Cool Springs Blvd.
Franklin, TN 37067
***Tel: (615) 261-6500***
***www.providentmusicgroup.com***

**Radio One, Inc.**
5900 Princess Garden Pkwy., 7th Fl.
Lanham, MD 20706

***www.radio-one.com***

**The Recording Academy**
National Academy of Recording Arts & Sciences (NARAS)
3030 Olympic Blvd.
Santa Monica, CA 90404
***Tel: (310) 392-3777***
***www.grammy.com***

**Rolling Stone Magazine**
1290 Ave. of the Americas
New York, NY 10104
***Tel: (212) 484-1616***
***www.rollingstone.com***

**SIRIUS XM Radio, Inc.**
1221 Ave. of the Americas
New York, NY 10020
***Tel: (212) 584-5100***
***www.careers-siriusxm.icims.com***
***www.sirius.com***

**Sony Music Entertainment**
9830 Wilshire Blvd.
Beverly Hills, CA 90212
***Tel: (310) 272-2100***
***www.sonymusic.com***

**Sony Music Entertainment**
550 Madison Avenue
New York, NY 10022
***Tel: (212) 833-8000***
***www.sonymusic.com***

**Sony Nashville**
1400 18th Avenue S. - 4th Fl.
Nashville, TN 37212
***Tel: (615) 301-4300***
***www.sonymusic.com***

**Universal Music Group**
2220 Colorado Ave.
Santa Monica, CA 90404
***Tel: (310) 865-5000***
***www.universalmusic.com***

**Universal Music Group**
1755 Broadway
New York, NY 10019
***Tel: (212) 841-8000***
***www.universalmusic.com***

**Warner Music Group**
75 Rockefeller Plaza
New York, NY 10019
***Tel: (212) 275-2000***
***www.wmg.com***

**WHUR-WHBC Internship Program**
529 Bryant Street, NW
Washington, DC 20059
***Tel: (202) 806-3500***
***www.whur.com***

**5 Alarm Music**
35 W. Dayton Street
Pasadena, CA 91105
***Tel: (626) 304-1698***
***www.5alarmmusic.com***

**615 Music Library**
1030 16th Avenue S.
Nashville, TN 37212
***Tel: (615) 244-6515***
***Tel: (818) 846-1615 (CA)***
***Tel: (212) 315-1615 (NY)***
***www.615musiclibrary.com***

**Aircraft Production Music Library**
162 Columbus Avenue
Boston, MA 02116
***Tel: (617) 303-7600***
***www.aircraftmusiclibrary.com***

**Allegro Music**
20048 NE San Rafael
Portland, OR 97230
***Tel: (503) 257-8480/(800) 288-2007***
***www.allegro-music.com***

**Associated Production Music**
6255 Sunset Blvd., Ste. 820
Hollywood, CA 90028
***Tel: (323) 461-3211***
***www.apmmusic.com***

**Associated Production Music**
381 Park Ave., South - Ste. 1101
New York, NY 10016
***Tel: (212) 856-9800***
***www.apmmusic.com***

**AudioSparx**
Navarr Enterprises, Inc.
99 King Street, Ste. 2092
Saint Augustine, FL 32085
***Tel: (954) 791-9795***
***www.audiosparx.com***

**Autry National Center**
4700 Western Heritage Drive
Los Angeles, CA 90027
***Tel: (323) 667-2000***
***www.autrynationalcenter.org***

**Country Music Hall of Fame**
222 Fifth Avenue S.
Nashville, TN 37203
***Tel: (615) 416-2001***
***www.countrymusichalloffame.com***

**CSS Music**
1948 Riverside Dr.
Los Angeles, CA 90039
***Tel: (800) HOT-MUSIC***
***www.cssmusic.com***

**De Wolfe Music Library**
25 W. 45th St., Ste. 401
New York, NY 10036
***Tel: (212) 382-0220***
***www.dewolfemusic.com***

**Dick Clark Archives**
2900 Olympic Boulevard
Santa Monica, CA 90404
***Tel: (310) 255-4600***
***www.dickclarkproductions.com***

**FirstCom Music**
9255 W. Sunset Blvd., 2nd Fl.
Los Angeles, CA 90069
***Tel: (310) 865-4477***
***www.firstcom.com***

**FirstCom Music**
1325 Capital Pkwy., Ste. 109
Carrollton, TX 75006
***Tel: (972) 446-8742***
***www.firstcom.com***

**Fresh Music Library**
320 South Street
Agawam, MA 01001
***Tel: (413) 786-1450***
***www.freshmusic.com***

**Hollywood Edge**
7080 Hollywood Blvd., Ste. 519
Hollywood, CA 90028
***Tel: (323) 603-3252***
***www.hollywoodedge.com***

**HRS Studios**
420 Lexington Ave., Ste. 1934
New York, NY 10170
***Tel: (212) 687-4180***
***www.hsrny.com***

**IAMusic.com**
2653 2nd Avenue East
St. Paul, MN 55109
***Tel: (818) 528-4494***
***www.iamusic.com***

**JamSync**
Box 120969
Nashville, TN 37212
***Tel: (615) 320-5050***

www.jamsync.com

**Kamen Entertainment Group**
701 Seventh Ave., 6th Fl.
New York, NY 10036
*Tel: (212) 575-4660*
*www.kamen.com*

**Killer Tracks**
8750 Wilshire Boulevard
Beverly Hills, CA 90211
*Tel: (310) 358-4455*
*www.killertracks.com*

**MBA Music**
208 W. 23rd Street, Ste. 814
New York, NY 10011
*Tel: (212) 414-9601*
*www.mbamusic.com*

**Megatrax Production Music**
7629 Fulton Avenue
N. Hollywood, CA 91605
*Tel: (818) 255-7100*
*www.megatrax.com*

**The Music Bakery**
7522 Campbell Rd., Ste. 113
Dallas, TX 75248
*Tel: (972) 578-7863*
*www.themusicbakery.com*

**Music Library Association**
8551 Research Way, Ste. 180
Middleton, WI 53562
*Tel: (608) 836-5825*
*www.musiclibraryassoc.org*

**Non-Stop Music**
4605 Lankershim Blvd., Ste. 305
N. Hollywood, CA 91602
*Tel: (818) 752-1898*
*www.nonstopmusic.com*

**Non-Stop Music**
75 Rockefeller Plaza, 8th Fl.
New York, NY 10019
*Tel: (212) 275-3134*
*www.nonstopmusic.com*

**Non-Stop Music**
915 W. 100 South
Salt Lake City, UT 94104
*Tel: (801) 531-0060*
*www.nonstopmusic.com*

**Partners in Rhyme**
*Tel: (323) 774-1389*
*www.partnersinrhyme.com*

**Premier Tracks**
1775 E. Palm Canyon Drive
Suite 110-239
Palm Springs, CA 92264
*Tel: (760) 416-0805*
*www.premiertracks.com*

**Production Garden Music**
510 E. Ramsey, Ste. 4
San Antonio, TX 78216
*Tel: (210) 530-5200*
*www.productiongarden.com*

**Royalty Free Music Inc.**
Gary Lamb Music
P.O. Box 72008
San Clemente, CA 92673
*Tel: (800) 772-7701*
*www.royaltyfree.com*

**Royalty Free Music Library**
Prolific Arts, Inc.
23 Royal Oaks
Denton, TX 76210
*Tel: (940) 382-4191*
*www.royaltyfreemusiclibrary.com*

**Russo Grantham Productions**
37 W. 20th St., 8th Fl.
New York, NY 10011
*Tel: (212) 633-1175*
*www.russograntham.com*

**Screen Music International**
18034 Ventura Blvd., Ste. 450
Encino, CA 91316
*Tel: (818) 789-2954*
*www.screenmusicrecords.com*

**SFX Source.com**
*Tel: (877) 863-5639*
*www.sfxsource.com*

**Songs to Your Eyes Production Music Library**
22040 Del Valle Street
Woodland Hills, CA 91364
*Tel: (323) 988-9725*
*www.songstoyoureyes.com*

**SoperSound Music Library**
P.O. Box 869
Ashland, OR 97520
*Tel: (541) 552-0830*
*www.sopersound.com*

**Soundfx**
P.O. Box 6303
Kingman, AZ 86402
*Tel: (928) 565-7550*
*www.soundfx.com*

**Sound Dogs**
2633 Lincoln Blvd., Ste. 148
Santa Monica, CA 90405
*Tel: (877) 315-3647*
*www.sounddogs.com*

**Sync Sound**
450 W. 56th Street
New York, NY 10019
*Tel: (212) 246-5580*
*www.syncsound.com*

**TRF Music Libraries**
One International Blvd., Ste. 212
Mahwah, NJ 07495
*Tel: (201) 335-0005*
*www.trfmusic.com*

**Valentino Inc.**
7750 Sunset Boulevard
Los Angeles, CA 90046
*Tel: (323) 969-0968*
*www.tvmusic.com*

**VideoHelper**
18 W. 21st Street, 7th Fl.
New York, NY 10010
*Tel: (212) 633-7009*
*www.videohelper.com*

**Aspen Music Festival & School**
2 Music School Road
Aspen, CO 81611
***Tel: (970) 925-3254***
***www.aspenmusicfestival.com***

**Audio Engineering Institute**
10925 West Avenue
San Antonio, TX 78216
***Tel: (210) 698-9666***
***www.audio-eng.com***

**Berklee College of Music**
1140 Boylston Street
Boston, MA 02218
***Tel: (617) 266-1400***
***www.berklee.edu***

**Blair School of Music**
Vanderbilt University
2400 Blakemore Avenue
Nashville, TN 37212
***Tel: (615) 322-7651***
***www.vanderbilt.edu/blair***

**Brooklyn Conservatory of Music**
58 Seventh Avenue
Brooklyn, NY 11217
***Tel: (718) 622-3300***
***www.brooklynconservatory.com***

**The Collective School of Music**
541 Ave. of the Americas
New York, NY 10011
Tempe, AZ 85282
***Tel: (212) 741-0091***
***www.thecoll.com***

**Conservatory of Recording Arts & Sciences**
2300 E. Broadway Rd.
Tempe, AZ 85282
***Tel: (480) 858-0764***
***www.cras.org***

**Curtis Institute of Music**
1726 Locust Street
Philadelphia, PA 19103
***Tel: (215) 893-5252***
***www.curtis.edu***

**Eastman School of Music**
University of Rochester
26 Gibbs Street
Rochester, NY 14604
***Tel: (585) 274-1000***
***www.rochester.edu/eastman***

**Full Sail University**
3300 University Boulevard
Winter Park, FL 32792
***Tel: (407) 679-6333/(800) 226-7625***
***www.fullsail.edu***

**Globe Institute of Recording & Production**
739 Bryant Street
San Francisco, CA 94107
***Tel: (650) 324-0464/(800) 900-0MIX***
***www.globerecording.com***

**Hollywood Pop Academy**
6801 Hollywood Blvd., Ste. 223
Hollywood, CA 90028
***Tel: (323) 463-4080/(877) SING-POP***
***www.hollywoodpopacademy.com***

**Howard University**
**College of Arts & Sciences**
**Div. of Fine Arts/Dept. of Music**
2455 Sixth Street, NW
Washington, D.C. 20059
***Tel: (202) 806-7082***
***www.howard.edu/collegefinearts***

**Institute of Audio Research**
64 University Place
New York, NY 10003
***Tel: (212) 777-8550***
***audioschool.com***

**Institute of Production & Recording**
312 Washington Avenue N.
Minneapolis, MN 55401
***Tel: (612) 375-1900***
***www.iprschool.com***

**International College of Broadcasting**
6 S. Smithville Road
Dayton, OH 45431
***Tel: (937) 258-8251***

*www.icbcollege.com*

**The Juilliard School**
60 Lincoln Center Plaza
New York, NY 10023
*Tel: (212) 799-5000*
*www.juilliard.edu*

**Levine School of Music**
2801 Upton Street, NW
Washington, D.C. 20008
*Tel: (202) 686-8000*
*www.levineschool.org*

**Los Angeles Music Academy**
370 S. Fair Oaks Avenue
Pasadena, CA 91105
*Tel: (626) 568-8850*
*www.lamusicacademy.com*

**Los Angeles Recording School**
6690 Sunset Boulevard
Hollywood, CA 90028
*Tel: (323) 464-5200*
*www.recordingcareer.com*

**Madison Media Institute**
2702 Agriculture Drive
Madison, WI 53719
*Tel: (608) 829-2728*
*www.madisonmedia.com*

**Manhattan School of Music**
120 Claremont Avenue
New York, NY 10027
*Tel: (212) 749-2802*
*www.msmnyc.edu*

**McNally Smith College of Music**
19 Exchange Street East
Saint Paul, MN 55101
*Tel: (651) 291-0177/(800) 594-9500*
*www.mcnallysmith.edu*

**Merit School of Music**
38 S. Peoria Street
Chicago, IL 60607
*Tel: (312) 786-9428/(312) 786-1830*
*www.meritmusic.org*

**Musicians Institute**
6752 Hollywood Blvd.
Hollywood, CA 90028
*Tel: (323) 462-1384*
*www.mi.edu*

**MusicTech College**
19 Exchange Street E.
St. Paul, MN 55101
*Tel: (651) 291-0177*
*www.musictech.com*

**NYU Tisch School of the Arts**
721 Broadway - Floor 9N
New York, NY 10003
*Tel: (212) 998-1800*
*www.tisch.nyu.edu*

**NYU Tisch School of the Arts**
Clive Davis Department of
Recorded Music
194 Mercer Street, 5th Fl.
New York, NY 10012
*Tel: (212) 992-8400*
*www.nyu.edu/tisch/recordedmusic*

**Oberlin Conservatory of Music**
39 W. College Street
Oberlin, OH 44074
*Tel: (440) 775-8413*
*www.oberlin.edu*

**Omega Studios' School of Applied Recording Arts & Sciences**
5609 Fishers Lane
Rockville, MD 20852
*Tel: (301) 230-9100*
*www.omegastudios.com*

**Peabody Institute of the Johns Hopkins University**
1 East Mount Vernon Place
Baltimore, MD 21202
*Tel: (410) 659-8100*
*www.peabody.jhu.edu*

**Recording Connection**
6253 Hollywood Blvd., Ste. 302
Los Angeles, CA 90028
*Tel: (800) 755-7597/(310) 456-9624*
*www.recordingconnection.com*

**Recording Institute of Detroit**
14611 E. Nine Mile Road
Eastpointe, MI 48201
*Tel: (586) 779-1388/(800) 683-1743*
*www.recordinginstitute.com*

**Recording Workshop**
455 Massieville Rd.
Chillicothe, OH 45601
*Tel: (740) 663-1000*
*www.recordingworkshop.com*

**SAE Institute - L.A.**
6565 Sunset Blvd., Ste. 100
Los Angeles, CA 90028
*Tel: (323) 466-6323*
*www.sae.edu*

**SAE Institute - S.F.**
450 Bryant Street, Ste. 100
San Francisco, CA 94107
*Tel: (415) 344-0886*
*www.sae.edu*

**SAE Institute - Miami**
16051 W. Dixie Highway
N. Miami Beach, FL 33160
*Tel: (305) 944-7494*
*www.sae.edu*

**SAE Institute - Atlanta**
215 Peachtree Street, Ste. 300
Atlanta, GA 30303
*Tel. (404) 526-9366*
*www.sae.edu*

**SAE Institute - NY**
1293 Broadway, 9th Fl.
New York, NY 10001
*Tel: (212) 944-9121*
*www.sae.edu*

**SAE Institute - Nashville**
7 Music Circle North
Nashville, TN 37203
*Tel: (615) 244-5848*
*www.sae.edu*

**San Francisco Conservatory of Music**
50 Oak Street
San Francisco, CA 94102

***Tel: (415) 864-7326***
***www.sfcm.edu***

**School Without Walls**
Dirk Price Music
1237 Ashland Mine Road
Ashland, OR 97520
***Tel: (541) 552-9605/(800) 994-7683***
***www.dickgrove.com***

**Pinnacle College**
1000 S. Fremont Avenue
Bldg. A11/Ste. 11010
Alhambra, CA 91803
***Tel: (626) 284-0050***
***www.pinnaclecollege.edu***

**Syracuse University**
College of Visual & Performing Arts
202 Crouse College
Syracuse, NY 13244
***Tel: (315) 443-2769***
***vpa.syr.edu***

**The Technology Institute for Music Educators/TI:ME**
3300 Washtenaw Ave., Ste 220
Ann Arbor, MI 48104
***Tel: (734) 677-2270***
***www.ti-me.org***

**UCLA Department of Music**
2539 Schoenberg Music Bldg.
Box 951616
Los Angeles, CA 90095
***Tel: (310) 825-4761***
***www.music.ucla.edu***

**University of Alabama School of Music**
Box 870366
Tuscaloosa, AL 35487
***Tel: (205) 348-7110***
***www.music.ua.edu***

**Univ. of Southern California/(USC)**
Thornton School of Music
Department of Music Industry
Los Angeles, CA 90089
***Tel: (213) 740-3224***
***www.usc.edu/music***

Homework!
10+ Resources to Help YOU Understand Copyrights, Royalties, Song Registrations, Statistics & More.
* ASCAP - www.ascap.com
* BMI - www.bmi.com
* Nielsen BDS - en-us.nielsen.com
* Nielsen SoundScan - www.soundscan.com
* Recording Industry Association of America - www.riaa.com. Get YOUR Gold & Platinum Certification.
* SESAC - www.sesac.com
* SoundScan - www.soundscan.com
* SoundExchange - www.soundexchange.com
* TuneCore.com - www.tunecore.com. One of MANY affordable ways to sell your music online (starting at $9.99) on iTunes, Rhapsody, Zune Marketplace & many other digital sites.
* U.S. Copyright Office - www.copyright.gov. Protect your work for $35 online, registration lasts your lifetime PLUS 70 years.

**American Christian Radio Network (ACN)**
P.O. Box 31000
Spokane, WA 99223
***Tel: (509) 443-1000***
***www.acn-network.com***

**American Forces Radio & TV Network**
***Tel: (703) 428-0622***
***afrts.dodmedia.osd.mil***

**American Urban Radio Networks**
432 Park Avenue S., 14th Fl.
New York, NY 10016
***Tel: (212) 883-2100***
***www.aurnol.com***

**AP Broadcast News Center**
1100 13th Street, Ste. 700
Washington, D.C. 20005
***Tel: (202) 641-9500***
***www.apbroadcast.com***

**Bible Broadcasting Network**
11530 Carmel Commons Blvd.
Charlotte, NC 28226
***Tel: (704) 523-5555***
***www.bbnradio.org***

**Black University Radio Network**
B.E. Advertising & Promotions
6125 Clybourn Ave., Ste. #47
N. Hollywood, CA 91606
***Tel: (818) 766-0087***
***www.eurweb.com***

**Buckley Radio**
166 W. Putnam Avenue
Greenwich, CT 06830
***Tel: (203) 661-4307***
***www.buckleyradio.com***

**CBS Radio**
40 West 57th Street
New York, NY 10019
***Tel: (212) 846-3939***
***www.cbsradio.com***

**Citadel Broadcasting**
7201 W. Lake Mead Blvd., Ste. 400
Las Vegas, NV 89128
***Tel: (702) 804-5200***
***www.citadelbroadcasting.com***

**Citadel Media**
261 Madison Avenue
New York, NY 10016
***Tel: (212) 735-1700***
***www.citadelmedianetworks.com***

**Citadel Media**
13725 Montfort Drive
Dallas, TX 75240
***Tel: (972) 991-9200***
***www.citadelmedianetworks.com***

**Clear Channel**
200 E. Basse Road
San Antonio, TX 78209
***Tel: (210) 822-2828***
***www.clearchannel.com***

**Cox Radio**
6205 Peachtree Dunwoody Rd.
Atlanta, GA 30328
***Tel: (678) 645-0000***
***www.coxradio.com***

**Cumulus Media & Broadcasting**
3280 Peachtree Rd., NW - Ste. 2300
Atlanta, GA 30305
***Tel: (404) 949-0700***
***www.cumulus.com***

**Electronic Urban Report (EUR Web.com)**
P.O. Box 412081
Los Angeles, CA 90041
***Tel: (323) 254-9599/(661) 250-7300***
***www.eurweb.com***

**Emmis Communications**
One Emmis Plaza
40 Monument Circle, Ste. 700
Indianapolis, IN 46204
***Tel: (317) 266-0100***
***www.emmis.com***

**Entercom Communications Corp.**
401 City Ave., Ste. 809

Bala Cynwyd, PA 19004
***Tel: (610) 660-5610***
***www.entercom.com***

**ESPN Radio**
ESPN Radio
Bristol, CT 06010
***Tel: (860) 766-2000***
***www.espnradio.com***

**Inner City Broadcasting**
1900 Pineview Drive
Columbia, SC 29209
***Tel: (803) 695-8600***
***www.innercitysc.com***

**Katz Media Corp.**
125 W. 55th Street
New York, NY 10019
***Tel: (212) 424-6000***
***www.katz-media.com***

**Latino Broadcasting Company**
2100 Coral Way, Ste. 126
Miami, FL 33145
***Tel: (305) 857-6657***
***www.latinobroadcasting.com***

**Moody Radio**
820 N. LaSalle Blvd.
Chicago, IL 60610
***Tel: (800) 621-7031***
***www.moodyradio.org***

**MRN Radio - Motor Racing Network**
1801 W. Int'l. Speedway Blvd.
Daytona Beach, FL 32114
***Tel: (386) 947-6400***
***www.mrnradio.com***
***www.racingone.com***

**National Public Radio**
635 Massachusetts Ave., NW
Washington, D.C. 20001
***Tel: (202) 513-2000***
***www.npr.org***

**Premiere Radio Networks**
15260 Ventura Blvd., 5th Fl.
Sherman Oaks, CA 91403
***Tel: (818) 377-5300***
***www.premrad.com***

**Public Radio International**
100 N. Sixth Street, Ste. 900A
Minneapolis, MN 55403
***Tel: (612) 338-5000***
***www.pri.org***

**Pulse of Radio**
1065 6th Avenue, 3rd Fl.
New York, NY 10018
***Tel: (212) 536-3600***
***pulseofradio.com***

**Radio One, Inc.**
5900 Princess Garden Pkwy., 7th Fl.
Lanham, MD 20706
***Tel: (301) 306-1111***
***www.radio-one.com***

**Salem Radio Network**
4800 Santa Rosa Road
Camarillo, CA 93012
***Tel: (805) 987-0400***
***www.salem.cc***

**Sheridan Broadcasting**
960 Penn Avenue, Ste. 200
Pittsburgh, PA 15222
***Tel: (412) 456-4000***
***www.sgnthelight.com***

**SIRIUS XM Radio, Inc.**
1221 Avenue of the Americas
New York, NY 10020
***Tel: (212) 584-5100***
***www.sirius.com***
***www.careers-siriusxm.icims.com***

**Triton Radio Networks**
220 W. 42nd Street
New York, NY 10036
***Tel: (212) 419-2929***
***www.tritonradionetworks.com***

**United Stations Radio Networks**
11400 W. Olympic Blvd., Ste. 750
Los Angeles, CA 90064
***Tel: (310) 268-9292***
***www.unitedstations.com***

**United Stations Radio Networks**
1065 Ave. of the Americas, 3rd Fl.
New York, NY 10018
***Tel: (212) 869-1111***
***www.unitedstations.com***

**Voice of America**
330 Independence Ave., SW
Washington, D.C. 20237
***Tel: (202) 203-4959***
***www.voanews.com***

**Westwood One**
40 W. 57th Street, 5th Fl.
New York, NY 10019
***Tel: (212) 641-2000***
***www.westwoodone.com***

# RADIO STATIONS

# WHO OWNS RADIO?

Radio Stations are going through a major metamorphosis (changing formats, call letters, programming agendas and more) -- as is the entire music industry. Below is our *EPP: 4* QUICK LIST of resources for locating your FAVORITE RADIO STATION. *For a complete list of THOUSANDS of RADIO STATIONS contact the RADIO NETWORKS listed on Pages 176-177 & the MEDIA GIANTS listed on Page 97.

## RADIO STATION CENTRAL:

**Arbitron**
***www.arbitron.com***

**Live-Radio.net**
***www.live-radio.net***

**Online Radio Stations.com**
***www.onlineradiostations.com***

**Radio Locator**
***www.radio-locator.com***

**Radio Row**
***www.radiorow.com***

**Radio Stations**
***www.radiostations.com***

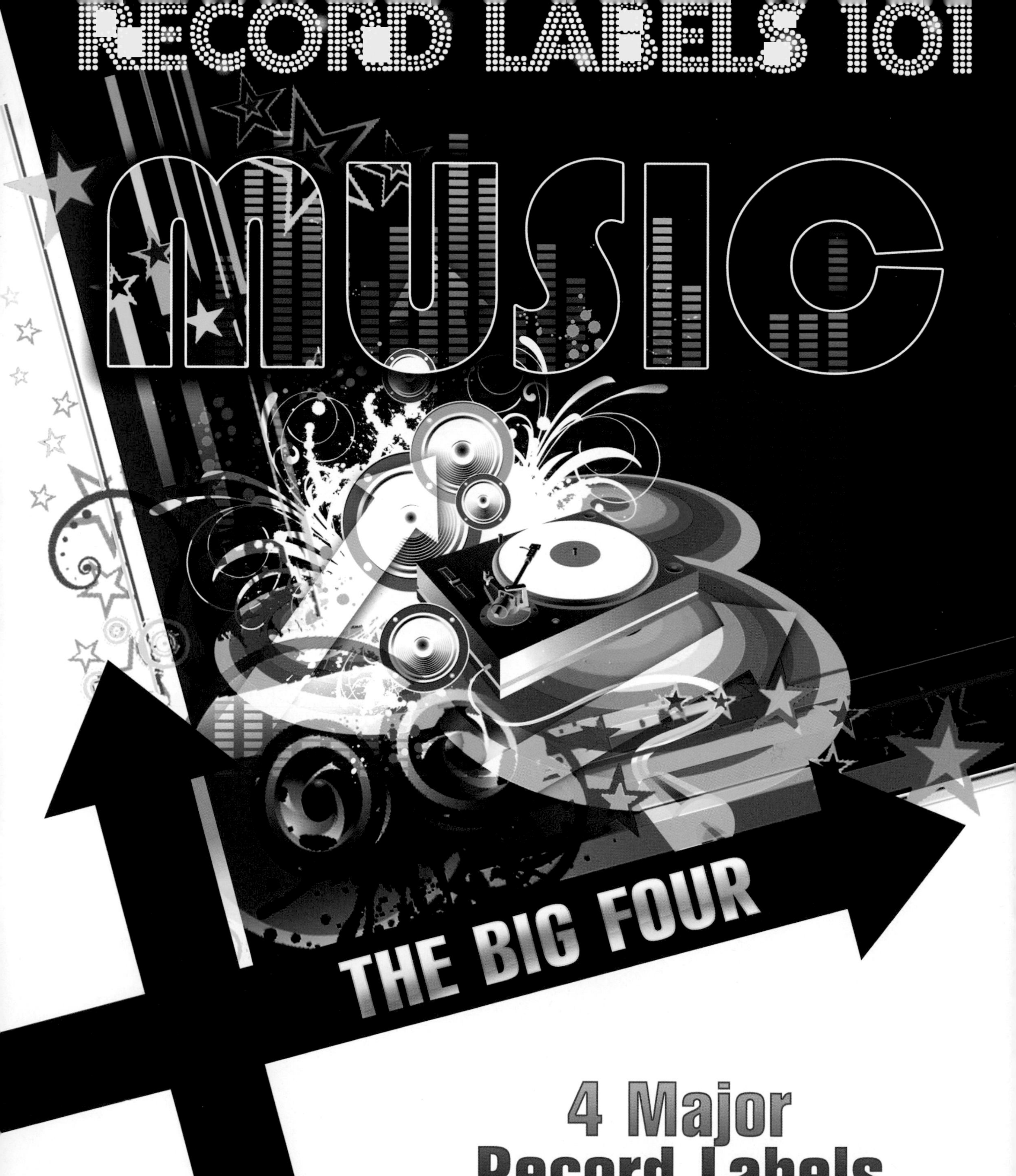
RECORD LABELS 101
MUSIC
THE BIG FOUR
4 Major
Record Labels

# ***The World's Four Largest Record Labels***

(New York headquarters are listed first)

The Big Four Labels and their subsidiary labels are listed below. These POWERHOUSES also have scores of affiliated labels under their subsidiary labels.

## EMI Group

150 Fifth Avenue
New York, NY 10011
***Tel: (212) 786-8000***
***www.emigroup.com***

## EMI Music

1750 N. Vine St.
Los Angeles, CA 90028
***Tel: (323) 871-5000***
***www.emigroup.com***

*Labels include*: Angel; Astralwerks; Blue Note; Capitol; Capitol Nashville; EMI Classics; EMI Christian Music Group; EMI Records; EMI Televisa Music; Manhattan; Mute; Parlophone; Virgin

## Sony Music Entertainment

550 Madison Avenue
New York, NY 10022
***Tel: (212) 833-8000***
***www.sonymusic.com***

## Sony Music Entertainment

9830 Wilshire Blvd.
Beverly Hills, CA 90212
***Tel: (310) 272-2100***
***www.sonymusic.com***

## Sony Nashville

1400 18th Avenue S. - 4th Fl.
Nashville, TN 37212
***Tel: (615) 301-4300***
***www.sonymusic.com***

*Labels include*: Arista; Arista Nashville; BNA Records Label; Columbia; Columbia Nashville; Epic; J Records; Jive; Legacy; Masterworks; Provident Label Group; RCA; Sony Music; Sony Music Latin; Sony Music Nashville; Verity; Zomba Label Group

## Universal Music Group

1755 Broadway
New York, NY 10019
***Tel: (212) 841-8000***
***www.universalmusic.com***

## Universal Music Group

2220 Colorado Ave.
Santa Monica, CA 90404
***Tel: (310) 865-5000***
***www.universalmusic.com***

*Labels include*: A&M/Octone; Bad Boy; Decca Label Group; Interscope Geffen A&M; Island Def Jam Music Group; Universal Motown Republic Group; Universal Music Enterprises; Universal Music Group Nashville; Universal Music Latin Entertainment; Universal Records South; Verve Music Group

## Warner Music Group

75 Rockefeller Plaza
New York, NY 10019
***Tel: (212) 275-2000***
***www.wmg.com***

## Warner Music Group

3400 W. Olive Avenue
Burbank, CA 91505
***Tel: (818) 238-6500***
***www.wmg.com***

*Labels include*: Asylum; Atlantic Records; East West Records; Elektra; Independent Label Group (ILG); Nonesuch; Reprise; Rhino; Road Runner Records; Rykodisc; Sire; Warner Bros. Records; Warner Bros. Records Nashville; Word Label Group

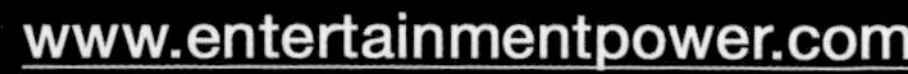

You can find a current listing of hundreds of Record Labels on our www.entertainmentpower.com website. Digital downloads available too.

RECORDING STUDIOS

**Acacia Recording**
13005 Purden Court
Mt. Airy, MD 21771
***Tel: (301) 829-8088***
***www.acaciarecording.com***

**Afterhours Recording Company**
1616 Victory Blvd., Ste. 104G
Glendale, CA 91201
***Tel: (818) 246-6583***

**Allusion Studios**
248 W. Elm Street
Tucson, AZ 85705
***Tel: (520) 622-3895***
***www.allusionstudios.com***

**American Recording Company**
22301 Mulholland Highway
Calabasas, CA 91302
***Tel: (818) 223-8030***

**Apparatus**
19752 Observation Dr.
Topanga, CA 90290
***Tel: (310) 455-3332***

**Ardent Studios**
2000 Madison Ave.
Memphis, TN 38104
***Tel: (901) 725-0855***
***www.ardentstudios.com***

**Arrow Records Recording Studio**
5917 Old National Highway
College Park, GA 30349
***Tel: (770) 210-5708***
***www.arrowrecords.org***

**Audio Productions**
1102 17th Ave. South, Ste. 200
Nashville, TN 37212
***Tel: (615) 321-3612***
***www.audioproductions.com***

**Avex Honolulu Studios**
377 Keahole Street, D-03
Honolulu, HI 96825
***Tel: (808) 393-2021***
***www.avexhonolulustudios.com***

**Baker Sound Studios Inc.**
1821 Ranstead St.
Philadelphia, PA 19103
***Tel: (215) 567-0400***
***www.bakersound.com***

**Bates Brothers Recording Studio**
3427 Davey Allison Rd., Ste. 101
Hueytown, AL 35023
***Tel: (205) 491-4066***
***www.batesbrothersrecording.com***

**Battery Studios**
321 W. 44th Street, 10th Fl.
New York, NY 10036
***Tel: (212) 833-7373***
***www.batterystudios.com***

**Bay Records Recording Studios**
1741 Alcatraz Avenue
Berkeley, CA 94703
***Tel: (510) 428-2002***
***www.bayrec.com***

**Bias Studios**
5400 Carolina Place
Springfield, VA 22151
***Tel: (703) 941-3333***
***www.biasrecording.com***

**Blackstar Studios**
12187 SW 132 Court
Miami, FL 33186
***Tel: (305) 235-5043***
***www.blackstarstudiomiami.com***

**Boss Studios**
1005 Market Street
San Francisco, CA 94103
***Tel: (415) 626-1234***
***www.pboss.com***

**Capitol Studios**
1750 N. Vine Street
Hollywood, CA 90028
***Tel: (323) 875-5001***
***www.capitolstudios.com***

**Castle Recording Studios**
1393 Old Hilsboro Road
Franklin, TN 37069
***Tel: (615) 791-0810***
***www.castlerecordingstudios.com***

**Cherokee Recording Studio**
751 N. Fairfax Avenue
Los Angeles, CA 90046
***Tel: (323) 653-3412***
***www.cherokeestudios.com***

**Chicago Recording Company**
232 E. Ohio Street
Chicago, IL 60611
***Tel: (312) 822-9333***
***www.chicagorecording.com***

**Clear Lake Audio**
10520 Burbank Blvd.
N. Hollywood, CA 91601
***Tel: (818) 762-0707***
***www.clearlakeaudio.com***

**Commercial Recording Studios**
6001 W. Creek Road
Independence, OH 44131
***Tel: (216) 642-1000***
***www.commercialrecording.com***

**Complex Studios**
2323 Corinth Avenue
Los Angeles, CA 90064
***Tel: (310) 477-1938***
***www.thecomplexstudios.com***

**Concord Music Studios**
2600 10th St.
Berkeley, CA 94710
***Tel: (510) 549-2500***
***www.concordmusicgroup.com***

**Crescent Moon**
6205 Bird Road
Miami, FL 33155
***Tel: (305) 663-8924***
***www.crescentmoon.com***

**Cue Recording Studios**
109 Park Avenue, Ste. E.
Falls Church, VA 22046
***Tel: (703) 532-9033***
***www.cuerecording.com***

**Cups 'N Strings**
23281 Ventura Blvd.
Woodland Hills, CA 91364
***Tel: (818) 222-4600***
***www.cupsnstrings.com***

**The Cutting Room**
14 E. 4th Street, 6th Fl.
New York, NY 10012
***Tel: (212) 260-0905***
***www.thecuttingroom.com***

**DARP - Dallas Austin Recording Projects**
582 Trabert Ave. NW
Atlanta, GA 30309
***Tel: (404) 351-3736***

**Darkchild Records**
503 Doughty Rd.
Pleasantville, NJ 08323
***www.darkchild.com***

**Dixiana Music**
1024 17th Avenue S.
Nashville, TN 37212
***Tel: (615) 329-2199***
***www.dixiana.com***

**Doppler Studios**
1922 Piedmont Circle NE
Atlanta, GA 30324
***Tel: (404) 873-6941***
***www.dopplerstudios.com***

**Echo Beach Studios**
947 Alternate A-1-A
Jupiter, FL 33477
***Tel: (800) 795-3246***
***www.echobeach.com***

**XM Productions-Effanel Music**
***Tel: (212) 807-1100***
***effanel.com***

**Exstasy Recording Studio North**
5253 Lankershim Blvd.
N. Hollywood, CA 91601
***Tel: (818) 761-3882***
***www.exstasyrecordingstudios.com***

**Exstasy Recording Studio South**
8000 Beverly Boulevard
Los Angeles, CA 90048
***Tel: (323) 655-9200***
***www.exstasyrecordingstudios.com***

**Fever Recording Studios**
5739 TaJunga Blvd.
N. Hollywood, CA 91601
***Tel: (818) 487-8772***
***www.feverrecordingstudios.com***

**Firehouse Recording Studios**
35 W. Dayton Street
Pasadena, CA 91105
***Tel: (626) 405-0411***
***www.firehouserecordingstudios.com***

**Foxfire Recording**
16760 Stagg St., Ste. 210
Van Nuys, CA 91406
***Tel: (818) 787-4843***
***www.foxfirerecording.com***

**Full House Studios**
123 W. 18th Street, 7th Fl.
New York, NY 10011
***Tel: (212) 645-2228***
***www.fullhouseny.com***

**Golden Track Recording Studio**
6526 El Cajon Blvd.
San Diego, CA 92115
***Tel: (619) 252-8763***
***www.goldentrackstudio.com***

**Harmonic Ranch**
59 Franklin Street
New York, NY 10013
***Tel: (212) 966-3141***
***www.harmonicranch.com***

**Harmonie Park Studios**
1427 Randolph St., #200
Detroit, MI 48226
***Tel: (313) 965-4343***
***www.harmoniepark.com***

**Hen House Studios**
P.O. Box 742
Venice, CA 90294
***Tel: (310) 577-9150***
***www.henhousestudios.com***

**Herringbone Recording Studio**
559 Brewer Drive
Antioch, TN 37211
***Tel: (615) 331-6567***
***www.herringbonerecords.com***

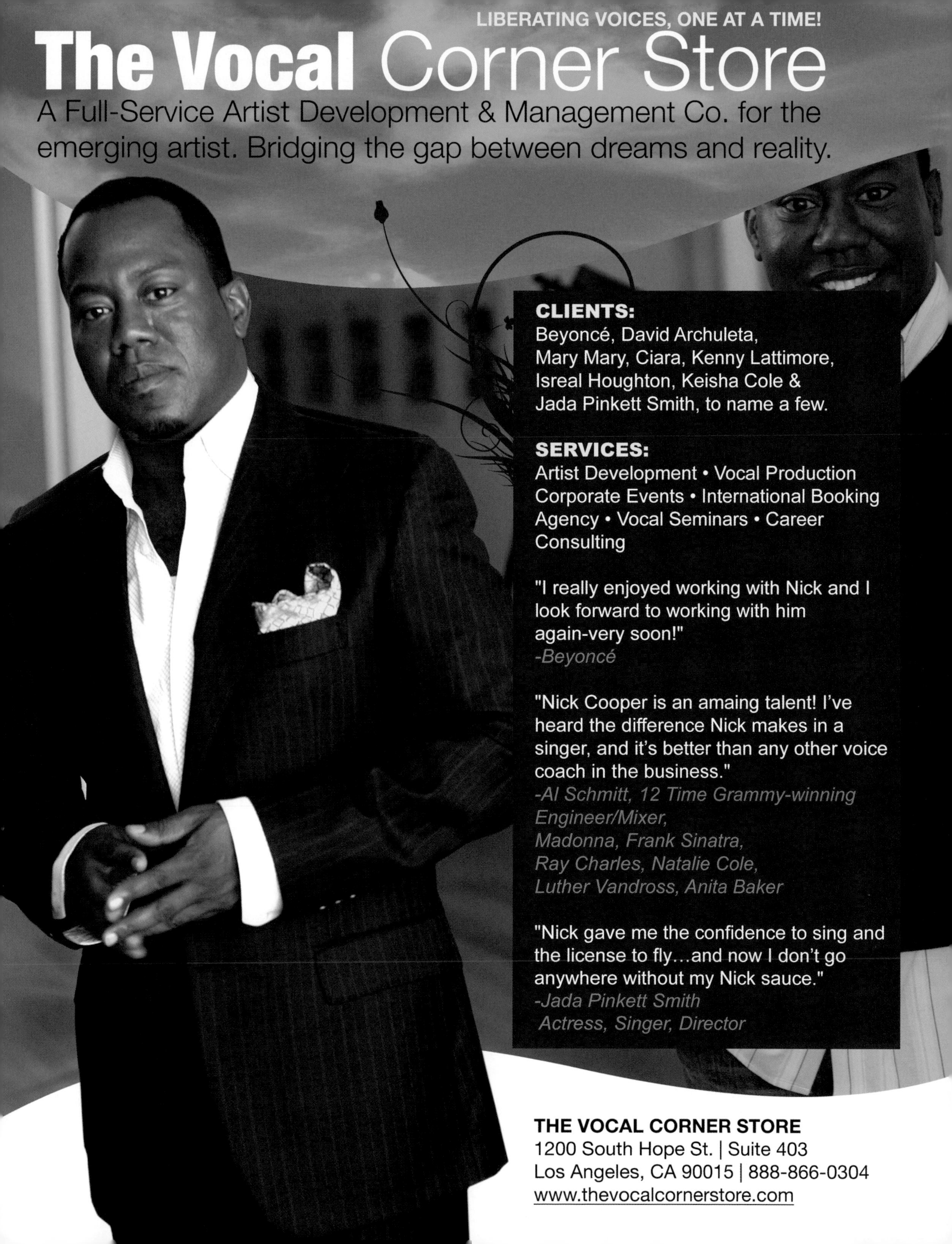
LIBERATING VOICES, ONE AT A TIME!
The Vocal Corner Store
A Full-Service Artist Development & Management Co. for the emerging artist. Bridging the gap between dreams and reality.
CLIENTS:
Beyoncé, David Archuleta, Mary Mary, Ciara, Kenny Lattimore, Isreal Houghton, Keisha Cole & Jada Pinkett Smith, to name a few.
SERVICES:
Artist Development • Vocal Production Corporate Events • International Booking Agency • Vocal Seminars • Career Consulting
"I really enjoyed working with Nick and I look forward to working with him again-very soon!"
-Beyoncé
"Nick Cooper is an amaing talent! I've heard the difference Nick makes in a singer, and it's better than any other voice coach in the business."
-Al Schmitt, 12 Time Grammy-winning Engineer/Mixer, Madonna, Frank Sinatra, Ray Charles, Natalie Cole, Luther Vandross, Anita Baker
"Nick gave me the confidence to sing and the license to fly…and now I don't go anywhere without my Nick sauce."
-Jada Pinkett Smith
Actress, Singer, Director
THE VOCAL CORNER STORE
1200 South Hope St. | Suite 403
Los Angeles, CA 90015 | 888-866-0304
www.thevocalcornerstore.com

**The Hit Factory Criteria Studios**
1744 NE 149th Street
Miami, FL 33181
***Tel: (305) 947-5611/(212) 664-1000***
***www.criteriastudios.com.com***

**House of Blues Studios**
4431 Petit Avenue
Encino, CA 91436
***Tel: (818) 990-1296***
***www.houseofbluesstudios.com***
****Memphis studio too***

**House of Blues Studios**
518 E. Iris Drive
Nashville, TN 37204
***Tel: (615) 777-9080***
***www.houseofbluesstudios.com***
****Memphis studio too***

**Hunnicutt Recording**
737 W. Lynwood St.
Phoenix, AZ 85007
***Tel: (602) 254-6000***

**Hyde Street Studios**
245 Hyde Street
San Francisco, CA 94102
***Tel: (415) 441-8934***
***www.hydestreet.com***

**Kamen Entertainment Group**
701 Seventh Ave., 6th Fl.
New York, NY 10036
***Tel: (212) 575-4660***
***www.kamen.com***

**King Street Sounds**
115 W. 30th St., #306
New York, NY 10001
***Tel: (212) 594-3737***
***www.kingstreetsounds.com***

**The Lodge**
740 Broadway, Ste. 605
New York, NY 10003
***Tel: (212) 353-3895***
***www.thelodge.com***

**Mad Dog Studios Inc.**
293 S. Lake Street
Burbank, CA 91502
***Tel: (818) 557-0100***
***www.maddogstudio.com***

**Maximedia Recording Studios**
13300 Branch View Lane
Dallas, TX 75234
***Tel: (972) 488-8814***
***www.maximedia.us***

**National Public Radio Studios**
635 Massachusetts Ave., NW
Washington, D.C. 20001
***Tel: (202) 513-2000***
***www.npr.org***

**Nightbird Recording Studios**
Sunset Marquis Hotel
1200 Alta Loma Road
W. Hollywood, CA 90069
***Tel: (310) 657-8405***
***www.nightbirdrecordingstudios.com***

**Night Flight Recording Studios**
9537 Fort Foote Road
Fort Washington, MD 20774
***Tel: (301) 567-3483***
***www.nightflightonline.com***

**Nightingale Studios**
156 W. Providencia Avenue
Burbank, CA 91502
***Tel: (818) 562-6660***
***www.nightingalestudios.com***

**Ocean Way**
6050 Sunset Blvd.
Hollywood, CA 90028
***Tel: (323) 467-9375***
***www.oceanwayrecording.com***

**Odds On Records & Studios**
14 Sunset Way
Henderson, NV 89014
***Tel: (702) 318-6001***
***www.oddsonrecording.com***

**Omega Recording Studios**
5609 Fishers Lane
Rockville, MD 20852
***Tel: (301) 230-9100***
***www.omegastudios.com***

**Patchwerk Recording Studios**
1094 Hemphill Avenue
Atlanta, GA 30318
***Tel: (404) 874-9880***
***www.patchwerk.com***

**Phat Planet Recording Studios**
3473 Parkway Center Court
Orlando, FL 32808
***Tel: (407) 295-7270***
***www.phatplanetstudios.com***

**Philadelphia International Records Recording Studios**
309 S. Broad Street
Philadelphia, PA 19107
***Tel: (215) 985-0900***
***www.gamble-huffmusic.com***

**Pilot Recording Studios**
The Birkshires, MA
***Tel: (212) 255-5544***
***www.pilotrecording.com***

**Pressure Point Recording Studios**
2239 South Michigan Ave.
Chicago, IL 60616
***Tel: (312) 842-8099***
***www.pressurepointrecording.com***

**Quad Recording Studios**
723 7th Avenue, 10th Fl.
New York, NY 10019
***Tel: (212) 730-1035***
***www.quadstudios.com***

**Quad Recording Studios**
1802 Grand Avenue
Nashville, TN 37212
***Tel: (615) 321-9500***
***www.quadstudios.com***

**Race Horse Studios**
3780 Shelby Avenue
Los Angeles, CA 90034
***Tel: (310) 280-0175***
***www.racehorsestudios.com***

**Record Plant Recording Studio**
1032 N. Sycamore Avenue
Los Angeles, CA 90038
***Tel: (323) 993-9300***
***www.recordplant.com***

POWER QUOTES&
Notes

# Want To Be In The Music Industry?

If you can answer YES to any of the questions below, you NEED......

"7 Steps to Put Yourself Into the Music Industry"

1. Do you have a CD but don't know how to do marketing & promotion past the local level?

2. Do you need to get airplay?

3. Do you want to recieve rolyalties from your music from traditional radio and internet radio?

4. Do you want to learn about the business side (the legal stuff) of the industry?

5. Do you want to record a CD and just don't know how to get started?

*Get the answers to these questions & more!*

More than 20 years of industry experience at your fingertips. These Key 7 Steps is what Everyone Should know, but MOST don't!
*(Even the ones who "claim" to be already in the industry)*

Your Key To Success!

**ORDER YOUR COPY TODAY!**
(301) 459-2558
www.bgrstar.com

**WWW.BGRSTAR.COM** Contact (301) 459-2558 **Get Ready For Success!**

*Available for workshops and speaking engagements. Call today to reserve your date.* Postcard by LA Designs. 240 593-2345

**Royaltone Studios**
10335 Magnolia Boulevard
Hollywood, CA 91602
***Tel: (818) 769-2596***
***www.royaltonestudios.com***

**RPM Studios**
180 Oxford Rd.
Fern Park, FL 32730
***Tel: (407) 331-0588***
***www.rennmusic.com***

**The Saltmine**
48 S. Macdonald Street
Mesa, AZ 85210
***Tel: (480) 220-4007***
***www.thesaltmine.com***

**Scream Studios**
23679 Calabasas Road, #7
Calabasas, CA 91302
***Tel: (818) 505-0755***
***www.screamstudios.com***

**Sigma Sound House**
212 N. 12th Street
Philadelphia, PA 19107
***Tel: (215) 561-3660***
***www.sigmasound.com***

**Skywalker Sound**
***Tel: (415) 662-1000***
***www.skysound.com***

**SoundByte Digital Audio Productions**
Lewis Tower
225 S. 15th St., Ste. 2020
Philadelphia, PA 19102
***Tel: (215) 893-3004***
***www.soudbytedigital.com***

**SoundCastle Recording Studios**
1334 Third St. Promenade, Ste. 228
Santa Monica, CA 90401
***Tel: (310) 394-6014***
***www.soundcastle.com***

**Sound City Studios**
15456 Cabrito Rd.
Van Nuys, CA 91406
***Tel: (818) 787-3722***
***www.soundcitystudios.com***

**Soundelux**
7080 Hollywood Boulevard
Hollywood, CA 90028
***Tel: (323) 603-3200***
***www.soundelux.com***

**Stankonia Recording**
677 Antone Street
Atlanta, GA 30318
***Tel: (404) 355-2121***
***www.outcast.com/stankonia***

**Sterling Sound**
88 Tenth Ave., 6th Fl.
New York, NY 10011
***Tel: (212) 604-9433***
***www.sterlingsound.com***

**Studio 88**
829 27th Avenue
Oakland, CA 94601
***Tel: (510) 533-0880***
***www.studio88.com***

**The Studio**
413 N. 7th Street, 3rd Fl.
Philadelphia, PA 19123
***Tel: (215) 629-5557***
***www.thestudiophilly.com***

**Studio West**
11021 Via Frontera
San Diego, CA 92127
***Tel: (858) 592-9497***
***www.studiowest.com***

**Sugarhill Recording Studios**
5626 Brock Street
Houston, Tx 77023
***Tel: (713) 926-4431***
***www.sugarhillstudios.com***

**Sunset Sound**
6650 Sunset Blvd.
Hollywood, CA 90028
***Tel: (323) 469-1186***
***www.sunsetsound.com***

**Surreal Sound Studios**
2046 Castor Ave., 2nd Fl.
Philadelphia, PA 19134
***Tel: (215) 288-8863***
***www.surrealsoundstudios.com***

**Threshold Music**
440 W. 41st Street, Plaza 6
New York, NY 10036
***Tel: (212) 24-1871***
***www.thresholdmusic.com***

**Threshold Sound + Vision**
2114 Pico Boulevard
Santa Monica, CA 90405
***Tel: (310) 571-0500***
***www.thresholdsound.com***

**Universal Music Publishing Recording Studio**
1904 Adelicia Street
Nashville, TN 37212
***Tel: (615) 340-5400***
***www.umpgnashville.com***

**The Village**
1616 Butler Ave.
W. Los Angeles, CA 90025
***Tel: (310) 478-8227***
***www.villagestudios.com***

**Westbeach Recorders**
6035 Hollywood Blvd.
Hollywood, CA 90028
***Tel: (323) 461-6959***
***www.westbeachrecorders.com***

**Westlake Recording Studios**
7265 Santa Monica Blvd.
Los Angeles, CA 90046
***Tel: (323) 851-9800***
***www.thelakestudios.com***

# RETAIL OUTLETS

**AmazonMP3.com**
***www.amazon.com***
***www.createspace.com***

**Amoeba Music**
2455 Telegraph Avenue
Berkeley, CA 94704
***Tel: (510) 549-1125***
***www.amoebamusic.com***

**Amoeba Music**
6400 Sunset Boulevard
Hollywood, CA 90028
***Tel: (323) 245-6400***
***www.amoebamusic.com***

**Amoeba Music**
1855 Haight
San Francisco, CA 94117
***Tel: (415) 831-1200***
***www.amoebamusic.com***

**Apple iTunes**
***www.apple.com/itunes***
***www.itunes.com***

**Barnes & Noble.com**
76 Ninth Avenue, 9th Fl.
New York, NY 10011
***Tel: (212) 414-6100***
***www.barnesandnoble.com***

**Best Buy**
7601 Penn Avenue South
Richfield, MN 55423
***Tel: (612) 291-1000***
***www.bestbuy.com***

**Borders Books & Music**
Borders Group, Inc.
100 Phoenix Drive
Ann Arbor, MI 48108
***Tel: (734) 477-1100***
***www.bordersgroupinc.com***

**CD Baby**
5925 NE 80 Avenue
Portland, OR 97218
***Tel: (503) 595-3000***
***www.cdbaby.com***

**eMusic**
244 5th Avenue, Ste. 2070
New York, NY 10001
***Tel: (212) 201-9240***
***www.emusic.com***

**Family Christian Stores**
5300 Patterson Ave., SE
Grand Rapids, MI 49530
***Tel: (888) 319-0319***
***www.familychristian.com***

**iTunes**
***www.itunes.com***

**Rasputin Music**
2401 Telegraph Avenue
Berkeley, CA 94704
***Tel: (800) 350-8700***
***www.rasputinmusic.com***

**Rasputin Music**
920 Admiral Callaghan Lane
Vallejo, CA 94591
***Tel: (800) 350-8700***
***www.rasputinmusic.com***

**Rhapsody**
***www.rhapsody.com***

**Target Stores**
100 Nicollet Mall
Minneapolis, MN 55403
***Tel: (612) 304-6073***
***www.target.com***

**TransWorld Entertainment**
38 Corporate Circle
Albany, NY 12203
***Tel: (518) 452-1242***
***www.twec.com***
***www.fye.com***
***Includes: fye.com; Wherehouse.com***

**Wal-Mart Stores, Inc.**
702 S.W. 8th Street
Bentonville, AR 72716
***Tel: (479) 273-4000***
***www.walmart.com***

**Word of Life**
7223 S. Main Street
Los Angeles, CA 90003
***Tel: (323) 758-2733/(323) 295-8223***
***www.shopwordoflife.com***

Apple's iTunes Store is now the largest seller of music in the world, surpassing all record stores, Wal-Mart, Amazon.com, Best Buy and Target. Technological innovation and digital distribution have leveled the playing field. Emerging and established artists now have a host of outlets for selling music and being heard, both online and in stores.

# SONGWRITING COMPETITIONS

**American Songwriter Amateur Lyric Contest**
1303 16th Avenue S., 2nd Fl.
Nashville, TN 37212
***Tel: (615) 321-6096***
***www.americansongwriter.com***

**Chris Austin Songwriting Contest**
Wilkes Community College
P.O. Box 120
Wilkesboro, NC 28697
***Tel: (336) 838-6100***
***www.merlefest.org***

**Billboard Song Contest**
***www.billboard.com***

**BMI Student Composer Awards**
320 W. 57th Street
New York, NY 10019
***Tel: (212) 586-2000***
***www.bmi.com***

**CMT NSAI Song Contest**
Nashville Songwriters Assoc.
1710 Roy Acuss Place
Nashville, TN 37203
***Tel: (615) 256-3354/(800) 321-6008***
***www.nashvillesongwriters.com***
***www.nsai.cmt.com***

**Contemporary Christian Music Network Songwriting Contest**
P.O. Box 7483
Springdale, AR 72766
***ccmni.mmgi.org***

**Dallas Songwriters Song Contest**
Dallas Songwriters Association
Sammons Center for the Arts
3630 Harry Hines Blvd., Box 20
Dallas, TX 75219
***Tel: (214) 750-0916 ext. 1***
***www.dallassongwriters.org***

**Goodnight Kiss Songwriting, Lyric & Music Competition**
Goodnight Music
10153 1/2 Riverside Dr., #239
Toluca Lake, CA 9160
***Tel: (831) 479-9993***
***www.goodnightkiss.com***

**Gospel Music Association (GMA) Music in the Rockies National Songwriting Competition**
1205 Division Street
Nashville, TN 37203
***Tel: (615) 242-0303***
***www.gospelmusic.org***

**Gospel Music Association (GMA) Academy Artist Song National Competition**
1205 Division Street
Nashville, TN 37203
***Tel: (615) 242-0303***
***www.gospelmusic.org***

**John Lennon Songwriting Contest**
***Tel: (212) 873-9300***
***www.jlsc.com***

**Mid-Atlantic Song Contest**
Songwriters' Association of Washington
4200 Wisconsin Avenue, NW
PMB 106-137
Washington, D.C. 20016
***Tel: (301) 654-8434***
***www.saw.org***

**Nashville International Song & Lyric Competition**
Paramount Group
P.O. Box 23705
Nashville, TN 37202
***www.paramountsong.com***

**CMT Nashville Songwriters Association International Song Contest**
1710 Roy Acuss Place
Nashville, TN 37203
***Tel: (615) 256-3354/(800) 321-6008***
***www.nashvillesongwriters.com***
***www.nsai.cmt.com***

**San Diego Songwriters Guild Song Contest**
3368 Governor Dr., Ste. F-326
San Diego, CA 92122
***www.sdsongwriters.org***

**Song of the Year**
21175 Tomball Parkway, Ste. 242
Houston, TX 77070
***www.songoftheyear.com***

**Star Search Nashville**
***www.nashvillesymposium.com***

**The Ten-Minute Musicals Project Annual Competition**
P.O. Box 461194
West Hollywood, CA 90046
***www.tenminutemusicals.org***

**USA Songwriting Competition**
***www.songwriting.net***

# Sara Light

*President & Co-Founder*, SongU.com

Founded by husband and wife songwriting team Danny Arena and Sara Light, and technology specialist Martin Bell, SongU.com is one of the hippest and happening songwriting websites in the world, offering more than 70 online courses, coaching, co-writing and industry connections -- all at a reasonable price. The SongU.com team, whose remarkable combined credits include a Best Original Score Tony nomination for the Broadway musical *"Urban Cowboy,"* ASCAP and SESAC awards, hit songs with 2 million+ radio plays, and staff publishing deals with majors like Warner/Chappell Music, Curb Magnatone Music Publishing and Zamalama Music, has created a top-notch service with an educational slant designed to help beginning to master-level songwriters hone their skills.

**POWER QUOTE #1:**

*"We basically created a resource with everything we wished we had when we moved to Nashville to start songwriting. It's a wonderful thing when you can help someone else realize their dream. I love that about SongU.com because we're constantly getting e-mails from people who are getting their first royalty checks, their first publishing contracts, or even just getting a coach to say 'Hey, your song is great. You finally got it.'"*

***If you're a songwriter in search of contacts, information and inspiration to help advance your career, then SongU.com might be the resource you've been looking for.***

What are the SongU.com success stories? Many are impressive. For starters, more than 2,000 SongU.com members have received single-song music publishing contracts since 2008! On the worldwide stage, 100+ SongU.com songwriters' songs were featured in the 2008 Beijing Olympic Games, further advancing SongU.com's international appeal. Everyday, around the globe emerging and established songwriters are logging on to SongU.com and moving closer and closer to achieving songwriting success.

**POWER QUOTE #2:**

*"We take every member at whatever level they're at and help them find their path - so they can succeed at whatever their particular songwriting desire is, whether it's to have a huge hit or to just get better at the craft."*

## EPPers is SongU. com for you?

*To find out more about **www.SongU.com**, log onto to their website.*

**A & R Registry**
7510 Sunset Blvd., #1041
Los Angeles, CA 90046
***Tel: (818) 995-7458***
***www.musicregistry.com***

**Acoustic Guitar**
P.O. Box 767
San Anselmo, CA 94979
***Tel: (415) 485-6946***
***www.acousticguitar.com***

**American Music Press Online**
P.O. Box 1070
Martinez, CA 94553
***Tel: (925) 228-1423***
***www.ampmagazine.com***

**American Songwriter Magazine**
1303 16th Ave., South - 2nd Fl.
Nashville, TN 37203
***Tel: (615) 321-6096***
***www.americansongwriter.com***

**AudioXPress**
P.O. Box 876
305 Union Street
Peterborough, NH 03458
***Tel: (603) 924-9464***
***www.audioxpress.com***

**Bass Player**
New Bay Media
1111 Bayhill Dr., Ste. 125
San Bruno, CA 94066
***Tel: (650) 238-0300***
***www.bassplayer.com***

**Billboard**
5055 Wilshire Boulevard
Los Angeles, CA 90036
***Tel: (323) 525-2300***
***www.billboard.com***

**Billboard**
770 Broadway
New York, NY 10003
***Tel: (646) 654-4400***
***www.billboard.com***

**Black Talent News**
8306 Wilshire Blvd., Ste. 2057
Beverly Hills, CA 90211
***Tel: (310) 929-5297***
***www.blacktalentnews.com***

**Bluegrass Unlimited**
P.O. Box 771
Warrenton, VA 22014
***Tel: (540) 349-8181***
***www.bluegrassmusic.com***

**BRE-Black Radio Exclusive**
15030 Ventura Blvd., Ste. 864
Sherman Oaks, CA 91403
***Tel: (818) 907-9959***
***www.bremagazine.com***

**Christian Musician**
4427 S. Meridian, C275
Puyallup, WA 98373
***Tel: (253) 770-0650***
***www.christianmusician.com***

**CMJ - College New Music Monthly**
100 5th Avenue, 11th Fl.
New York, NY 10011
***Tel: (212) 277-7120***
***www.cmj.com***

**Contemporary Christian Music**
750 Old Hickory Blvd., Ste. 1-150
Brentwood, TN 37027
***Tel: (800) 527-5226***
***www.ccmmagazine.com***

**Country Line Magazine**
9508 Chishom Trail
Austin, TX 78748
***Tel: (512) 292-1113***
***www.countrylinemagazine.com***

**Country Weekly**
118 16th Ave. South, Ste. 230
Nashville, TN 37203
***Tel: (615) 743-0257***
***www.countryweekly.com***

**Drum Magazine**
95 S. Market Street, Ste. 200
San Jose, CA 95113
***Tel: (408) 971-9794***
***www.drummagazine.com***

**Ebony Magazine**
Johnson Publishing Company
820 S. Michigan Avenue
Chicago, IL 60605
***Tel: (312) 322-9200***
***www.ebony.com***

**Electronic Musician**
6400 Hollis St., Ste. 12
Emeryville, CA 94608
***Tel: (510) 653-3307***
***www.emusician.com***

**EQ Magazine**
New Bay Media
1111 Bayhill Drive, Ste. 125
San Bruno, CA 94066
***Tel: (650) 238-0300***
***www.eqmag.com***

**Essence Magazine**
135 W. 50th Street, 4th Fl.
New York, NY 10020
***Tel: (212) 522-1866/(212) 522-1212***
***www.essence.com***

**EUR Web (Electronic Urban Report)**
P.O. Box 412081
Los Angeles, CA 90041
***Tel: (323) 254-9599/(661) 250-7300***
***www.eurweb.com***

**Fader Magazine**
71 W. 23rd Street, 13th Fl.
New York, NY 10010
***Tel: (212) 741-7100***
***www.thefader.com***

**Film & TV Music Guide**
7510 Sunset Blvd., #1041
Los Angeles, CA 90046
***Tel: (818) 995-7458***
***www.musicregistry.com***

**Film Score Monthly**
6311 Romaine St., Ste. 7109
Hollywood, CA 90038
***Tel: (323) 461-2240***
***www.filmscoremonthly.com***

**Giant Magazine**
Interactive One
205 Hudson Street, 6th Fl.
New York, NY, 10013
***Tel: (212) 431-4477***
***www.giantmag.com***
***www.interactiveone.com***

**Gospel Music Industry Round-Up**
P.O. Box 451848
Los Angeles, CA 90045
***Tel: (310) 677-6011***
***www.gospelroundup.com***

**Gospel Today Magazine**
P.O. Box 800
Fiarburn, GA 30213
***Tel: (770) 719-4825***
***www.gospeltoday.com***

**Gospel Truth Magazine**
P.O. Box 38218
Houston, TX 77382
***Tel: (832) 912-7700***
***www.gospeltruthmagazine.com***

**Gospel USA Magazine**
P.O. Box 970704
Miami, FL 33197
***Tel: (305) 234-8689***
***www.gospelusamagazine.com***

**Guitar Legends**
Future US
4000 Shoreline Court, Ste. 400
San Francisco, CA 94080
***Tel: (650) 872-1642***
***www.guitarworld.com***

**Guitar Legends**
Future US
149 Fifth Avenue, 9th Fl
New York, NY 10010
***Tel: (646) 723-5400***
***www.guitarworld.com***

**Guitar One**
Future US
4000 Shoreline Court, Ste. 400
San Francisco, CA 94080
***Tel: (650) 944-9279***
***www.guitarworld.com***

**Guitar One**
Future US
149 Fifth Avenue, 9th Fl
New York, NY 10010
***Tel: (646) 723-5400***
***www.guitarworld.com***

**Guitar Player**
New Bay Media
1111 Bayhill Dr., Ste. 125
San Bruno, CA 94066
***Tel: (650) 238-0300***
***www.guitarplayer.com***

**Guitar World**
Future US
4000 Shoreline Court, Ste. 400
San Francisco, CA 94080
***Tel: (650) 872-1642***
***www.guitarworld.com***

**Guitar World**
Future US
149 Fifth Avenue, 9th Fl.
New York, NY 10010
***Tel: (646) 723-5400***
***www.guitarworld.com***

**Guitar World Acoustic**
Future US
4000 Shoreline Court, Ste. 400
San Francisco, CA 94080
***Tel: (650) 872-1642***
***www.guitarworld.com***

**Guitar World Acoustic**
Future US
149 Fifth Avenue, 9th Fl
New York, NY 10010
***Tel: (212) 944-9279***
***www.guitarworld.com***

**Harp Magazine**
8737 Colesville Road, 9th Fl.
Silver Spring, MD 20910
***Tel: (301) 588-4114***
***www.harpmagazine.com***

**Jazz Times Magazine**
8737 Colesville Road, 9th Fl.
Silver Spring, MD 20910
***Tel: (301) 588-4114***
***www.jazztimes.com***

**JAZZIZ Magazine**
2650 N. Military Trail
Fountain Square Bldg. II, Ste. 140
Boca Ratan, FL 33431
***Tel: (561) 893-6868 ext. 303***
***www.jazziz.com***

**Jet Magazine**
Johnson Publishing Company
820 S. Michigan Avenue
Chicago, IL 60605
***Tel: (312) 322-9200***
***www.ebonyjet.com***

**Keyboard Magazine**
New Bay Media
1111 Bayhill Dr., Ste. 125
San Bruno, CA 94066
***Tel: (650) 238-0300***
***www.keyboardmag.com***

**L.A. Weekly**
3861 Sepulveda Blvd.
Culver City, CA 90230
***Tel: (310) 574-7100***
***www.laweekly.com***

**Latin Beat**
15900 Crenshaw Blvd., Ste. 1-223
Gardena, CA 90249
***Tel: (310) 516-6767***
***www.latinbeatmagazine.com***

**Louisville Music News**
3705 Fairway Lane
Louisville, KY 40207
***Tel: (502) 893-9933***
***www.louisvillemusic.com***

**Magnet Magazine**
1218 Chestnut Street, Ste. 508
Philadelphia, PA 19107
***Tel: (215) 413-8570***
***www.magnetmagazine.com***

**The Metropolitan Opera Guide**
70 Lincoln Center Plaza
New York, NY 10023
***Tel: (212) 769-7000***
***www.metoperafamily.org***

**Mix**
6400 Hollis Street, Ste. 12
Emeryville, CA 94608
***Tel: (510) 653-3307***
***www.mixonline.com***

**Modern Drummer**
12 Old Bridge Road
Cedar Grove, NJ 07009
***Tel: (973) 239-4140***
***www.moderndrummer.com***

**Music Attorney, Legal & Business Affairs Guide**
7510 Sunset Blvd., #1041
Los Angeles, CA 90046
***Tel: (818) 995-7458***
***www.musicregistry.com***

**Music Connection Magazine**
14654 Victory Blvd., 1st Fl.
Van Nuys, CA 91411
***Tel: (818) 995-0101***
***www.musicconnections.com***

**Music Education Technology Magazine**
***www.metmagazine.com***

**Music Monthly**
2807 Goodwood Road
Baltimore, MD 21214
***Tel: (410) 426-9000***
***www.musicmonthly.com***

**Music Business Registry**
7510 Sunset Blvd., #1041
Los Angeles, CA 90046
***Tel: (818) 995-7458***
***www.musicregistry.com***

**Music Publisher Registry**
7510 Sunset Blvd., #1041
Los Angeles, CA 90046
***Tel: (818) 995-7458***
***www.musicregistry.com***

**Music Row**
1231 17th Ave. South
Nashville, TN 37212
***Tel: (615) 321-3617***
***www.musicrow.com***

**Musician's Atlas**
Music Resource Group
32 Ann Street
Clifton, NJ 07013
***Tel: (973) 767-1800***
***www.musiciansatlas.com***

**Musician's Friend**
P.O. Box 4370
Medford, OR 97501
***Tel: (800) 391-8762***
***www.musiciansfriend.com***

**OffBeat Music Magazine**
421 Frenchmen Street, Ste. 200
New Orleans, LA 70116
***Tel: (504) 944-4300***
***www.offbeat.com***

**Outburn**
P.O. Box 3187
Thousand Oaks, CA 91359
***Tel: (323) 344-1200***
***www.outburn.com***

**Paste Magazine**
P.O. Box 1606
Decatur, GA 30031
***Tel: (404) 378-8677***
***www.pastemagazine.com***

**Pennsylvania Musician Magazine**
P.O. Box 362
Millerstown, PA 17062
***Tel: (717) 444-2423***
***www.pamusician.com***

**Performing Songwriter Magazine**
2805 Azalea Place
Nashville, TN 37204
***Tel: (615) 385-7796***
***www.performingsongwriter.com***

**Pollstar**
4697 Jacquelyn Ave.
Fresno, CA 93722
***Tel: (559) 271-7900***
***www.pollstar.com***

**Pop Culture Press**
P.O. Box 4990
Austin, TX 78765
***Tel: (512) 445-3208***
***www.popculturepress.com***

**Pro Sound News**
***www.prosoundnews.com***

**Radio & Production Magazine**
P.O. Box 630071
Irving, TX 75063
***Tel: (972) 432-8100***
***www.rapmag.com***

**Radio Ink Magazine**
224 Datura Street, Ste. 1015
W. Palm Beach, FL 33401
***Tel: (561) 655-8778***
***www.radioink.com***

**Recording Magazine**
5412 Idylwild Trail, #100
Boulder, CO 80301
***Tel: (303) 516-9118***
***www.recordingmag.com***

**Reggae Report Int'l. Magazine**
P.O. Box 1823
Hallandale, FL 33309
***Tel: (305) 933-9918***
***www.reggaereport.com***

**Relix**
104 W. 29th Street, 11th Fl.
New York, NY 10011
***Tel: (646) 230-0100***
***www.relix.com***

**Remix Magazine**
P.O. Box 16886
N. Hollywood, CA 91606
***Tel: (818) 487-2020***
***www.remixmag.com***

**Right On Magazine**
***www.rightonmag.com***

**Rolling Out**
Steed Media Group
1269 Pryor Road
Atlanta, GA 30315
***Tel: (404) 635-1313***
***www.rollingout.com***

**Rolling Stone Magazine**
1290 Ave. of the Americas
New York, NY 10104
***Tel: (212) 484-1616***
***www.rollingstone.com***

**S.F. Weekly**
185 Berry, Lobby 5, Ste. 3800
San Francisco, CA 94107
***Tel: (415) 536-8100***
***www.sfweekly.com***

**Sing Out!**
P.O. Box 5460
Bethlehem, PA 18015
***Tel: (610) 865-5366***
***www.singout.org***

**Singing News Magazine**
P.O. Box 2810
330 University Hall Dr.
Boone, NC 28607
***Tel: (828) 264-3700***
***www.singingnews.com***

**Sister 2 Sister**
2008 Enterprise Road
Bowie, MD 20721
***Tel: (301) 270-5999***
**www.s2smagazine.com**

**Spin**
205 Lexington Avenue, 3rd Fl.
New York, NY 10016
***Tel: (212) 231-7400***
***www.spin.com***

**Stereophile**
261 Madison Avenue
New York, NY 10016
***Tel: (212) 915-4157***
***www.stereophile.com***

**Strings Magazine**
P.O. Box 469120
Escondido, CA 92046
***Tel: (760) 233-3768***
***www.stringsmagazine.com***

**The Source**
11 Broadway, Ste. 315
New York, NY 10004
***Tel: (212) 253-3700***
***www.thesource.com***

**Tape Op Magazine**
P.O. Box 14517
Portland, OR 97293
***Tel: (503) 232-6047***
***www.tapeop.com***

**UPSCALE**
600 Bronner Brothers Way, SW
Atlanta, GA 30310
***Tel: (404) 758-7467***
***Tel: (770) 988-0015***
***www.upscalemagazine.com***

**Urban Network Magazine**
3255 Wilshire Blvd., 815
Los Angeles, CA 90010
***Tel: (213) 388-4155***
***www.urbannetwork.com***

**Vibe**
***www.vibe.com***

**The Village Voice**
36 Cooper Square
New York, NY 10003
***Tel: (212) 475-3300***
***www.villagevoice.com***

**XXL**
1115 Broadway, 8th Fl.
New York, NY 10010
***Tel: (212) 807-7100***
***www.xxlmag.com***

# The only four music business directories you will ever need.

"The A&R and Music Publisher Registry are the most complete and reliable information sources... assembled by someone who really knows the business.

*— MIKE MCCARTY, PRESIDENT*
*EMI MUSIC PUIBLISHING, CANADA*

The A&R Registry is the most accurate and up-to-date A&R source I have ever seen. No producer should be without this."

*— JELLYBEAN, PRODUCER OF MADONNA, WHITNEY HOUSTON*

***All Directories Available on Disk***

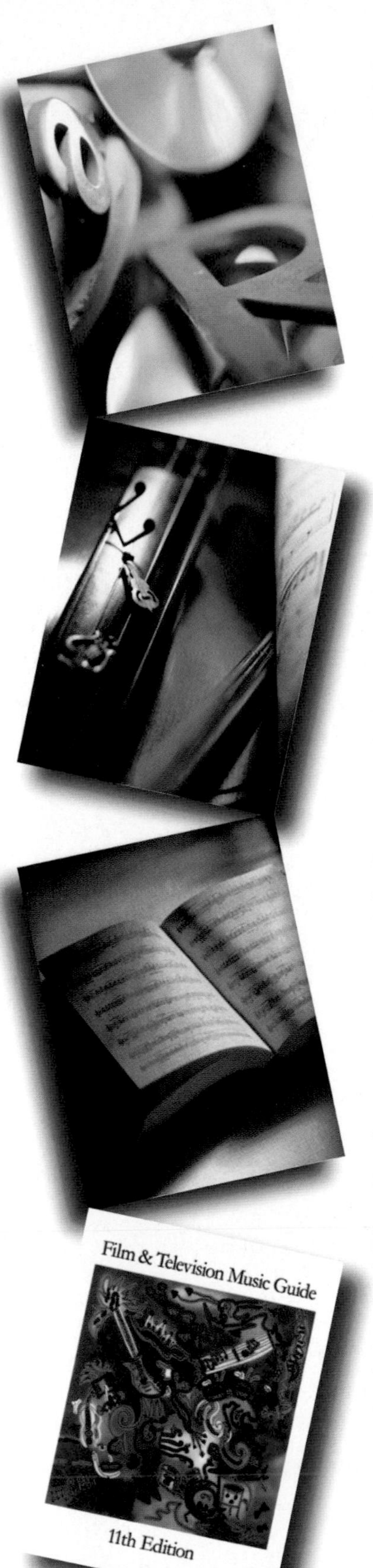


**A&R Registry**
The music industry's only A&R directory updated and published every 8 weeks listing all major and independent record labels throughout the U.S., Canada, and the UK including LA, NY, Nashville, Atlanta, Miami, Toronto and London. Listings include entire A&R staff ***including the style of music they focus on***, their titles, assistant's names, direct dial phone and fax numbers, e-mail and company web sites. All this for only $400 a year (6 issue subscription in **PDF FORMAT**) or get a single issue **(PDF FORMAT)** for only $75.

**Music Publisher Registry**
The only directory of its kind that is updated twice a year lists all major publishers as well as significant independent publishers in LA, NY, Nashville, Atlanta, Miami, Toronto and London. Here you will find listings for the entire creative staff, their titles, assistant's names, direct dial phone and fax numbers, e-mail and company web sites. Receive all of this for only $135 a year (2 issue subscription in **PDF FORMAT**) or get a single issue **(PDF FORMAT)** for only $75.

**Music Business**
**Attorney, Legal & Business Affairs Registry**
Our latest exclusive directory lists all music business attorneys (including the services they provide), their assistant's names, direct dial phone and fax numbers, e-mail and web sites. In addition this directory includes all Legal and Business Affairs personnel at all of the record labels, music publishers film studios and television network music departments. Receive all of this for only $95 **(PDF FORMAT)**.

**Film & Television Music Guide**
The only directory of its kind listing the contacts that can get your music into films, television shows and video games. Lists all movie studios, television network and independent production company music departments, all music supervisors, film composers and their agents, music clearance companies, music libraries, music editors, ASCAP, BMI, and SESAC film/TV divisions, scoring stages, and music preparation services. All of this for only $100 **(PDF FORMAT)**.

***CALIFORNIA RESIDENTS PLEASE ADD 9.25% SALES TAX***

## The Music Business Registry

7510 SUNSET BOULEVARD, #1041, LOS ANGELES, CA 90046-3400 USA
**(800) 377-7411 • 818-995-7458 fax: 800-228-9411 or 740-587-3916**
WWW.MUSICREGISTRY.COM INFO@MUSICREGISTRY.COM

# SPORTS

**American Hockey League**
One Monarch Place, Ste. 2400
Springfield, MA 01144
***Tel: (413) 781-2030***
***www.theahl.com***

**American Powerboating Association**
17640 Nine Mile Road
Eastpointe, MI 48021
***Tel: (586) 773-9700***
***www.apba-racing.com***

**Association of Tennis Professionals Tour**
201 ATP Tour Boulevard
Ponte Vedra Beach, FL 32082
***Tel: (904) 285-8000***
***www.atptour.org***

**Association of Volleyball Professionals**
6100 Center Drive, 9th Fl.
Los Angeles, CA 90045
***Tel: (310) 426-8000***
***www.avp.com***

**Black Entertainment & Sports Lawyers Association (BESLA)**
P.O. Box 441485
Fort Washington, MD 20749
***Tel: (301) 248-1818***
***www.besla.org***

**Black Sports Agents Association**
9255 Sunset Blvd., Ste. 1120
Beverly Hills, CA 90069
***Tel: (310) 858-6565***
***www.blacksportsagents.com***

**Championship Auto Racing Teams (CART)**
5350 Lakeview Parkway S. Drive
Building 36 - Inner Park/Park 100
Indianpolis, IN 46268
***Tel: (317) 715-4100***
***www.cart.com***

**Iditarod Trail Committee**
Mile 2.2 Knik Goose Bay Road
Wasilla, AK 99687
***Tel: (907) 376-5155 ext. 108***
***www.iditarod.com***

**Indy Racing League**
4565 16th Street
Indianapolis, IN 46222
***Tel: (317) 484-6526***
***www.indyracing.com***

**International Game Fish Association**
300 Gulf Stream Way
Dania Beach, FL 33004
***Tel: (954) 927-2628***
***www.igfa.org***

**International Motor Sports Association**
1394 Broadway Avenue
Braselton, GA 30517
***Tel: (706) 658-2120***
***www.imsaracing.net***

**The Jockey's Guild, Inc.**
103 Wind Haven Dr., Ste. 200
Nicholasville, KY 40356
***Tel: (859) 305-0606***
***www.jockeysguild.com***

**Ladies Professional Golf Association**
100 International Golf Drive
Daytona Beach, FL 32124
***Tel: (386) 274-6200***
***www.lpga.com***

**Little League Baseball, Inc.**
539 US Route 15 Hwy./P.O. Box 3485
Williamsport, PA 17701
***Tel: (570) 326-1921***
***www.littleleague.org***

**Major Indoor Soccer League**
1175 Post Road East
Westport, CT 06880
***Tel: (203) 222-4900***
***www.misl.net***

**Major League Baseball**
245 Park Avenue, 31st Fl.

New York, NY 10167
***Tel: (212) 931-7800***
***www.mlb.com***

**Major League Baseball Players Association**
12 E. 49th Street, 24th Fl.
New York, NY 10017
***Tel: (212) 826-0808***
***www.mlbplayers.com***

**Major League Soccer**
420 Fifth Avenue, 7th Fl.
New York, NY 10018
***Tel: (212) 450-1200***
***www.mlsnet.com***

**Minor League Baseball**
201 Bayshore Dr., SE
P.O. Box A
St. Petersburg, FL 33731
***Tel: (727) 822-6937***
***www.minoreaguebaseball.com***

**National Association for Stock Car Auto Racing/NASCAR**
1801 W. Int'l. Speedway Blvd.
Daytona Beach, FL 32114
***Tel: (386) 253-0611***
***www.nascar.com***

**National Basketball Association**
645 Fifth Avenue
New York, NY 10022
***Tel: (212) 407-8000***
***www.nba.com***

**National Basketball Association Players Association**
2 Penn Plaza, Ste. 2430
New York, NY 10121
***Tel: (212) 655-0880***
***www.nbpa.com***

**National Football League**
280 Park Avenue
New York, NY 10017
***Tel: (212) 450-2000***
***www.nfl.com***

**NFL Players Association**
1133 20th Street, NW
Washington, D.C. 20036
***Tel: (202) 572-7500/(800) 372-2000***
***www.nflplayers.com***

**National Hockey League**
1251 Ave. of the Americas, 47th Fl.
New York, NY 10020
***Tel: (212) 789-2999***
***www.nhl.com***

**National Hockey League Players Association**
777 Bay Street, Ste. 2400
Toronto, Ontario M5G 2C8 Canada
***Tel: (416) 313-2300***
***www.nhlpa.com***

**National Hot Rod Association**
2035 E. Financial Way
Glendora, CA 91741
***Tel: (626) 914-4761***
***www.nhra.com***

**National Thoroughbred Racing Association**
800 Third Avenue, Ste. 901
New York, NY 10022
***Tel: (212) 230-9500***
***www.ntra.com***

**PGA Tour**
112 PGA Tour Boulevard
Ponte Vedra Beach, FL 32124
***Tel: (904) 285-3700***
***www.pgatour.com***

**Professional Bowlers Association**
719 Second Ave., Ste. 701
Seattle, WA 98104
***Tel: (206) 332-9688***
***www.pba.com***

**Professional Golfers' Association of America**
100 Avenue of the Champions
Box 109601
Palm Beach Gardens, FL 33410
***Tel: (561) 624-8400***
***www.pgaonline.com***

**Thoroughbred Racing Associations of America**
420 Fair Hill Drive, Ste. 1
Elkton, MD 21921
***Tel: (410) 393-9200***
***www.tra-online.com***

**United Soccer Leagues**
14497 N. Dale Mabry Hwy., Ste. 201
Tampa, FL 33618
***Tel: (813) 963-3909***
***www.uslsoccer.com***

**United States Golf Association**
Golf House
P.O. Box 708
Liberty Corner Road
Far Hills, NJ 07931
***Tel: (908) 234-2300***
***www.usga.org***

**United States Olympic Committee**
Olympic House/One Olympic Plaza
Colorado Spring, CO 80909
***Tel: (719) 632-5551***
***www.usolympicteam.com***

**U.S. Polo Association**
771 Corporate Dr., Ste. 505
Lexington, KY 40503
***Tel: (859) 219-1000***
***www.uspolo.org***

**USA Rugby Football Union**
1033 Walnut Street, Ste. 200
Boulder, CO 80302
***Tel: (303) 539-0300***
***www.usarugby.org***

**Women's National Basketball Association (WNBA)**
645 Fifth Avenue
New York, NY 10022
***Tel: (212) 688-9622***
***www.wnba.com***

**World Boxing Council**
***www.wbcboxing.com***

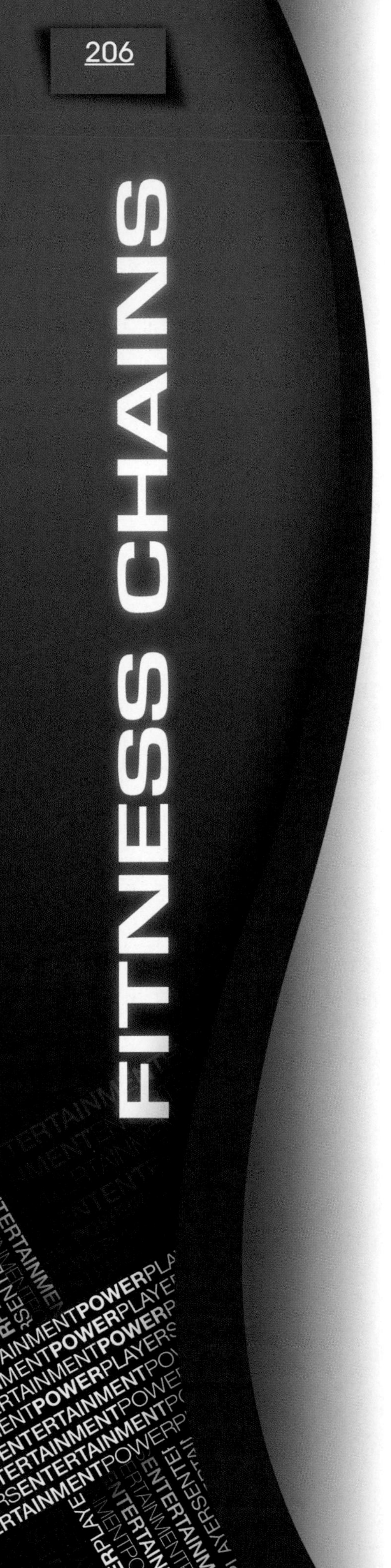


**24-Hour Fitness Worldwide**
12647 Alcosta Blvd., 5th Fl.
San Ramon, CA 94583
***Tel: (925) 543-3100***
***www.24hourfitness.com***

**Bally Total Fitness**
8700 W. Bryn Mawr Avenue
Chicago, IL 60631
***Tel: (800) 515-CLUB/(773) 380-3000***
***www.ballyfitness.com***

**Boston Sports Clubs**
***www.mysportsclubs.com***

**Crunch Fitness**
Old Chelsea Station/P.O. Box 1918
New York, NY 10011
***Tel: (888) 2-CRUNCH***
***www.crunch.com***

**Curves International**
100 Ritchie Road
Waco, TX 76712
***Tel: (800) 848-1096***
***www.curves.com***

**Gold's Gym International**
125 E. John Carpenter Fwy., Ste. 1300
Irving, TX 75062
***Tel: (214) 574-4653***
***www.goldsgym.com***

**L.A. Fitness International**
P.O. Box 54170
Irvine, CA 92619
***Tel: (949) 255-7200***
***www.lafitness.com***

**Life Start Fitness Centers**
117 N. Jefferson St., Ste. 203
Chicago, IL 60661
***Tel: (312) 627-1300***
***www.lifestart.net***

**Life Time Fitness**
2902 Corporate Place
Chanhassan, MN 55317
***Tel: (952) 947-0000***
***www.lifetimefitness.com***

**Health Fitness Centers/HFC**
3600 America Blvd., Ste. 560
Minneapolis, MN 55431
***Tel: (800) 639-7913***
***www.hfitcenter.com***

**New York Sports Clubs**
***www.mysportsclubs.com***

**Philadelphia Sports Clubs**
Town Sports International
***www.mysportsclubs.com***

**Sport Fit Total Fitness**
100 White Marsh Park Dr.
Bowie, MD 20715
***Tel: (301) 262-4553***
***www.sportfitclubs.c om***

**The Sports Club/LA**
***Tel: (310) 479-5200***
***www.thesportsclub/la.com***

**Washington Sports Clubs**
***www.mysportsclubs.com***

**Wellbridge**
8400 E. Crescent Pkwy., Ste. 200
Greenwood Village, CO 80111
***Tel: (303) 866-0800***
***www.wellbridge.com***

**World Gym/Planet Fitness**
T.R. World Gym, LLC
113 Crosby Rd., Ste. 15
Dover, NH 03820
***Tel: (603) 742-4443***
***www.worldgym.com***

**YMCA of the USA**
101 N. Wacker Drive
Chicago, IL 60606
***Tel: (800) 872-9622***
***www.ymca.net***

**YWCA USA**
1015 18th Street, NW - Ste. 1100
Washington, D.C. 20036
***Tel: (202) 467-0801***
***www.ywca.org***

**Baseball Hall of Fame**
National Baseball Hall
of Fame & Museum
P.O. Box 590/25 Main Street
Cooperstown, NY 13326
***Tel: (607) 547-7200***
***www.baseballhalloffame.org***

**Basketball Hall of Fame**
Naismith Memorial Basketball
Hall of Fame
1000 W. Columbus Avenue
Springfield, MA 01105
***Tel: (413) 781-6500***
***www.hoophall.com***

**Bowling Museum & Hall of Fame**
Int'l. Bowling Museum & Hall of Fame
111 Stadium Plaza
St. Louis, MO 63102
***Tel: (314) 231-6340***
***www.bowlingmuseum.com***

**Boxing Hall of Fame**
Int'l. Boxing Hall of Fame
One Hall of Fame Drive
Canastota, NY 13032
***Tel: (315) 697-7095***
***www.ibhof.com***

**Football Hall of Fame**
Professional Football Hall of Fame
2121 George Halas Dr., NW
Canton, OH 44708
***Tel: (330) 456-8207***
***www.profootballhof.com***

**Ladies Pro Golf Association (LPGA) Hall of Fame**
100 International Golf Drive
Daytona Beach, FL 32124
***Tel: (386) 274-6200***
***www.lpga.com***

**Hockey Hall of Fame**
Brookfield Place
30 Yonge Street
Toronto, Ontario
Canada M5E 1X8
***Tel: (416) 360-7735***
***www.hhof.com***

**Museum of Racing & Hall of Fame**
National Museum of Racing &
Hall of Fame
191 Union Avenue
Saratoga Springs, NY 12866
***Tel: (518) 584-0400***
***www.racingmuseum.org***

**Negro League Legends Hall of Fame**
***Tel: (301) 647-2145***
***www.negroleaguelegendshalloffame.org***

**Soccer Hall of Fame**
National Soccer Hall of Fame
18 Stadium Circle
Oneonta, NY 13820
***Tel: (607) 432-3351***
***www.soccerhall.org***

**Swimming Hall of Fame**
International Swimming Hall of Fame
One Hall of Fame Drive
Ft. Lauderdale, FL 33316
***Tel: (954) 462-6536***
***www.ishof.org***

**Tennis Hall of Fame**
International Tennis Hall of Fame
194 Bellevue Avenue
Newport, RI 02840
***Tel: (401) 849-3990***
***www.tennisfame.com***

**Track & Field Hall of Fame**
National Track & Field Hall of Fame
216 Ft. Washington Avenue
New York, NY 10032
***Tel: (317) 261-0500***
***www.usaf.org***

**World Boxing Council Hall of Fame**
***www.wbcboxing.com***

# EVERY LISTING

## in this DIRECTORY can be an Internship Opportunity. Here's our List to get you going!!!



**Atlanta Braves**
755 Hank Aaron Drive
Atlanta, GA 30315
***Tel: (404) 522-7630***
***www.atlantabraves.com***

**Atlanta Falcons**
4400 Falcon Parkway
Flowery Branch, GA 30542
***Tel: (770) 965-3115***
***www.atlantafalcons.com***

**Baltimore Orioles**
Camden Yards
333 West Camden Street
Baltimore, MD 21201
***Tel: (410) 685-9800***
***www.theorioles.com***

**Baltimore Ravens**
One Winning Drive
Owings Mills, MD 21117
***Tel: (410) 701-4000***
***www.baltimoreravens.com***

**Black Entertainment & Sports Lawyers Association (BESLA)**
P.O. Box 441485
Fort Washington, MD 20749
***Tel: (301) 248-1818***
***www.besla.org***

**Boston Celtics**
226 Causeway Street
Boston, MA 02114
***Tel: (617) 523-6050***
***www.celtics.com***
***www.nba.com/celtics/contact/celtics-internship-opportunities.html***

**Boston Red Sox**
Fenway Park
4 Yawkey Way
Boston, MA 02215
***Tel: (617) 267-9440***
***www.redsox.com***

**Chicago Bulls**
1901 W. Madison Street
Chicago, IL 60612
***Tel: (312) 455-4000***
***www.bulls.com***

**Chicago Cubs**
Wrigley Field
1060 West Addison
Chicago, IL 60613-4397
***Tel: (773) 404-2827***
***www.cubs.com***

**Chicago White Sox**
U.S. Cellular Field
333 West 35th Street
Chicago, IL 60616
***Tel: (312) 674-1000***
***www.whitesox.com***

**Cleveland Cavaliers**
One Center Court
Cleveland, OH 44115
***Tel: (216) 420-2000***
***www.cavs.com***

**Dallas Cowboys**
One Legends Way
Arlington, TX 76011
***Tel: (817) 892-4161***
***www.dallascowboys.com***

**Detroit Pistons**
Six Championship Drive
Auburn Hills, MI 48326
***Tel: (248) 377-0100***
***www.pistons.com***

**Indianapolis Colts**
7001 West 56th Street
Indianapolis, IN 46254
***Tel: (317) 297-2658***
***www.colts.com***

**Jobs in Sports.com**
***www.jobsinsports.com***

**Los Angeles Clippers**
The Staples Center
1111 S. Figueroa St., Ste. 1100
Los Angeles, CA 90015
***Tel: (213) 742-7500***
***www.clippers.com***

**Los Angeles Dodgers**
Dodger Stadium
1000 Elysian Park Avenue
Los Angeles, CA 90012
***Tel: (323) 224-1500***
***www.dodgers.com***

**Los Angeles Lakers**
555 N. Nash Street
El Segundo, CA 90245
***Tel: (310) 426-6000***
***www.lakers.com***

**Major League Baseball Internships**
245 Park Avenue, 31st Fl.
New York, NY 10167
***Tel: (212) 931-7800***
***www.mlb.com***

**NASCAR Diversity Internship**
1801 W. Int'l. Speedway Blvd.
Daytona Beach, FL 32114
***Tel: (386) 253-0611***
***www.nascar.com***
***www.diversityinternships.com***

**National Basketball Association**
645 Fifth Avenue
New York, NY 10022
***Tel: (212) 407-8000***
***www.nba.com***

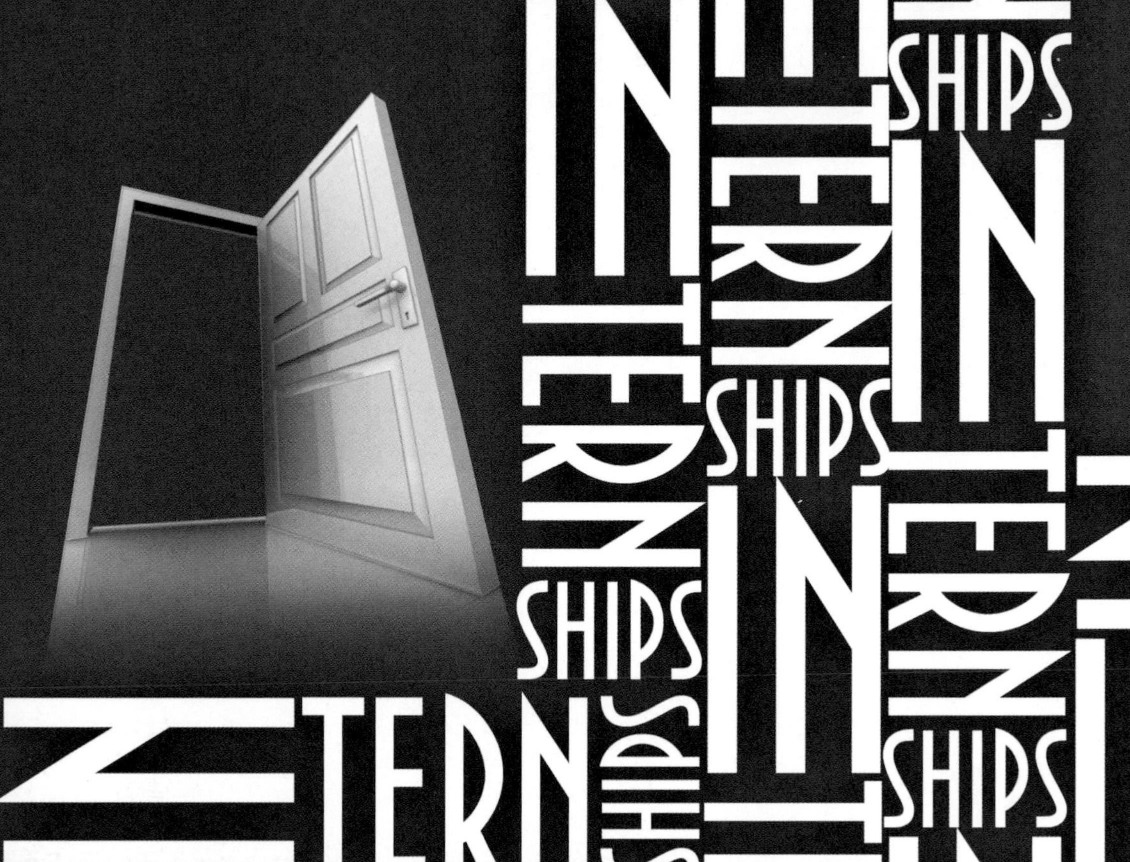

**National Football League Internships**
280 Park Avenue
New York, NY 10017
***Tel: (212) 450-2000***
***www.nfl.com***

**National Hockey League**
1251 Ave. of the Americas, 47th Fl.
New York, NY 10020
***Tel: (212) 789-2999***
***www.nhl.com***

**New York Giants**
Giants Stadium
East Rutherford, NJ 07073
***Tel: (201) 935-8111***
***www.giants.com***

**New York Yankees**
Yankee Stadium
One E. 161st Street
Bronx, NY 10451
***Tel: (718) 293-4300***
***www.yankees.com***

**Oakland Athletics**
Oakland Coliseum
7000 Coliseum Way
Oakland, CA 94621
***Tel: (510) 638-4900***
***www.oaklandathletics.com***

**Oakland Raiders**
1220 Harbor Bay Parkway
Alameda, CA 945202
***Tel: (510) 864-5000***
***www.raiders.com***

**Philadelphia 76ers**
3601 S. Broad Street
Philadelphia, PA 19148
***Tel: (215) 339-7600***
***www.sixers.com***

**Philadelphia Eagles**
1 NovaCare Way
Philadelphia, PA 19145
***Tel: (215) 463-2500***
***www.philadelphiaeagles.com***

**Philadelphia Phillies**
One Citizens Bank Way
Philadelphia, PA 19148
***Tel: (215) 463-6000***
***www.phillies.com***

**Washington Redskins**
21300 Redskins Park Dr.
Ashburn, VA 20147
***Tel: (703) 726-7000***
***www.redskins.com***

**Arizona Diamondbacks**
401 East Jefferson Street
Phoenix, AZ 85004
***Tel: (602) 462-6500***
***www.azdiamondbacks.com***

**Atlanta Braves**
755 Hank Aaron Drive
Atlanta, GA 30315
***Tel: (404) 522-7630***
***www.atlantabraves.com***

**Baltimore Orioles**
Oriole Park
333 West Camden Street
Baltimore, MD 21201
***Tel: (410) 685-9800***
***www.theorioles.com***

**Boston Red Sox**
Fenway Park
4 Yawkey Way
Boston, MA 02215
***Tel: (617) 267-9440***
***www.redsox.com***

**Chicago Cubs**
Wrigley Field
1060 West Addison
Chicago, IL 60613
***Tel: (773) 404-2827***
***www.cubs.com***

**Chicago White Sox**
U.S. Cellular Field
333 West 35th Street
Chicago, IL 60616
***Tel: (312) 674-1000***
***www.whitesox.com***

**Cincinnati Reds**
100 Joe Nuxhall Way
Cincinnati, OH 45202
***Tel: (513) 765-7000***
***www.cincinnatireds.com***

**Cleveland Indians**
Progressive Field
2401 Ontario Street
Cleveland, OH 44115
***Tel: (216) 420-4200***
***www.indians.com***

**Colorado Rockies**
2001 Blake Street
Denver, CO 80205
***Tel: (303) 292-0200***
***www.coloradorockies.com***

**Detroit Tigers**
Comerica Park
2100 Woodward Avenue
Detroit, MI 48201
***Tel: (313) 471-2000***
***www.detroittigers.com***

**Florida Marlins**
2269 Dan Marino Boulevard
Miami, FL 33056
***Tel: (305) 626-7400***
***www.floridamarlins.com***

**Houston Astros**
Minute Maid Park
501 Crawford Street
Houston, TX 77002
***Tel: (713) 259-8000***
***www.astros.com***

**Kansas City Royals**
Kauffman Stadium
1 Royal Way
Kansas City, MO 64141
***Tel: (816) 921-8000***
***www.kcroyals.com***

**Los Angeles Angels of Anaheim**
Angel Stadium
2000 Gene Autry Way
Anaheim, CA 92806
***Tel: (714) 940-2000***
***www.angelsbaseball.com***

**Los Angeles Dodgers**
Dodger Stadium
1000 Elysian Park Avenue
Los Angeles, CA 90012
***Tel: (323) 224-1500***
***www.dodgers.com***

**Milwaukee Brewers**
Miller Park
One Brewers Way
Milwaukee, WI 53214
***Tel: (414) 902-4400***

**www.milwaukeebrewers.com**

**Minnesota Twins**
The Metrodome
34 Kirby Puckett Place
Minneapolis, MN 55415
***Tel: (612) 375-1366***
***www.twinsbaseball.com***

**New York Mets**
Citi Field
Flushing, NY 11368
***Tel: (718) 507-6387***
***www.mets.com***

**New York Yankees**
Yankee Stadium
One E. 161st Street
Bronx, NY 10451
***Tel: (718) 293-4300***
***www.yankees.com***

**Oakland Athletics**
Oakland Coliseum
7000 Coliseum Way
Oakland, CA 94621
***Tel: (510) 638-4900***
***www.oaklandathletics.com***

**Philadelphia Phillies**
Citizens Bank Park
One Citizens Bank Way
Philadelphia, PA 19148
***Tel: (215) 463-6000***
***www.phillies.com***

**Pittsburgh Pirates**
PNC Park
115 Federal Street
Pittsburgh, PA 15212
***Tel: (412) 323-5000***
***www.pittsburghpirates.com***

**San Diego Padres**
PETCO Park
100 Park Boulevard
San Diego, CA 92101
***Tel: (619) 795-5000***
***www.padres.com***

**San Francisco Giants**
AT & T Park
24 Willie Mays Plaza
San Francisco, CA 94107
***Tel: (415) 972-2000***
***www.sfgiants.com***

**Seattle Mariners**
Safeco Field
1250 First Avenue S.
Seattle, WA 98134
***Tel: (206) 346-4000***
***www.seattlemariners.com***

**St. Louis Cardinals**
Busch Stadium
700 Clark Street
St. Louis, MO 63102
***Tel: (314) 345-9600***
***www.stlcardinals.com***

**Tampa Bay Rays**
Tropicana Field
One Tropicana Drive
St. Petersburg, FL 33705
***Tel: (727) 825-3137***
***www.tampabayrays.com***

**Texas Rangers**
1000 Ballpark Way
Arlington, TX 76011
***Tel: (817) 273-5222***
***www.texasrangers.com***

**Toronto Blue Jays**
Rogers Centre
1 Blue Jays Way, Ste. 3200
Toronto, Ontario, Canada M5V1J1
***Tel: (416) 341-1000***
***www.bluejays.com***

**Washington Nationals**
Nationals Park
1500 S. Capitol Street, SE
Washington, D.C. 20003
***Tel: (202) 349-0400***
***www.nationals.com***

## ***For All YOUR MLB Questions, CONTACT:***

**Major League Baseball**
245 Park Avenue, 31st Fl.
New York, NY 10167
***Tel: (212) 931-7800***
***www.mlb.com***

**Major League Baseball Players Association**
12 E. 49th Street, 24th Fl.
New York, NY 10017
***Tel: (212) 826-0808***
***www.mlbplayers.com***

**Chicago Fire Main**
Toyota Park
7000 S. Harlem Avenue
Bridgeview, IL 60455
***Tel: (708) 594-7200***
***www.chicago-fire.com***

**Chivas USA**
18400 Avalon Blvd., Ste. 500
Carson, CA 90746
***Tel: (310) 630-4569***
***http://web.mlsnet.com/t120/***

**Colorado Rapids**
Dick's Sporting Goods Park
6000 Victory Way
Commerce Park, CO 80022
***Tel: (303) 727-3500***
***www.coloradorapids.com***

**Columbus Crew**
One Black & Gold Blvd.
Columbus, OH 43211
***Tel: (614) 447-CREW (2739)***
***http://web.mlsnet.com/t102/***

**D.C. United**
2400 East Capitol Street, SE
Washington, DC 20003
***Tel: (202) 587-5000***
***www.dcunited.com***

**FC Dallas**
9200 World Cup Way, Ste. 202
Frisco, TX 75034
***Tel: (214) 705-6700***
***www.fcdallas.com***

**Houston Dynamo**
1415 Louisiana Ste. 3400
Houston, TX 77002
***Tel: (713) 276-7500***
***www.houstondynamo.com***

**Kansas City Wizards**
8900 State Line Road
Leawood, KS 66206
***Tel: (913) 387-3400***
***www.kcwizards.com***

**Los Angeles Galaxy**
The Home Depot Center
18400 Avalon Blvd., Ste. 200
Carson, CA 90746
***Tel: (310) 630-2200***
***www.lagalaxy.com***

**New England Revolution**
Gillette Stadium
One Patriot Place
Foxborough, MA 02035
***Tel: (508) 543-8200***
***www.revolutionsoccer.net***

**New York Red Bulls**
One Harmon Plaza, 3rd Fl.
Secaucus, NJ, 07094
***Tel: (201) 583-7000***
***www.newyorkredbulls.com***

**Portland Timbers**
1844 SW Morrison
Portland, OR 97205
***Tel: (503) 553-5400***
***www.portlandtimbers.com***

**Real Salt Lake**
9256 S. State Street
Sandy, UT 84070
***Tel: (801) 727-2700***
***www.realsaltlake.com***

**Toronto FC**
Maple Leaf Sports & Entertainment
40 Bay Street, Ste. 400
Toronto, ON M5J 2X2
***Tel: (416) 815-5400***
***http://web.mlsnet.com/t280/***

**Vancouver MLS 2011**
The Landing
375 Water Street, Ste. 550
Vancouver, BC V6B 5C6
***Tel: (604) 669-WAVE***

**Atlanta Hawks**
101 Marietta Street, Ste. 1900
Atlanta, GA 30303
***Tel: (404) 878-3800***
***www.hawks.com***

**Boston Celtics**
226 Causeway Street
Boston, MA 02114
***Tel: (617) 523-6050***
***www.celtics.com***

**Charlotte Bobcats**
333 E. Trade Street
Charlotte, NC 28202
***Tel: (617) 523-6050***
***www.bobcatsbasketball.com***

**Chicago Bulls**
1901 W. Madison Street
Chicago, IL 60612
***Tel: (312) 455-4000***
***www.bulls.com***

**Cleveland Cavaliers**
One Center Court
Cleveland, OH 44115
***Tel: (216) 420-2000***
***www.cavs.com***

**Dallas Mavericks**
2909 Taylor Street
Dallas, TX 75224
***Tel: (214) 747-6287***
***www.dallasmavericks.com***

**Denver Nuggets**
1000 Chopper Circle
Denver, CO 80204
***Tel: (303) 405-1100***
***www.nuggets.com***

**Detroit Pistons**
Six Championship Drive
Auburn Hills, MI 48326
***Tel: (248) 377-0100***
***www.pistons.com***

**Golden State Warriors**
1011 Broadway
Oakland, CA 94607
***Tel: (510) 986-2200***
***www.gs-warriors.com***

**Houston Rockets**
1510 Polk Street
Houston, TX 77002
***Tel: (713) 627-3865***
***www.rockets.com***

**Indiana Pacers**
125 S. Pennsylvania Street
Indianapolis, IN 46204
***Tel: (317) 917-2500***
***www.pacers.com***

**Los Angeles Clippers**
The Staples Center
1111 S. Figueroa St., Ste. 1100
Los Angeles, CA 90015
***Tel: (213) 742-7500***
***www.clippers.com***

**Los Angeles Lakers**
555 N. Nash Street
El Segundo, CA 90245
***Tel: (310) 426-6000***
***www.lakers.com***

**Memphis Grizzlies**
191 Beale Street
Memphis, TN 38103
***Tel: (901) 888-4667***
***www.grizzlies.com***

**Miami Heat**
601 Biscayne Boulevard
Miami, FL 33132
***Tel: (786) 777-1000***
***www.heat.com***

**Milwaukee Bucks**
1001 N. Fourth Street
Milwaukee, WI 53203
***Tel: (414) 227-0599***
***www.bucks.com***

**Minnesota Timberwolves**
600 First Avenue North
Minneapolis, MN 55403
***Tel: (612) 673-1600***
***www.timberwolves.com***

**New Jersey Nets**
390 Murray Hill Parkway
E. Rutherford, NJ 07073
***Tel: (201) 935-8888***
***www.njnets.com***

**New Orleans Hornets**
1250 Poydras St., 9th Fl.
New Orleans, LA 70113
***Tel: (504) 593-4700***
***www.hornets.com***

**New York Knicks**
Two Pennsylvania Plaza
New York, NY 10121
***Tel: (212) 465-6471***
***www.nyknicks.com***

**Oklahoma City Thunder**
Two Leadership Square
211 N. Robinson Ave., Ste. 300
Oklahoma City, OK 73102
***Tel: (405) 208-4800***
***www.nba.com/thunder***

**Orlando Magic**
8701 Maitland Blvd.
Orlando, FL 32810
***Tel: (407) 916-2400***
***www.orlandomagic.com***

**Philadelphia 76ers**
3601 S. Broad Street
Philadelphia, PA 19148
***Tel: (215) 339-7600***
***www.sixers.com***

**Phoenix Suns**
201 E. Jefferson Street
Phoenix, AZ 85004
***Tel: (602) 379-7900***
***www.suns.com***

**Portland Trail Blazers**
One Center Court, Ste. 200
Portland, OR 97227
***Tel: (503) 234-9291***
***www.blazers.com***

**Sacramento Kings**
One Sports Parkway
Sacramento, CA 95834
***Tel: (916) 928-0000***
***www.kings.com***

**San Antonio Spurs**
One AT & T
San Antonio, TX 78219
***Tel: (210) 444-5000***
***www.spurs.com***

**Toronto Raptors**
40 Bay Street, Ste. 400
Toronto, Ontario
M5J 2X2 Canada
***Tel: (416) 815-5600***
***www.raptors.com***

**Utah Jazz**
301 W. South Temple
Salt Lake City, UT 84101
***Tel: (801) 325-2500***
***www.utahjazz.com***

**Washington Wizards**
601 F Street, NW
Washington, D.C. 20004
***Tel: (202) 661-5000***
***www.nba.com/wizards***

## *For All Your NBA Questions CONTACT:*

**National Basketball Association (NBA)**
645 Fifth Avenue
New York, NY 10022
***Tel: (212) 407-8000***
***www.nba.com***

**National Basketball Association Players Association**
2 Penn Plaza, Ste. 2430
New York, NY 10121
***Tel: (212) 655-0880***
***www.nbpa.com***

**Arizona Cardinals**
P.O. Box 888
Phoenix, AZ 85001
***Tel: (602) 379-0101***
***www.azcardinals.com***

**Atlanta Falcons**
4400 Falcon Parkway
Flowery Branch, GA 30542
***Tel: (770) 965-3115***
***www.atlantafalcons.com***

**Baltimore Ravens**
One Winning Drive
Owings Mills, MD 21117
***Tel: (410) 701-4000***
***www.baltimoreravens.com***

**Buffalo Bills**
One Bills Drive
Orchard Park, NY 14127
***Tel: (716) 648-1800***
***www.buffalobills.com***

**Carolina Panthers**
800 South Mint Street
Charlotte, NC 28202
***Tel: (704) 358-7000***
***www.panthers.com***

**Chicago Bears**
Halas Hall
1000 Football Drive
Lake Forest, IL 60045
***Tel: (847) 295-6600***
***www.chicagobears.com***

**Cincinnati Bengals**
One Paul Brown Stadium
Cincinnati, OH 45202
***Tel: (513) 621-3550***
***www.bengals.com***

**Cleveland Browns**
76 Lou Groza Boulevard
Berea, OH 44017
***Tel: (440) 891-5000***
***www.clevelandbrowns.com***

**Dallas Cowboys**
One Legends Way
Arlington, TX 76011
***Tel: (817) 892-4161***
***www.dallascowboys.com***

**Dallas Cowboys**
One Cowboys Parkway
Irving, TX 75063
***Tel: (972) 556-9900***
***www.dallascowboys.com***

**Denver Broncos**
13655 Broncos Parkway
Englewood, CO 80112
***Tel: (303) 649-9000***
***www.denverbroncos.com***

**Detroit Lions**
222 Republic Drive
Allen Park, MI 48101
***Tel: (313) 216-4000***
***www.detroitlions.com***

**Green Bay Packers**
Lambeau Field Atrium
1265 Lombardi Avenue
Green Bay, WI 54304
***Tel: (920) 569-7500***
***www.packers.com***

**Houston Texans**
Two Reliant Park
Houston, TX 77054
***Tel: (832) 667-2000***
***www.houstontexans.com***

**Indianapolis Colts**
7001 West 56th Street
Indianapolis, IN 46254
***Tel: (317) 297-2658***
***www.colts.com***

**Jacksonville Jaguars**
One Stadium Place
Jacksonville, FL 32202
***Tel: (904) 633-6000***
***www.jaguars.com***

**Kansas City Chiefs**
One Arrowhead Drive
Kansas City, MO 64129
***Tel: (816) 920-9300***

**www.kcchiefs.com**

**Miami Dolphins**
7500 SW 30th Street
Davie, FL 33314
***Tel: (954) 452-7000***
***www.miamidolphins.com***

**Minnesota Vikings**
9520 Viking Drive
Eden Prairie, MN 55344
***Tel: (952) 828-6500***
***www.vikings.com***

**New England Patriots**
Gillette Stadium
One Patriot Place
Foxboro, MA 02035
***Tel: (508) 543-8200***
***www.patriots.com***

**New Orleans Saints**
5800 Airline Drive
Metairie, LA 70003
***Tel: (504) 733-0255***
***www.neworleanssaints.com***

**New York Giants**
Giants Stadium
East Rutherford, NJ 07073
***Tel: (201) 935-8111***
***www.giants.com***

**New York Jets**
One Jets Drive
Florham Park, NJ 07932
***Tel: (9730 549-4800***
***www.newyorkjets.com***

**Oakland Raiders**
1220 Harbor Bay Parkway
Alameda, CA 945202
***Tel: (510) 864-5000***
***www.raiders.com***

**Philadelphia Eagles**
NovaCare Complex
1 NovaCare Way
Philadelphia, PA 19145
***Tel: (215) 463-2500***
***www.philadelphiaeagles.com***

**Pittsburgh Steelers**
3400 S. Water Street
Pittsburgh, PA 15203
***Tel: (412) 432-7800***
***www.steelers.com***

**St. Louis Rams**
One Rams Way
St. Louis, MO 63045
***Tel: (314) 982-7267***
***www.stlouisrams.com***

**San Diego Chargers**
4020 Murphy Canyon Road
San Diego, CA 92123
***Tel: (858) 874-4500***
***www.chargers.com***

**San Francisco 49ers**
4949 Centennial Boulevard
Santa Clara, CA 95054
***Tel: (408) 562-4949***
***www.49ers.com***

**Seattle Seahawks**
12 Seahawks Way
Renton, WA 98056
***Tel: (888) 635-4295***
***www.seahawks.com***

**Tampa Bay Buccaneers**
One Buccaneer Place
Tampa, FL 33607
***Tel: (813) 870-2700***
***www.buccaneers.com***

**Tennessee Titans**
460 Great Circle Road
Nashville, TN 37228
***Tel: (615) 565-4000***
***www.titansonline.com***

**Washington Redskins**
21300 Redskins Park Drive
Ashburn, VA 20147
***Tel: (703) 726-7000***
***www.redskins.com***

***For All Your NFL Questions Go to THE Source:***

**National Football League (NFL)**
280 Park Avenue
New York, NY 10017
***Tel: (212) 450-2000***
***www.nfl.com***

**NFL Players Association**
1133 20th Street, NW
Washington, D.C. 20036
***Tel: (202) 572-7500/(800) 372-2000***
***www.nflplayers.com***

**Anaheim Ducks**
2695 E. Katella Avenue
Anaheim, CA 92806
***Tel: (877) 945-9464***
***www.mightyducks.com***

**Atlanta Thrashers**
101 Marietta St. NW, Ste. 1900
Atlanta, GA 30303
***Tel: (404) 878-3800***
***www.atlantathrashers.com***

**Boston Bruins**
100 Legends Way
Boston, MA 02114
***Tel: (617) 624-1900***
***www.bostonbruins.com***

**Buffalo Sabres**
HSBC Arena
One Seymour H. Knox III Plaza
Buffalo, NY 14203
***Tel: (716) 855-4100***
***www.sabres.com***

**Calgary Flames**
P.O. Box 1540 Stn. M
Calgary, Alberta T2P 3B9
***Tel: (403) 777-2177***
***www.calgaryflames.com***

**Carolina Hurricanes**
1400 Edwards Mill Rd.
Raleigh, NC 27607
***Tel: (919) 467-7825***
***www.carolinahurricanes.com***

**Chicago Blackhawks**
United Center
1901 W. Madison Street
Chicago, IL 60612
***Tel: (312) 455-7000***
***www.chicagoblackhawks.com***

**Colorado Avalanche**
1000 Chopper Circle
Denver, CO 80204
***Tel: (303) 405-1100***
***www.coloradoavalanche.com***

**Columbus Blue Jackets**
200 W. Nationwide Blvd.
Columbus, OH 43215
***Tel: (614) 246-4625***
***www.bluejackets.com***

**Dallas Stars**
2601 Avenue of the Stars
Frisco, TX 75034
***Tel: (214) 387-5500***
***www.dallasstars.com***

**Detroit Red Wings**
19 Steve Yzerman Drive
Detroit, MI 48226
***Tel: (313) 396-7444***
***www.detroitredwings.com***

**Edmonton Oilers**
11230 110th Street
Edmonton, Alberta T5G 3H7
***Tel: (780) 414-4000***
***www.edmontonoilers.com***

**Florida Panthers**
One Panther Parkway
Sunrise, FL 33323
***Tel: (954) 835-7000***
***www.floridapanthers.com***

**Los Angeles Kings**
1111 S. Figueroa Street, Ste. 3100
Los Angeles, CA 90015
***Tel: (213) 742-7100***
***www.lakings.com***

**Minnesota Wild**
317 Washington Street
St. Paul, MN 55102
***Tel: (651) 602-6000***
***www.wild.com***

**Montreal Canadiens**
1275 St. Antoine Street W.
Montreal, Quebec H3C 5L2
***Tel: (514) 925-2525***
***www.canadiens.com***

**Nashville Predators**
501 Broadway
Nashville, TN 37203
***Tel: (615) 770-2300***
***www.nashvillepredators.com***

**New Jersey Devils**
165 Mulberry Street
Newark, NJ 07102
***Tel: (973) 757-6100***
***www.newjerseydevils.com***

**New York Islanders**
1535 Old Country Road
Plainview, NY 11803
***Tel: (516) 501-6700***
***www.newyorkislanders.com***

**New York Rangers**
2 Pennsylvania Plaza
New York, NY 10121
***Tel: (212) 465-6000***
***www.newyorkrangers.com***

**Ottawa Senators**
1000 Palladium Drive
Ottawa, Ontario
K2V 1A5 Canada
***Tel: (613) 599-0250***
***www.ottawasenators.com***

**Philadelphia Flyers**
3601 S. Broad Street
Philadelphia, PA 19148
***Tel: (215) 465-4500***
***www.philadelphiaflyers.com***

**Phoenix Coyotes**
6751 N. Sunset Blvd., #200
Glendale, AZ 85305
***Tel: (623) 772-3200***
***www.phoenixcoyotes.com***

**Pittsburgh Penguins**
1 Chatham Center, Ste. 400
Pittsburgh, PA 15219
***Tel: (412) 642-1300***
***www.pittsburghpenguins.com***

**St. Louis Blues**
1401 Clark Avenue
St. Louis, MO 63103
***Tel: (314) 622-2500***
***www.stlouisblues.com***

**San Jose Sharks**
525 W. Santa Clara Street
San Jose, CA 95113
***Tel: (408) 287-7070***
***www.sjsharks.com***

**Tampa Bay Lightning**
401 Channelside Drive
Tampa, FL 33602
***Tel: (813) 301-6500***
***www.tampabaylightning.com***

**Toronto Maple Leafs**
Air Canada Centre
40 Bay Street - Ste. 400
Toronto, Ontario M5J 2X2 Canada
***Tel: (416) 815-5500***
***www.mapleleafs.com***

**Vancouver Canucks**
General Motors Place
800 Griffiths Way
Vancouver, B.C. V6B 6G1
***Tel: (604) 899-4600***
***www.canucks.com***

**Washington Capitals**
627 N. Glebe Road, Ste. 850
Arlington, VA 22203
***Tel: (202) 266-2200***
***www.washingtoncaps.com***

***For ALL the Latest NHL Information, CONTACT:***

**National Hockey League**
1185 Ave. of the Americas, 12th Fl.
New York, NY 10020
***Tel: (212) 789-2000***
***www.helvetica.com***

**National Hockey League Players Association**
20 Bay Street, Ste. 1700
Toronto, Ontario M5J 2N8
***Tel: (416) 313-2300***
***www.nhlpa.com***

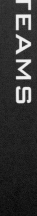

**Atlanta Dream**
83 Walton Street, NW - Ste. 500
Atlanta, GA 30303
***Tel: (404) 604-2626***
***www.atlantadream.net***

**Chicago Sky**
20 W. Kinzie Street, Ste. 1020
Chicago, IL 60654
***Tel: (312) 829-9550***
***www.chicagosky.net***

**Connecticut Sun**
One Mohegan Sun Blvd.
Uncasville, CT 06382
***Tel: (860) 862-4000***
***www.connecticutsun.com***

**Detroit Shock**
Six Championship Drive
Auburn Hills, MI 48326
***Tel: (248) 377-0100***
***www.detroitshock.com***

**Indiana Fever**
125 S. Pennsylvania Street
Indianpolis, IN 46204
***Tel: (317) 917-2500***
***www.wnba.com/fever***

**Los Angeles Sparks**
888 S. Figueroa St., Ste. 2010
Los Angeles, CA 90017
***Tel: (213) 929-1300***
***www.lasparks.com***

**Minnesota Lynx**
600 First Avenue North
Minneapolis, MN 55403
***Tel: (612) 673-8400***
***www.wnba.com/lynx/***

**New York Liberty**
Madison Square Garden
Two Pennsylvania Plaza, 14th Fl.
New York, NY 10121
***Tel: (212) 564-9622***
***www.nyliberty.com***

**Phoenix Mercury**
201 E. Jefferson Street
Phoenix, AZ 85004
***Tel: (602) 514-8333***
***www.phoenixmercury.com***

**Sacramento Monarchs**
One Sports Parkway
Sacramento, CA 95834
***Tel: (916) 928-0000***
***www.sacramentomonarchs.com***

**San Antonio Silver Stars**
One AT & T Center
San Antonio, TX 78219
***Tel: (210) 444-5090***
***www.sanantoniosilverstars.com***

**Seattle Storm**
3421 Thorndyke Ave., W.
Seattle, WA 98119
***Tel: (206) 281-5800***
***www.wnba.com/storm***

**Washington Mystics**
Verizon Center
601 F Street, NW - 3rd Fl.
Washington, D.C. 20004
***Tel: (202) 527-7540***
***www.washingtonmystics.com***

## *For All Your WNBA Contacts:*

**Women's National Basketball Association (WNBA)**
645 Fifth Avenue
New York, NY 10022
***Tel: (212) 688-9622***
***www.wnba.com***

**Women's National Basketball Players Association**
310 Lenox Avenue
New York, NY 10027
***Tel: (212) 655-0880***
***www.wnbpa.com***

## Pace & Brace Yourself

Working in the industry is
a long journey, with mountains to climb,
rivers to cross & races to run.
Limit stress. Limit undue pressure.
Enjoy it.

www.entertainmentpower.com

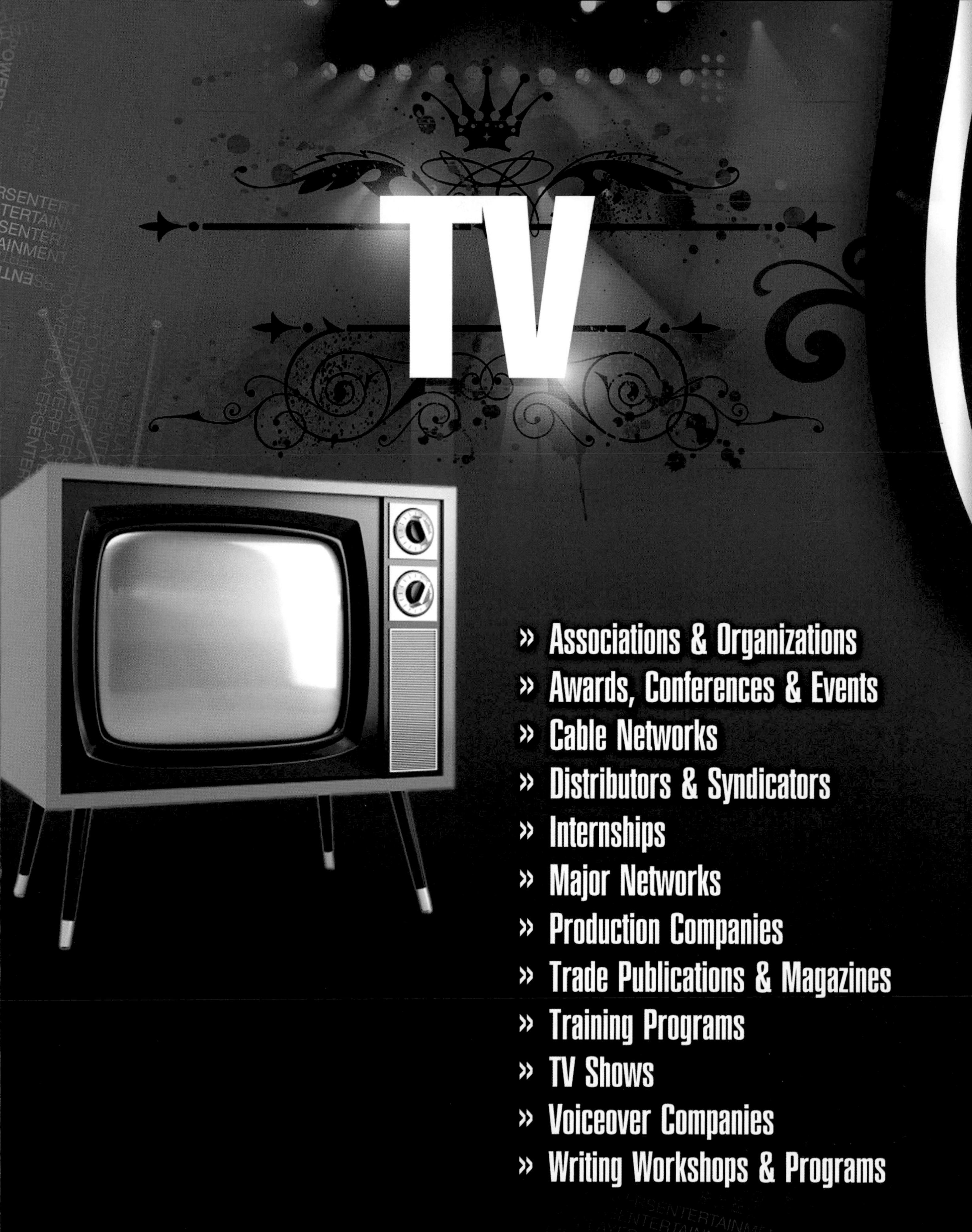

# TV

- Associations & Organizations
- Awards, Conferences & Events
- Cable Networks
- Distributors & Syndicators
- Internships
- Major Networks
- Production Companies
- Trade Publications & Magazines
- Training Programs
- TV Shows
- Voiceover Companies
- Writing Workshops & Programs

**Academy of Interactive Arts & Sciences**
23622 Calabasas Rd., Ste. 220
Calabasas, CA 91302
***Tel: (818) 876-0826***
***www.interactive.org***

**Academy of Television Arts & Sciences**
5220 Lankershim Boulevard
N. Hollywood, CA 91601
***Tel: (818) 754-2800***
***www.emmys.tv***

**Actors Equity Association**
165 W. 46th Street
New York, NY 10036
***Tel: (212) 869-8530***
***www.actorsequity.org***

**Actors Equity Association**
6755 Hollywood Blvd., 5th Fl.
Hollywood, CA 90028
***Tel: (323) 978-8080***
***www.actorsequity.org***

**Affiliated Property Craftspersons IATSE Local 44**
12021 Riverside Drive
N. Hollywood, CA 91607
***Tel: (818) 769-2500***
***www.local44.org***

**Alliance of Motion Picture & Television Producers (AMPTP)**
15301 Ventura Boulevard
Sherman Oaks, CA 91403
***Tel: (818) 995-3600***
***www.amptp.org***

**American Federation of TV & Radio Artists (AFTRA)**
5757 Wilshire Blvd., 9th Fl.
Los Angeles, CA 90036
***Tel: (323) 634-8100***
***www.aftra.org***

**American Federation of TV & Radio Artists (AFTRA)**
260 Madison Ave., 7th Fl.
New York, NY 10016
***Tel: (212) 532-0800***
***www.aftra.org***

**American Women in Radio & TV**
1760 Old Meadow Road, Ste. 500
McLean, VA 22102
***Tel: (703) 506-3290***
***www.awrt.org***

**American Guild of Variety Artists (AGVA)**
4741 Laurel Canyon Blvd., Ste. 208
Valley Village, CA 91607
***Tel: (818) 508-9984***

**American Guild of Variety Artists (AGVA)**
363 7th Avenue, 17th Fl.
New York, NY 10010
***Tel: (212) 675-1003***

**American Women in Radio & TV (AWRT)**
1760 Old Meadow Road, Ste. 500
McLean, VA 22102
***Tel: (703) 506-3290***
***www.awrt.org***

**Art Directors Guild & Scenic, Title & Graphic Design**
11969 Ventura Blvd., 2nd Fl.
Studio City, CA 91604
***Tel: (818) 762-9995***
***www.artdirectors.org***

**Association of Celebrity Personal Assistants**
914 Westwood Blvd., #507
Los Angeles, CA 90024
***Tel: (310) 281-7755***
***www.celebrityassistants.org***

**Association of Independent Commercial Editors (AICE)**
308 W. 107th Street, Ste. 5F
New York, NY 10025
***Tel: (212) 665-2679***
***www.aice.org***

**Association of Independent Commercial Producers (AICP)**
3 W. 18th Street, 5th Fl.
New York, NY 10011
***Tel: (212) 929-3000***
***www.aicp.com***

**Association of Independent Commercial Producers (AICP)**
650 N. Bronson Avenue, Ste. 223B
Los Angeles, CA 90004
***Tel: (323) 960-4763***

**_www.aicp.com_**

**Association of Talent Agents**
9255 Sunset Blvd., Ste. 930
Los Angeles, CA 90069
***Tel: (310) 274-0628***
***www.agentassociation.com***

**Association for Women in Communications**
3337 Duke Street
Alexandria, VA 22314
***Tel: (703) 370-7436***
***www.womcom.org***

**Association of Cable Communicators**
P.O. Box 75007
Washington, D.C. 20013
***Tel: (202) 222-2371***
***www.cablecommunicators.org***

**Assoc. of Public TV Stations**
2100 Crystal Drive, Ste. 700
Arlington, VA 22202
***Tel: (202) 654-4200***
***www.apts.org***

**Bay Area Video Coalition**
2727 Mariposa St., 2nd Fl.
San Francisco, CA 94110
***Tel: (415) 861-3282***
***www.bavc.org***

**Black Entertainment & Sports Lawyers Association (BESLA)**
P.O. Box 441485
Fort Washington, MD 20749
***Tel: (301) 248-1818***
***www.besla.org***

**Breaking Into Hollywood**
P.O. Box 3909
Hollywood, CA 90078
***Tel: (310) 712-3459***
***www.breakingintohollywood.org***

**Broadcast Education Association**
1771 N Street NW
Washington, D.C. 20036
***Tel: (202) 429-3935***
***www.beaweb.org***

**Cable In The Classroom**
25 Massachusetts Ave., NW/Ste. 100

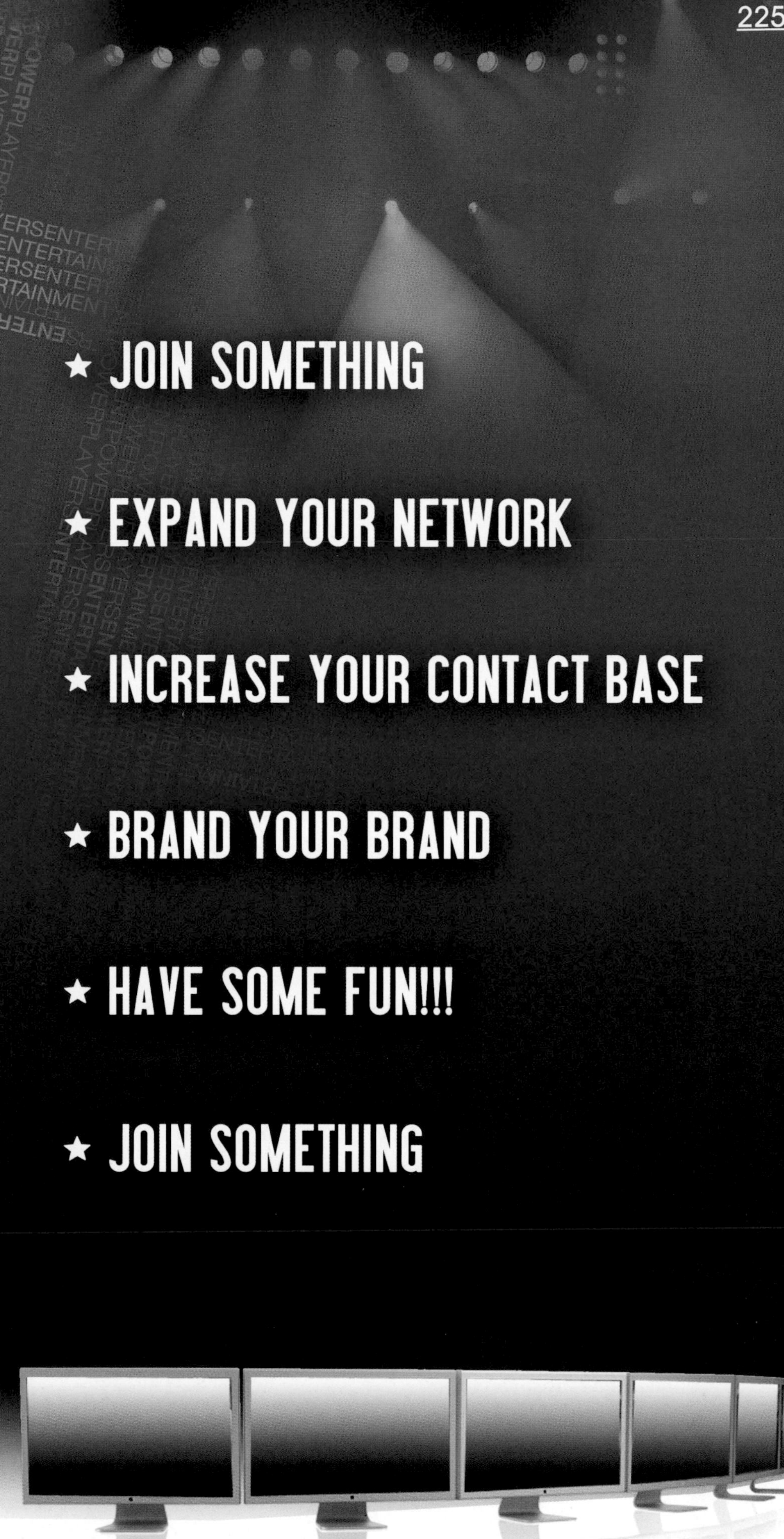

★ JOIN SOMETHING
★ EXPAND YOUR NETWORK
★ INCREASE YOUR CONTACT BASE
★ BRAND YOUR BRAND
★ HAVE SOME FUN!!!
★ JOIN SOMETHING

Washington, D.C. 20001
***Tel: (202) 222-2335***
***www.ciconline.com***

**Cable Telecommunications Association For Marketing**
201 N. Union St., Ste. 440
Alexandria, VA 22314
***Tel: (703) 549-4200***
***www.ctam.com***

**Cable Television Laboratories**
858 Coal Creek Circle
Louisville, CO 80027
***Tel: (303) 661-9100***
***cablelabs.com***

**Cable TV Advertising Bureau**
830 Third Avenue, 2nd Fl.
New York, NY 10022
***Tel: (212) 508-1200***
***www.cabletvadbureau.com***

**California Broadcasters Assoc.**
915 L Street, Ste. 1150
Sacramento, CA 95814
***Tel: (916) 444-2237***
***www.yourcba.com***

**California Cable TV Association**
360 22nd Street, Ste. 750
Oakland, CA 94612
***Tel: (510) 628-8043***
***www.calcable.org***

**California Cable TV Association**
1121 L Street., Ste. 400
Sacramento, CA 95814
***Tel: (916) 446-7732***
***www.calcable.org***

**California Chicano News Media Association**
USC Annenberg School of Journ.
One California Plaza
Los Angeles, CA 90071
***Tel: (213) 437-4408***
***www.ccnma.org***

**Casting Society of America**
606 N. Larchmont Blvd., Ste. 4-B
Los Angeles, CA 90004
***Tel: (323) 463-1925***
***www.castingsociety.com***

**Casting Society of America**
311 W. 43rd St., 10th Fl.
New York, NY 10019
***Tel: (212) 868-1260***

**Center for Asian American Media (CAAM)**
145 Ninth Street, Ste. 350
San Francisco, CA 94103
***Tel: (415) 863-0814***
***www.asianamericanmedia.org***

**Christian Writers Guild**
5525 N. Union Blvd., Ste. 200
Colorado Springs, CO 80918
***Tel: (719) 495-5177***
***www.christianwritersguild.com***

**Coalition of Asian Pacifics in Entertainment**
P.O. Box 251855
Los Angeles, CA 90025
***Tel: (310) 278-2313***
***www.capeusa.org***

**Collegiate Broadcasters, Inc.**
UPS - Hershey Square Center
1152 Mae Street
Hummelstown, PA 17036
***Tel: (713) 348-2935***
***www.collegebroadcasters.org***

**Corporation for Public Broadcasting**
401 Ninth Street, NW
Washington, DC 20004
***Tel: (202) 879-9600***
***www.cpb.org***

**Costume Designers Guild**
11969 Ventura Blvd., 1st Fl.
Studio City, CA 91604
***Tel: (818) 752-2400***
***www.costumedesignersguild.com***

**Digital Entertainment Group**
9229 Sunset Blvd., Ste. 405
Los Angeles, CA 90069
***Tel: (310) 888-2823***
***www.dvdinformation.com***

**Digital Video Professionals Association**
135 Interstate Blvd., Ste. 1
Greenville, SC 29615
***Tel: (888) 339-DVPA (3872)***
***www.dvpa.com***

**Directors Guild of America**
7920 Sunset Boulevard
Los Angeles, CA 90046
***Tel: (310) 289-2000***
***www.dga.org***

**Directors Guild of America**
110 W. 57th Street
New York, NY 10019
***Tel: (212) 581-0370***
***www.dga.org***

**Entertainment Industries Council**
2600 W. Olive Street, Ste. 574
Burbank, CA 91505
***Tel: (818) 333-5001***
***www.eiconline.org***

**Entertainment Industries Council**
1856 Reston Parkway, Ste. 215
Reston, VA 20190
***Tel: (703) 481-1414***
***www.eiconline.org***

**Entertainment Merchant Assoc.**
16530 Ventura Blvd., Ste. 400
Encino, CA 91436
***Tel: (818) 385-1500***
***www.vsda.org***

**Federal Communications Commission**
445 12th Street, SW
Washington, DC 20554
***Tel: (888) CALL-FCC/(888) 225-5322***
***www.fcc.gov***

**Guild of Italian Amer. Actors**
Canal Street Station
P.O. Box 123
New York, NY 10013
***Tel: (212) 420-6590***
***www.nygiaa.org***

**Hispanic Organization of Latin Actors (HOLA)**
107 Suffolk Street, Ste. 302
New York, NY 10002
***Tel: (212) 253-1015***
***www.hellohola.org***

**Hollywood Connect**
1763 North Gower Street
Hollywood, CA 90028
***www.hollywoodconnect.com***

**Hollywood Radio & TV Society**
13701 Riverside Dr., Ste. 205
Sherman Oaks, CA 91423
***Tel: (818) 789-1182***
***www.hrts.org***

**Independent Film & TV Alliance**
10850 Wilshire Blvd., 9th Fl.
Los Angeles, CA 90024
***Tel: (310) 446-1000***
***www.ifta-online.org***

**Int'l. Association of Lighting Designers**
The Merchandise Mart, Ste. 9-104
Chicago, IL 60654
***Tel: (312) 527-3677***
***www.iald.org***

**Int'l. Assoc. of Theatrical Stage Employees - IATSE Local 33**
1720 W. Magnolia Boulevard
Burbank, CA 91506
***Tel: (818) 841-9233***
***ia33.org***

**Int'l. Alliance of Theatrical Stage Employees (IATSE)**
10045 Riverside Drive
Toluca Lake, CA 91602
***Tel: (818) 980-3499***
***www.iatse-intl.org***

**Int'l. Alliance of Theatrical Stage Employees (IATSE)**
1430 Broadway, 20th Fl.
New York, NY 10018
***Tel: (212) 730-1770***
***www.iatse-intl.org***

**Illustrators & Matte Artists IATSE Local 790**
13949 Ventura Blvd., Ste. 301
Sherman Oaks, CA 91423
***Tel: (818) 784-6555***

**International Documentary Association**
1201 W. 5th Street, Ste. M270
Los Angeles, CA 90017
***Tel: (213) 534-3600***
***www.documentary.org***

**International Radio & Television Society Foundation**
420 Lexington Ave., Ste. 1601
New York, NY 10170
***Tel: (212) 867-6650***
***www.irts.org***

**Media Communications Assoc.**
2810 Crossroads Dr., Ste. 3800
Madison, WI 53718
***Tel: (608) 443-2464***
***www.mca-i.org***

**Media Education Foundation**
60 Masonic Street
Northhampton, MA 01060
***Tel: (413) 584-8500***
***www.mediaed.org***

**Media Fellowship International**
P.O. Box 82685
Kenmore, WA 98028
***Tel: (425) 488-3965***
***www.mediafellowship.org***

**National Academy of Television Arts & Sciences**
111 West 57th Street, Ste. 600
New York, NY 10019
***Tel: (212) 586-8424***
***www.emmyonline.tv***

**National Association of Black Female Executives in Music & Entertainment (NABFEME)**
59 Maiden Lane, 27th Fl.
New York, NY 10038
***Tel: (212) 424-9568***
***www.nabfeme.org***

**National Association of Black Journalists (NABJ)**
***Tel: (301) 445-7100***
***www.nabj.org***

**National Black Public Relations Society**
9107 Wilshire Blvd., Ste. 450
Beverly Hills, CA 90210
***Tel: (888) 976-0005***
***www.nbprs.com***

**National Assoc. of Black-Owned Broadcasters (NABOB)**
1155 Connecticut Ave., NW - Ste. 600
Washington, D.C. 20036
***Tel: (202) 463-8970***
***www.nabob.org***

**National Association of Black Telecom Professionals**
2020 Pennsylvania Ave., NW/Box 735
Washington, D.C. 20006
***Tel: (800) 946-6228***
***www.nabtp.org***

**National Association of Broadcast Employees & Technicians (NABET)**
80 West End Ave., Room 501
New York, NY 10023
***Tel: (212) 757-7191***
***www.nabet16.org***

**National Association of Broadcasters (NAB)**
1771 N Street, NW
Washington, D.C. 20036
***Tel: (202) 429-5300***
***www.nab.org***

**National Association of Latino Independent Producers**
1323 Lincoln Blvd., Ste. 220
Santa Monica, CA 90401
***Tel: (310) 395-8880***
***www.nalip.org***

**National Association of Latino Independent Producers (NALIP)**
c/o POV
32 Broadway, 14th Fl.
New York, NY 10004
***Tel: (646) 336-6333***
***www.nalip.org***

**National Association of Minority Media Executives**
7950 Jones Branch Drive
McLean, VA 22107
***Tel: (703) 854-7178***
***www.namme.org***

**National Association of Multi-Ethnicity In Communications (NAMIC)**
336 W. 37th Street, Ste. 302
New York, NY 10018
***Tel: (212) 594-5985***
***www.namic.com***

**National Association of Talent Representatives**
The Gage Group
315 W. 57th St., Ste. 48
New York, NY 10019

***Tel: (212) 541-5250***

**National Association of Television Program Executives (NATPE)**
5757 Wilshire Blvd., Penthouse 10
Los Angeles, CA 90036
***Tel: (310) 453-4440***
***www.natpe.org***

**National Black Programming Consortium**
68 E. 131st Street, 7th Fl.
New York, NY 10037
***Tel: (212) 234-8200***
***www.nbpc.tv***

**National Broadcasting Society**
P.O. Box 4206
Chesterfield, MO 63006
***Tel: (636) 536-1943***
***www.nbs1.org***

**National Cable & Television Association**
25 Massachusetts Ave., NW/Ste. 100
Washington, D.C. 20001
***Tel: (202) 222-2300***
***www.ncta.com***

**National Cable Television Cooperative**
11200 Corporate Avenue
Lenexa, KS 66219
***Tel: (913) 599-5900***
***www.cabletvco-op.org***

**National Communications Association**
1765 N Street, NW
Washington, D.C. 20036
***Tel: (202) 464-4622***
***www.natcom.org***

**National Educational Telecommunications Assoc.**
939 South Stadium Road
Columbia, SC 29201
***Tel: (803) 799-5517***
***www.netaonline.org***

**National Hispanic Media Coalition**
55 S. Grand Avenue
Pasadena, CA 91105
***Tel: (626) 792-6462***
***www.nhmc.org***

**National Newspaper Publishers Association**
3200 13th Street, NW
Washington, DC 20010
***Tel: (202) 588-8764***
***www.nnpa.org***

**New York Women In Film & TV**
6 E. 39th Street, Ste. 1200
New York, NY 10016
***Tel: (212) 679-0870***
***www.nywift.org***

**Organization of Black Screenwriters (OBS)**
Golden State Mutual
Life Insurance Building
1999 W. Adams Blvd./Rm. Mezzanine
Los Angeles, CA 90018
***Tel: (323) 735-2050***
***www.obswriter.com***

**Pacific Islanders in Communications**
1221 Kapiolani Blvd., Ste. 6A-4
Honolulu, HI 96814
***Tel: (808) 591-0059***
***www.piccom.org***

**PBS**
2100 Crystal Drive
Arlington, VA 22202
***Tel: (703) 739-5000***
***www.pbs.org***

**Producers Guild of America**
8530 Wilshire Blvd., Ste. 450
Beverly Hills, CA 90211
***Tel: (310) 358-9020***
***www.producersguild.org***

**Producers Guild of America**
1000 Ave. of the Americas, 11th Fl.
New York, NY 10013
***Tel: (212) 894-4016***
***www.producersguild.org***

**Production Equipment Rental Association**
101 W. 31st Street, Ste. 1005
New York, NY 10001
***Tel: (646) 839-0430***
***www.peraonline.org***

**PROMAX BDA**
1522e Cloverfield Blvd.
Santa Monica, CA 90404
***Tel: (310) 788-7600***
***www.promaxbda.org***

**Public Relations Society of America (PRSA)**
33 Maiden Lane, 11th Fl.
New York, NY 10038
***Tel: (212) 460-1400***
***www.prsa.org***

**Public Relations Student Society of America (PRSSA)**
33 Maiden Lane, 11th Fl.
New York, NY 10038
***Tel: (212) 460-1474***
***www.prssa.org***

**Radio-Television News Directors Association (RTNDA)**
529 14th Street, NW - Ste. 425
Washington, D.C. 20045
***Tel: (202) 659-6510***
***www.rtnda.org***

**Radio & TV Broadcast Engineers**
225 W. 34th Street, Ste. 1120
New York, NY 10122
***Tel: (212) 354-6770***
***www.ibew1212.org***

**Screen Actors Guild (SAG)**
5757 Wilshire Boulevard
Los Angeles, CA 90036
***Tel: (323) 954-1600***
***www.sag.org***

**Screen Actors Guild (SAG)**
360 Madison Avenue, 12th Fl.
New York, NY 10036
***Tel: (212) 944-1030***
***www.sag.org***

**Script Supervisors & Continuity Coordinators**
1159 Chandler Boulevard
N. Hollywood, CA 91601
***Tel: (818) 509-7871***
***www.ialocal871.org***

**Script Supervisors, Continuity Coordinators**
630 Ninth Avenue, Ste. 1103
New York, NY 10036

***Tel: (212) 977-9655***
***www.local161.org***

**Set Decorators Society of America**
7100 Tujuna Avenue, Ste. #A
N. Hollywood, CA 91605
***Tel: (818) 255-2425***
***www.setdecorators.org***

**Society of Cable Telecommunications Engineers**
140 Philips Road
Exton, PA 19341
***Tel: (610) 363-6888***
***www.scte.org***

**Society of Motion Picture & Television Engineers (SMPTE)**
3 Barker Avenue
White Plains, NY 10601
***Tel: (914) 761-1100***
***www.smpte.org***

**Society of Professional Journalists**
Eugene S. Pulliam National Journalism Center
3909 N. Meridian Street
Indianapolis, IN 46208
***Tel: (317) 927-8000***
***www.spj.org***

**Society of Stage Directors & Choreographers**
1501 Broadway, Ste. 1701
New York, NY 10036
***Tel: (212) 391-1070***
***www.ssdc.org***

**Southern California Cable & Telecommunications Assoc.**
1070 East Orange Grove
Burbank, CA 91501
***Tel: (818) 569-5100***
***www.sccta.org***

**Stagehands - IATSE Local 33**
1720 W. Magnolia Blvd.
Burbank, CA 91506
***Tel: (818) 841-9233***
***ia33.org***

**Studio Electrical Lighting Technicians - IATSE Local 728**
***Tel: (818) 985-0728***
***www.iatse728.org***

**Syndicated Network TV Assoc.**
One Penn Plaza, Ste. 5310
New York, NY 10111
***Tel: (212) 259-3740***
***www.snta.com***

**Television Bureau of Advertising**
3 E. 54th Street
New York, NY 10022
***Tel: (212) 486-1111***
***www.tvb.org***

**Television Critics Assoc. (TCA)**
5459 Boem Drive
Fairfield, OH 45014
***Tel: (818) 754-4757***
***www.tvcritics.org***

**Theatrical Stage Employees**
1720 W. Magnolia Blvd.
Burbank, CA 91506
***Tel: (818) 841-9233***
***www.iatselocalone.org***

**Theatrical Stage Employees**
320 W. 46th Street
New York, NY 10036
***Tel: (212) 333-2500***
***www.iatselocalone.org***

**United Stuntmen's Association**
10924 Mukilteo Speedway, #272
Mukilteo, WA 98275
***Tel: (425) 290-9957***
***www.stuntschool.com***

**United Stunt Women's Assoc.**
26893 Bouquet Canyon Rd.
Suite C331
Saugus, CA 91350
***Tel: (818) 774-3889***
***www.usastunts.com***

**University Film & Video Assoc.**
Peter J. Bukalski
Box 1777
Edwardsville, IL 62026
***Tel: (866) 647-8382***
***www.ufva.org***

**Women In Cable & Telecommunications**
14555 Avion Pkwy., Ste. 250
Chantilly, VA 20151
***Tel: (703) 234-9810***
***www.wict.org***

**Women in Film & Video (WIFV)**
3628 12th Street, NE
Washington, DC 20017
***Tel: (202) 429-WIFV (9438)***
***www.wifv.org***

**Women in Film & TV Atlanta**
P.O. Box 52726
Atlanta, GA 30355
***Tel: (770) 621-5071***
***www.wifa.org***

**Workplace Hollywood**
1201 W. 5th Street, Ste. T-550
Los Angeles, CA 90017
***Tel: (213) 250-9921***
***www.workplacehollywood.org***

**Writers Guild of America, east**
555 W. 57th Street, Ste. 1230
New York, NY 10019
***Tel: (212) 767-7800***
***www.wgaeast.org***

**Writers Guild of America, west**
7000 W. Third Street
Los Angeles, CA 90048
***Tel: (323) 951-4000***
***www.wga.org***

**Academy Awards (Oscars)**
8949 Wilshire Boulevard
Beverly Hills, CA 90211
***Tel: (310) 247-3000***
***www.oscars.org***

**ActorFest L.A.**
Back Stage
5055 Wilshire Boulevard
Los Angeles, CA 90036
***Tel: (323) 525-2356***
***www.backstage.com***

**ActorFest NY**
Back Stage
770 Broadway
New York, NY 10003
***Tel: (646) 654-5700***
***www.backstage.com***

**Alma Awards**
National Council of La Raza (NCLR)
1126 16th Street, NW
Washington, D.C. 20036
***Tel: (202) 785-1670***
***www.nclr.org***

**Angel Awards**
***www.angelawards.com***

**ASCAP Film & TV Music Awards**
7920 Sunset Blvd., 3rd Fl.
Los Angeles, CA 90046
***Tel: (323) 883-1000***
***www.ascap.com***

**Artios Awards**
Casting Society of America
606 N. Larchmont Blvd., Ste. 4-B
Los Angeles, CA 90004
***Tel: (323) 463-1925***
***www.castingsociety.com***

**Aurora Awards**
299 S. Main Street, 17th Fl.
Salt Lake City, UT 84111
***Tel: (801) 535-4339***
***www.auroraawards.com***

**BET Awards**
1235 W Street, NE
Washington, D.C. 20018
***Tel: (202) 608-2000***
***www.bet.com***

**Cindy Awards**
P.O. Box 270779
Flower Mound, TX 75027
***www.cindys.com***

**CINE Golden Eagle Award**
1112 16th Street, NW - Ste. 510
Washington, D.C. 20036
***Tel: (202) 785-1136***
***www.cine.org***

**Clio Awards**
770 Broadway, 15th Fl.
New York, NY 10003
***Tel: (212) 683-4300***
***www.clioawards.com***

**College Television Awards**
Academy of Television Arts &
Sciences Foundation
5220 Lankershim Boulevard
N. Hollywood, CA 91601
***Tel: (818) 754-2800***
***www.emmys.tv/foundation***

**The Diversity Awards**
Multicultural Motion Pic. Assoc.
6100 Wilshire Boulevard, Ste. 230
Los Angeles, CA 90048
***Tel: (310) 358-8300***
***www.thediversityawards.org***

**Emmy Awards**
Academy of TV Arts & Sciences
5220 Lankershim Boulevard
N. Hollywood, CA 91601
***Tel: (818) 754-2800***
***www.emmys.org***

**Film, Stage & ShowBiz Expo**
440 9th Avenue, 8th Fl.
New York, NY 10001
***Tel: (212) 404-2456***
***www.TheShowBizExpo.com***

**Golden Globe Awards**
Hollywood Foreign Press. Assoc.
646 N. Robertson Boulevard
W. Hollywood, CA 90069
***Tel: (310) 657-1731***
***www.hfpa.org***

**Int'l. Broadcasting Awards**
Hollywood Radio & TV Society

13701 Riverside Dr., Ste. 205
Sherman Oaks, CA 91423
***Tel: (818) 789-1182***
***www.hrts.org***

**Latino Media Market**
National Association of Latino Independent Producers (NALIP)
1323 Lincoln Blvd., Ste. 220
Santa Monica, CA 90401
***Tel: (310) 395-8880***
***www.nalip.org***

**MTV Video Music Awards**
1515 Broadway
New York, NY 10036
***Tel: (212) 258-8000***
***www.mtv.com***

**NAACP Image Awards**
4929 Wilshire Blvd., Ste. #310
Los Angeles, CA 90010
***Tel: (323) 938-5268***
***www.naacpimageawards.net***

**National Commendation Awards**
American Women in Radio & TV
1760 Old Meadow Road, Ste. 500
McLean, VA 22102
***Tel: (703) 506-3290***
***www.awrt.org***

**National Media Market**
***Tel: (520) 743-7735***
***www.nmm.net***

**NATPE Conference**
National Association of Television Program Executives
5757 Wilshire Blvd., Penthouse 10
Los Angeles, CA 90036
***Tel: (310) 453-4440***
***www.natpe.org***

**NATPE LATV Fest**
National Association of Television Program Executives
5757 Wilshire Blvd., Penthouse 10
Los Angeles, CA 90036
***Tel: (310) 453-4440***
***www.latvfest.net***
***www.natpe.org***

**New York Women in Film & TV**
6 E. 39th Street, Ste. 1200
New York, NY 10016
***Tel: (212) 679-0870***
***www.nywift.org***

**News & Documentary Emmy Awards**
National Television Academy
111 W. 57th Street, Ste. 600
New York, NY 10019
***Tel: (212) 586-8424***
***www.emmyonline.org***

**Omni Awards**
3735 Palomar Center Dr., Ste. 150
Lexington, KY 40513
***Tel: (888) 914-OMNI***
***www.omniawards.com***

**The Paley Festival**
25 W. 52nd Street
New York, NY 10019
***Tel: (212) 621-6800***
***www.paleycenter.org***

**Peabody Awards**
University of Georgia
Grady College of Journalism
Sanford Dr. @ Baldwin Street
Athens, GA 30602
***Tel: (706) 542-3787***
***www.peabody.uga.edu***

**People's Choice Awards**
***www.cbs.com***

**PRISM Awards**
Entertainment Industries Council
1856 Old Reston Ave, Ste 215
Reston, VA 20190
***Tel: (703) 481-1414***
***www.prismawards.com***

**Producers Guild Awards**
8350 Wilshire Blvd., Ste. 450
Beverly Hills, CA 90211
***Tel: (310) 358-9020/(212) 894-4016***
***www.producersguild.com***

**Screen Actors Guild Awards**
5757 Wilshire Blvd., 7th Fl.
Los Angeles, CA 90036
***Tel: (310) 235-1030***
***www.sagawards.org***

**Screenwriting Expo**
6404 Hollywood Blvd., Ste. 415
Los Angeles, CA 90028
***Tel: (323) 857-1405***
***www.screenwritingexpo.com***

**ShoWest/ShoEast**
770 Broadway
New York, NY 10003
***Tel: (646) 654-7680***
***www.showest.com***

**Spirit Awards**
Film Independent
9911 W. Pico Blvd., 11th Fl.
Los Angeles, CA 90035
***Tel: (310) 432-1240***
***www.filmindependent.org***

**Telly Awards**
22 W. 21st Street, 7th Fl.
New York, NY 10010
***Tel: (212) 675-3555***
***www.tellyawards.com***

**Tony Awards**
American Theatre Wing
570 Seventh Avenue
New York, NY 10018
***Tel: (212) 765-0606***
***www.tonyawards.com***

**Trumpet Awards**
101 Marietta Street, Ste. 1010
Atlanta, GA 30303
***Tel: (404) TRUMPET/(404) 878-6738***
***www.trumpetfoundation.org***

**Visual Effects Society Awards**
5535 Balboa Blvd., Ste. 205
Encino, CA 91316
***Tel: (818) 981-7861***
***www.vesawards.com***
***www.visualeffectssociety.com***

**UNITY Conference**
UNITY: Journalists of Color, Inc.
7950 Jones Branch Drive
McLean, VA 22107
***Tel: (703) 854-3585***
***www.unityjournalists.org***

**ABC Family Channel**
3800 W. Alameda Ave.
Burbank, CA 91505
***Tel: (818) 560-1000***
***www.abcfamily.com***

**A & E Television Networks**
1925 Century Park E., Ste. 1000
Los Angeles, CA 90067
***Tel: (310) 286-3000***
***www.aetv.com***

**A & E Television Networks**
111 E. Wacker Dr., Ste. 2206
Chicago, IL 60601
***Tel: (312) 819-0191***
***www.aetv.com***

**A & E Television Networks**
235 E. 45th Street
New York, NY 10017
***Tel: (212) 210-1400***
***www.aetv.com***

**A & E Television Networks**
One Buckhead Plaza
3060 Peachtree Road, Ste. 875
Atlanta, GA 30305
***Tel: (404) 816-8880***
***www.aetv.com***

**AMC**
11 Penn Plaza, 15th Fl.
New York, NY 10001
***Tel: (212) 324-8500***
***www.amctv.com***

**AMC**
2425 W. Olympic Blvd., Ste. 5050W
Santa Monica, CA 90404
***Tel: (310) 998-9300***
***www.amctv.com***

**Animal Planet**
One Discovery Place
Silver Spring, MD 20910
***Tel: (240) 662-2000***
***www.discovery.com***

**AmericanLife Network**
5057 Keller Springs Rd., Ste. 110
Dallas, TX 75001
***Tel: (571) 730-6115***
***www.americanlifetv.com***

**BBC America**
4144 Lankershim Blvd., Ste. 200
Burbank, CA 91602
***Tel: (818) 299-9660***
***www.bbcamerica.com***

**BBC Americas**
747 Third Avenue
New York, NY 10017
***Tel: (212) 705-9300***
***www.bbcamerica.com***

**BET Networks**
One BET Plaza
1235 W Street, NE
Washington, D.C. 20018
***Tel: (202) 608-2000***
***www.bet.com***

**BET Networks**
10635 Santa Monica Blvd., 2nd Fl.
Los Angeles, CA 90025
***Tel: (310) 481-3700***
***www.bet.com***

**BET Networks**
1540 Broadway, 27th Fl.
New York, NY 10036
***Tel: (212) 205-3000***
***www.bet.com***

**Better Black TV (BBTV)**
***www.betterblacktv.com***

**Bio**
1925 Century Park E., Ste. 1000
Los Angeles, CA 90067
***Tel: (310) 286-3000***
***www.biography.com***

**Bio**
235 E. 45th Street
New York, NY 10017
***Tel: (212) 210-1400***
***www.biography.com***

**Bloomberg Information Channel**
731 Lexington Ave.
New York, NY 10021

Tel: (212) 318-2000
www.bloomberg.com

**Book TV**
400 N. Capitol Street, NW - Ste. 650
Washington, D.C. 20001
*Tel: (202) 737-3220*
*www.booktv.org*
*www.c-span.org*

**Bravo**
3000 Alameda Avenue
Burbank, CA 91523
*Tel: (818) 840-2200*
*www.bravotv.com*

**Bravo**
30 Rockefeller Plaza, Ste. 14E
New York, NY 10112
*Tel: (212) 664-4444*
*www.bravotv.com*

**The California Channel**
1121 L Street, Ste. 110
Sacramento, CA 95814
*Tel: (916) 444-9792*
*www.calchannel.com*

**Cartoon Network**
1050 Techwood Dr., NW
Atlanta, GA 30318
*Tel: (404) 885-2263*
*www.cartoonnetwork.com*

**CBN**
Christian Broadcasting Network
977 Centerville Turnpike
Virginia Beach, VA 23463
*Tel: (757) 226-7000*
*www.cbn.org*

**CMT: Country Music Television**
2600 Colorado Avenue
Santa Monica, CA 90404
*Tel: (310) 752-8248*
*www.cmt.com*

**CMT: Country Music Television**
330 Commerce Street
Nashville, TN 37201
*Tel: (615) 335-8400*
*www.cmt.com*

**CNBC**
3000 Alameda Blvd., Ste. #C296
Burbank, CA 91523
*Tel: (818) 840-4444*
*www.nbcumv.com/cnbc*

**CNBC**
900 Sylvan Avenue
Englewood Cliff, NJ 07632
*Tel: (201) 735-2622*
*www.nbcumv.com/cnbc*

**CNN**
One Time Warner Center
New York, NY 10019
*Tel: (212) 275-7800*
*www.cnn.com*

**CNN**
One CNN Center
Atlanta, GA 30303
*Tel: (404) 827-1500*
*www.cnn.com*

**Comcast SportsNet**
7700 Wisconsin Ave., Ste. 200
Bethesda, MD 20814
*Tel: (301) 718-3200*
*www.comcastsportsnet.com*

**Comcast SportsNet**
3601 South Broad Street
Philadelphia, PA 19148
*Tel: (215) 336-3500*
*www.csnphilly.com*

**Comedy Central**
2049 Century Park E., Ste. 4170
Los Angeles, CA 90067
*Tel: (310) 407-4700*
*www.comedycentral.com*

**Comedy Central**
345 Hudson Street, 9th Fl.
New York, NY 10019
*Tel: (212) 767-8600*
*www.comedycentral.com*

**C-SPAN**
400 N. Capitol St., NW - Ste. 650
Washington, D.C. 20001
*Tel: (202) 737-3220*
*www.c-span.org*

**Current TV**
118 King Street
San Francisco, CA 94107
*Tel: (415) 995-8200*
*www.current.tv*

**Daystar**
3901 Highway 121
Bedford, TX 76021
*Tel: (817) 571-1229*
*www.daystar.com*

**DISH Network**
9601 S. Meridian Blvd.
Englewood, CO 80112
*Tel: (303) 723-1000*
*www.dishnetwork.com*

**Discovery Networks**
One Discovery Place
Silver Spring, MD 20910
*Tel: (240) 662-2000*
*www.discovery.com*

**Disney Channels Worldwide**
3800 W. Alameda Ave.
Burbank, CA 91505
*Tel: (818) 569-7500*
*www.disneychannel.com*

**DIY Network**
9721 Sherrill Blvd.
Knoxville, TN 37932
*Tel: (865) 694-2700*
*www.diynetwork.com*

**The Documentary Channel**
142 Rosa Parks Blvd.
Nashville, TN 37203
*Tel: (615) 297-4410*
*www.documentarychannel.com*

**E! Entertainment Television**
5750 Wilshire Boulevard
Los Angeles, CA 90036
*Tel: (323) 954-2400*
*www.eonline.com*

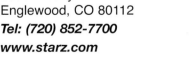

**Encore**
8900 Liberty Circle
Englewood, CO 80112
*Tel: (720) 852-7700*
*www.starz.com*

**ESPN**
ESPN Plaza
Bristol, CT 06010
***Tel: (860) 766-2000***
***www.espn.go.com***

**Fine Living**
9721 Sherrill Blvd.
Knoxville, TN 37932
***Tel: (865) 694-2700***
***www.fineliving.com***

**FitTV**
One Discovery Place
Silver Spring, MD 20910
***Tel: (240) 662-2000***
***www.discovery.com***

**Food Network**
75 Ninth Avenue
New York, NY 10011
***Tel: (212) 398-8836***
***www.foodtv.com***

**Fox News Channel**
1440 S. Sepulveda Blvd.
Los Angeles, CA 90025
***Tel: (310) 444-8752***
***www.foxnews.com***

**Fox News Channel**
1211 Ave. of the Americas
New York, NY 10036
***Tel: (212) 301-3000***
***www.foxnews.com***

**Fox Sports Network**
10201 W. Pico Blvd., Bldg. 101
Los Angeles, CA 90035
***Tel: (310) 369-1000***
***www.foxsports.com***

**Fuel TV**
***Tel: (877) 4 FUEL-TV***
***www.fuel.tv***

**FUSE Network/Rainbow Media**
2425 W. Olympic Blvd., Ste. 5050W
Santa Monica, CA 90404
***Tel: (310) 453-4493***
***www.fuse.tv***

**Fuse**
11 Penn Plaza, 15th Fl.
New York, NY 10001
***Tel: (212) 324-3400***
***www.fuse.tv***

**FX Networks**
10201 W. Pico Blvd.
Bldg. 103, 4th Fl.
Los Angeles, CA 90035
***Tel: (310) 369-1000***
***www.fxnetworks.com***

**G4**
5750 Wilshire Boulevard
Los Angeles, CA 90036
***Tel: (323) 954-2400***
***www.g4tv.com***

**Golf Channel**
7580 Commerce Center Dr.
Orlando, FL 32819
***Tel: (407) 355-4653***
***www.thegolfchannel.com***

**Gospel Music Channel**
1895 Phoenix Blvd., Ste. 355
Atlanta, GA 30349
***Tel: (770) 969-7936***
***www.gospelmusicchannel.com***

**Great American Country/GAC**
49 Music Square West, Ste. 301
Nashville, TN 37203
***Tel: (615) 255-4620***
***www.gactv.com***

**GSN Game Show Network**
2150 Colorado Ave., Ste. 100
Santa Monica, CA 90404
***Tel: (310) 255-6800***
***www.gsn.com***

**Hallmark Channel**
12700 Ventura Blvd., Ste. 200
Studio City, CA 91604
***Tel: (818) 755-2400***
***www.hallmarkchannel.com***

**Home Box Office (HBO)**
2500 Broadway, Ste. 400
Santa Monica, CA 90404
***Tel: (310) 382-3000***
***www.hbo.com***

**Home Box Office (HBO)**
1100 Ave. of the Americas
New York, NY 10036
***Tel: (212) 512-1000***
***www.hbo.com***

**HDNet**
8269 E. 23rd Avenue
Denver, CO 80238
***Tel: (303) 542-5600***
***www.hd.net***

**HDNet**
320 S. Walton Street
Dallas, TX 75226
***Tel: (214) 651-1740***
***www.hd.net***

**HGTV**
9721 Sherrill Boulevard
Knoxville, TN 37932
***Tel: (865) 694-2700***
***www.hgtv.com***

**History Channel**
235 E. 45th Street
New York, NY 10017
***Tel: (212) 210-1400***
***www.historychannel.com***

**HSN**
1 HSN Drive
St. Petersburg, FL 3379
***Tel: (800) 284-3900***
***www.hsn.com***

**iaTV**
ImaginAsian Entertainment
1515 Broadway, 12th Fl.
New York, NY 10036
***Tel: (212) 520-1027***
***www.iaei.tv***

**IFC Independent Film Channel**
11 Penn Plaza, 15th Fl.
New York, NY 10001
***Tel: (212) 324-8500***
***www.ifctv.com***

**In Demand Networks**
345 Hudson Street
New York, NY 10014
***Tel: (646) 638-8200***
***www.indemand.com***

**Ion Media Networks**
601 Clearwater Park Road
W. Palm Beach, FL 33401
***Tel: (561) 659-4122***
***www.ionmedia.tv***

**Inspiration Network**
P.O. Box 7750
Charlotte, NC 28241
***Tel: (803) 578-1000***
***www.insp.com***

**Lifetime Television**
2049 Century Park E., Ste. 840
Los Angeles, CA 90067
***Tel: (310) 556-7500***
***www.mylifetime.com***

**Lifetime Television**
309 W. 49th Street
New York, NY 10019
***Tel: (212) 424-7000***
***www.mylifetime.com***

**MLB Network**
40 Hartz Way, Ste. 110
Secaucus, NJ 07094
***Tel: (201) 520-6400***
***www.mlbnetwork.com***

**MSNBC**
30 Rockefeller Plaza
New York, NY 10112
***Tel: (212) 664-4444***
***www.msnbc.com***

**MTV Networks**
2600 Colorado Avenue
Santa Monica, CA 90404
***Tel: (310) 752-8000***
***www.mtv.com***

**MTV Networks**
1515 Broadway
New York, NY 10036
***Tel: (212) 258-8000***
***www.mtv.com***

**National Geographic Channel**
1145 17th Street, NW
Washington, D.C. 20036
***Tel: (202) 912-6500***
***www.nationalgeographic.com/tv/channel***

**NBC Universal Cable**
3000 W. Alameda Avenue
Burbank, CA 91523
***Tel: (818) 840-4444***
***www.nbcuni.com***

**NFL Network**
One NFL Plaza
Mt. Laurel, NJ 08054
***Tel: (856) 222-3500***
***www.nfl.com/network***

**NFL Network**
10950 Washington Blvd., Ste. 100
Culver City, CA 90232
***Tel: (310) 840-4635***
***www.nfl.com/network***

**Nickelodeon**
231 Olive Avenue
Burbank, CA 91502
***Tel: (818) 736-3000***
***www.nick.com***

**Nickelodeon**
2600 Colorado Avenue
Santa Monica, CA 90404
***Tel: (310) 752-8000***
***www.nick.com***

**Nickelodeon**
1515 Broadway
New York, NY 10036
***Tel: (212) 258-7500***
***www.nick.com***

**Oasis TV**
2029 Century Park E., Ste. 1400
Los Angeles, CA 90067
***Tel: (310) 553-4300***
***www.oasistv.com***

**Outdoor Channel**
43445 Business Park Dr., Ste. 103
Temecula, CA 92590
***Tel: (800) 770-5750***
***www.outdoorchannel.com***

**Ovation - The Arts Network**
2800 28th St., Ste. 240
Santa Monica, CA 90405
***Tel: (310) 430-7580***
***www.ovationtv.com***

**OWN: The Oprah Winfrey Network**
5700 Wilshire Blvd., Ste. 120
Los Angeles, CA 90036
***Tel: (323) 602-5500***

**Oxygen Media**
75 Ninth Avenue, 7th Fl.
New York, NY 10011
***Tel: (212) 651-2000***
***ww.oxygen.com***

**PBS**
2100 Crystal Drive
Arlington, VA 22202
***Tel: (703) 739-5000***
***www.pbs.org***

**Product Information Network**
2600 Michelson Drive, Ste. 1650
Irvine, CA 92612
***Tel: (949) 263-9900***
***www.pinnet.com***

**QVC, Inc.**
1200 Wilson Drive
West Chester, PA 19308
***Tel: (484) 701-1000***
***www.qvc.com***

**Scripps Networks**
312 Walnut Street
2800 Scripps Center
Cincinnati, OH 45202
***Tel: (513) 977-3000***
***www.scripps.com***

**Shop At Home**
5388 Hickory Hollow Pkwy.
Nashville, TN 37013
***Tel: (615) 263-8000***

***www.shopathometv.com***

**Showtime Networks, Inc.**
10880 Wilshire Blvd., Ste. 1600
Los Angeles, CA 90024
***Tel: (310) 234-5200***
***www.sho.com***

**Showtime Networks, Inc.**
1633 Broadway
New York, NY 10019
***Tel: (212) 708-1600***
***www.sho.com***

**Sleuth/NBC Universal Cable**
900 Sylvan Avenue
One CNBC Plaza
Englewood Cliffs, NJ 07632
***Tel: (201) 735-3600***
***www.sleuthchannel.com***

**SoapNet**
2300 W. Riverside Dr.
Burbank, CA 91506
***Tel: (818) 558-5917***
***www.soapnet.com***

**Speed Channel**
***www.speedtv.com***

**Spike TV**
345 Hudson St., 7th Fl.
New York, NY 10014
***Tel: (212) 767-4001***
***www.spiketv.com***

**Starz Entertainment**
8900 Liberty Circle
Englewood, CO 80112
***Tel: (720) 852-7700***
***www.starz.com***

**Style Network**
5750 Wilshire Boulevard
Los Angeles, CA 90036
***Tel: (323) 954-2400***
***www.stylenetwork.com***

**Sundance Channel**
1633 Broadway, 8th Fl.
New York, NY 10019
***Tel: (212) 654-1500***
***www.sundancechannel.com***

**Syfy**
30 Rockefeller Center, 21st Fl.
New York, NY 10112
***Tel: (212) 664-4444***
***www.syfy.com***

**Syfy**
100 Universal City Plaza
Bldg. 1440, 14th Fl.
Universal City, CA 91608
***Tel: (818) 777-6898***
***www.syfy.com***

**TBS**
3500 W. Olive Ave., 15th Fl.
Burbank, CA 91505
***Tel: (818) 977-5500***
***www.tbs.com***

**TBS**
1050 Techwood Dr., NW
Atlanta, GA 30318
***Tel: (404) 827-1700***
***www.tbs.com***

**TCM Turner Classic Movies**
1050 Techwood Drive NW
Atlanta, GA 30318
***Tel: (404) 827-1700***
***Tel: (404) 885-5535***
***www.tcm.com***

**Telemundo Network Group**
2290 W. 8th Avenue
Hialeah, FL 33010
***Tel: (315) 884-8200***
***www.telemundo.com***

**TFC The Filipino Channel**
150 Shoreline Drive
Redwood City, CA 94065
***Tel: (650) 508-6000***
***www.abs-cbnglobal.com***

**The Word Network**
20733 W. Ten Mile
Southfield, MI 48075
***Tel: (248) 357-4566***
***www.thewordnetwork.org***

**TLC**
Discovery Communications
10100 Santa Monica Blvd., Ste. 1500
Los Angeles, CA 90067
***Tel: (310) 551-1611***
***www.discovery.com***

**TLC**
One Discovery Place
Silver Spring, MD 20910
***Tel: (240) 662-2000***
***www.discovery.com***

**TNT**
3500 W. Olive Ave., 15th Fl.
Burbank, CA 91505
***Tel: (818) 977-5500***
***www.tnt.tv***

**TNT**
1050 Techwood Dr., NW
Atlanta, GA 30318
***Tel: (404) 827-1700***
***www.tnt.tv***

**Travel Channel**
5425 Wisconsin Ave., Ste. 500
Chevy Chase, MD 20815
***Tel: (301) 244-7500***
***www.travelchannel.com***

**Trinity Broadcasting Network**
P.O. Box A
Santa Ana, CA 92711
***Tel: (714) 832-2950***
***www.tbn.org***

**tru TV**
600 Third Avenue
New York, NY 10016
***Tel: (212) 973-2800***
***www.trutv.com***

**Turner Classic Movies**
1050 Techwood Drive NW
Atlanta, GA 30318
***Tel: (404) 827-1700***
***Tel: (404) 885-5535***
***www.tcm.com***

**TV Guide Network**
6922 Hollywood Blvd., 12th Fl.

Los Angeles, CA 90028
***Tel: (323) 817-4600***
***www.tvguide.com***

**TV Guide Network**
1211 Ave. of the Americas, 28th Fl.
New York, NY 10036
***Tel: (212) 626-2500***
***www.tvguide.com***

**TV Land**
345 Hudson Street
New York, NY 10014
***Tel: (212) 846-7356***
***www.tvland.com***

**TV ONE**
1010 Wayne Ave., 10th Fl.
Silver Spring, MD 20910
***Tel: (301) 755-0400***
***www.tv-one.tv***

**Univision**
9405 NW 41st Street
Miami, FL 33178
***Tel: (305) 471-3900***
***www.univision.net***

**Univision Communications**
5999 Center Drive
Los Angeles, CA 90045
***Tel: (310) 216-3434***
***www.univision.com***

**USA Network**
100 Universal City Plaza
Universal City, CA 91608
***Tel: (818) 777-6898***
***www.usanetwork.com***

**USA Network**
30 Rockefeller Plaza, 21st Fl.
New York, NY 10112
***Tel: (212) 664-4444***
***www.usanetwork.com***

**Veria TV Network**
Natural Wellness USA, Inc.
701 Highlander Blvd., #200
Arlington, TX 76015
***Tel: (2866) 91-VERIA***
***www.veriatv.com***

**Versus**
One Comcast Center
Philadelphia, PA 19103
***Tel: (203) 276-8000***
***www.versus.com***

**VH1**
2600 Colorado Avenue
Santa Monica, CA 90404
***Tel: (310) 752-8000***
***www.vh1.com***

**VH1**
1515 Broadway
New York, NY 10036
***Tel: (212) 258-8000***
***www.vh1.com***

**Viacom/MTV Networks**
1515 Broadway
New York, NY 10036
***Tel: (212) 258-6000***
***www.viacom.com***

**VideoFashion Network**
611 Broadway, Ste. 307
New York, NY 10012
***Tel: (212) 274-1600***
***www.videofashion.com***

**WE: Women's Entertainment**
11 Penn Plaza, 19th Fl.
New York, NY 10001
***Tel: (212) 324-8500***
***www.we.tv***

**Wealth TV Network**
Herring Broadcasting, Inc.
4757 Morena Blvd.
San Diego, CA 92117
***Tel: (858) 270-6900***
***www.wealthtv.com***

**The Weather Channel**
1875 Century Park E., Ste. 900
Los Angeles, CA 90067
***Tel: (310) 785-0511***
***www.weather.com***

**The Weather Channel**
300 Interstate N. Parkway SE
Atlanta, GA 30339
***Tel: (770) 226-0000***
***www.weather.com***

**The Word Network**
20733 W. Ten Mile
Southfield, MI 48075
***Tel: (248) 357-4566***
***www.thewordnetwork.org***

**YES Network -Yankees Entertainment & Sports Network**
405 Lexington Ave., 36th Fl.
New York, NY 10174
***Tel: (646) 487-3600***
***www.yesnetwork.com***

**A & E Network**
235 E. 45th Street
New York, NY 10017
***Tel: (212) 210-1400***
***www.aetv.com***

**ABC Cable Networks Group**
3800 Alameda Avenue
Burbank, CA 91505
***Tel: (818) 569-7500***
***www.disney.com***

**BBC Worldwide Americas**
3500 W. Alameda Avenue
Burbank, CA 91505
***Tel: (818) 840-9770***
***www.bbcworldwide.com***

**BBC America**
747 Third Ave., 6th Floor
New York, NY 10017
***Tel: (212) 705-9300***
***www.bbcamerica.com***

**Broadway Video Distribution**
1619 Broadway
New York, NY 10019
***Tel: (212) 265-7600/(212) 603-1829***
***www.broadwayvideo.com***

**Buena Vista Home Entertainment Television**
350 S. Buena Vista St.
Burbank, CA 91521
***Tel: (818) 560-1000***
***www.disney.com***

**California Newsreel**
500 Third Street, Ste. 505
San Francisco, CA 91407
***Tel: (415) 284-7800***
***www.newsreel.org***

**CBS Television Distribution**
2401 Colorado Avenue, Ste. 110
Santa Monica, CA 90404
***Tel: (310) 264-3300***
***www.cbstvd.com***

**CBS Television Distribution**
455 N. Cityfront Plaza Dr., Ste. 2910
Chicago, IL 60611
***Tel: (312) 644-3600***
***www.cbstvd.com***

**CBS Television Distribution**
1700 Broadway, 32nd Floor
New York, NY 10019
***Tel: (212) 315-4000***
***www.cbstvd.com***

**Central City Productions**
212 E. Ohio Street, Ste. 300
Chicago, IL 60611
***Tel: (312) 654-1100***
***www.ccptv.com***

**CinemaNow, Inc.**
4553 Glencoe Ave., Ste. 380
Marina del Rey, CA 90292
***Tel: (310) 314-2000***
***www.cinemanow.com***

**Codeblack Entertainment**
111Universal Hollywood Dr./Ste. 2260
Universal City, CA 91608
***Tel: (818) 286-8600***
***www.codeblackentertainment.com***

**Debmar-Mercury**
225 Santa Monica Blvd., 8th Fl.
Santa Monica, CA 90401
***Tel: (310) 393-6000***
***www.debmarmercury.com***

**Debmar-Mercury**
75 Rockefeller Plaza, 16th Fl.
New York, NY 10010
***Tel: (212) 669-5025***
***www.debmarmercury.com***

**Discovery Networks**
One Discovery Place
Silver Spring, MD 20910
***Tel: (240) 662-2000***
***www.discovery.com***

**Distribution Video & Audio**
133 Candy Lane
Palm Harbor, FL 34683
***Tel: (727) 447-4147***
***www.dva.com***

**Documentary Educational Resources, Inc.**
101 Morse Street
Watertown, MA 02472
***Tel: (617) 926-0491***
***www.der.org***

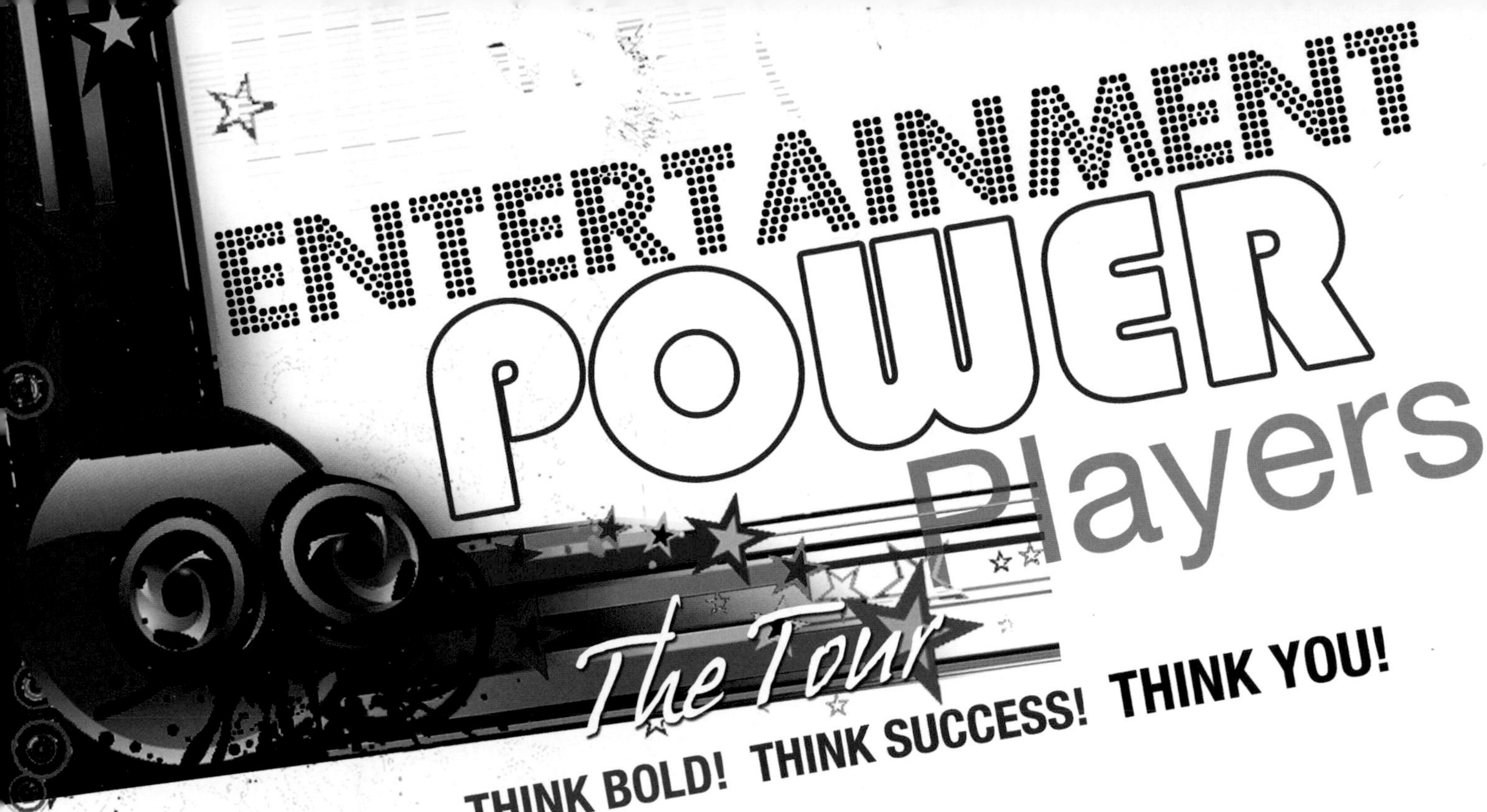


**THINK BOLD! THINK SUCCESS! THINK YOU!**

*Featuring*

# Fashion, Film, Music, Sports & TV

**FREE Admission**

- Creating YOUR Entertainment Career POWER PLAN.
- 10 Things You Can Do TODAY to POWER UP YOUR Career.
- How to Land the Perfect Entertainment Internship or Job.
- Make it Happen! Challenge
- 100+ Entertainment Job Websites.
- Prize Giveaways & More!

For more information about ***EPP: The Tour***, call (323) 533-1971.

**www.entertainmentpower.com**

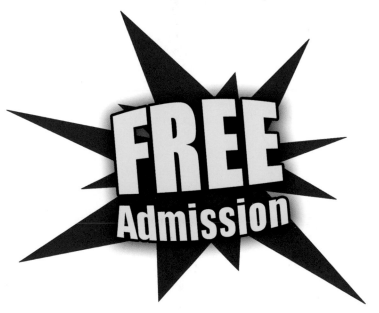

**Facets Multimedia**
1517 W. Fullerton Avenue
Chicago, IL 60614
***Tel: (773) 281-9075***
***www.facets.org***

**FilmCore**
1010 N. Highland Avenue
Hollywood, CA 90038
***Tel: (323) 464-8600***
***www.filmcore.net***

**FilmCore**
500 Sansome St., 7th Fl.
San Francisco, CA 94111
***Tel: (415) 397-8400***
***www.filmcore.net***

**FilmCore**
1619 Broadway, Ste. 612
New York, NY 10019
***Tel: (212) 459-0290***
***www.filmcore.net***

**FremantleMedia**
4000 W. Alameda Ave., 3rd Fl.
Burbank, CA 91505
***Tel: (818) 748-1100***
***www.fremantlemedia.com***

**GRB Entertainment**
13400 Riverside Dr., Ste. 300
Sherman Oaks, CA 91423
***Tel: (818) 728-7600***
***www.grbtv.com***

**GoTV Networks, Inc.**
14144 Ventura Blvd., Ste. 300
Sherman Oaks, CA 91423
***Tel: (818) 933-2100***
***www.gotvnetworks.com***

**Alfred Haber Distribution**
111 Grand Avenue, Ste. 203
Palisades Park, NJ 07650
***Tel: (201) 224-8000***
***www.alfredhaber.com***

**Hearst Entertainment**
300 W. 57th Street
New York, NY 10019
***Tel: (212) 969-7553***
***www.hearstent.com***

**HSN/Home Shopping Network**
1 HSN Drive
St. Petersburg, FL 33729
***Tel: (800) 284-3900***
***www.hsn.com***

**Image Entertainment**
20525 Nordhoff St., Ste. 200
Chatsworth, CA 91311
***Tel: (972) 671-5200***
***www.homevision.com***

**Independent Film Channel/IFC**
11 Penn Plaza, 15th Fl.
New York, NY 10001
***Tel: (212) 324-8500***
***www.ifctv.com***

**IndieVest**
1416 N. La Brea Avenue
Los Angeles, CA 90028
***Tel: (888) 299-9961***
***www.indievest.com***

**HBO Enterprises**
1100 Avenue of the Americas
New York, NY 10036
***Tel: (212) 512-1000***
***www.hbo.com***

**Janson Media**
88 Semmens Road
Harrington Park, NJ 07640
***Tel: (201) 784-8488***
***www.janson.com***

**Koch Entertainment Distribution**
22 Harbor Park Drive
Port Washington, NY 11050
***Tel: (516) 484-1000***
***www.kochdistribution.com***

**Manga Entertainment**
521 Fifth Ave., Ste. 1900
New York, NY 10175
***Tel: (212) 905-4228***
***www.manga.com***

**Maverick Entertainment Group**
1191 E. Newport Ctr. Dr., Ste. 210
Deerfield Beach, FL 33442
***Tel: (954) 422-8811***
***www.maverickentertainment.cc***

**MGM Home Entertainment & Worldwide Television Group**
10250 Constellation Blvd.
Los Angeles, CA 90067
***Tel: (310) 449-3000***
***www.mgm.com***

**MySpace TV**
c/o Fox Interactive Media (FIM)
407 N. Maple Dr.
Beverly Hills, CA 90210
***Tel: (310) 969-7000***
***www.myspacetv.com***

**Namesake Entertainment**
P.O. Box 436492
Louisville, KY 40253
***Tel: (502) 243-3185***
***www.namesakeentertainment.com***

**NBC Universal Home Entertainment/Television Distribution**
100 Universal City Plaza
Universal City, CA 91608
***Tel: (818) 777-1300***
***www.nbcuni.com***

**Netflix**
100 Winchester Circle
Los Gatos, CA 9503
***Tel: (408) 540-3700***
***www.netflix.com***

**Paramount Home Entertainment**
5555 Melrose Avenue
Los Angeles, CA 90038
***Tel: (323) 956-5000***
***www.paramount.com***

**PBS**
2100 Crystal Drive
Arlington, VA 22202
***Tel: (703) 739-5000***
***www.pbs.org***

**RHI Entertainment**
1325 Ave. of the Americas, 21st Fl.
New York, NY 10019
***Tel: (212) 977-9001***
***www.rhitv.com***

**Reveille, LLC**
100 Universal City Plaza

Bungalows 5180/5170
Universal City, CA 91608
***Tel: (818) 733-1218***

**Showtime Pay Per View**
1633 Broadway
New York, NY 10019
***Tel: (212) 708-1600***
***www.sho.com***

**Sony Pictures Television & Home Entertainment**
10202 W. Washington Blvd.
Culver City, CA 90232
***Tel: (310) 244-4000***
***www.sonypicturestelevision.com***

**Starz!**
8900 Liberty Circle
Englewood, CO 80112
***Tel: (720) 852-7700***
***www.starz.com***

**Summit Entertainment**
1630 Stewart St., Ste. 120
Santa Monica, CA 90404
***Tel: (310) 309-8400***
***www.summit-ent.com***

**Tapestry International**
3 Church Street
Sea Bright, NJ 07760
***Tel: (732) 559-1300***
***www.tapestry.tv***

**Tapeworm Video Distribution**
25876 The Old Rd., #141
Stevenson Ranch, CA 91381
***Tel: (661) 257-4904***
***www.tapeworm.com***

**Telemundo Network Group**
2290 W. 8th Avenue
Hialeah, FL 33010
***Tel: (315) 884-8200***
***www.telemundo.com***

**Telepictures Productions**
3500 W. Olive Ave., 10th Fl.
Burbank, CA 91505
***Tel: (818) 972-0777***
***www.telepicturestv.com***

**Teleproductions International**
4520 Daly Drive
Chantilly, VA 20151
***Tel: (703) 222-2408***
***www.tpiltd.com***

**The Television Syndication Co.**
501 Sabal Lake Drive, Ste. 105
Longwood, FL 32779
***Tel: (407) 788-6407***
***www.tvsco.com***

**Time-Life Video/Direct Holdings**
***Tel: (800) 950-7887***
***www.timelife.com***

**Twentieth Century Fox Home Entertainment**
2121 Ave. of the Stars, 11th Fl.
Los Angeles, CA 90067
***Tel: (310) 369-5369***
***www.fox.com***

**Universal Studios Home Entertainment**
10 Universal City Plaza
Universal City, CA 91608
***Tel: (818) 777-1000***
***www.universalstudios.com***

**Vivendi Entertainment**
111 Universal Hollywood Dr., Ste. 400
Universal City, CA 91608
***Tel: (877) 252-4144***
***www.vivendient.com***

**Warner Bros. Domestic Television Distribution**
4000 Warner Blvd.
Burbank, CA 91522
***Tel: (818) 954-5652***
***www.warnerbros.com***

**Warner Horizon Television**
4000 Warner Blvd.
Burbank, CA 91522
***Tel: (818) 954-6000***
***www.warnerbros.com***

**WWE (World Wrestling Entertainment)**
1241 E. Main St.
Stamford, CT 06902
***Tel: (203) 352-8600***
***www.wwe.com***

**WWE (World Wrestling Entertainment)**
780 Third Avenue, 11th Fl.
New York, NY 10017
***Tel: (212) 593-2228***
***www.wwe.com***

**Xenon Pictures**
1440 Ninth Street
Santa Monica, CA 90401
***Tel: (301) 451-5510***
***www.xenonpictures.com***

**York Entertainment**
4565 Sherman Oaks Ave.
Sherman Oaks, CA 91403
***Tel: (818) 788-4050***
***www.yorkentertainment.com***

**YouTube**
***www.youtube.com***

# EVERY LISTING

## in this DIRECTORY can be an Internship Opportunity. Here's our List to get you going!!!



**Academy of Television Arts & Sciences Summer Internship Program**
5220 Lankershim Boulevard
N. Hollywood, CA 91601
***Tel: (818) 754-2800***
***www.emmys.tv/foundation***

**BET**
One BET Plaza
1235 W Street, NE
Washington, D.C. 20018
***Tel: (202) 608-2000***
***www.bet.com***

**Jerry Bruckheimer Films & TV**
1631 Tenth Street
Santa Monica, CA 90404
***Tel: (310) 664-6260***
***www.jbfilms.com***

**CBS Internship & Page Program**
7800 Beverly Boulevard
Los Angeles, CA 90036
***Tel: (323) 575-2345***
***www.cbscareers.com***

**CBS Internship & Page Program**
51 W. 52nd Street, 4th Fl.
New York, NY 10019
***Tel: (212) 975-4321***
***www.cbsdiversity.com***

**Current TV**
118 King Street
San Francisco, CA 94107
***Tel: (415) 995-8200***
***www.current.tv***

**Emma Bowen Foundation**
1299 Pennsylvania Ave., NW-11th Fl.
Washington, DC 20004
***Tel: (202) 637-4494 (D.C.)***
***Tel: (818) 655-5708 (CA)***
***Tel: (212) 975-2545 (NY)***
***www.emmabowenfoundation.com***

**Entertainment Weekly**
1675 Broadway
New York, NY 10019
***Tel: (212) 522-1212***
***www.ew.com***

**ESPN**
ESPN Plaza
Bristol, CT 06010
***Tel: (860) 766-2000***
***www.espn.com/joinourteam***

**Fox Broadcasting Co.**
10201 W. Pico Boulevard
Los Angeles, CA 90035
***Tel: (310) 369-1000***
***www.foxcareers.com***
***www.fox.com/diversity***

**Fox Broadcasting Co.**
1211 Ave. of the Americas
New York, NY 10036
***Tel: (212) 556-2400***
***www.foxcareers.com***
***www.fox.com/diversity***

**Harpo**
110 N. Carpenter Street
Chicago, IL 60607
***Tel: (312) 633-1000***
***www.harpocareers.com***

**Harpo Films**
345 N. Maple Dr., Ste. 315
Beverly Hills, CA 90210
***Tel: (310) 278-5559***
***www.harpocareers.com***

**Hearst Corporation**
300 W. 57th Street
New York, NY 10019
***Tel: (212) 969-7553***
***www.hearst.com***

**The Jim Henson Company**
1416 N. LaBrea Avenue
Hollywood, CA 90028
***Tel: (323) 802-1500***
***www.henson.com***

**The Jim Henson Company**
627 Broadway, 9th Fl.
New York, NY 10012
***Tel: (212) 794-2400***
***www.henson.com***

**MTV**
2600 Colorado Avenue
Santa Monica, CA 90404
***Tel: (310) 752-8000***
***www.mtvncareers.com***

**MTV**
1515 Broadway
New York, NY 10036
***Tel: (212) 258-8000***
***www.mtvncareers.com***

**NATPE Conference**
National Association of Television Program Executives
5757 Wilshire Blvd., PH 10
Los Angeles, CA 90036
***Tel: (310) 453-4440***
***www.natpe.org***

**NBC Internship & Page Program**
3000 W. Alameda Avenue
Burbank, CA 91523
***Tel: (818) 840-4444***
***www.nbcunicareers.com***

**NBC Universal Internships**
100 Universal City Plaza
Universal City, CA 91608
***Tel: (818) 777-1000***
***www.nbcunicareers.com***

**NBC Universal Internship & Page Program**
30 Rockefeller Plaza
New York, NY 10112
***Tel: (212) 664-4444***
***www.nbcunicareers.com***

**News Corporation**
1211 Avenue of the Americas
New York, NY 10036
***Tel: (212) 852-7000***
***www.newscorp.com***

**Pie Town Productions**
5433 Laurel Canyon Blvd.
N. Hollywood, CA 91607
***Tel: (818) 255-9300***
***www.pietown.tv***

**Showtime Networks, Inc.**
10880 Wilshire Blvd., Ste. 1600
Los Angeles, CA 90024
***Tel: (310) 234-5200***
***www.sho.com/careers***

**Showtime Networks, Inc.**
1633 Broadway
New York, NY 10019
***Tel: (212) 708-1600***
***www.sho.com/careers***

**Starz Entertainment Group**
8900 Liberty Circle
Englewood, CO 80112
***Tel: (720) 852-7700***
***www.starz.com***

**T. Howard Foundation**
601 13th Street, NW - 710 N
Washington, D.C. 20005
***Tel: (202) 639-8847***
***www.t-howard.org***

**Time Warner, Inc.**
1 Time Warner Center
New York, NY 10019
***Tel: (212) 484-8000***
***www.timewarner.com/careers***

**Turner Broadcasting System**
1050 Techwood Dr., NW
Atlanta, GA 30318
***Tel: (404) 827-1500/(404) 827-1700***
***www.turnerjobs.com***

**Viacom**
1515 Broadway
New York, NY 10036
***Tel: (212) 258-6000***
***www.viacomcareers.com***

**Workplace Hollywood**
1201 W. 5th Street, Ste. T-550
Los Angeles, CA 90017
***Tel: (213) 250-9921***
***www.workplacehollywood.org***

# MAJOR NETWORKS

**ABC**
500 S. Buena Vista Street
Burbank, CA 91521
***Tel: (818) 460-7777***
***www.abc.com***

**ABC**
77 W. 66th Street
New York, NY 10023
***Tel: (212) 456-7777***
***www.abc.com***

**CBS Television City**
7800 Beverly Boulevard
Los Angeles, CA 90036
***Tel: (323) 575-2345***
***www.cbs.com***

**CBS Television Studios**
4024 Radford Avenue
Studio City, CA 91604
***Tel: (818) 655-5000***
***www.cbstelevisionstudios.com***

**CBS**
51 W. 52nd Street
New York, NY 10019
***Tel: (212) 975-4321***
***www.cbs.com***

**The CW**
3300 W. Olive Avenue
Burbank, CA 91505
***Tel: (818) 977-2500***
***www.cwtv.com***

**The CW**
1325 Ave. of the Americas, 32nd Fl.
New York, NY 10019
***Tel: (212) 636-5000***
***www.cwtv.com***

**Fox Broadcasting Co.**
10201 W. Pico Boulevard
Los Angeles, CA 90035
***Tel: (310) 369-1000***
***www.fox.com***

**Fox Broadcasting Co.**
1211 Ave. of the Americas
New York, NY 10036
***Tel: (212) 556-2400***
***www.fox.com***

**NBC Universal**
3000 W. Alameda Ave.
Burbank, CA 91523
***Tel: (818) 840-4444***
***www.nbcuni.com***

**NBC Universal**
100 Universal City Plaza
Universal City, CA 91608
***Tel: (818) 777-1000***
***www.nbcuni.com***

**NBC Universal**
30 Rockefeller Plaza
New York, NY 10112
***Tel: (212) 664-4444***
***www.nbcuni.com***

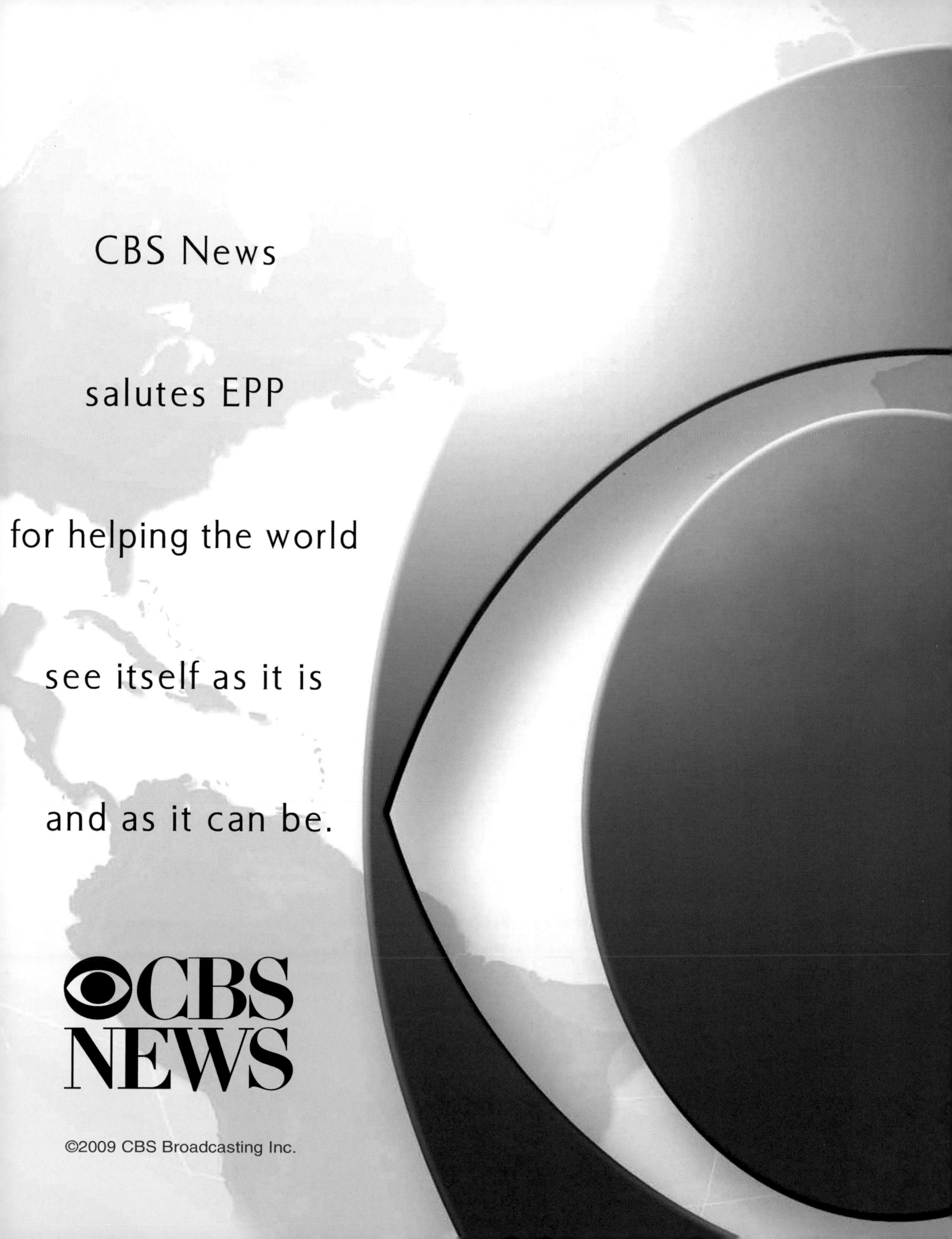

CBS News

salutes EPP

for helping the world

see itself as it is

and as it can be.

**10 x 10 Entertainment**
1640 S. Sepulveda Blvd., Ste. 450
Los Angeles, CA 90025
***Tel: (310) 575-1235***
***Credits: America's Next Top Model; Made in the U.S.A.; Stylista***

**19 Entertainment**
8560 W. Sunset Blvd., 9th Fl.
W. Hollywood, CA 90069
***Tel: (310) 777-1940***
***www.19.co.uk***
***Credits: American Idol; So You Think You Can Dance***

**3 Arts Entertainment**
9460 Wilshire Blvd., 7th Fl.
Beverly Hills, CA 90212
***Tel: (310) 888-3200***
***Credits: 30 Rock; Chelsea Lately; Everybody Hates Chris; Parks & Recreation; The Office***

**3 Ball Productions**
1600 Rosecrans Ave., Bldg. 7
Manhattan Beach, CA 90266
***Tel: (310) 727-3337***
***www.3ballproductions.com***
***Credits: Beauty and the Geek; The Biggest Loser***

**34th St. Films**
8200 Wilshire Blvd., Ste. 300
Beverly Hills, CA 90211
***Tel: (323) 315-5743***

**40 Acres & a Mule Filmworks**
75 S. Elliot Place
Brooklyn, NY 11217
***Tel: (718) 624-3703***
***www.40acres.com***
***Credits: 4 Little Girls; Passing Strange; When the Levees Broke***

**44 Blue Productions**
4040 Vineland Ave., Ste. 105
Studio City, CA 91604
***Tel: (818) 760-4442***
***Credits: Investigative Reports; Lock Up; the True Story of Black Hawk Down***

**51 Minds Entertainment**
6565 Sunset Blvd., Ste. 301
Los Angeles, CA 90028
***Tel: (323) 466-9200***
***Credits: Flavor of Love; I Love New York; The Surreal Life; Rock of Love***

**900 Films**
1203 Activity Drive
Vista, CA 92081
***Tel: (760) 477-2470***
***www.900films.com***
***Credits: Tony Hawk Projects***

**Actual Reality Pictures**
6725 Sunset Blvd., Ste. 350
Los Angeles, CA 90028
***Tel: (310) 202-1272***
***Credits: Black.White; Flip That House***

**AEI-Atchity Entertainment**
518 S. Fairfax Avenue
Los Angeles, CA 90036
***Tel: (310) 932-0407***
***Credits: Life or Something Like It; Shadow of Obsession***

**Alchemy Television Group**
8530 Wilshire Blvd., Ste. 400
Beverly Hills, CA 90211
***Tel: (310) 289-7766***
***Credits: Coco Chanel; Karol: A Man Who Became Pope***

**Craig Anderson Productions**
444 N. Larchmont Blvd., Ste. 109
Los Angeles, CA 90004
***Tel: (323) 463-2000***
***Credits: Sally Hemings; The Piano Lesson***

**Apatow Productions**
11788 W. Pico Blvd.
Los Angeles, CA 90064
***Tel: (310) 943-4400***
***Credits: Freaks and Geeks; The Ben Stiller Show; The Larry Sanders Show***

**Apostle**
568 Broadway, #301
New York, NY 10012
***Tel: (212) 541-4323***
***Credits: Rescue Me; The Job***

**Asylum Entertainment**
7920 W. Sunset Blvd., 2nd Fl.
Los Angeles, CA 90046
***Tel: (310) 696-4600***
***Credits: American Gangster; Beyond the Glory; The Gift***

**POWER QUOTE:**
*"You can't just brown-nose your way to the top. Impress your colleagues by taking work off their plates too..."*

**JENNIFER DAVIDSON**
*Executive Producer/Co-Founder*
*Pie Town Productions*

Tara Sandler, Scott Templeton & Jennifer Davidson

Pie Town Productions, headquartered in North Hollywood, CA, is one of ***EPP***'s all-time favorites production companies. Ever since their 1995 launch, Executive Producers Jennifer Davidson, Tara Sandler and Scott Templeton, have been busy developing and producing more than 3,000 episodes of some of the best, most refreshing, original, reality shows on television, including *"House Hunters," "Design on a Dime," "$40 A Day," "Chefs vs. City,"* and *"Diet Tribe,"* to name a few.

***EPP: 4*** caught up with Jennifer Davidson, a graduate of Northwestern University in Evanston, IL, whose success at producing cost-efficient programming for HGTV, the Food Network, Lifetime, TLC and Paramount is also a shining example of how to put a Radio, TV & Film major to good use. ***Here Jennifer shares her 123 POWER ADVICE for Succeeding in the Industry:***

***On Pie Town's Big Break:***
***JD:*** "We received our first commission from TLC for an half-hour show called "Great Country Inns." It was a very simple show we did on literally $17k per episode. So that was the challenge - trying to figure out logistically how to get that much material through the pipeline. All three of us going through film school came in handy because we each had to do basically every job on the show. We had an assistant, two editors and then all three of us had to pitch in in every way possible."

***EPP:*** So it was the guerilla filmmaking style of tv producing?

***JD:*** "Completely."

***On Breaking Into the Industry:***
***JD:*** "Look around and see who you have connections to. You don't have to know someone to get involved in television production and do well - but it certainly helps. Send out as many e-mails, and make as many phone calls as you possibly can to figure out who's doing what, then you pursue those people. Once you land the job, do the job to the absolute best of your ability, even if it's not something that's challenging you intellectually. Even if it's running errands and cleaning out the refrigerator at the office. Excel at it and be visible to your colleagues and higher ups."

***On Rising to the Top:***
***JD:*** "Your colleagues are probably the next source of your next job, not necessarily your bosses - so you can't just brown-nose your way to the top. Impress your colleagues by taking work off their plates too. When I was starting out, every next job I got was from somebody who was in my department who got onto the next show."

***On Succeeding in the Industry:***
***JD:*** "Be efficient, but don't be so quietly efficient that you're not noticed. If you're doing your job well we notice that. Every time you come into contact with bosses, as well as your colleagues, have a friendly, optimistic, helpful point of view. If you grasp that attitude as early in your career as possible, the better off you're going to be."

***On POWER TOOLS:***
***JD:*** "In terms of communication, Tara and Scott and I all have iPhones and Macs and we tend to upgrade fairly often. They're nice toys and they're great business tools too."

*To contact Pie Town Productions, visit them online at www.pietown.tv.*

**Atlas Media Corporation**
242 W. 36th St., 11th Fl.
New York, NY 10018
***Tel: (212) 714-0222***
***Credits: American Eats; Dr. G: Medical Examiner***

**Atmosphere Entertainment**
4751 Wilshire Blvd., 3rd Fl.
Los Angeles, CA 90010
***Tel: (310) 860-5446***
***Credits: Godsend; Taking Lives***

**Avalon Television**
8332 Melrose Ave., 2nd Fl.
W. Hollywood, CA 90069
***Tel: (323) 930-6010***
***Credits: Greg Behrendt's Wake Up Call; Special Delivery***

**Bad Hat Harry Productions**
4000 Warner Boulevard
Bldg. 81, Ste. 200
Burbank, CA 91522
***Tel: (818) 954-4043***
***Credits: House***

**Bad Robot Productions**
5555 Melrose Ave., Drier, 2nd Fl.
Los Angeles, CA 90038
***Tel: (323) 956-2995***
***Credits: Alias; Cloverfield; Fringe; Lost***

**Bankable Productions**
4000 Warner Boulevard
Bldg., 139, Rm. 207 C
Burbank, CA 91522
***Tel: (818) 954-1600***
***Credits: America's Next Top Model; The Tyra Banks Show***

**Bankable Productions**
221 W. 26th Street
New York, NY 10001
***Tel: (646) 638-5760***
***Credits: America's Next Top Model; The Tyra Banks Show***

**Banyan Productions**
100 Ross Road, Ste. 150
King of Prussia, PA 19406
***Tel: (215) 928-1414***
***Credits: A Wedding Story; Ambush Makeover; Birth Day***

**Belisarius Productions**
4024 Radford Ave., Bung. 16
Studio City, CA 91604
***Tel: (818) 655-5190***
***Credits: Jag; Magnum, P.I.; NCIS***

**Berlanti Television**
500 S. Buena Vista St.
Old Animation Bldg., 2B-5
Burbank, CA 91521
***Tel: (818) 560-7800***
***Credits: Brothers & Sisters; Eli Stone***

**BermanBraun**
2900 W. Olympic Blvd., 3rd Fl.
Santa Monica, CA 90404
***Tel: (310)255-7272***
***Credits: America's Toughest Jobs; Duel; Mercy***

**Steven Bochco Productions**
3000 W. Olympic Blvd., Ste. 1310
Santa Monica, CA 90404
***Tel: (310) 566-6900***
***Credits: Commander-in-Chief; NYPD Blue***

**Boku Films**
1501 Calvert Street
Van Nuys, CA 91411
***Tel: (818) 373-4155***
***Credits: My So-Called Life; Six Feet Under***

**Boyett Theatricals**
268 W. 44th St, 4th Fl.
New York,  NY 10036
***Tel: (212) 702-9779***
***Credits: Family Matters; Happy Days; Mork & Mindy; Theater - Fiddler on the Roof; Spamalot***

**Brancato/Salke Productions**
500 S. Buena Vista Street
Old Animation Bldg. 1E, Ste. 6
Burbank, CA 91521
***Tel: (818) 560-1520***
***Credits: Crossing Jordan; X-Files***

**Braverman Productions**
3000 Olympic Boulevard
Santa Monica, CA 90404
***Tel: (310) 264-4184***
***Credits: Debutantes; Sextuplets; Prison Medical; Yellowstone Bison***

**Brillstein Entertainment Partners**
9150 Wilshire Blvd., Ste. 350
Beverly Hills, CA 90212
***Tel: (310) 275-6135***
***Credits: According the Jim; Samantha Who?; Real Time With Bill Maher; The Sopranos***

**Broadway Video**
1619 Broadway, Brill Bldg. 10th Fl.
New York, NY 10019
***Tel: (212) 265-7600***
***Credits: Saturday Night Live***

**Brookwell McNamara Entertainment**
1600 Rosecrans Avenue
Building 2B, 3rd Fl.
Manhattan Beach, CA 90266
***Tel: (310) 727-3353***
***www.bmetvfilm.com***
***Credits: That's So Raven; Wild Grizzly***

**Jerry Bruckheimer Films & Television**
1631 Tenth Street
Santa Monica, CA 90404
***Tel: (310) 664-6260***
***www.jbfilms.com***
***Credits: Amazing Race; Cold Case; CSI Franchise; Without a Trace***

**Bunim/Murray Productions**
6007 Sepulveda Boulevard
Van Nuys, CA 91411
***Tel: (818) 756-5100***
***www.bunim-murray.com***
***Credits: Living Lohan; Keeping Up with the Kardashians; Making the Band***

**Mark Burnett Productions**
640 N. Sepulveda Blvd.
Los Angeles, CA 90049
***Tel: (310) 903-5400***
***Credits: Are You Smarter Than a 5th Grader?; Martha Stewart; Survivor; The Celebrity Apprentice***

**Cannell Studios**
7083 Hollywood Blvd., Ste. 600
Hollywood, CA 90028
***Tel: (323) 465-5800***
***Credits: 21 Jump Street; A-Team; The***

*Greatest American Hero*

**Anne Carlucci Productions**
9200 Sunset Blvd., Penthouse 20
Los Angeles, CA 90069
***Tel: (310) 550-9545***
***Credits: Don't Look Back; Flirting with Danger; Going for Broke***

**Carrie Productions**
2625 Alcatraz Ave., Ste. 243
Berkeley, CA 94705
***Tel: (510) 450-2500***
***Credits: Buffalo Soldiers; Freedom Song***

**The Thomas Carter Company**
3000 W. Olympic Blvd.
Santa Monica, CA 90404
***Tel: (310) 264-3990***
***Credits: Ali: An American Hero; Coach Carter; Don King: Only in America***

**Cates/Doty Productions**
10920 Wilshire Blvd., Ste. 1840
Los Angeles, CA 90024
***Tel: (310) 208-2134***
***Credits: The Academy Awards***

**Central City Productions**
212 E. Ohio, Ste. 300
Chicago, IL 60611
***Tel: (312) 654-1100***
***www.ccptv.com***
***Credits: Minority Business Report; Stellar Gospel Music Awards***

**Charles Bros.**
4024 Radford Avenue
Bldg. CNB, Ste. 310
Studio City, CA 91604
***Tel: (818) 655-7558***
***Credits: Cheers; Will & Grace***

**Chotzen/Jenner Productions**
1626 N. Wilcox Ave., Ste. 1381
Hollywood, CA 90028
***Tel: (323) 465-9877***
***Credits: Matter of Justice; The Rosa Parks Story***

**Chris/Rose Productions**
3131 Torreyson Place
Los Angeles, CA 90046
***Tel: (323) 851-8772***
***Credits: An Accidental Friendship; Autobiography of Miss Jane Pittman***

**City Entertainment**
266-1/2 S. Rexford Dr.
Beverly Hills, CA 90212
***Tel: (310) 273-3101***
***Credits: Introducing Dorothy Dandridge; The Pentagon Papers***

**Dick Clark Productions**
2900 Olympic Boulevard
Santa Monica, CA 90404
***Tel: (310) 255-4600***
***www.dickclarkproductions.com***
***Credits: Dick Clark's New Year's Rockin' Eve; Golden Globe Awards***

**Codeblack Entertainment**
111 Universal Hollywood Dr./Ste. 2260
Universal City, CA 91608
***Tel: (818) 286-8600***
***www.codeblackentertainment.com***
***Credits: Mama, I Want to Sing!; Why We Laugh: Black Comedians on Black Comedy***

**The Collective**
9100 Wilshire Blvd., Ste. 700W
Beverly Hills, CA 90212
***Tel: (310) 288-8181***
***Credits: College Road Trip; One on One; Wild 'n' Out***

**Comedy Arts Studios**
2500 Broadway, Ste. 400
Santa Monica, CA 90404
***Tel: (310) 382-3677***
***Credits: Everybody Loves Raymond; U.S. Comedy Arts Festival***

**Connection III Entertainment**
5900 Wilshire Blvd., Ste. 545
Los Angeles, CA 90036
***Tel: (323) 937-8700***
***www.connection3.com***
***Credits: Made in Hollywood; The Garage Band; What About Your Friends***

**Corymore Productions**
9171 Wilshire Blvd., Ste. 400
Beverly Hills, CA 90210
***Tel: (310) 274-7891***
***Credits: Mrs. Pollifaz; Mrs. Santa Claus; Murder, She Wrote***

**Cosgrove-Meurer Productions**
4303 W. Verdugo Ave.
Burbank, CA 91505
***Tel: (818) 843-5600***
***Credits: A Friend's Betrayal; Unsolved Mysteries***

**Cossette Productions**
8899 Beverly Blvd., Ste. 100
Los Angeles, CA 90048
***Tel: (310) 278-3366***
***Credits: BET Awards; Grammy Awards***

**Curious Pictures**
440 Lafayette St., 6th Fl.
New York, NY 10003
***Tel: (212) 674-1400***
***www.curiouspictures.com***
***Credits: Avenue Amy; Little Einsteins; The Offbeats***

**Current TV, LLC**
118 King Street
San Francisco, CA 94107
***Tel: (415) 995-8200***
***www.current.tv***

**Dan Curtis Productions**
725 Arizona Ave., Ste. 301
Santa Monica, CA 90401
***Tel: (310) 395-9935***
***Credits: The Love Letter; War & Remembrance***

**De Passe Entertainment**
9200 Sunset Blvd., Ste. 510
W. Hollywood, CA 90069
***Tel: (310) 858-3734***
***Credits: NAACP Image Awards; Showtime at the Apollo; Sister Sister; The Temptations Miniseries***

**Dreyfuss/James Productions**
2420 Laurel Pass
Los Angeles, CA 90046
***Tel: (323) 822-0140***
***Credits: Having Our Say***

**The Edelstein Company**
500 S. Buena Vista Street
Animation Bldg., Ste. 204
Burbank, CA 91521
***Tel: (818) 560-3884***
***Credits: Desperate Housewives; Threat Matrix***

**Edmonds Entertainment**
1635 N. Cahuenga Blvd., 6th Fl.
Los Angeles, CA 90028
***Tel: (323) 860-1550***
***Credits: College Hill; David E. Talbert Presents Stage Black; DMX: Soul of a Man; Soul Food***

**Endemol USA, Inc.**
9255 Sunset Blvd., Ste. 1100
Los Angeles, CA 90069
***Tel: (310) 860-9914***
***Credits: Big Brother; Deal or No Deal; Extreme Makeover: Home Edition; Fear Factor; I Want to Be a Hilton; Wipe Out***

**Evolution**
3310 W. Vanowen Street
Burbank, CA 91505
***Tel: (818) 260-0300***
***Credits: Big Brother; Clean Sweep; Desperate Spaces; Fear Factor***

**Film 44**
1526 Cloverfield Blvd., Ste. D
Santa Monica, CA 90404
***Tel: (310) 586-4949***
***Credits: Friday Night Lights; Trauma***

**Firm Television**
9465 Wilshire Blvd., 6th Fl.
Beverly Hills, CA 90212
***Tel: (310) 860-8000***
***Credits: Campus Confidential; Freddie***

**Flame Ventures**
1416 N. La Brea Ave.
Los Angeles, CA 90028
***Tel: (323) 802-1700***
***Credits: 24; Felicity; NASCAR Drivers: 360***

**FremantleMedia**
4000 W. Alameda Ave., 3rd Fl.
Burbank, CA 91505
***Tel: (818) 748-1100***
***www.fremantlemedia.com***
***Credits: American Idol; America's Got Talent; Family Feud; The Price is Right***

**Fuse Entertainment**
1041 N. Formosa Ave.
Formosa Bldg., Ste. 195
West Hollywood, CA 90046
***Tel: (323) 850-3873***
***Credits: Burn Notice***

**Gallant Entertainment**
16161 Ventura Blvd., Ste. 664
Encino, CA 91436
***Tel: (818) 905-9848***
***Credits: Bionic Ever After; Stompin' At The Savoy; Ten Attitudes***

**Generate**
1545 26th Street, Ste. 200
Santa Monica, CA 90404
***Tel: (310) 255-0460***
***Credits: Chocolate News; Comedy Tours***

**Generate**
845 3rd Avenue, 6th Fl. - Ste. 652
New York, NY 10022
***Tel: (212) 242-1602***
***Credits: Chocolate News: Comedy Tours***

**Genrebend Productions**
233 Wilshire Blvd., 7th Fl.
Santa Monica, CA 90401
***Tel: (310) 917-1064***
***Credits: Smallville; The Mentalist; West Wing; Without a Trace***

**Good Humor Television**
9255 Sunset Blvd., Ste. 1040
West Hollywood, CA 90069
***Tel: (310) 205-7367***
***Credits: Hank; Happy Hour; Playing Chicken***

**GoTV Networks, Inc.**
14144 Ventura Blvd., Ste. 300
Sherman Oaks, CA 91423
***Tel: (818) 933-2100***
***www.gotvnetworks.com***
***Credits: Attitude; Es Música; Hip Hop Central***

**Grammnet Productions**
23852 Pacific Coast Highway, #350
Malibu, CA 90265
***Tel: (310) 317-4231***
***Credits: Girlfriends; Medium; The Game***

**Granada America**
15303 Ventura Blvd., Bldg. C/Ste. 800
Sherman Oaks, CA 91403
***Tel: (818) 455-4600***
***www.granadaamerica.com***
***Credits: Bought & Sold; Celebrity Fit Club; Chopping Block; First 48; Nanny 911***

**Grand Productions, Inc.**
15303 Ventura Blvd., Ste. 9027
Sherman Oaks, CA 91403
***Tel: (818) 380-3009***
***Credits: Any Day Now; Beauty; Saving Grace; A Song from the Heart Any***

**GRB Entertainment**
13400 Riverside Dr., Ste. 300
Sherman Oaks, CA 91423
***Tel: (818) 728-7600***
***Credits: Growing Up Gotti; Intervention; Medal of Honor; Next Action Star***

**Robert Greenwald Productions**
10510 Culver Boulevard
Culver City, CA 90232
***Tel: (310) 204-0404***
***Credits: Audrey Hepburn; Livin' for Love: The Natalie Cole Story; The Book of Ruth***

**Greif Company**
280 S. Beverly Drive, PH
Beverly Hills, CA 90212
***Tel: (310) 385-1200***
***www.greifcompany.com***
***Credits: A & E Biography; Gene Simmons Family Jewels; Headliners & Legends; Weddings of a Lifetime***

**Merv Griffin Entertainment**
130 S. El Camino Drive
Beverly Hills, CA 90212
***Tel: (310) 385-2727***
***www.merv.com***
***Creator: Jeopardy!; Wheel of Fortune***

**Gross-Weston Productions**
10560 Wilshire Blvd., Ste. 801
Los Angeles, CA 90024
***Tel: (310) 777-0010***
***Credits: A Place for Annie; Hallmark Billionaire Boys Club; Decoy; Invisible Child; Louis Armstrong***

**Beth Grossbard Productions**
5168 Otis Avenue
Tarzana, CA 91356
***Tel: (818) 758-2500***
***Credits: Meltdown; No One Could Protect Her; The Christmas Shoes***

**The Gurin Company**
11846 Ventura Blvd., Ste. 303
Studio City, CA 91604

Tel: (818) 623-9393
www.gurinco.com
Credits: FOX New Year's Eve Live; Miss Teen USA: Miss Universe; Miss USA

**Hallmark Hall of Fame Prods.**
12001 Ventura Place, Ste. 300
Studio City, CA 91604
Tel: (818) 505-9191
Credits: A Painted House; Candles on Bay Street; The Magic of Ordinary Days

**Harpo Films, Inc.**
345 N. Maple Dr., Ste. 315
Beverly Hills, CA 90210
Tel: (310) 278-5559
Credits: The Wedding; Their Eyes Were Watching God; Tuesdays with Morrie

**Harpo Productions**
110 N. Carpenter Street
Chicago, IL 60607
Tel: (312) 633-1000
www.oprah.com
Credits: The Oprah Winfrey Show

**Heel & Toe Films**
9100 Wilshire Blvd., Ste. 1000W
Beverly Hills, CA 90212
Tel: (310) 369-3466
Credits: Gideon's Crossing; House

**The Jim Henson Company**
1416 N. LaBrea Avenue
Hollywood, CA 90028
Tel: (323) 802-1500
www.henson.com
Credits: Muppets; World of Dr. Seuss

**The Jim Henson Company**
627 Broadway, 9th Fl.
New York, NY 10012
Tel: (212) 794-2400
www.henson.com
Credits: Muppets; World of Dr. Seuss

**High Noon Entertainment**
12233 W. Olympic Blvd., Ste. 328
Los Angeles, CA 90064
Tel: (310) 820-7500
www.highnoonproductions.com
Credits: Carter Can; Food Network Challenge; If Walls Could Talk; Rachel's Vacation

**Hollywood East Entertainment**
900 Wheeler Road, Ste. 230
Hauppauge, NY 11788
Tel: (631) 584-4371
www.hollywoodeast.tv
Credits: Hollywood East; Unique Whips

**Homerun Entertainment**
13428 Maxella Ave., #508
Marina del Rey, CA 90293
Tel: (310) 338-1500
www.homerunent.com
Credits: Celebrity Hobbies; RV Roadtrips; Weekend Gardening

**Hypnotic/Dutch Oven**
12233 W. Olympic Blvd., Ste. 256
Los Angeles, CA 90064
Tel: (310) 806-6930
Credits: Heist; Knight Rider; The O.C.

**Imagine Television**
9465 Wilshire Blvd., 7th Fl.
Beverly Hills, CA 90212
Tel: (310) 858-2000
Credits: 24; Friday Night Lights

**Industry Entertainment Partners**
955 S. Carrillo Dr., 3rd Fl.
Los Angeles, CA 90048
Tel: (323) 954-9000
Credits: Becker; War Stories

**Ion Television**
601 Clearwater Park Road
W. Palm Beach, FL 33401
Tel: (561) 659-4122
www.iontelevision.com
Credits: America's Most Talented Kids; It's a Miracle; Shop 'Til You Drop

**ITV Studios**
15303 Ventura Blvd.
Bldg. C., Ste. 800
Sherman Oaks, CA 91403
Tel: (818) 455-4600
www.itv-america.com
Credits: Celebrity Fit Club; I'm a Celebrity, Get Me Out of Here!; Kitchen Nightmare; Nanny 911

**Jaffe/Braunstein Films**
12301 Wilshire Blvd., Ste. 110
Los Angeles, CA 90025
Tel: (310) 207-6600
Credits: 100 Centre Street; 10.5 Apocalypse; Faith of My Fathers; Martha, Inc.; The Gilda Radner; The Rosa Parks Story

**Charles Floyd Johnson Productions**
1438 N. Gower St., 4th Fl.
Los Angeles, CA 90028
Tel: (323) 468-4520
Credits: Jag; NCIS; Quantum Leap

**David E. Kelley Productions**
1600 Rosecrans Ave., Bldg. 4-B
Manhattan Beach, CA 90266
Tel: (310) 727-2200
Credits: Boston Legal; Boston Public; The Practice

**Kornerstone Film**
Tel: (240) 535-1371
Credits: Premier MD/DC/VA Area Productions; Event Management; Music Videos

**Lifetime Television**
2049 Century Park East, Ste. 840
Los Angeles, CA 90067
Tel: (310) 556-7500
www.lifetimetv.com
Credits: Intimate Portrait; Missing; The Division

**Lifetime Television**
309 W. 49th Street
New York, NY 10019
Tel: (212) 424-7000
www.lifetimetv.com
Credits: Intimate Portrait; Missing; The Division

**Liquid Theory**
6725 Sunset Blvd., Ste. 240
Los Angeles, CA 90028
Tel: (323) 460-5658
www.liquid-theory.com
Credits: MTV Movie Awards; People's Choice Awards; VH1 Fashion Awards

**LMNO Productions**
15821 Ventura Blvd., Ste. 320
Encino, CA 91436
Tel: (818) 380-8000
www.lmnotv.com
Credits: Amazing Medical Stories; Babies:

*Special Delivery; Race to the Altar*

**Lost Marbles TV**
144 S. Beverly Dr., 5th Fl.
Beverly Hills, CA 90210
***Tel: (310) 860-5502***
***Credits: Prison Break; Tru Calling***

**The Tom Lynch Company**
8750 Wilshire Blvd., Ste. 250
Beverly Hills, CA 90211
***Tel: (310) 724-6900***
***Credits: Class of 3000; Lil' Romeo!; Scout's Safari; Secret World of Alex Mack***

**Magic Elves**
453 S. Spring St., Ste. 1100
Los Angeles, CA 90013
***Tel: (213) 630-6530***
***www.magicelves.com***
***Credits: Last Comic Standing; Project Runway; Top Chef***

**Mandalay Entertainment**
4751 Wilshire Blvd., 3rd Fl.
Los Angeles, CA 90010
***Tel: (323) 549-4300***
***Credits: Go For It; Million Dollar Shootout; The Quest for Nutrition***

**Millar/Gough Ink**
500 S. Buena Vista St.
Animation 1E17
Burbank, CA 91521
***Tel: (818) 560-4260***
***Credits: Hannah Montana: The Movie; Smallville***

**Moffitt-Lee Productions**
2500 Broadway Ave., Ste. 400
Santa Monica, CA 90404
***Tel: (310) 382-3469***
***Credits: 50 Years of Television; Comic Relief; Hollywood Squares; U.S. Comedy Arts Festival***

**MRB Productions, Inc.**
311 N. Robertson Blvd., Ste. 513
Beverly Hills, CA 90211
***Tel: (323) 465-7676***
***Credits: ESPY Awards; Monday Night Football***

**Namesake Entertainment**
P.O. Box 436492
Louisville, KY 40253
***Tel: (502) 243-3185***
***www.namesakeentertainment.com***
***Credits: Hangman's Curse; Eli; Left Behind***

**Overbrook Entertainment**
450 N. Roxbury Dr., 4th Fl.
Beverly Hills, CA 902210
***Tel: (310) 432-2400***
***www.overbrookent.com***
***Credits: All of Us***

**Pariah**
9744 Wilshire Blvd., Ste. 205
Los Angeles, CA 90036
***Tel: (310) 276-3500***
***Credits: Curb Your Enthusiasm; Gilmore Girls; My Boys; Tell Me You Love Me***

**Pie Town Productions**
5433 Laurel Canyon Blvd.
N. Hollywood, CA 91607
***Tel: (818) 255-9300***
***www.pietown.tv***
***Credits: $40 A Day; Chefs vs. City; Design on a Dime; Designed to Sell; House Hunters***

**RDF USA**
225 Santa Monica Blvd., 5th Fl.
Santa Monica, CA 90401
***Tel: (310) 460-4490***
***www.rdfusa.com***
***Credits: Don't Forget the Lyrics; Junkyard Wars; Secret Millionaire; Wife Swap***

**Red Varden Studios**
2716 Ocean Park Blvd., Ste. 1065
Santa Monica, CA 90405
***Tel: (310) 450-5860***
***www.redvarden.com***
***Credits: The Othersiders***

**Regency Television**
10201 W. Pico Blvd., Bldg. 12
Los Angeles, CA 90035
***Tel: (310) 369-8300***
***Credits: Living with Fran; Malcolm in the Middle; The Bernie Mac Show***

**Reveille**
100 Universal City Plaza
Bungalow 5180/5170
Burbank, CA 91608
***Tel: (818) 733-1218***
***Credits: The Biggest Loser; Kath & Kim; Nashville Star; The Office; Ugly Betty***

**RHI Entertainment**
1325 Ave. of the Americas, 21st Fl.
New York, NY 10019
***Tel: (212) 977-9001***
***www.rhitv.com***
***Credits: Cleopatra; Dinotopia; Temptations***

**Al Roker Productions**
250 W. 57th St., Ste. 1525
New York, NY 10019
***Tel: (212) 757-8500***
***Credits: Chef Jeff; Recipe for Success; Roker on the Road***

**RVI Motion Media**
4518 Beech Road, Ste. 100
Temple Hills, MD 20748
***Tel: (301) 423-6884***
***Credits: Apple Crumb Panic; Lex Vector; Maryland State Teacher's Association***

**Scholastic Entertainment**
557 Broadway
New York, NY 10012
***Tel: (212) 389-3964***
***www.scholastic.com***
***Credits: Clifford the Big Red Dog; the Golden Compass; The Magic School Bus***

**Scott Free Productions**
614 N. La Peer Dr.
West Hollywood, CA 90069
***Tel: (310) 360-2250***
***Credits: Numb3rs;The Company; The Good Wife***

**Arnold Shapiro Productions**
c/o LA Digital Post
11311 Camarillo St., 2nd Fl.
Toluca Lake, CA 91602
***Tel: (818) 487-5125***
***www.arnoldshapiroproductions.com***
***Credits: Big Brother; Border Security; Rescue 911; Scared Straight; Specials***

**Shed Media U.S.**
3800 Barham Blvd., Ste. 410
Los Angeles, CA 90068
***Tel: (323) 904-4680***
***www.shedmediaus.com***

*Credits: The Marriage Ref; The Real Housewives of New York; Supernanny*

**Simmons Lathan Media Group**
6100 Wilshire Blvd., Ste. 1110
Los Angeles, CA 90048
*Tel: (323) 634-6400*
*www.simmonslathan.com*
*Credits: Daddy's Girls; Run's House*

**A. Smith & Co. Productions**
9911 W. Pico Blvd., Ste. 250
Los Angeles, CA 90035
*Tel: (310) 432-4800*
*www.asmithco.com*
*Clients: American Gangster; I Survived a Japanese Game Show; Unsung*

**SRB Communications**
1819 L Street, NW - 7th Fl.
Washington, D.C. 20036
*Tel: (202) 775-7721*
*www.srbcommunications.com*
*Clients: TV One; U.S. Dept. of Housing and Urban Development (HUD); Washington Gas*

**Darren Star Productions**
10202 W. Washington Blvd.
David Lean Bldg., Ste. 430
Culver City, CA 90232
*Tel: (310) 244-4000*
*Credits: Beverly Hills, 90210; Sex and the City*

**Martha Stewart Living Omnimedia, Inc.**
11 W. 42nd Street
New York, NY 10036
*Tel: (212) 827-8000*
*www.marthastewart.com*
*Credits: Martha; The Apprentice: Martha Stewart*

**Storyline Entertainment**
8355 Sunset Blvd., Ste. 207
Hollywood, CA 90069
*Tel: (323) 210-7263*
*www.storyline-entertainment.com*
*Credits: Annie; Cinderella; Double Platinum; Drop Dead Diva; Life with Judy Garland; Lucy; The Three Stooges*

**Tantamount Studios**
10202 W. Washington Blvd.
Astaire Bldg., Ste. 2310
Culver City, CA 90232
*Tel: (310) 244-1822*
*Credits: Brothers; Two and a Half Men*

**Telepictures Productions**
3500 W. Olive Ave., 10th Fl.
Burbank, CA 91505
*Tel: (818) 972-0777*
*Credits: Judge Mathis; The Bachelor; The Tyra Banks Show; TMZ*

**Tenth Planet Productions**
833 N. LaCienega Blvd., Ste. 200
Los Angeles, CA 90069
*Tel: (818) 659-8001*
*Credits: MTV Movie Awards; VH1 Fashion Awards*

**Tollin Productions**
3702 Eureka Drive
Studio City, CA 91604
*Tel: (818) 755-3000*
*Credits: All That; Hardball; One Tree Hill; Smallville; What I Like About You*

**Universal Media Studios**
100 Universal City Plaza
Universal City, CA 91608
*Tel: (818) 777-1000*
*www.nbcuni.com*

**Vin Di Bona Productions**
12233 W. Olympic Blvd., Ste. 170
Los Angeles, CA 90064
*Tel: (310) 442-5600*
*www.vdbp.com*
*Credits: America's Funniest Videos*

**Weller/Grossman Productions**
5200 Lankershim Blvd., Ste. 500
N. Hollywood, CA 91601
*Tel: (818) 755-4800*
*Credits: Bar-B-Que with Bobby Flay; It's A Miracle; Wolfgang Puck*

**John Wells Productions**
4000 Warner Blvd., Bldg. 1
Burbank, CA 91522
*Tel: (818) 954-1687*
*Credits: China Beach; ER; The West Wing; Southland; Third Watch*

**Whoop Inc./One Ho Productions/Lil' Whoop Prods.**
333 W. 52nd St., Ste. 602
New York, NY 10019
*Tel: (212) 245-6900*
*Credits: Hollywood Squares; Just For Kicks; Whoopi*

**Wind Dancer Productions**
315 S. Beverly Dr., Ste. 502
Beverly Hills, CA 90212
*Tel: (310) 601-2720*
*Credits: Home Improvement; What Women Want*

**Wind Dancer Productions**
200 W. 57th St., Ste. 601
New York, NY 10019
*Tel: (212) 765-4772*
*Credits: Home Improvement; What Women Want*

**Wolf Films, Inc.**
100 Universal City Plaza, Bldg. 2252
Universal City, CA 91608
*Tel: (818) 777-6969/(212) 627-0088*
*Credits: Law & Order Franchise*

**The Wolper Organization**
4000 Warner Boulevard
Bldg. 14, Suites 200/202
Burbank, CA 91522
*Tel: (818) 954-1421/(818) 954-3505*
*Credits: LA Confidential; Queen; Roots; War on Drugs*

**Worldwide Pants, Inc.**
1697 Broadway
New York, NY 10019
*Tel: (212) 975-5300*
*Credits: Late Show with David Letterman*

**World Wrestling Entertainment (WWE)**
1241 East Main Street
Stamford, CT 06902
*Tel: (203) 352-8600*
*www.wwe.com*
*Credits: Friday Night Smackdown; Raw; Wrestle Mania*

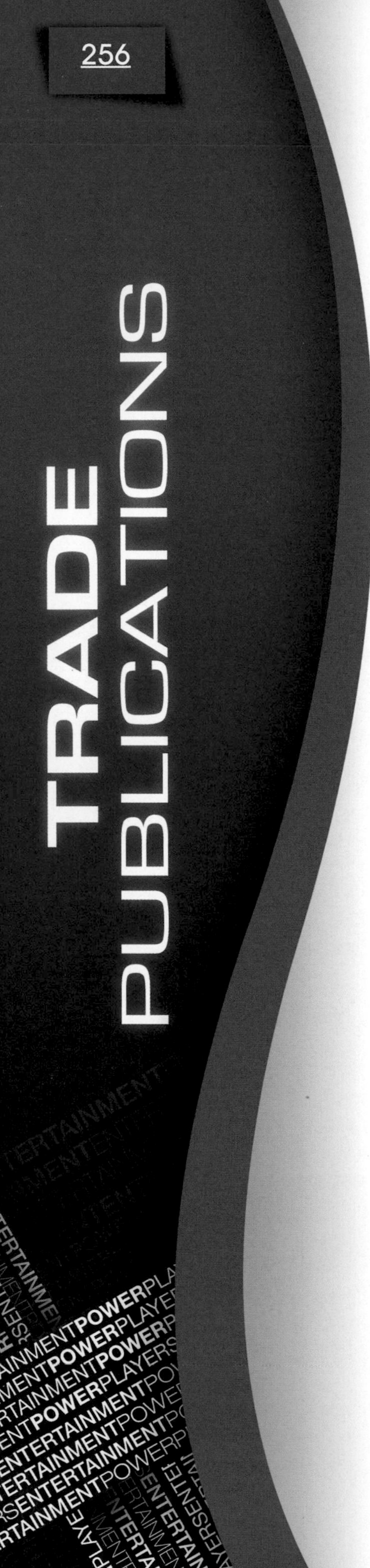


**Academy Players Directory**
1313 N. Vine Street
Hollywood, CA 90028
***Tel: (310) 247-3058***
***www.playersdirectory.com***

**Advertising Age**
711 Third Avenue
New York, NY 10017
***Tel: (212) 210-0100***
***www.adage.com***

**Advertising Age**
6500 Wilshire Blvd., Ste. 2300
Los Angeles, CA 90048
***Tel: (323) 651-3710***
***www.adage.com***

**Adweek**
5055 Wilshire Blvd.
Los Angeles, CA 90036
***Tel: (323) 525-2270***
***www.adweek.com***

**Adweek**
770 Broadway, 7th Fl.
New York, NY 10003
***Tel: (646) 654-5421***
***www.adweek.com***

**Animation Magazine**
30941 W. Agoura Rd., Ste. 102
Westlake Village, CA 91361
***Tel: (818) 991-2884***
***www.animationmagazine.net***

**Back Stage**
5055 Wilshire Boulevard
Los Angeles, CA 90036
***Tel: (323) 525-2356***
***www.backstage.com***

**Back Stage**
770 Broadway
New York, NY 10003
***Tel: (646) 654-5700***
***www.backstage.com***

**Black Talent News**
8306 Wilshire Blvd., Ste. 2057
Beverly Hills, CA 90211
***Tel: (310) 929-5297***
***www.blacktalentnews.com***

**Breakdown Services**
2140 Cotner Avenue, 3rd Fl.
Los Angeles, CA 90025
***Tel: (310) 276-9166***
***www.breakdownservices.com***

**Breakdown Services**
850 7th Ave., Ste. 600
New York, NY 10019
***Tel: (212) 869-2003***
***www.breakdownservices.com***

**Broadcasting & Cable**
360 Park Avenue South
New York, NY 10010
***Tel: (646) 746-6400***
***www.broadcastingcable.com***

**Call Sheet**
770 Broadway
New York, NY 10003
***Tel: (323) 525-2231***
***www.backstage.com/callsheet***

**The Costume Designer**
Costume Designers Guild
11969 Ventura Blvd., 1st Fl.
Studio City, CA 91604
***Tel: (818) 752-2400***
***www.costumedesignersguild.com***

**Create Magazine**
***www.createmagazine.com***

**Creative Handbook**
10152 Riverside Drive
Toluca Lake, CA91602
***Tel: (818) 752-3200***
***www.creativehandbook.com***

**Creative Screenwriting**
6404 Hollywood Blvd., Ste. 415
Los Angeles, CA 90028
***Tel: (323) 957-1405***
***www.creativescreenwriting.com***

**Debbie's Book**
P.O. Box 6488

Altadena, CA 91003
***Tel: (626) 798-7968***
***www.debbiesbook.com***

**DGA Magazine**
7920 Sunset Boulevard
Los Angeles, CA 90046
***Tel: (310) 289-2000***
***www.dga.org***

**Digital Video (DV) Magazine**
New Bay Media
810 Seventh Avenue, 27th Fl.
New York, NY 10019
***Tel: (212) 378-0400***
***www.dv.com***

**Ebony Magazine**
Johnson Publishing Company
820 S. Michigan Avenue
Chicago, IL 60605
***Tel: (312) 322-9200***
***www.ebony.com***

**Emmy Magazine**
5220 Lankershim Blvd.
N. Hollywood, CA 91601
***Tel: (818) 754-2800***
***www.emmys.tv***

**Entertainment Today**
12021 Wilshire Blvd., Ste. 398
Los Angeles, CA 90025
***Tel: (213) 387-2060 ext 1***
***www.entertainmenttoday.net***

**Entertainment Weekly**
11766 Wilshire Blvd., Ste. #1700
Los Angeles, CA 90025
***Tel: (310) 268-7200***
***www.ew.com***

**Entertainment Weekly**
1675 Broadway
New York, NY 10019
***Tel: (212) 522-1400***
***www.ew.com***

**Essence**
135 W. 50th Street, 4th Fl.
New York, NY 10020
***Tel: (212) 522-1212***
***www.essence.com***

**EUR Web/Electronic Urban Report**
P.O. Box 412081
Los Angeles, CA 90041
***Tel: (323) 254-9599/(661) 250-7300***
***www.eurweb.com***

**Film & Video Magazine**
110 William Street, 11th Fl.
New York, NY 10038
***Tel: (212) 621-4900***
***www.filmandvideomagazine.com***

**Film/Tape World**
21 Orinda Way, Ste. C#343
Orinda, CA 94563
***Tel: (415) 543-6100***
***www.filmtapeworld.com***

**Film & TV Music Guide**
7510 Sunset Blvd., #1041
Los Angeles, CA 90046
***Tel: (818) 995-7458***
***www.musicregistry.com***

**Giant Magazine**
Interactive One
205 Hudson Street, 6th Fl.
New York, NY, 10013
***Tel: (212) 431-4477***
***www.giantmag.com***
***www.interactiveone.com***

**The Hair, Makeup & Fashion Styling Career Guide**
7119 W. Sunset Blvd., Ste. 392
Los Angeles, CA 90046
***Tel: (323) 913-0500***
***www.makeuphairandstyling.com***

**Hollywood Creative Directory**
5055 Wilshire Boulevard
Los Angeles, CA 90036
***Tel: (323) 525-2369***
***www.hcdonline.com***

**Hollywood Life**
Mail.com Media Corporation
9800 S. La Cienega Blvd 14th Fl.
Los Angeles, CA 90301
***Tel: (310) 321-5000***
***www.hollywoodlife.com***

**The Hollywood Reporter**
5055 Wilshire Blvd., 6th Fl.
Los Angeles, CA 90036
***Tel: (323) 525-2000***
***www.hollywoodreporter.com***

**The Hollywood Reporter Blu-Book**
5055 Wilshire Blvd., 6th Fl.
Los Angeles, CA 90036
***Tel: (323) 525-2000/(323) 525-2369***
***www.hcdonline.com/blubook***

**Jet Magazine**
Johnson Publishing Company
820 S. Michigan Avenue
Chicago, IL 60605
***Tel: (312) 322-9200***
***www.ebonyjet.com***

**Kemps Production Services Handbook**
***www.kftv.com***

**LA 411**
5900 Wilshire Blvd., Ste. 3100
Los Angeles, CA 90036
***Tel: (323) 617-9100***
***www.la411.com***

**LA 411**
360 Park Ave. South
New York, NY 10010
***Tel: (646) 746-6400***
***www.la411.com***

**Locations Magazine**
Association of Film Commissioners International
109 E. 17th St., Ste. 18
Cheyenne, WY 82001
***Tel: (307) 637-4422***
***www.afci.org***

**Media Week**
770 Broadway, 7th Fl.
New York, NY 10003
***Tel: (646) 654-5553***
***www.mediaweek.com***

**Motion Picture TV & Theatre Directory**
P.O. Box 276
Tarrytown, NY 10591
*Tel: (212) 245-0969*
*www.mpe.net*

**NY 411**
360 Park Avenue S. - 17th Fl.
New York, NY 10010
*Tel: (646) 746-6400*
*Tel: (646) 746-6891*
*www.newyork411.com*

**O, The Oprah Magazine**
1700 Broadway
New York, NY 10019
*Tel: (212) 903-5366*
*www.oprah.com*

**P3 Update**
1438 N. Gower, Box 65
Hollywood, CA 90028
*Tel: (323) 315-9477*
*www.p3update.com*

**Post Magazine**
*Tel: (516) 526-6103*
*www.postmagazine.com*

**PR Week**
PRWeek / Haymarket Media, Inc.
114 W. 26th St., 4th Fl.
New York, NY 10001
*Tel: (646) 638-6000*
*www.prweekus.com*

**Premiere Magazine**
1633 Broadway
New York, NY 10019
*Tel: (212) 767-5400*
*www.premieremag.com*

**Production Hub**
1809 E. Winter Park Rd.
Orlando, FL 32803
*Tel: (407) 629-4122*
*www.productionhhub.com*

**Production Weekly**
3001 Bridgeway Blvd.
Sausality, CA 94965
*Tel: (415) 223-3994*
*www.productionweekly.com*

**Screen Actor Magazine**
Screen Actors Guild
5757 Wilshire Blvd., 7th Fl.
Los Angeles, CA 90036
*Tel: (323) 549-6654*
*www.sag.org*

**Screen Magazine**
340 B Quadrangle Drive
Bolingbrook, IL 60440
*Tel: (312) 640-0800*
*www.screenmag.tv*

**Script Magazine**
Final Draft
26707 W. Agoura Rd. Ste. 205
Calabasas, CA 91302
*Tel: (818) 995-8995*
*www.scriptmag.com*

**Script Magazine**
5638 Sweet Air Road
Baldwin, MD 21013
*Tel: (888) 245-2228*
*www.scriptmag.com*

**Shoot**
650 N. Brunson Ave., #B140
Los Angeles, CA 90004
*Tel: (323) 960-8035*
*www.shootonline.com*

**Showbiz Labor Guide**
500 S. Sepulveda Blvd., 4th Fl.
Los Angeles, CA 90049
*Tel: (310) 471-9330*
*www.showbizsoftware.com*

**Sister 2 Sister**
2008 Enterprise Road
Bowie, MD 20721
*Tel: (301) 270-5999*
**www.s2smagazine.com**

**The Independent**
*www.aivf.org*
*www.independent-magazine.org*

**Television Week**
Crain Communications
6500 Wilshire Blvd., Ste. 2300
Los Angeles, CA 90047
*Tel: (323) 370-2400*
*www.tvweek.com*

**TV Guide**
11 W. 42nd St., 17th Fl.
New York, NY 10036
*Tel: (212) 852-7500*
*www.tvguide.com*

**UPSCALE**
600 Bronner Brothers Way, SW
Atlanta, GA 30310
*Tel: (404) 758-7467*
*www.upscalemagazine.com*

**US Weekly**
1290 Ave. of the Americas, 2nd Fl.
New York, NY 10104
*Tel: (212) 484-1616*
*www.usmagazine.com*

**Variety**
5900 Wilshire Blvd., Ste. 3100
Los Angeles, CA 90036
*Tel: (323) 617-9100*
*www.dailyvariety.com*

**Variety**
360 Park Ave. South
New York, NY 10010
*Tel: (646) 746-7001*
*www.variety.com*

**Videography**
CMP Entertainment Media
810 Seventh Ave., 27th Fl.
New York, NY 10019
*Tel: (212) 378-0400*
*www.cmpmedia.com*

**Videomaker Magazine**
P.O. Box 4591
Chico, CA 95927
*Tel: (530) 891-8410*
*www.videomaker.com*

**Written By Magazine**
7000 W. Third Street
Los Angeles, CA 90048
*Tel: (323) 951-4000*
*www.wga.org*

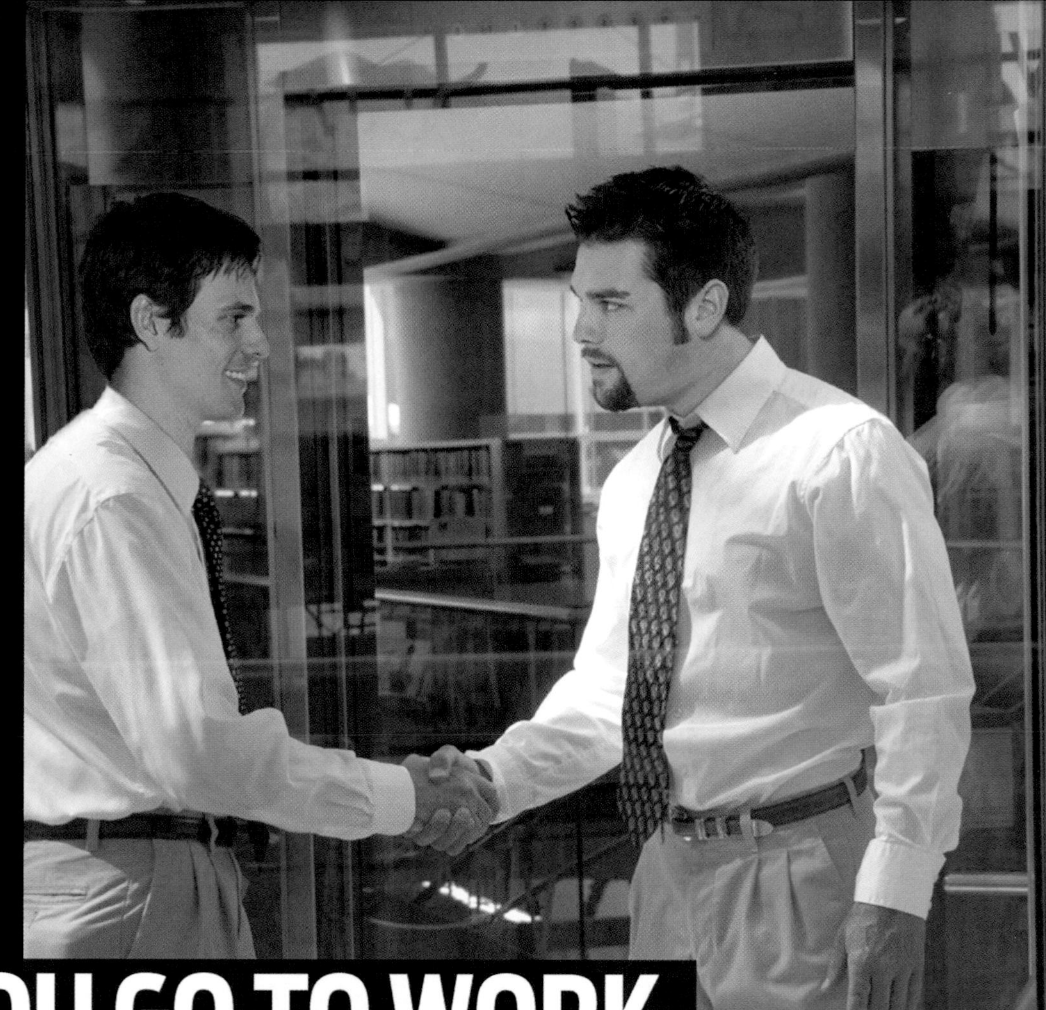

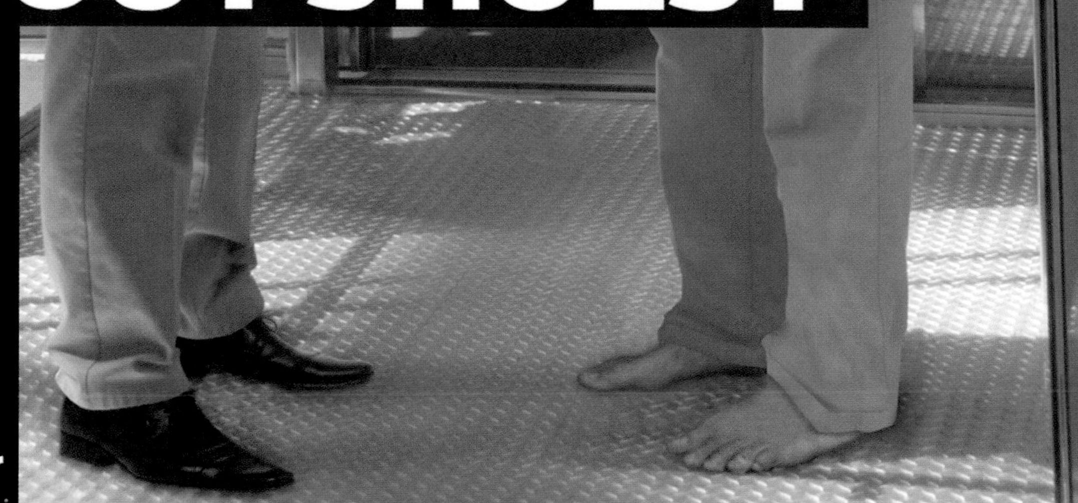

# WRITER'S BLOCK

## May Chan

TV/Animation Writer

**POWER QUOTE:**
*"I watch a lot of tv and movies. The fun part for me is when I walk out of a movie like 'how would I have done it differently?' Or, a few times I say 'this movie is perfect the way it is.'"*

**Education:** B.A. in Film Studies - U.C., Santa Barbara; UCLA Professional Program for Screenwriting; UCLA Advanced Writing for Sitcom TV
**Big Break:** Getting into the Nickelodeon Writing Fellowship
**Writing Credits:** *"Hank," "Phineas & Ferb," "AVATAR: The Last Airbender" & "Ni-Hao, Kai-Lan"*
**Writing Inspirations:** Classic, classic sitcoms: *"I Love Lucy," "Seinfeld" &"Golden Girls"*
**POWER Tools:** Computer. Final Draft software & New Yorker magazine
**In Development:** Working on/trying to sell a tv pilot

***EPP: How do you deal with Writer's Block?***

*MC: "Brainstorming. I'll open a blank page on Microsoft Word and start listing possible story ideas. I do that for at least a day. The second day I'll go back and see if there's anything there - and if not, I keep brainstorming. It always works. Eventually I come up with something I can work with, the plot, sometimes the emotional arc, the real story behind the character's story. Just letting your mind go free and writing whatever you want, you'll hone in on something."*

***EPP: Your 123 POWER ADVICE to all writers?***

*MC: "#1 Always keep writing. Never give up. That's the only thing you can control - you sitting down in that chair and writing.*

*"#2 - Keep writing.*

*"#3 - Try not to take things too personally - whether it's getting notes from your boss or your close circle of friends. Some of the notes I get are pretty brutal. You have to know they're trying to help you. You asked for this help, or if it's a showrunner, this is their show. You are there to support them. Don't take it personal. Everybody gets notes. Everybody gets rewritten."*

## Kerri Grant

TV Writer & Script Coordinator

**POWER QUOTE:**
*"I have three notebooks in my purse at any given moment. Paper and pen. Back to basics."*

**Education:** B.A. in Business from George Washington University; Writing Classes at Parsons: The New School in New York
**Big Break:** Getting into the Nickelodeon Fellowship
**Writing Credits:** *"The Fresh Beat Band; "The Backyardigans"*
**Favorite Writers:** Gabriel García Márquez; Ntozake Shange; Toni Morrison; Amy Tan,Isabel Allende, Milan Kundera & Tom Robbins. TV & Film writers Alan Ball; Jill Soloway; Bryan Fuller
**POWER Tools:** Listening to the world around me and writing things down. Pen and paper.
**POWER Exercise:** Writing haiku poems, sticking to the 5, 7, 5 structure

***EPP: How do you deal with Writer's Block?***

*KG: "#1 is the Pre-Warm Up Phase of doing something repetitive that is decidedly not writing - such as dishes, cleaning, scrubbing something, daydreaming, re-piling piles. Doing something repetitive soothes your mind, calms it, where you're not focused on anything but that task. It also serves as a kind of cleanse for your mind.*

*"#2 is the Warm-Up Phase. Surf the web a little bit. Check e-mail. Do research. Read things that get you inspired and feeling good about yourself.*

*"Phase 3 is get in gear and start writing. I force myself to write something down on the page, and I give myself permission for it to be bad."*

***EPP: Why do you write and what's your advice to emerging writers who need a little inspiration?***

*KG: "Try to find the thing that reminds why you want to be a writer. That's what the haiku does for me. When I write it, I remember why I want to do this. One day I picked up my mother's notepad that she uses for groceries and started writing a poem because I was in pain as a teenager. That's what I chose to do, was driven to do. I know a lot of artists say this, but I write because I have to. It's something I need to maintain, to live -- and it's what makes me feel like me."*

*Four tv and film writers share their POWER ADVICE on dealing with Writer's Block, a gripping combination of fear, procrastination and mental blocks that makes established and emerging writers **really** focus on the fact that they're not writing. Buckle down, keep writing and be inspired by these profiles. Glean from their advice. Watch for their names in the credits too! These are writers on the move!*

# Jordan Harper

TV Writer

**POWER QUOTE:**
*"Hollywood is a small town with a lot of really high fences. If you can find a door through one of the fences, you're through and everybody knows everybody. They're willing to be friendly to you once you're through the door - but you've gotta get through*

**Current Job:** Staff Writer on *"The Mentalist"*
**Big Break:** Getting into the Warner Bros. Writers Workshop
**Education:** B.A. in Creative Writing, University of Missouri
**First Writing Jobs:** Rock Critic for the Riverfront Times, a weekly newspaper in St. Louis, MO; music and movies reviews for the Village Voice
**POWER Tools:** Reading writing books like *Story* by Robert McKee
**In Development:** More tv writing, features, short stories and novels

***EPP:* What's your POWER ADVICE for overcoming Writer's Block?**

*JH: "The most important thing to do when you have writer's block is acknowledge that you have it. You're not being lazy. It's not that you're not creative anymore. There's a phrase we have in Missouri that sometimes you get the bear and sometimes the bear gets you. Acknowledge the anxiety, let it go through you and then get back to your work."*

***EPP:* What's your POWER ADVICE for anyone who wants to travel down this writing road?**

*JH: "Everybody says to write often and that's absolutely true. But, you can't forget to read often. Read things that are challenging too. We don't have the luxury of only reading things that are fun -- and anybody who does is going to end up being a weak writer. Challenge yourself. Do a lot of research and read. Also, a basic thing for writers is when nobody is willing to pay you, then you write for free. Write a lot for free. And then once you start getting paid, never write for free again, at least not in that field.*

*"Trying to get into programs like the Warner Bros. Workshop or the ABC Program is really your best bet these days. They're really, really competitive but the results you can get are amazing. Hollywood is a small town with a lot really high fences, so if you can find a door through one of the fences, once you're through. Everybody knows everybody and they're willing to be friendly to you once you're through the door - but you've gotta get through the door."*

# Kenneth Rance

Film & TV Writer

**POWER QUOTE #1:** *"First spec script I went out with, praise God, it was sold...."*

**POWER QUOTE #2:** *"One of the ways to alleviate frustration as a features or television writer is to write in a different genre. Some stories are better as a play, an internet short, a webisode, a graphic novel, a manga, a self-published book, a poem. There's an audience for everything.*

**Education:** B.A. in Radio, TV & Film Production Howard University
**Big Break:** Optioning first screenplay *"Scary Dates"* to 20th Century FOX & becoming a member of the Writers Guild of America, west -- at 26 years old
**Writing Credits:** *"New in Town"* starring Renée Zellweger and Harry Connick, Jr.; TV and film projects for 20th Century Fox Films, Destination Films, Universal Pictures; Marriage Columnist for *Insight News*, a Minneapolis, MN-based newspaper.
**Scripts & Screenplays Sold:** At least 7.
**POWER Tools:** Movie Magic Screenwriter software; the internet; the legal tablet
**POWER Exercise:** Writing on a tablet; keeping the writing flowing
**In Development:** More feature films and tv show writing; working on first book

***EPP:* How do you deal with Writer's Block?**

*KR: "At any point in time I'm writing multiple projects. I have one in development; one in what I view as production where I'm actually physically writing a script. And then I have a third one in post where I'm editing and I'm doing the revision. So, if I get stuck on one project I'll switch to the next and keep it working that way."*

***EPP:* What's your process for writing screenplays?**

*KR: "I outline a film and I'm able to move much faster when I write screenplays out by hand. The left margin on the legal tablet is where I'll write notes and comments. Then I'll hand my tablets off to a typist and have that individual load them into the computer for me. This affords me the ability to continue my flow."*

***EPP:* What's your 123 POWER ADVICE for the emerging writer?**

*KR: "Make sure you have income to support yourself through the lean years. There is no shame in your game in having the day-to-day job. I've had six-figure years and I've had $6 years. I wrote my first screenplay while I was a phone operator at 1-800-DENTIST. Also, think about writing a different genre and mediums because you want to be able to share your God-given gift with the rest of the world. Start looking at ways in which you can get your product directly to the people - whether it's a column, a blog, a short. At the end of the day, writers write.*

**ABC Daytime Writer Development Program**
ABC Daytime
77 W. 66th Street
New York, NY 10023
***www.disneyabctalentdevelopment.com***

**CBS Directing Initiative**
51 W. 52nd Street, 4th Fl.
New York, NY 10019
***Tel: (212) 975-4321***
***www.cbscareers.com***

**CBS Diversity Institute Writers Mentoring Program**
7800 Beverly Boulevard
Los Angeles, CA 90036
***Tel: (323) 575-2000***
***www.cbsdiversity.com***

**CBS Page Program**
7800 Beverly Boulevard
Los Angeles, CA 90036
***Tel: (323) 575-2008***
***www.cbsdiversity.com***
***www.cbscareers.com***

**CBS Internship & Page Program**
7800 Beverly Boulevard
Los Angeles, CA 90036
***Tel: (323) 575-2008***
***www.cbscareers.com***

**CBS Internship & Page Program**
51 W. 52nd Street, 4th Fl.
New York, NY 10019
***Tel: (212) 975-4321***
***www.cbscareers.com***

**CBS News Development Program**
c/o Dir. of Development & Diversity
524 W. 57th Street
514 Building/Room 6215
New York, NY 10019
***Tel: (212) 975-4321***
***www.cbscareers.com***

**CBS Page Program**
7800 Beverly Boulevard
Los Angeles, CA 90036
***Tel: (323) 575-2008***
***www.cbsdiversity.com***
***www.cbscareers.com***

**Creative Artists Agency Agent Trainee Program**
2000 Avenue of the Stars
Los Angeles, CA 90067
***Tel: (424) 288-2000***
***www.caa.com***

**Directors Guild Assistant Directors Training Program**
15301 Ventura Blvd., Bldg E #1075
Sherman Oaks, CA 91403
***Tel: (818) 386-2545***
***www.trainingplan.org***

**Directors Guild Producer Training Plan**
15301 Ventura Blvd., Bldg E #1075
Sherman Oaks, CA 91403
***Tel: (818) 386-2545***
***www.trainingplan.org***

**Disney | ABC Casting Project**
Disney | ABC Television Group
Talent Development & Diversity
500 S. Buena Vista Street
Burbank, CA 91521
***www.disneyabctalentdevelopment.com***

**Disney | ABC DGA Directing Program**
Disney | ABC Television Group
Talent Development & Diversity
500 S. Buena Vista Street
Burbank, CA 91521
***www.disneyabctalentdevelopment.com***

**Disney | ABC Production Associates Program**
Disney | ABC Television Group
Talent Development & Diversity
500 S. Buena Vista Street
Burbank, CA 91521
***www.disneyabctalentdevelopment.com***

**Disney | ABC Talent Development Programs**
Disney | ABC Television Group
Talent Development & Diversity
500 S. Buena Vista Street
Burbank, CA 91521
***www.disneyabctalentdevelopment.com***

The Write Stuff: The search to discover and develop new and creative writing talent continues...

Nickelodeon is offering writing fellowships in live action and animated television to writers with diverse backgrounds and experiences. Participants will have hands-on interaction with executives writing spec scripts and pitching story ideas.

The program, developed to broaden Nickelodeon's outreach efforts, provides a salaried position for up to one year.

Website: www.nickwriting.com

Email: info.writing@nick.com

Hotline: (818) 736-3663

**Disney | ABC Institute of American Indian Arts Summer TV & Film Workshop**
Disney | ABC Television Group
Talent Development & Diversity
500 S. Buena Vista Street
Burbank, CA 91521
*www.disneyabctalentdevelopment.com*

**Disney | ABC National Hispanic Media Coalition Writers Workshop**
Disney | ABC Television Group
Talent Development & Diversity
500 S. Buena Vista Street
Burbank, CA 91521
*www.disneyabctalentdevelopment.com*

**Disney | ABC Television Writing Fellowship**
Disney | ABC Television Group
Talent Development & Diversity
500 S. Buena Vista Street
Burbank, CA 91521
*www.disneyabctalentdevelopment.com*

**ESPN Production Assistant Trainee Program**
ESPN Plaza
Bristol, CT 06010
*Tel: (860) 766-2000*
*www.espn.com*

**FOX Entertainment Group Programs**
*Tel: (310) 369-1000*
*www.fox.com/diversity*
*www.foxcareers.com*

**Guy A. Hanks & Marvin Miller Screenwriting Program/The Cosby Program**
USC School of Cinematic Arts
900 W. 34th Street, Rm. 235
Los Angeles, CA 90089
*Tel: (213) 740-8194*
*www.cosbyprogram.com*

**Hollywood Cinema Production Resources (CPR)**
9700 S. Sepulveda Blvd.
Los Angeles, CA 90045
*Tel: (310) 258-0123*
*www.hollywoodcpr.org*

**Hollywood Mentorship Program**
*www.hollywoodmentorship program.org*

**ICM Agent Trainee Program**
10250 Constellation Blvd.
Los Angeles, CA 90067
*Tel: (310) 550-4000*
*www.icmtalent.com*

**ICM Agent Trainee Program**
825 8th Avenue, 26th Fl.
New York, NY 10019
*Tel: (212) 556-5600*
*www.icmtalent.com*

**Katz Media Associates Program**
125 W. 55th Street
New York, NY 10019
*Tel: (212) 424-6000*
*www.katz-media.com*

**Latino Producers Academy**
National Assoc. of Latino Independent Producers (NALIP)
1323 Lincoln Blvd., Ste. 220
Santa Monica, CA 90401
*Tel: (310) 395-8880*
*www.nalip.org*

**Latino Writers Lab**
National Assoc. of Latino Independent Producers (NALIP)
1323 Lincoln Blvd., Ste. 220
Santa Monica, CA 90401
*Tel: (310) 395-8880*
*www.nalip.org*

**Minorities in Broadcasting Training Program**
P.O. Box 67132
Century City, CA 90067
*Tel: (310) 652-0271*
*www.thebroadcaster.com*

**Minority Media & Telecommunications Council Legal Training Program**
Earle K. Moore Fellowships
3636 16th Street, NW - Ste. B-366
Washington, D.C. 20011
*Tel: (202) 332-0500*
*www.mmtconline.org*

**Moviola**
1135 N. Mansfield Avenue
Hollywood, CA 90038
*Tel: (323) 467-3107*
*www.moviola.com*

**National Association of Broadcasters (NAB) Education Foundation Training Programs**
1771 N Street, NW
Washington, D.C. 20036
*Tel: (202) 429-5300*
*www.nabef.org*

**National Hispanic Media Coalition Latino Television Writers Program**
55 S. Grand Avenue
Pasadena, CA 91105
*Tel: (626) 792-6462*
*www.nhmc.org*

**NATPE Diversity Fellowship Program**
National Association of Television Programming Executives
5757 Wilshire Blvd., PH 10
Los Angeles, CA 90036
*Tel: (310) 453-4440*
*www.natpemarket.com/conference*

**NBC Universal Commercial Leadership Program**
*www.nbcunicareers.com/early careerprograms/commercialleader ship.shtml*

**NBC Universal Entertainment Associates Program**
3000 W. Alameda Avenue
Burbank, CA 91523
*Tel: (818) 840-4444*
*www.nbcunicareers.com/early careerprograms/entassociates program.shtml*

**NBC Universal Minority Fellowship Program**
30 Rockefeller Plaza, Rm. 1678

New York, NY 10012
***Tel: (212) 664-7870***
***www.nbcunicareers.com***

**NBC Universal News Associate Program**
***www.nbcunicareers.com***

**NBC Universal Page Program (East Coast)**
30 Rockefeller Plaza, Rm. 1678
New York, NY 10012
***Tel: (212) 664-7870***
***www.nbcunicareers.com/early careerprograms/***

**NBC Universal Page Program (West Coast)**
3000 W. Alameda Avenue
Burbank, CA 91523
***Tel: (818) 840-4444***
***www.nbcunicareers.com/early careerprograms/***

**Newsroom Training Program**
Society of Professional Journalists
Eugene S. Pulliam National Journalism Center
3909 N. Meridian Street
Indianapolis, IN 46208
***Tel: (317) 927-8000***
***www.spj.org***

**New York DGA Assistant Director Training Program**
1697 Broadway, Ste. 600
New York, NY 10019
***Tel: (212) 397-0930***
***www.dgatrainingprogram.org***

**New York Voiceover Academy**
31 Merrick Ave., Ste. 150
Merrick, NY 11566
***Tel: (516) 208-5480***
***www.newyorkvoiceoveracademy.com***

**Nickelodeon Writing Fellowship**
231 W. Olive Ave.
Burbank, CA 91502
***Tel: (818) 736-3663***
***www.nickwriting.com***

**The Nielsen Company Emerging Leaders Program**
770 Broadway
New York, NY 10003
***Tel: (646) 654-5000***
***www.nielsen.com***

**Paradigm Talent Agency Agent Training Program**
360 N. Crescent Dr. - North Bldg.
Beverly Hills, CA 90210
***Tel: (310) 288-8000***
***www.paradigmagency.com***

**Paradigm Talent Agency Agent Training Program**
360 Park Avenue South, 16th Fl.
New York, NY 10010
***Tel: (212) 897-6400***
***www.paradigmagency.com***

**Paradigm Talent Agency Agent Training Program**
124 12th Avenue S. - Ste. 410
Nashville, TN 37203
***Tel: (615) 251-4400***
***www.paradigmagency.com***

**Tim Russert Fellowship**
***www.nbcunicareers.com/early careerprograms/TimRussertFellowship.shtml***

**Peter Stark Producing Program**
USC School of Cinematic Arts
University Park, SCA 366
900 W. 34th Street
Los Angeles, CA 90089
***Tel: (213) 740-3304***
***cinema.usc.edu/stark***

**Streetlights Production Assistant Program**
Raleigh Studios
662 N. Van Ness Ave., Rm. 105
Hollywood, CA 90004
***Tel: (323) 960-4540***
***www.streetlights.org***

**Sundance Screenwriters Lab**
Sundance Institute
8530 Wilshire Blvd., 3rd Fl.
Beverly Hills, CA 90211
***Tel: (310) 360-1981/(801) 328-3456***
***www.sundance.org***

**Television News Center's Anchor, Reporter, Producer & Writing Training Programs**
184 New Mark Esplanade
Rockville, MD 20850
***Tel: (866) 415-4129/(301)-340-6160***
***www.televisionnewscenter.org***

**Turner Trainee Team Program(T3)**
***www.turner.com/t3***

**United Talent Agency (UTA) Agent Training Program**
9560 Wilshire Boulevard
Beverly Hills, CA 90212
***Tel: (310) 273-6700***
***www.unitedtalent.com/training***

**Voicetrax Voiceover Workshops**
1207 D Bridgeway
Sausalito, CA 94965
***Tel: (415) 331-8800***
***www.voiceover-training.com***

**Warner Bros. Television Comedy Writers Workshop**
4000 Warner Boulevard
Bldg. 35, Rm. 155
Burbank, CA 91505
***Tel: (818) 954-5700***
***writersworkshop.warnerbros.com/***

**Writers Guild of America, west Writers Training Program**
7000 W. Third Street
Los Angeles, CA 90048
***Tel: (323) 782-4548***
***www.wga.org***

**Writers on the Verge**
***www.nbcunicareers.com/early careerprograms/writersontheverge.shtml***

**24**
21050 Lassen Street
Chatsworth, CA 91311
***Tel: (818) 717-5400***
***www.fox.com/24***

**30 Rock**
Silvercup Studios
42-22 22nd Street, Ste. 320
Long Island City, NY 11101
***Tel: (718) 906-2223***
***www.nbc.com/30_rock***

**Access Hollywood**
3000 W. Alameda Ave.
Admin. Bldg., 3rd Fl.
Burbank, CA 91523
***Tel: (818) 526-7000 or 7023 (news)***
***www.accesshollywood.com***

**All My Children**
320 W. 66th Street
New York, NY 10023
***Tel: (212) 456-0800***
***www.abc.com***

**The Amazing Race**
World Race Productions
7800 Beverly Blvd.
Los Angeles, CA 90036
***Tel: (310) 577-9381***

**America's Funniest Home Videos**
12233 W. Olympic Blvd., Ste. 170
Los Angeles, CA 90064
***Tel: (310) 442-5600***
***www.afv.tv***

**America's Got Talent**
7800 Beverly Blvd., Bung. 25
Los Angeles, CA 90036
***Tel: (323) 575-8500***
***www.nbc.com/americas-got-talent***

**America's Next Top Model**
Bankable Productions
10 x 10 Entertainment
1640 S. Sepulveda Blvd., Ste. 450
Los Angeles, CA 90025
***Tel: (310) 575-1235***
***www.cwtv.com/shows/americas-next-top-model13***

**American Idol**
7800 Beverly Boulevard, Ste. 251
Los Angeles, CA 90036
***Tel: (323) 575-8000***
***www.americanidol.com***

**The Apprentice**
Mark Burnett Productions
640 N. Sepulveda Blvd.
Los Angeles, CA 90049
***Tel: (310) 903-5400***
***www.nbc.com/the_apprentice***

**The Bachelor**
10200 Riverside Dr., Ste. 200
Toluca Lake, CA 91602
***Tel: (818) 308-5200***
***abc.go.com/primetime/bachelor***

**The Bachelor**
12100 Olympic Blvd., Ste. 420
Los Angeles, CA 90064
***Tel: (310) 954-2300***
***abc.go.com/primetime/bachelor***

**The Biggest Loser**
3 Ball Productions
3650 Redondo Beach Ave.
Redondo Beach, CA 90278
***Tel: (424) 236-7500***
***www.nbc.com/the-biggest-loser***

**The Bold and the Beautiful**
7800 Beverly Blvd., Ste. 3371
Los Angeles, CA 90036
***Tel: (323) 575-4138***
***www.boldandbeautiful.com***

**Brothers & Sisters**
ABC Television Studio
500 S. Buena Vista Street
Burbank, CA 91521
***Tel: (818) 560-3277***
***http://abc.go.com/primetime/brothersandsisters***

**Celebrity Apprentice**
Mark Burnett Productions
640 N. Sepulveda Blvd.

# HILL HARPER

Actor/Author/Entrepreneur

## POWER QUOTE

***"I've always been a person who has wanted to have a positive impact on the world. I've been working very hard to do my best in that regard."***

Hill Harper's success as a talented television, film and stage actor, bestselling author, Harvard-educated scholar and down-to-earth mentor is commendable. As a thespian, he's been rocking the boob tube for close to two decades, most recently with his starring role as Dr. Sheldon Hawkes on the CBS hit drama "*CSI: NY*." Despite his busy shooting schedule, ***EPP*** managed to catch up with Harper, whose primary inspirations are Paul Robeson, Meryl Streep and Morgan Freeman, and asked him what's his POWER ADVICE for achieving longevity in the industry.

"Really know yourself and stay true," Harper shares.

"This is a journey, a career, not a sprint to the top. It's not, 'I just need to be discovered.' It's about strategically doing something on a daily basis that moves your career and artistry forward - whether it's relationships, perfecting your acting or performing abilities, getting your body together and prepared to do the things that are required, or to look a certain way. All these things actually move the ball forward."

"One of the biggest problems with the entertainment business is the pathos of fear," Harper says. "People are so afraid that they can't figure out how to crack the code and that's why your book is very valuable," he shares, emphasizing the importance of being entrepreneurial and doing the homework necessary to sustain a career.

Like an architect building a masterpiece, Harper's career continues to take unpredictable twists and turns that keep landing him in the spotlight at industry events, on the red carpet at awards shows and at the top of the ratings charts and the *New York Times* Bestseller List - for his books *Letters to a Young Brother*, *Letters to a Young Sister* and his most recent, critically-acclaimed book, *The Conversation*. ***EPP*** is honored to shine our spotlight on Hill Harper!

Los Angeles, CA 90049
***Tel: (310) 903-5400***
***www.nbc.com/the_apprentice***

**CSI: Crime Scene Investigation**
100 Universal City Plaza
Building 2128, Ste. F
Universal City, CA 91608
***Tel: (818) 777-4274***
***www.cbs.com/primetime/csi***

**CSI: Miami**
1600 Rosecrans Avenue
Building 4A, 2nd Fl.
Manhattan Beach, CA 90266
***Tel: (310) 727-5959***
***www.cbs.com/primetime/csi_miami***

**CSI: NY**
4024 Radford Avenue
Building 2, Ste. 200
Studio City, CA 91604
***Tel: (818) 655-5511***
***www.cbs.com/primetime/csi_ny***

**Dancing with the Stars**
7800 Beverly Blvd., Bung. 1
Los Angeles, CA 90036
***Tel: (323) 575-8100***
***www.abc.go.com/primetime/dancing/index.html***

**Days of Our Lives**
3000 W. Alameda Ave., Stages 2 & 4
Burbank, CA 91505
***Tel: (818) 840-4089***
***www.nbc.com/days_of_our_lives***

**Deal or No Deal**
9336 W. Washington Blvd., Bldg. O
Culver City, CA 90232
***Tel: (310) 202-3333***
***www.nbc.com***

**Desperate Housewives**
100 Universal City Plaza
Bldg. 2128, Ste. G
Universal City, CA 91608
***Tel: (818) 733-3773***
***abc.go.com/primetime/desperate/index.html***

**Dr. Phil**
5555 Melrose Avenue
Mae West Bldg. 151
Los Angeles, CA 90038
***Tel: (323) 956-3300***
***www.drphil.com***

**Entertainment Tonight**
4024 Radford Ave., Bldg. R
Studio City, CA 91604
***Tel: (818) 655-4400***
***www.etonline.com***

**Extreme Makeover: Home Edition**
Endemol USA, Inc.
9255 Sunset Blvd., Ste. 1100
Los Angeles, CA 90069
***Tel: (323) 785-2262***
***abc.go.com/primetime/xtremhome***

**General Hospital**
ABC Daytime
4151 Prospect Ave.
Los Angeles, CA 90027
***Tel: (323) 671-4588***

**Grey's Anatomy**
4151 Prospect Avenue
Producer's Bldg., 2nd Fl.
Los Angeles, CA 90027
***Tel: (323) 671-4650***
***abc.go.com/primetime/greys anatomy***

**Heroes**
1438 N. Gower Street
Hollywood, CA 90028
***Tel: (323)468-7900***
***www.nbc.com/heroes***

**House**
10201 W. Pico Boulevard
Bldg. 89, Rm. 230
Los Angeles, CA 90035
***Tel: (310) 369-3100***
***www.fox.com/house***

**Jimmy Kimmel Live**
6834 Hollywood Blvd., Ste. 600
Hollywood, CA 90028
***Tel: (310) 860-5900***
***abc.go.com/shows/jimmy-kimmel-live***

**Jeopardy!**
10202 W. Washington Blvd.
Culver City, CA 90232
***Tel: (310) 244-8855***
***www.jeopardy.com***

**Larry King Live**
6430 Sunset Boulevard
Los Angeles, CA 90028
***Tel: (323) 993-5100***
***www.cnn.com/CNN/Programs/larry.king.live***

**Law & Order**
Chelsea Piers, Pier 62, Rm. 215
New York, NY 10011
***Tel: (212) 627-0088***
***www.nbc.com/law_and_order***

**Law & Order: Criminal Intent**
Chelsea Piers, Pier 62, Rm. 305
New York, NY 10011
***Tel: (212) 336-6350***
***www.nbc.com/law_&_order:_criminal_intent***

**Law & Order: SVU**
100 Universal City Plaza
Universal City, CA 91608
***Tel: (818) 777-4038***
***www.nbc.com/law_&_order:_special_victims_unit***

**Live! with Regis & Kelly**
7 Lincoln Square, 5th Fl.
New York, NY 10023
***Tel: (212) 456-3605***
***www.liveregisandkelly.com***

**Martha**
226 W. 26th Street, 3rd Fl.
New York, NY 10001
***Tel: (917) 438-5700***
***www.marthastewart.com***

**One Life To Live**
56 W. 66th Street
New York, NY 10023
***Tel: (212) 456-7777***

www.onelifetolive.com

**Praise the Lord**
P.O. Box A
Santa Ana, CA 92711
***Tel: (714) 832-2950***
***www.tbn.org***

**Private Practice**
5300 Melrose Ave., E. Bldg., 4th Fl.
Los Angeles, CA 90038
***Tel: (323) 960-4940***

**Project Runway**
Full Picture
517 N. Robertson Blvd., Ste. 200
West Hollywood, CA 90048
***Tel: (310) 860-0505***
***www.fulllpicture.com***

**Rachel Ray**
222 E. 44th Street
New York, NY 10017
***Tel: (212) 450-1600***
***www.rachelray.com***

**Saturday Night Live**
30 Rockefeller Plaza, 17th Fl.
New York, NY 10012
***Tel: (212) 664-4511***
***www.nbc.com/saturday_night_live***

**Smallville**
4000 Warner Boulevard
Building 160, Ste. 200
Burbank, CA 91522
***Tel: (818) 977-4050***

**So You Think You Can Dance**
7800 Beverly Blvd., Ste. 202
Los Angeles, CA 90036
***Tel: (323) 575-6100***
***www.fox.com/dance***

**The Amazing Race**
World Race Productions
7800 Beverly Blvd.
Los Angeles, CA 90036
***Tel: (310) 577-9381***

**The Apprentice**
Mark Burnett Productions
640 N. Sepulveda Blvd.
Los Angeles, CA 90049
***Tel: (310) 903-5400***

**The Bold And The Beautiful**
7800 Beverly Blvd., Ste. 3371
Los Angeles, CA 90036
***Tel: (323) 575-4138***
***www.cbs.com/daytime/bb***

**The Daily Show with Jon Stewart**
604 W. 52nd Street
New York, NY 10019
***Tel: (212) 468-1700***
***www.thedailyshow.com***

**The Jay Leno Show**
3000 W. Alameda Ave., Studio 11
Burbank, CA 91523
***Tel: (818) 840-2222***
***www.thejaylenoshow.com***

**The Late Show with David Letterman**
Ed Sullivan Theatre
1697 Broadway
New York, NY 10019
***Tel: (212) 975-5300***
***www.cbs.com/latenight/lateshow***

**The Mentalist**
4000 Warner Boulevard
Burbank, CA 91522
***Tel: (818) 954-1030***

**The Office**
100 Universal City Plaza
Universal City, CA 91608
***Tel: (818) 786-6666***
***www.nbc.com/the_office***

**The Oprah Winfrey Show**
110 N. Carpenter Street
Chicago, IL 60607
***Tel: (312) 633-1000***
***www.oprah.com***

**The Price is Right**
7800 Beverly Boulevard
Los Angeles, CA 90036
***Tel: (323) 575-2345***
***www.cbs.com/daytime/price***

**The Simpsons**
10201 W. Pico Blvd., Bldg. 203
Los Angeles, CA 90035
***Tel: (310) 369-3959***
***www.thesimpsons.com***

**The Tonight Show with Conan O'Brien**
100 Universal City Plaza
Bldg. 2220, 4th Fl.
Universal City, CA 91608
***Tel: (818) 684-3737***
***www.thetonightshowwithconanobrien.com***

**The Tyra Banks Show**
221 W. 26th Street, 4th Fl.
New York, NY 10001
***Tel: (646) 638-5600***
***www.tyrashow.com***

**The View**
77 W. 66th Street
New York, NY 10023
***Tel: (212) 456-7777***
***theview.abc.go.com***

**The Young and the Restless**
7800 Beverly Boulevard, Ste. 3305
Los Angeles, CA 90036
***Tel: (323) 575-2532***

**Two and a Half Men**
4000 Warner Blvd., Bldg. 136, 2nd Fl.
Burbank, CA 91522
***Tel: (818) 977-1777***

**Ugly Betty**
34-02 Starr Ave., 2nd Fl.
Long Island City, NY 11101
***Tel: (718) 906-3400***
***abc.go.com/shows/ugly-betty***

**Wheel of Fortune**
10202 W. Washington Blvd.
Culver City, CA 90232
***Tel: (310) 244-1234***
***www.wheeloffortune.com***

**Archer Productions**
390 Mallory Station Rd., Ste. 107
Franklin, TN 37067
***Tel: (615) 778-1237***
***www.archerproductions.com***

**Artist Management Agency**
835 5th Avenue, Ste. 411
San Diego, CA 92101
***Tel: (714) 972-0311***
***www.artistmanagementagency.com***

**Bert Berdis & Company**
1956 N. Cahuenga Blvd.
Hollywood, CA 90068
***Tel: (323) 462-7261***
***www.bertradio.com***

**Terry Berland Voice Casting**
2329 Purdue Avenue
Los Angeles, CA 90064
***Tel: (310) 775-6608***
***www.terryberlandcasting.com***

**Carroll Voiceover Casting Co.**
6767 Forest Lawn Dr., Ste. 203
Hollywood, CA 90068
***Tel: (323) 851-9966***
***www.carrollcasting.com***

**Elaine Craig Voice Casting**
6464 Sunset Blvd., 11th Fl.
Hollywood, CA 90028
***Tel: (323) 469-8773***
***www.elainecraig.com***

**Edge Studio's Voice Design Group**
1817 Black Rock Turnpike, Ste. 102
Fairfield, CT 06825
***Tel: (203) 334-EDGE***
***www.edgestudio.com***

**Edge Studio's Voice Design Group**
307 Seventh Ave., Ste. 1007
New York, NY 10001
***Tel: (212) 868-EDGE***
***www.edgestudio.com***

**Edge Studio's Voice Design Group**
307 Seventh Avenue, Ste. 1007
New York, NY 10001
***Tel: (212) 868-EDGE***
***www.edgestudio.com***

**Edge Studio's Voice Design Group**
7720 Wisconsin Ave., Ste. B101
Bethesda, MD 20814
***Tel: (202) 398-EDGE***
***www.edgestudio.com***

**Funny Farm Radio**
4470 Sunset Blvd., Ste. 200
Los Angeles, CA 90027
***Tel: (877) FUNNYFARM***
***Tel: (323) 667-2054***
***www.funnyfarmradio.com***

**Marc Graue Voiceover Recording Studios**
3421 W. Burbank Blvd.
Burbank, CA 91505
***Tel: (818) 953-8991***
***www.fixinthemix.com***

**The Great Voice Company**
110 Charlotte Place
Englewood Cliffs, NJ 07632
***Tel: (201) 541-8595***
***www.greatvoice.com***

**Nancy Hayes Casting**
400 Treat Avenue, Ste. #E
San Francisco, CA 94110
***Tel: (415) 558-1675***
***www.hayescasting.com***

**Innovative Artists Chicago**
541 N. Fairbanks, Ste. 2735
Chicago, IL 60611
***Tel: (312) 832-1113***
***www.voicesunlimited.com***

**Kalmenson & Kalmenson Voice Casting**
105 S. Sparks Street
Burbank, CA 91506
***Tel: (818) 377-3600***

*www.kalmenson.com*

**Sheila Manning Voice Casting**
332 S. Beverly Dr.
Beverly Hills , CA 90212
***Tel: (310) 557-9990***

**Metaphoria Ltd.**
1496 Lafayette Road
Claremont, CA 91711
***Tel: (909) 626-2626***
***www.metaphoria.com***

**Mix Magic Post Sound**
839 N. Highland Ave.
Hollywood, CA 90038
***Tel: (323) 466-2442***
***www.mixmagic.com***

**Larry Moss Speech & Dialect Services**
855 3rd St., Ste. 305
Santa Monica, CA 90403
***Tel: (310) 395-4284***

**New York Voiceover Academy**
31 Merrick Ave., Ste. 150
Merrick, NY 11566
***Tel: (516) 208-5480***
***www.newyorkvoiceoveracademy .com***

**Outlaw Sound**
1608 N. Argyle Avenue
Hollywood, CA 90028
***Tel: (323) 462-1873***
***www.outlawsound.com***

**Pacific Ocean Post Sound**
625 Arizona Ave.
Santa Monica, CA 90401
***Tel: (310) 458-9192***
***www.popsound.com***

**Nick Sommers Productions**
8320 S. Tamiami Trail
Sarasota, FL 34238
***Tel: (941) 870-8700***
***www.nicksommers.com***

**STS Foreign Language Services**
2109 W. Burbank Blvd.
Burbank, CA 91506
***Tel: (818) 563-3004***
***www.stsmedia.com***

**The Voicecaster**
1832 W. Burbank Boulevard
Burbank, CA 91506
***Tel: (818) 841-5300***
***www.voicecaster.com***

**The Voiceover Connection, Inc.**
691 S. Irolo, Ste. 212
Los Angeles, CA 90005
***Tel: (213) 384-9251***
***www.voconnection.com***

**The Voiceover Directory**
P.O. Box 20801
New York, NY 10129
***Tel: (866) 224-4101***
***www.voiceoverdirectory.com***

**The Voiceworks**
***www.thevoiceworks.com***

**Voice123**
P.O. Box 1167
Seacaucus, NJ 07094
***www.voice123.com***

**VoiceCasting**
8950 Laurel Way, Ste. 200
Alpharetta, GA 30022
***Tel: (678) 481-5026***
***Tel: (678) 457-6394***
***www.voicecasting.com***

**Voice Hunter**
P.O. Box 1266
Weston, CT 06883
***Tel: (866) 810-1922***
***Tel: (203) 341-0111***
***www.voicehunter.com***

**VoiceMedia/Susan & Friends**
69 Green Street
San Francisco, CA 94111
***Tel: (415) 956-3878***
***www.susansvoicemedia.com***

**Voice One**
665 Third Street, Ste. 227
San Francisco, CA 94107
***Tel: (415) 974-1103***
***www.voiceoneonline.com***

**Voice-Over Xtra**
P.O. Box 132
Trumbull, CT 06611
***Tel: (203) 459-8834***
***www.voiceoverxtra.com***

**Voiceover Universe**
***www.vouniverse.com***

**Voiceovers Unlimited**
123 W. 18th Street, 7th Fl.
New York, NY 10011
***Tel: (917) 363-9877/(800) 888-8364***
***www.voiceoversunlimited.com***

**Voice Recruiters.com**
***www.voicerecruiters.com***

**Voices In Media.com**
***www.voicesinmedia.com***

**Voicetrax West**
12215 Ventura Blvd., Ste. 205
Studio City, CA 91604
***Tel: (818) 487-9007***
***www.voicetraxwest.com***

**Voicetrax**
1207 D Bridgeway
Sausalito, CA 94965
***Tel: (415) 331-8800***
***www.voiceover-training.com***

**ABC Daytime Writer Development Program**
ABC Daytime
77 W. 66th Street
New York, NY 10023
*www.disneyabctalentdevelopment.com*

**CBS Diversity Institute Writers Mentoring Program**
7800 Beverly Boulevard
Los Angeles, CA 90036
*Tel: (323) 575-2345*
*www.cbsdiversity.com*

**Disney | ABC Television Writing Fellowship**
Disney | ABC Television Group
Talent Development & Diversity
500 S. Buena Vista Street
Burbank, CA 91521
*www.disneyabctalentdevelopment.com*

**Disney | ABC National Hispanic Media Coalition Writers Workshop**
Disney | ABC Television Group
Talent Development & Diversity
500 S. Buena Vista Street
Burbank, CA 91521
*www.disneyabctalentdevelopment.com*

**FOX Writers Initiative**
FOX Diversity Development
P.O. Box 900
Beverly Hills, CA 90213
*Tel: (310) 369-1000*
*www.fox.com/diversity*
*www.foxcareers.com*

**Gotham Writers' Workshop**
555 Eighth Avenue, Ste. 1402
New York, NY 10018
*Tel: (212) 974-8377*
*www.writingclasses.com*

**Guy A. Hanks & Marvin Miller Screenwriting Program/The Cosby Program**
USC School of Cinematic
900 W. 34th Street, Rm. 235
Los Angeles, CA 90089
*Tel: (213) 740-8194*
*www.cosbyprogram.com*

**Michael Hauge's Screenplay Mastery**
P.O. Box 57498
Sherman Oaks, CA 91413
*Tel: (818) 995-4209*
*www.screenplaymastery.com*

**Hollywood Film Institute**
P.O. Box 481252
Los Angeles, CA 90048
*Tel: (310) 399-6699*
*www.hollywoodu.com*

**International Reporting Project/PEW Fellowships**
The Johns Hopkins University
School of Advanced Int'l. Studies
1619 Massachusetts Ave, NW
Washington, D.C. 20036
*Tel: (202) 663-7761*
*www.spj.org*

**Robert McKee's Story Seminar**
Two Arts, Inc.
P.O. Box 452930
Los Angeles, CA 90045
*Tel: (888) 676-2533*
*www.mckeestory.com*

**Latino Writers Lab**
National Association of Latino
Independent Producers (NALIP)
1323 Lincoln Blvd., Ste. 220
Santa Monica, CA 90401
*Tel: (310) 395-8880*
*www.nalip.org*

**National Hispanic Media Coalition Latino Television Writers Program**
55 S. Grand Avenue
Pasadena, CA 91105
*Tel: (626) 792-6462*
*www.nhmc.org*

**NAMIC Writers Workshop**
National Association for Multi-Ethnicity in Communications
320 W. 37th Street, 8th Fl.
New York, NY 10018

Tel: (212) 594-5985
www.namic.com

**New York Film Academy**
100 E. 17th Street
New York, NY 10003
*Tel: (212) 674-4300/(818) 733-2600*
*www.nyfa.com*

**Nickelodeon Writing Fellowship**
231 W. Olive Ave.
Burbank, CA 91502
*Tel: (818) 736-3663*
*www.nickwriting.com*

**On the Page**
13907 Ventura Boulevard, Ste. 101
Sherman Oaks, CA 91423
*Tel: (818) 905-8124*
*www.onthepage.tv*

**Organization of Black Screenwriters (OBS)**
Golden State Mutual Life Insur. Bldg.
1999 West Adams Blvd., Rm. Mezz.
Los Angeles, CA 90018
*Tel: (323) 735-2050*
*www.obswriter.com*

**Planet DMA**
14622 Ventura Blvd., #333
Sherman Oaks, CA 91403
*Tel: (818) 461-9211*
*www.planetdma.com*

**Truby's Writers Studio**
664 Brooktree Road
Santa Monica, CA 90402
*Tel: (310) 573-9630*
*www.truby.com*

**UCLA Extension Screenwriting Programs**
10995 Le Conte Ave., Rm. 437
Los Angeles, CA 90024
*Tel: (310) 825-9971/(818) 784-7006*
*www.uclaextension.edu*

**Warner Bros. Writers Workshop**
4000 Warner Boulevard
Burbank, CA 91505
*Tel: (818) 954-5700*
*www2.warnerbros.com/writersworkshop*

**Writers Boot Camp**
Bergamot Station Arts Center
2525 Michigan Ave., Bldg. I
Santa Monica, CA 90404
*Tel: (800) 800-1733*
*www.writersbootcamp.com*

**Writers Guild of America, west Writers Training Program**
7000 W. Third Street
Los Angeles, CA 90048
*Tel: (323) 782-4548/(323) 951-4000*
*www.wga.org*

**Writers on the Verge**
*www.nbcunicareers.com/earlycareerprograms/writersontheverge.shtml*

**Writers University**
The Writers Store
2040 Westwood Boulevard
Los Angeles, CA 90025
*Tel: (310) 441-5151/(866) 229-7483*
*www.writersuniversity.com*

**Writing for Screen & TV Program**
USC School of Cinematic Arts
900 W. 34th Street, Rm. 335
Los Angeles, CA 90089
*Tel: (213) 740-3303*
*http://cinema.usc.edu*

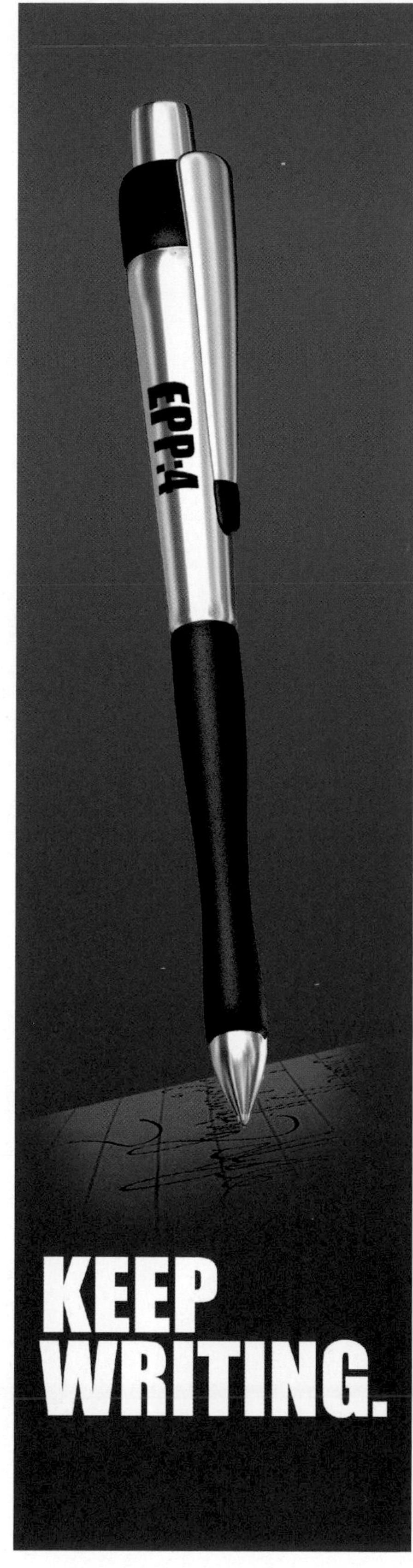

# TOTAL SATURATION

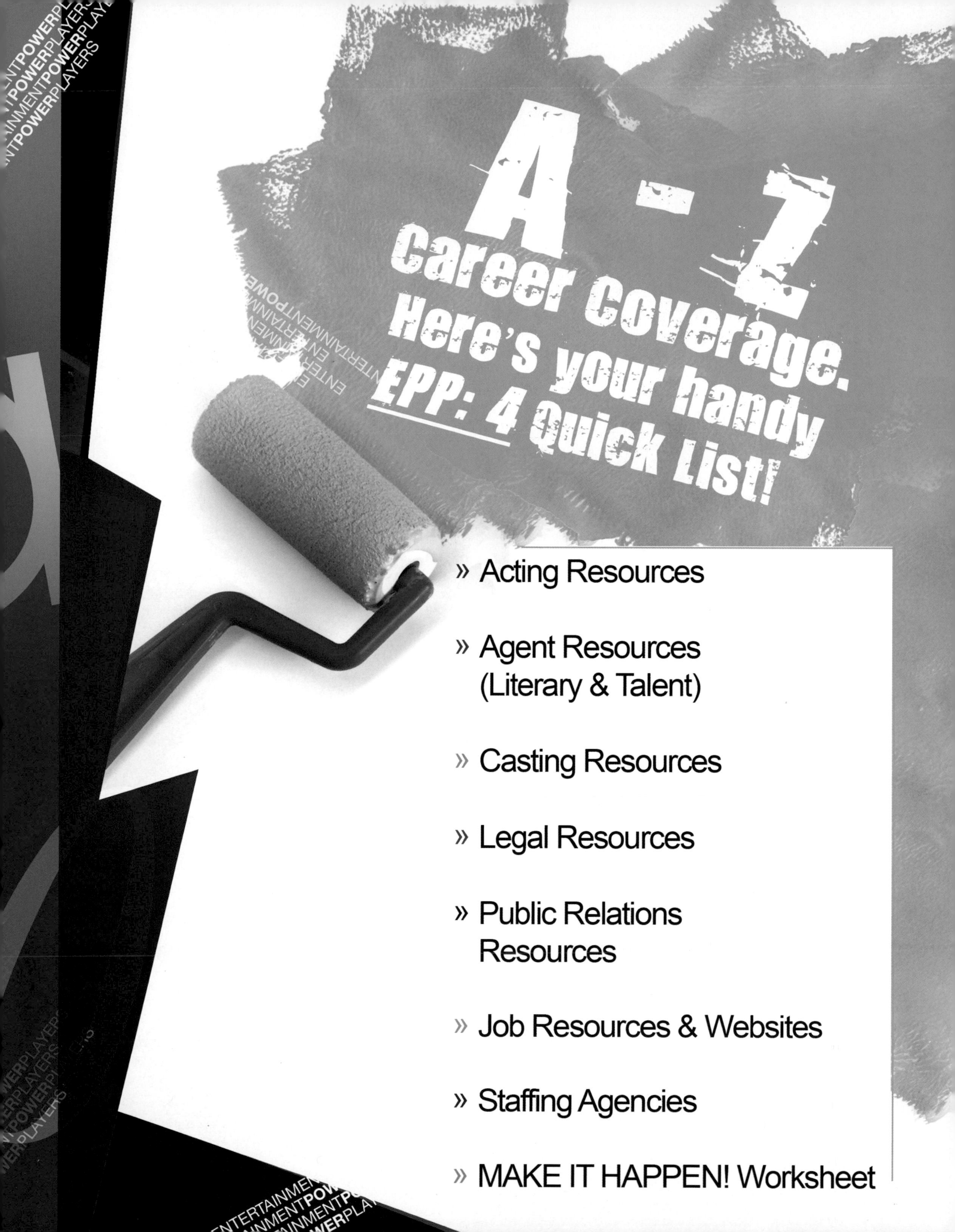
A - Z
Career Coverage.
Here's your handy
EPP: 4 Quick List!

- » Acting Resources
- » Agent Resources (Literary & Talent)
- » Casting Resources
- » Legal Resources
- » Public Relations Resources
- » Job Resources & Websites
- » Staffing Agencies
- » MAKE IT HAPPEN! Worksheet

## Acting Resources

**Actors Equity Association**
6775 Hollywood Blvd., 5th Fl.
Hollywood, CA 90028
***Tel: (323) 978-8080***
***Tel: (312) 641-0393 (Chicago)***
***Tel: (407) 345-8600 (Orlando)***
***www.actorsequity.org***

**Actors Equity Association**
165 W. 46th Street
New York, NY 10036
***Tel: (212) 869-8530***
***www.actorsequity.org***

**Back Stage**
5055 Wilshire Boulevard
Los Angeles, CA 90036
***Tel: (323) 525-2356***
***www.backstage.com***

**Back Stage & Call Sheet**
770 Broadway
New York, NY 10003
***Tel: (646) 654-5700 (Back Stage)***
***Tel: (323) 525-2231 (Call Sheet)***
***www.backstage.com***
***www.backstage.com/callsheet***

**Screen Actors Guild (SAG)**
5757 Wilshire Blvd, 18th Fl.
Los Angeles, CA 90036
***Tel: (323) 954-1600***
***www.sag.org***

**Screen Actors Guild (SAG)**
360 Madison Avenue, 12th Fl.
New York, NY 10036
***Tel: (212) 944-1030***
***www.sag.org***

**Show Fax**
2140 Cotner Avenue
Los Angeles, CA 90025
***Tel: (310) 385-6920***
***www.showfax.com***

## Literary & Talent Agencies

**APA**
Agency for the Performing Arts
405 S. Beverly Dr.
Beverly Hills, CA 90212
***Tel: (310) 888-4200***
***www.apa-agency.com***

**APA**
Agency for the Performing Arts
250 W. 57th Street, Ste. 1701
New York, NY 10107
***Tel: (212) 687-0092***
***www.apa-agency.com***

**CAA - Creative Artists Agency**
2000 Avenue of the Stars
Los Angeles, CA 90067
***Tel: (424) 288-2000***
***www.caa.com***
****Nashville & St. Louis offices too.***

**CAA - Creative Artists Agency**
1625 5th Avenue, 6th Fl.
New York, NY 10010
***Tel: (212) 277-9000***
***www.caa.com***
****Nashville & St. Louis offices too.***

**Gersh**
9465 Wilshire Blvd., 6th Fl.
Beverly Hills, CA 90212
***Tel: (310) 274-6611***
***www.gershagency.com***

**Gersh**
41 Madison Ave., 33rd Fl.
New York, NY 10010
***Tel: (212) 997-1818***
***www.gershagency.com***

**Innovative Artists**
1505 Tenth Street
Santa Monica, CA 90401
***Tel: (310) 656-0400***
***www.innovativeartists.com***
****NY & Chicago offices too.***

**ICM**
Int'l. Creative Management
10250 Constellation Blvd.
Los Angeles, CA 90067
***Tel: (310) 550-4000***
***www.icmtalent.com***

**ICM**
Int'l. Creative Management
825 Eighth Avenue
New York, NY 10019
***Tel: (212) 556-5600***
***www.icmtalent.com***

**Paradigm Talent Agency**
360 N. Crescent Dr. - North Bldg.
Beverly Hills, CA 90210
***Tel: (310) 288-8000***
***www.paradigmagency.com***
****Nashville & Monterey, CA offices too.***

**Paradigm Talent Agency**
360 Park Avenue South, 16th Fl.
New York, NY 10010
***Tel: (212) 897-6400***
***www.paradigmagency.com***
****Nashville & Monterey, CA offices too.***

**UTA - United Talent Agency**
9560 Wilshire Blvd., Ste. 500
Beverly Hills, CA 90212
***Tel: (310) 273-6700***
***www.unitedtalent.com***

**William Morris Endeavor Entertainment Agency**
151 El Camino Dr.
Beverly Hills, CA 90212
***Tel: (310) 274-7451***
***www.wmeentertainment.com***

**William Morris Endeavor Entertainment Agency**
9601 Wilshire Boulevard
Beverly Hills, CA 90210
***Tel: (310) 285-9000/(310) 248-2000***
***www.wmeentertainment.com***
****Nashville office too.***

**William Morris Endeavor Entertainment Agency**
1325 Avenue of the Americas
New York, NY 10019
***Tel: (212) 586-5100***
***www.wmeentertainment.com***

## Casting Resources

**Back Stage & Call Sheet**
***Tel: (323) 525-2356 (Back Stage)***
***Tel: (646) 654-5700 (Back Stage)***
***Tel: (323) 525-2231 (Call Sheet)***
***www.backstage.com***
***www.backstage.com/callsheet***

**Casting Society of America**
606 N. Larchmont Blvd., Ste. 4B
Los Angeles, CA 90004
***Tel: (323) 463-1925***
***www.castingsociety.com***

**Casting Society of America**
311 W. 43rd St., 10th Fl.
New York, NY 10019
***Tel: (212) 868-1260***

**Central Casting**
220 S. Flower St.
Burbank, CA 91502
***Tel: (818) 562-2700/(818) 562-2755***
***www.centralcasting.org***

**Central Casting New York**
***Tel: (646) 205-8244***
***www.centralcasting.org***

**Playbill**
525 Seventh Avenue
New York, NY 10018
***Tel: (212) 557-5757***
***www.playbill.com***

**Screen Actors Guild (SAG)**
5757 Wilshire Blvd, 18th Fl.
Los Angeles, CA 90036
***Tel: (323) 954-1600***
***www.sag.org***

**Screen Actors Guild (SAG)**
360 Madison Avenue, 12th Fl.
New York, NY 10036
***Tel: (212) 944-1030***
***www.sag.org***

**Talent6**
5419 Hollywood Blvd., Ste. C727
Hollywood, CA 90027
***Tel: (800) 846-9470***
***www.talent6.com***

## Legal Resources

**American Bar Association**
321 N. Clark Street
Chicago, IL 60610
***Tel: (312) 988-5000***
***www.abanet.org***

**American Bar Association**
740 15th Street, NW
Washington, D.C. 20005
***Tel: (202) 662-1000***
***www.abanet.org***

**Beverly Hills Bar Association**
300 S. Beverly Dr., Ste. 201
P.O. Box 7277
Beverly Hills, CA 90212
***Tel: (310) 601-BHBA***
***www.bhba.org***
****Barristers Committee for the Arts***

**Black Entertainment & Sports Lawyers Association (BESLA)**
P.O. Box 441485
Fort Washington, MD 20749
***Tel: (301) 248-1818***
***www.besla.org***

**California Lawyers for the Arts**
1641 18th Street
Santa Monica, CA 90404
***Tel: (310) 998-5590 (Santa Monica)***
***Tel: (415) 775-720 (San Francisco)***
***Tel: (916) 442-6210 (Sacramento)***
***www.calawyersforthearts.org***

**Library of Congress**
**U.S. Copyright Office**
101 Independence Ave., SE
Washington, D.C. 20540
***Tel: (202) 707-3000***
***www.copyright.gov***

**Volunteer Lawyers for the Arts**
1 E. 53rd Street, 6th Fl.
New York, NY 10022
***Tel: (212) 319-2878***
***www.vlany.org***

## Public Relations Resources

**National Black Public Relations Society (NBPRS)**
9107 Wilshire Blvd., Ste. 450
Beverly Hills, CA 90210
***Tel: (888) 976-0005***
***www.nbprs.com***

**National Publicity Summit**
Bradley Communications Corp.
390 Reed Road, 1st Fl.
Broomall, PA 19008
***Tel: (484) 477-4220 ext. 106***
***www.nationalpublicitysummit.com***

**O'Dwyer's Inside News of Public Relations & Marketing Communications**
271 Madison Avenue, #600
New York, NY 10016
***Tel: (212) 679-2471***
***www.odwyerpr.com***

**PR Newswire**
***www.prnewswire.com***

**PR Week**
PRWeek / Haymarket Media, Inc.
114 W. 26th St., 4th Fl.
New York, NY 10001
***Tel: (646) 638-6000***
***www.prweekus.com***

**Public Relations Society of America (PRSA)**
33 Maiden Lane, 11th Fl.
New York, NY 10038
***Tel: (212) 460-1400***
***www.prsa.org***

**Public Relations Student Society of America (PRSSA)**
33 Maiden Lane, 11th Fl.
New York, NY 10038
***Tel: (212) 460-1474***
***www.prssa.org***

**24 Seven Inc.**
*www.24seveninc.com*

**4 Entertainment Jobs**
*www.4entertainmentjobs.com*

**Atlantic Television**
*www.atlantictv.com*

**Berklee Music**
*www.berkleemusic.com*

**Billboard.com Career Center**
*www.billboard.com*

**CareerBuilder**
*www.careerbuilder.com*

**Career Connection**
*www.film-connection.com*

**CBS**
*www.cbscareers.com*

**Comcast Entertainment Group**
*www.comcast.com*

**Craigslist.com**
*www.craigslist.com*

**Creative Heads.net**
*www.creativeheads.net*

**Creative Jobs Central**
*www.creativejobscentral.com*

**Crew Net**
*www.crewnet.com*

**Crew Star**
*www.crewstar.com*

**Disney | ABC**
*www.disneyabcjobs.com*

**Employ Now**
*www.employnow.com*

**Entertainment Careers**
*www.entertainmentcareers.net*

**Entertainment Workers.com**
*www.entertainmentworkers.com*

**Fashion Career Center.com**
*www.fashioncareercenter.com*

**Fashion Career Expo**
*www.fashioncareerexpo.com*

**Fashion Job Site.com**
*www.fashionjobsite.com*

**Filmstaff.com**
*www.filmstaff.com*

**Find Film Work.com**
*www.findfilmwork.com*

**FOX Entertainment Group**
*www.foxcareers.com*

**FOX Interactive Media**
*www.fimcareers.com*

**Game Face**
*www.gamefacesportsjobs.com*

**Gig Directory**
*www.gigdirectory.net*

**Gigs List**
*www.gigslist.org*

**Hot Jobs**
*www.hotjobs.yahoo.com*

**Indeed**
*www.indeed.com*

**Jobs.Com**
*www.jobs.com*

**Jobs in Sports.com**
*www.jobsinsports.com*

**Jobs Radar**
*www.jobsradar.com*

**Journalism Jobs.com**
*www.journalismjobs.com*

**Kelly Services**
*www.kellyservices.com*

**LA Times.com**
*www.latimes.com/classified/jobs*

**The Ladders**
*www.theladders.com*

**Magic Workforce Solutions**
*www.magicworkforce.com*

**Mandy**
*www.mandy.com*

**Maslow Media**
*www.maslowmedia.com*

**Media Bistro**
*www.mediabistro.com*

**Media Match**
*www.media-match.com*

**Media Web Source**
*www.mediawebsource.com*

**Monster**
*www.monster.com*

**MTV Networks**
*www.mtvncareers.com*

**Music 444.com**
*www.music444.com*

**Musicians Contact Service**
*www.musicianscontact.com*

**My Music Job**
*www.mymusicjob.com*

**National Association of Broadcasters (NAB) Career Development Programs**
*www.nab.org*
*www.nabef.org*

**Nat'l. Assoc. of Record Industry Professionals (NARIP) Job Bank**
*www.narip.com*

**NBA Associate Program**
*www.nba.com/careers*

**NBA Internship Program**
*www.nba.com/careers*

**NBC Universal**
*www.nbcunicareers.com*

**News Corporation**
*careers.newscorp.com*

**NY Times.com**
*www.nytimes.com/jobs*

**Onlinegigs.com**
*www.onlinegigs.com*

**Production Hub**
*www.productionhub.com*

**Reality Staff.com**
*www.realitystaff.com*

**Reel Dirt**
*www.reeldirt.com*

**Reel TV.com**
*www.reeltv.com/jobs*

**Reel View.tv**
*www.reeltv.com/jobs*

**Showbiz Data**
*www.showbizdata.com*

**Showbiz Jobs**
*www.showbizjobs.com*

**Sony Pictures Entertainment**
*www.sonypicturesjobs.com*

**Sports Careers**
*www.sportscareers.com*

**Sports Jobs Now.com**
*www.sportsjobsnow.com*

**Sports Management Worldwide**
*www.smww.com*

**StyleCareers.com**
*www.stylecareers.com*

**Team People**
*www.teampeople.tv*

**Team Work Online.com**
*www.teamworkonline.com*

**Time Warner**
*www.timewarner.com/careers*

**Turner Broadcasting System**
*www.turnerjobs.com*

**TV & Radio Jobs**
*www.tvandradiojobs.com*

**TV Jobs**
*www.tvjobs.com*

**Variety Media Careers.com**
*www.varietymediacareers.com*

**Viacom**
*www.viacomcareers.com*

**Voice Recruiters.com**
*www.voicerecruiters.com*

**Walt Disney Company**
*www.disneycareers.com*

**Warner Music Group**
*www.wmg.com/joblist*

**Warner Bros. Entertainment**
*www.warnerbroscareers.com*

**Well Threaded.com**
*www.wellthreaded.com*

**Work In Sports.com**
*www.workinsports.com*

**Working World**
*www.workingworld.com*

**Yahoo! Hot Jobs**
*www.yahoohotjobs.com*

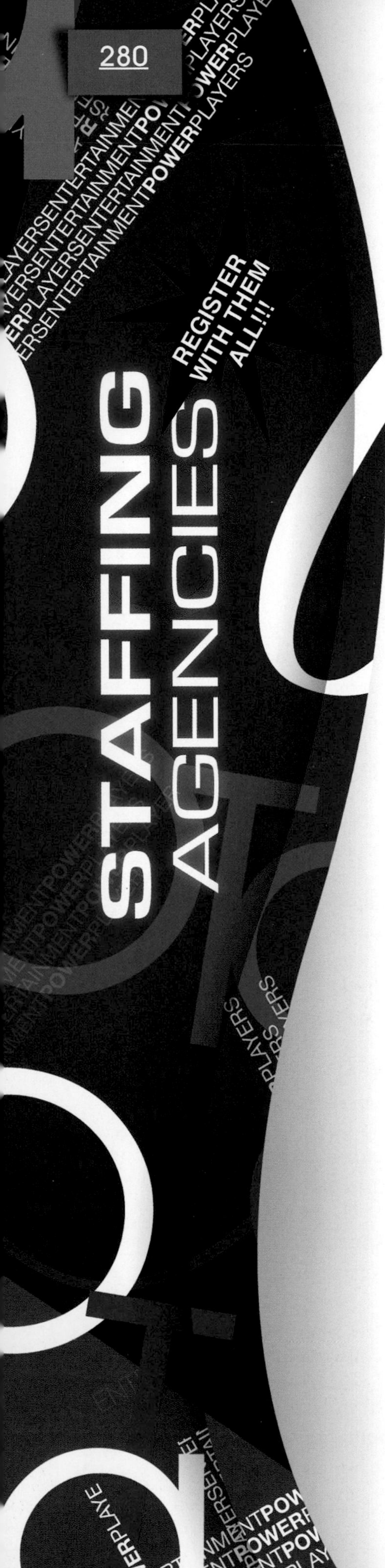


**24 Seven**
120 Wooster Street, 4th Fl.
New York, NY 10012
***Tel: (212) 966-4426***
***www.24seveninc.com***

**24 Seven**
325 Wilshire Blvd., Ste. 202
Santa Monica, CA 90401
***Tel: (310) 587-2772***
***www.24seveninc.com***

**24 Seven**
California Market Center
110 East 9th Street, Ste. #A793
Los Angeles, CA 90079
***Tel: (213) 412-2260***
***www.24seveninc.com***

**24 Seven**
49 Geary Street, Ste. 402
San Francisco, CA 94108
***Tel: (415) 989-2424***
***www.24seveninc.com***

**24 Seven**
2901 W. Coast Hwy., Ste. 250
Newport Beach, CA 92663
***Tel: (949) 258-6540***
***www.24seveninc.com***

**24 Seven**
1525 4th Avenue, Ste. 200
Seattle, WA 98101
***Tel: (206) 340-0247***
***www.24seveninc.com***

**A+ The Employment Company**
2749 W. Magnolia Blvd., Ste. 205
Burbank, CA 91505
***Tel: (818) 840-0998***
***www.theemploymentco.com***

**Act •1 Personnel**
1999 W. 190th Street
Torrance, CA 90504
***Tel: (800) 365-ACT1***
***www.act-1.com***

**Advantage Integrated Talent Services**
55 Main Street, 7th Fl.
Bridgeport, CT 06604
***Tel: (203) 394-5200***
***www.advhr.com***
*****Nationwide Locations***

**Advantage Integrated Talent Services**
575 Fifth Ave.
New York, NY 10017
***Tel: (212) 661-2020***
***www.thefutureofwork.com***

**Apple One**
***Tel: (800) 564-5644***
***www.appleone.com***

**Blaine And Associates**
2029 Century Park E., Ste. 1080
Los Angeles, CA 90067
***Tel: (310) 385-0560***
***www.blaineandassociates.com***

**Comar Agency**
6500 Wilshire Blvd., Ste. 2240
Los Angeles, CA 90048
***Tel: (310) 248-2700***
***www.comaragency.com***

**Corestaff Services**
6100 Wilshire Blvd., Ste. 150
Los Angeles, CA 90048
***Tel: (323) 857-1225***
***www.corestaffservices.com***

**Corestaff Services**
1775 St. James Place, Ste. 300
Houston, TX 77056
***Tel: (713) 438-1400***
***www.corestaffservices.com***
*****100+ Offices Nationwide***

**The Crew Works**
1500 Sulgrave Avenue
Baltimore, MD 21209
***Tel: (800) CW 4-CREW***
***www.thecrewworks.com***

**Elizabeth Rose Agency**
9151 Sunset Blvd.
W. Hollywood, CA 90069
***Tel: (310) 276-2555***
***www.elizabethroseagency.com***

**Emma Bowen Foundation**
CBS Studio Center
4024 Radford Avenue
Editorial 2, Ste. 1
Studio City, CA 91604
***Tel: (818) 655-5708***
***www.emmabowenfoundation.com***

**Emma Bowen Foundation**
1299 Pennsylvania Ave., NW - 9th Fl.
Washington, DC 20004
***Tel: (202) 637-4494***
***www.emmabowenfoundation.com***

**Emma Bowen Foundation**
524 West 57th Street
New York, NY 10019
***Tel: (212) 975-2545***
***www.emmabowenfoundation.com***

**Executive Temps**
2321 W. Olive Avenue, Ste. F
Burbank, CA 91506
***Tel: (818) 563-2939***
***www.executive-temps.com***

**Force One Entertainment**
1601 Broadway, 11th Fl.
New York, NY 10019
***Tel: (212) 922-9898***
***www.forceoneentertainment.com***

**Friedman Personnel Agency**
9000 Sunset Blvd., Ste. 1000
W. Hollywood, CA 90069
***Tel: (310) 550-1002***
***www.friedmanpersonnel.com***

**Kelly Services**
999 West Big Beaver Road
Troy, MI 48084
***Tel: (248) 362-4444***
***www.kellyservices.com***

**Ken Lindner & Assoc.**
2049 Century Park E., Ste. 1000
Los Angeles, CA 90067
***Tel: (310) 277-9223***
***www.kenlindner.com***

**Magic Workforce Solutions**
***Tel: (888) MAGIC-05***
***www.magicworkforce.com***

**Maslow Media**
2233 Wisconsin Ave., NW - Ste. 400
Washington, D.C. 20007
***Tel: (202) 965-1100***
***www.maslowmedia.com***

**Metropolitan Temps**
110 E. 42nd Street, Ste. 802
New York, NY 10017
***Tel: (212) 983-6060***
***www.metstaff.com***

**National Association of Broadcasters Education Foundation Career Center**
1771 N Street, NW
Washington, D.C. 20036
***Tel: (202) 429-5300***
***www.nabef.org***

**Olsten Temp Services**
500 Fifth Ave., Ste. 910
New York, NY 10010
***Tel: (212) 391-7000***
***www.worknow.com***

**Paladin Atlanta**
1050 Crown Pointe Pkwy., Ste. 1750
Atlanta, GA 30338
***Tel: (404) 495-0900***
***www.paladinstaff.com***

**Paladin Boston**
35 Corporate Drive, Ste. 220
Burlington, MA 01803
***Tel: (617) 951-0250***
***www.paladinstaff.com***

**Rindi Media**
***Tel: (202) 495-1054***
***www.rindimedia.com***

**Staffmark**
***www.staffmark.com***
****300 Locations Nationwide***

**Staffmark**
350 S. Grand Ave., Ste. 1610
Los Angeles, CA 90071
***Tel: (323) 931-9400***
***www.staffmark.com***

**Team People**
4455 Connecticut Ave, NW
Ste. C-100
Washington, DC 20008
***Tel: (202) 587-411***
***www.teampeople.tv***

**TemPositions**
420 Lexington Ave., 21st Fl.
New York, NY 10170
***Tel: (212) 490-7400***
***www.tempositions.com***

**Thor Agency**
360 Aviation Blvd., Ste. 3900
Manhattan Beach, CA 90266
***Tel: (310) 727-1777***
***www.thorgroup.com***

**Top Tempo Technical & Future Personnel**
3731 Wilshire Blvd., Ste. 512
Los Angeles, CA 90010
***Tel: (323) 388-7444***
***www.topjobsusa.net***

**Total Production Services**
Television Crewing Service
292 Hughes Road
Gulph Mills, PA 19406
***Tel: (888) 877-1178***
***www.tpsweb.com***

**Winston Temps**
122 East 42nd Street, Ste. 320
New York, NY 10168
***Tel: (212) 557-5000***
***www.winstonresources.com***

**Working World Magazine**
***www.workingworld.com***

**Workplace Hollywood**
1201 W. 5th Street, Ste. T-550
Los Angeles, CA 90017
***Tel: (213) 250-9921***
***www.workplacehollywood.org***

# ENTERTAINMENT POWER PLAYERS EDITION 4

## LEGAL RESOURCES

## 4 FINAL POWER NOTES:

1). ALWAYS PROTECT YOURSELF & YOUR WORK.
2). COPYRIGHT YOUR MATERIAL.
3). WORK WITH A GREAT LAWYER.
4). CREATE A REAL GAME PLAN/POWER PLAN FOR YOUR CAREER.

American Bar Association
321 N. Clark Street
Chicago, IL 60610
*Tel: (312) 988-5000*
*www.abanet.org*

American Bar Association
740 15th Street, NW
Washington, D.C. 20005
*Tel: (202) 662-1000*
*www.abanet.org*

Beverly Hills Bar Association
300 S. Beverly Dr., Ste. 201
P.O. Box 7277
Beverly Hills, CA 90212
*Tel: (310) 601-BHBA*
*www.bhba.org*
**Barristers Committee for the Arts*

Black Entertainment & Sports Lawyers Association (BESLA)
P.O. Box 441485
Fort Washington, MD 20749
*Tel: (301) 248-1818*
*www.besla.org*

California Lawyers for the Arts
1641 18th Street
Santa Monica, CA 90404
*Tel: (310) 998-5590 (Santa Monica)*
*Tel: (415) 775-720 (San Francisco)*
*Tel: (916) 442-6210 (Sacramento)*
*www.calawyersforthearts.org*

Library of Congress
U.S. Copyright Office
101 Independence Ave., SE
Washington, D.C. 20540
*Tel: (202) 707-3000*
*www.copyright.gov*

Volunteer Lawyers for the Arts
1 E. 53rd Street, 6th Fl.
New York, NY 10022
*Tel: (212) 319-2878*
*www.vlany.org*

POWER NOTE:
Intellectual Property and creativity leads to royalties, residuals and revenue streams. Make no mistake about it, this entertainment industry we all love is a multi-billion dollar industry. Make sure YOU get paid by copyrighting and registering your work (scripts/songs/lyrics, etc.) AND consulting with expert entertainment attorneys, agents and managers capable of negotiating and securing great deals for YOU. No short cuts. No "poor man's copyrights." Please, from the desk of *EPP*, PLEASE pick up the phone and start meeting the POWER PLAYERS you need to advance your career today!!! We're rooting for you! E-mail us your success stories.

# EPP POWER PLAN

## Questions to Accelerate MY Career

Where do I want to work or intern?

1.________________________________________

2.________________________________________

3.________________________________________

How many phone calls did I make today?

____ 0-5

____ 5-10

____ Not enough

Who do I want to meet?

1.________________________________________

2.________________________________________

3.________________________________________

What trade magazines will I read/organizations will I join?

1.________________________________________

2.________________________________________

3.________________________________________

What industry events will I attend?

1.________________________________________

2.________________________________________

3.________________________________________

Where are my Copyright Forms - for my songs, scripts & manuscripts?

____ Filed with the Copyright Office

____ I don't know

____ Ready to download/upload

Do I need the digital version of ***EPP: 4***?

____ Yes

____ No

____ Probably

My Career Notes, Thoughts, Dreams & Goals:

______________________________________________________________

______________________________________________________________

______________________________________________________________

______________________________________________________________

______________________________________________________________

think bold.

think success.

think YOU.

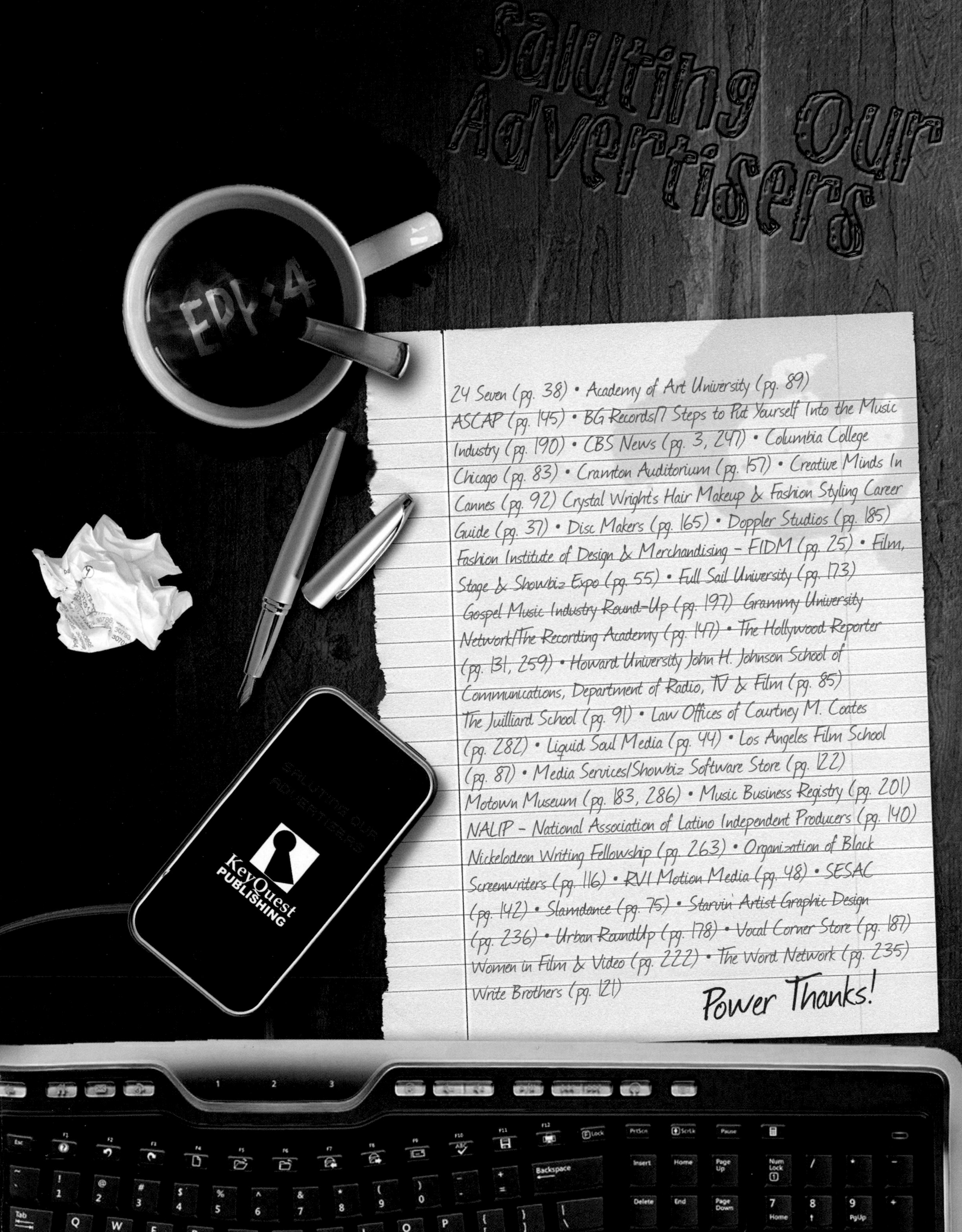
Saluting Our Advertisers
EPK:4
24 Seven (pg. 38) • Academy of Art University (pg. 89)
ASCAP (pg. 145) • BG Records/7 Steps to Put Yourself Into the Music
Industry (pg. 190) • CBS News (pg. 3, 247) • Columbia College
Chicago (pg. 83) • Cramton Auditorium (pg. 157) • Creative Minds In
Cannes (pg. 92) Crystal Wright's Hair Makeup & Fashion Styling Career
Guide (pg. 37) • Disc Makers (pg. 165) • Doppler Studios (pg. 185)
Fashion Institute of Design & Merchandising - FIDM (pg. 25) • Film,
Stage & Showbiz Expo (pg. 55) • Full Sail University (pg. 173)
Gospel Music Industry Round-Up (pg. 197) Grammy University
Network/The Recording Academy (pg. 147) • The Hollywood Reporter
(pg. 131, 259) • Howard University John H. Johnson School of
Communications, Department of Radio, TV & Film (pg. 85)
The Juilliard School (pg. 91) • Law Offices of Courtney M. Coates
(pg. 282) • Liquid Soul Media (pg. 44) • Los Angeles Film School
(pg. 87) • Media Services/Showbiz Software Store (pg. 122)
Motown Museum (pg. 183, 286) • Music Business Registry (pg. 201)
NALIP - National Association of Latino Independent Producers (pg. 140)
Nickelodeon Writing Fellowship (pg. 263) • Organization of Black
Screenwriters (pg. 116) • RVI Motion Media (pg. 48) • SESAC
(pg. 142) • Slamdance (pg. 75) • Starvin' Artist Graphic Design
(pg. 236) • Urban RoundUp (pg. 178) • Vocal Corner Store (pg. 187)
Women in Film & Video (pg. 222) • The Word Network (pg. 235)
Write Brothers (pg. 121)
Power Thanks!
KeyQuest PUBLISHING

EPP:5
Fashion + Film + Music + Sports + TV
Call us for inclusion:
(323) 533-1971
www.entertainmentpower.com